ESCAPE VIA BERLIN

THE BASQUE SERIES

Escape via Berlin

Eluding Franco in Hitler's Europe

José Antonio de Aguirre

Introductions and Annotations by Robert P. Clark

University of Nevada Press ▲▲ Reno & Las Vegas

Basque Series Editor:
William A. Douglass

This book was originally published in Spanish by Editorial Vasca Ekin in 1944 and entitled *De Guernica a Nueva York, Pasando Por Berlin*. The book was translated into English and originally published in the United States by Macmillan Company in 1945 under the title *Escape via Berlin*. The present volume duplicates the text of the Macmillan edition with the following changes: Robert P. Clark has provided a new introduction and annotations discussing differences between editions and commenting on historical events and political implications, and the front matter has been altered to reflect the new publisher.

In the Macmillan edition the author acknowledged Mrs. L. J. Navascues and Miss Nea Colton for the assistance they gave in the preparation of that version of the book.

Library of Congress Cataloging-in-Publication Data
Aguirre y Lecube, José Antonio de, 1904–1960.
    [De Guernica a Nueva York pasando por Berlin. English]
    Escape via Berlin : eluding Franco in Hitler's Europe / José Antonio de Aguirre ; introduction and annotations by Robert P. Clark.
        p. cm. — (The Basque series)
    Translation of: De Guernica a Nueva York pasando por Berlin.
    Reprint, with new introd. and annotations. Originally published: New York : Macmillan, 1944.
    Includes bibliographical references.
    ISBN 0-87417-167-9 (cloth ed. : acid-free paper)
    1. País Vasco (Spain)—History—Autonomy and independence movements. 2. Spain—History—Civil War, 1936–1939—Refugees. 3. Spain—History—Civil War, 1936–1939—Personal narratives. 4. World War, 1939–1945—Personal narratives, Basque. 5. Basques—Foreign countries. 6. Refugees, Political—Spain. 7. Aguirre y Lecube, José Antonio de, 1904–1960. I. Clark, Robert P., 1940– .
II. Title. III. Series.
DP302.B53A3413   1991
946.081—dc20   90-25136
                        CIP

University of Nevada Press,
Reno, Nevada 89557 USA
Designed by Richard Hendel.
Printed in the United States of America.

9 8 7 6 5 4 3 2 1

Contents

JOSÉ ANTONIO DE AGUIRRE

Our territory may have been conquered;
but not the soul of the Basque people;
it will never be.
—*José Antonio de Aguirre,*
  in his last message to the Basque people
  from Basque soil, June 1937

JOSÉ ANTONIO DE AGUIRRE

HIS LIFE AND HIS LEGACY

On very rare occasions when a whole people are locked in mortal struggle against overwhelming odds, a leader emerges so gifted with the sensitivity to recognize their yearnings and the expressive power to articulate those yearnings and turn them into real programs and policies, that he or she comes to symbolize that struggle and energize that people in their moment of trial. Following the sociologist Max Weber, we call these leaders "charismatic" for their ability to crystallize an entire people's dreams and to inspire them to greater heights of sacrifice and achievement in pursuit of those dreams.

The book you now hold in your hands was written by such a person—José Antonio de Aguirre y Lecube—who, for nearly twenty-four years from 1936 to his death in 1960, was the first president (or *lendakari*) of the Basque government. This book was one of many legacies he left behind to record his experiences and insights during a tragic time in the history of the Basque people, and indeed of people around the world. This new edition, issued nearly fifty years after the book first appeared, attests to the timeliness, the wisdom, and the foresight of his message.

The family of President Aguirre and the University of Nevada Press have honored me by asking me to provide an introduction and occasional notes to help the reader of today understand and appreciate more fully the wisdom of this truly exceptional man. In preparing my contributions to this edition, I have been guided by three objectives: first, to be faithful to both the English version and the "original" Spanish version, the latter of which was issued several years earlier and differs from the English book in that it offers different perspectives on Aguirre's thoughts and experiences; second, to interpret both versions for the enlightenment and enjoyment of the contemporary reader; and third, to avoid inserting too much of myself into the book, thereby placing myself between the reader and Aguirre. I hope the modern audience will enjoy and profit from this intensely personal account of an extraordinary adventure written by one of the shapers of twentieth-century Europe.

By the beginning of the twentieth century, Bilbao, capital of the Basque province of Vizcaya, was well on its way to becoming the dynamic center of Basque heavy industry and commerce, as well as the focal point of an emerging Basque nationalism. Thousands of Basques were drawn from the surrounding towns, villages, and farms to this burgeoning city, whose population had quadrupled to about 60,000 during the last half of the nineteenth century. Two of these were a young couple from the neighboring province of Guipúzcoa—Teodoro Aguirre Barrenechea-Arando from Vergara and his wife, Bernardina Lecube Aramburu, from Motrico. To this couple a son was born on March 6, 1904, the first of what was to be a typically large family of ten children. His name was José Antonio.

As a youth, José Antonio de Aguirre's principal concerns were language, sports, and religion. A speaker of the Basque language, *Euskera*, from childhood, he attended the first Basque-language school (or *ikastola*) in Bilbao; but he completed high school at the Jesuit academy in Orduña, where Euskera was not taught, and so had begun to lose his command of his mother tongue by his teenage years. As a young man, he returned from time to time to his father's hometown of Vergara to study Euskera and thus to recapture an essential part of the Basques' heritage. By the time he reached his twenties, he had already become well known in the area as a member of the Bilbao soccer team, the Athlétic, where he played forward. A devout Catholic, he was much influenced by Father Luigi Sturzo, founder of the Italian Christian Democratic movement in 1919. He became president of the church's social action group in Vizcaya, Catholic Youth, and eventually was elected to the organization's national governing board.

One of the early turning points in José Antonio's life came when the boy was only sixteen with the death of his father. Teodoro Aguirre was a lawyer noted for his defense of Basque nationalist political figures. In 1902, he participated in the legal defense of the founder of Basque nationalism, Sabino de Arana y Goiri, where he acted as assistant to the principal attorney, Daniel de Irujo. Upon his father's death, the young José Antonio accelerated his plans to follow in his footsteps. Entering law school at Bilbao's Deusto University (the training ground for several generations of Basque political and business leaders), he graduated in 1926 at the age of twenty-one. Upon the completion of his military service, he opened his law office in Bilbao in 1928.

Sometime before this, the family had moved to the Bilbao suburb of Guecho, then—as now—made up of the municipalities of Algorta, Las Arenas, Neguri, and Guecho itself. Located only a few kilometers from downtown Bilbao, the community had become the favored residential area for the city's up and coming middle-class professionals, many of whom assumed leading roles in Basque nationalist politics. During the dictatorship of Spanish General Primo de Rivera (1923–1930), José Antonio de Aguirre began to take a more activist role in the affairs of the leading nationalist group, the Partido Nacionalista Vasco (PNV). During the twenties, he divided his time between his law career, political activity, continued service in various Catholic social-action organizations, and personal responsibilities as the eldest son in a family without a father. He also began the courtship of his future wife, María de Zabala, daughter of a shipping company owner from Portugalete, a neighboring town of Bilbao. They were married in July 1933. Doña María, or Mari, as she was known more simply, would soon accompany José Antonio into exile and bear him three children: a daughter, Aintzane, born in Bilbao; and two sons, Joseba, born in Paris, and Iñaki, born in New York City.

Like many people in Spain, the life of José Antonio de Aguirre was altered fundamentally by the events of April 1931, when the Spanish monarchy fell and was replaced by the Second Republic. The restoration of republican government in Spain was marked throughout the country by the election of new municipal, provincial, and national assemblies. In the Basque Country, or *Euskadi* as it was known to the Basques, democracy in Spain meant renewed opportunities to struggle for Basque self-government. In these euphoric days, José Antonio de Aguirre rose to prominence as one of the leading spokesmen for Basque autonomy and Christian democracy. In 1931 Aguirre was elected to the municipal council of Guecho and then to the position of mayor of the city. He was thus plunged into the whirlwind of events described in such detail in this book:

1. The efforts to secure an autonomy statute for the Basque provinces, which met with failure until 1936;
2. The outbreak of the Spanish civil war in July 1936, followed by the Spanish government's granting of autonomy to the Basques and the election of Aguirre as the Basque government's first president in October 1936;
3. The bombing of Guernica, the fall of Bilbao, and the flight of the Basque government into exile in 1937;
4. The establishment of the government-in-exile in Paris, the fall of Barcelona, and the end of the civil war in 1939;

5. The outbreak of war between Germany and France in 1940, which trapped the Aguirre family behind German lines;

6. And finally, Aguirre's journey through Belgium, Germany, and Sweden, then by boat to Brazil, and to Uruguay and eventual safety by October 1941.

By December 1941, Aguirre, his wife, and their two children had reached New York City, their home for the next four years, and the birthplace of their third child.

The choice of New York as the new home for the Aguirre family, as well as for the Basque government-in-exile, stemmed from an interesting series of coincidences. Well before the end of the Spanish civil war, Aguirre had begun to dispatch Basque-government representatives, or "delegations" as they were known, to key cities around the world, from which they were supposed to influence local public opinion in favor of the Basque cause and raise money to support the Basque government and the tens of thousands of refugees in France and elsewhere. The first of these—in Madrid, Barcelona, Paris, London, and Brussels—were already opened by the end of 1936. New York was chosen as the site of the first delegation to be sent to the United States, partly because of the city's unequaled connections with Europe and the rest of the world, partly because there was a Basque Center in the city with some 175 members, and partly so as not to conflict with the efforts of the Spanish Republic's emissaries then residing in Washington, D.C.

The Basque-government delegation arrived in New York in August 1938. Shortly thereafter, in February 1939, a young Basque named Jon Bilbao learned of the existence of the delegation and volunteered his services to aid their cause. Bilbao had served in the Basque army during the civil war and, after a brief period as a refugee in Puerto Rico, had entered New York's Columbia University, where he received his master's degree in 1939. Also in early 1939, a wealthy and influential Basque, Manuel María de Ynchausti, likewise found himself in New York, also partly by accident. Although born in the Philippines, Ynchausti had retained his ties to, and identity with, his Basque ancestry; and at the outbreak of the

Spanish civil war he was in San Sebastián. He later went to France, where he worked extensively to aid the refugees from Euskadi. In April 1939 he was en route from Europe back to the Philippines via New York. Although he planned to stay in New York for only a brief time (he even left his baggage in the customs office), the spread of the war in Europe interrupted his trip, and he ended up living in New York more than eight years. From there, he was able to use his considerable wealth and personal contacts with powerful American opinion leaders—such as New York's Catholic Archbishop (later Cardinal) Spellman—to aid the Basque cause in the United States. The combination of the Basque delegation, Jon Bilbao's contacts with Columbia University, and Manuel Ynchausti's presence made New York the logical site for the Aguirre family to settle once their difficult escape from Nazi-controlled Europe had been achieved.

Until the end of the Second World War, Aguirre devoted himself tirelessly to keeping the Basque government-in-exile alive pending their return to Europe—perhaps to France, but preferably to Spain with Franco overthrown and the republic restored. Within days after arriving in New York, he issued orders reorganizing the government, and naming official representatives in London (Manuel de Irujo), Mexico City (Telesforo Monzón), and Buenos Aires (Ramón María Aldasoro). He also directed that the existing Basque delegations around the world continue to operate under the authority granted them by the government before the beginning of the war. Differences of ideology and party affiliation were set aside, to be settled once the war was over and the government returned to Euskadi. Unity was the overriding objective of the president. Because of the war, as well as conflicts within the Socialist party in the Basque Country, Aguirre was not able to convene a meeting of his full government in New York until February 1945, when they began planning their return to Europe.

While living in New York, Aguirre traveled to Latin America to work with local Basque communities and raise money for the government, as well as to shore up democracy against what he termed the "Latin dictatorships." His principal effort in this connection was a major two-month-long tour in 1942 of thirteen Latin American countries—Mexico, Guatemala, Panama, Colombia, Peru, Chile, Argentina, Uruguay, Brazil, Bolivia, Venezuela, the Dominican Republic, and Cuba. Throughout his tour, he was received with the honors appropriate to a head of state; and the local British and American embassies extended similar courtesies to him in virtually all the capital cities (much to the consternation of the local Spanish embassies).

Aguirre also wrote and spoke throughout the United States to try to counteract the anti-Basque propaganda that had emerged during the Spanish civil war, as well as to promote the cause of Christian democracy and human rights in Western Europe. We should not forget that during the 1930s he was as ardent an advocate for freedom of religious thought, and particularly of the rights of the Catholic church, as he was of Basque self-government. Some of his closest friends and advisors during this period were noted European leaders of Christian Democratic thought in exile in New York, including French intellectual Jacques Maritain and Italian priest Luigi Sturzo. Aguirre was one of a group of forty-two European intellectuals who, in November 1942, signed their important "manifesto," which addressed the "world crisis" and set forth the principles on which a liberal, post-war Europe would be established. In 1943 European Christian Democratic leaders began regular meetings in New York to plan for the post-war return of democracy to Europe. José Antonio de Aguirre was an active participant in these meetings and succeeded in having the cause of Basque self-governance placed on the Christian Democratic agenda.

One of the most controversial of President Aguirre's activities while in New York involved the close ties he established and maintained with the American government, specifically with the U.S. Department of State and with American intelligence services operating in Europe and Latin America. In fact, the Basque government had begun to cooperate with the Allies in late 1939. During the war, Basque nationalists aided downed American and British airmen in escaping from Nazi-held France via the Pyrenees, and Basque agents provided intelligence information to the Allies via the American consulate in Bilbao. As he stated in this book in his own words,

Aguirre placed great faith in America (by which he meant the Western Hemisphere) and the United States in particular. In later years, when the United States began to provide assistance and recognition to the Franco dictatorship, Aguirre would be sharply criticized for these pro-American policies; and the president himself became greatly disillusioned with what some regarded as a betrayal by the Western liberal democracies.

Finally, to keep his family and household intact, Aguirre lectured on contemporary European history at New York's Columbia University. His endowed chair at the university had been arranged in August 1941 (while Aguirre and his family were still in Brazil, traveling under their false names and passports) by Manuel Ynchausti and Columbia University history professor Carleton Hayes, a personal friend of President Franklin D. Roosevelt, and later assigned to the American embassy in Madrid from 1942 to 1945.

One of the principal achievements of Aguirre's stay in New York was this work, *Escape via Berlin*. The idea of writing such a book has been attributed to a Basque living in Buenos Aires, Andrés de Irujo, brother of Manuel de Irujo, one of Aguirre's closest advisors and a key member of the Basque government in London during the 1940s. In 1942 after considerable discussion and planning, Andrés de Irujo was preparing to form a publishing company in Buenos Aires called Editorial Ekin as an outlet for books about Basque culture and language. Irujo's collaborators in the project had insisted that the firm restrict itself to works about culture and avoid politics, but when Aguirre arrived in Buenos Aires en route to New York in late 1941, Irujo suggested that he write about his experiences since the outbreak of the Spanish civil war. This he did, completing most of the manuscript (as we learn from the book itself) by May 1942. The first Spanish edition was published on December 15, 1943, by Ekin in Buenos Aires, under the title *De Gernika a Nueva York, Pasando por Berlin* (*From Guernica to New York, Passing through Berlin*). The book quickly sold out its first edition in Spanish, and a second edition appeared on February 14, 1944. Eventually there would be six Spanish-language editions, four published in Buenos Aires (the third of which was distributed clandestinely in Spain), one in St.-Jean-de-Luz, France, and one included in Aguirre's collected works published in San Sebastián.

The person most responsible for the English-language version was Jon Bilbao, who selected writer Nea Colton to prepare the English translation. The English version was published in the United States as *Escape via Berlin* in November 1944, and subsequently in Britain as *Freedom Was Flesh and Blood* (recalling one of the memorable lines from the epic poem by British poet-laureate C. Day-Lewis, "The *Nabara*"). As the reader will note from the annotations in this volume, considerable liberties were taken by the translators in interpreting the Spanish version primarily, it seems, out of consideration for the sensibilities of the book's American audience. Nevertheless, a faithful interpretation of President Aguirre's experiences, ideas, and state of mind requires that we consider both texts more or less simultaneously. I consider the Spanish version to be the more authentic of the two because it was the original text. In any event, according to Basque historian Koldo San Sebastián, *Escape via Berlin* had a noticeable impact on American views of the war, at least among the opinion elite of New York. The book was reviewed by several newspapers, including the *New York Times*, and by such magazines as *The New Yorker* and *Harper's*.

In March 1945, President Aguirre returned to Europe for the first time since the outbreak of the war aboard an American Air Force bomber. Later that month, the Pact of Bayonne was signed by representatives of all the anti-Franco Basque political groups, in which they reaffirmed their support of the Spanish Second Republic government, still in exile. The pact also reaffirmed the commitment of all the parties to the support of the Basque government as the legitimate representative of the Basque people. In April Aguirre met in Paris with the leadership of the Basque Nationalist Party, as well as with leaders of the anti-Franco underground still operating in Spain. On April 21 he was reunited with soldiers of the Gernika Battalion, an all-Basque unit that had fought alongside the Allies in France. This brief visit was only preparatory, however; Aguirre's definitive return, along with his family, took place the following year. By mid-1946, the government was installed once again in Paris.

It is important to recall that in the years immediately following the end of the Second World War, many Basques believed that their day of liberation could not be far away. Within Spain, economic conditions and the average person's standard of living were worsening steadily. The Basques could count on an active clandestine network to support acts of resistance or sabotage; and in France, the Basque government had agreed to support the training of groups of guerrillas who would be infiltrated across the border to attack Spanish military and police targets. Financial support from Basques in exile abroad continued to flow at an increasing rate. In 1950 Aguirre attended the inauguration of the Basque Center in Caracas; from that point on, the Basque colony in Venezuela would play a key role in mobilizing and channeling funds to support the government in Paris and the activities of the resistance.

Moreover, Aguirre and many others still counted heavily on foreign intervention against Franco by the Western democracies, especially the United States. Now that fascism had been defeated in the rest of Europe, they believed the Americans and the British would turn their attention to Spain. Of course the democracies had their own reasons for wanting to overthrow Franco. But in addition there was—at least from the Basque perspective—an implicit agreement between the Basques and the Allies during the war, whereby the Basques supplied intelligence and espionage services as well as combat troops, and the Allies agreed to intervene against Franco once the war was over. (This understanding was contained, according to the Basques, in an oral agreement negotiated in 1942 between the PNV and American representatives, known as the "Umbe Pact.") Now, faced with American and British pressure against Franco combined with the Basque and Spanish republican resistance movements, the dictatorship could not last more than several years at the most. In 1948 the Basque government even went so far as to expel the Communists from the Aguirre cabinet in order (among other reasons) to meet what they understood to be American objections to the composition of the coalition government.

For several years events seemed to confirm the wisdom and feasibility of such a strategy. On May 1, 1947, the Basque resistance committee, together with the principal unions in the region, launched a seven-day-long general strike, the first such direct action against Franco's government. Despite fierce countermeasures by the regime, some 40,000 Vizcayan and Guipúzcoan workers eventually walked off their jobs. The strike was brought to a close by President Aguirre once the resistance had established its ability to conduct such audacious actions. A second strike, begun in Barcelona in March 1951 and seconded in Bilbao, spread even more widely to other parts of the Basque Country and even involved other cities in Spain. This time, the results included a two-day general strike in Euskadi on April 23 and 24, which eventually involved some 250,000 workers, about 85 percent of the work force of Vizcaya and Guipúzcoa. Resistance activists, however, were growing impatient, and many Basques, especially among the youth of the region, began to sense that the government in Paris was too cautious and slow in its conduct of the underground war against Franco. In fact, before long the 1951 strike would be seen clearly as the "last shot" to be fired by the resistance.

The decisive turning point that marked the collapse of this strategy came shortly after the 1951 strike. The United States, in the midst of the Cold War with the Soviet Union and the actual war in Korea, reversed its policy toward Franco and launched the conversations that led eventually to the United States–Spanish accord on American bases, signed in Madrid in September 1953. With the relaxation of American pressure came international recognition of the Franco regime, admission to various international bodies, and perhaps most important, the flow of American aid to Madrid. The French also began to pressure the Basques, first by expelling the government from its building on rue Marceau in Paris (and turning it over to the Spanish government, to add insult to injury) and then by closing the clandestine radio station that broadcast to the Basque Country (the station was eventually moved to Venezuela). Meanwhile in Bilbao a small number of Basque youths began to meet clandestinely to consider what might be done to accelerate the downfall of the Franco regime and the achievement of Basque independence. This group, which soon became known as "Ekin," after the title of their internal newsletter, soon challenged the legitimacy of the Basque government and of the PNV to conduct the resistance. For the next several years, through the mid-1950s, Aguirre and other PNV and government leaders would try to absorb the Ekin group into their more conservative organization, but without much success.

President Aguirre refused to give up on the Americans. In 1952 accompanied by the representative of the Basque government in the United States, Jesús de Galindez (who was allegedly kidnapped and executed four years later by agents of Dominican Republic dictator General Trujillo), Aguirre paid a visit to the American state department in a desperate—but failed—attempt to prevent the United States from aiding Franco. Even after the signing of the United States–Spanish bases agreement, Aguirre refused to condemn the United States, or to criticize his government's policy of collaborating with the Americans. Despite rising criticism within his own party (the PNV would officially condemn the United States for its support of Franco in 1958) and from other parties in the government coalition, Aguirre held steadfastly to his reliance on the United States until finally, in 1959, even he had to admit that the policy had failed. By that time, of course, changes in Spain and the world had produced a totally different dynamic that would affect ethnic movements like that of the Basques.

While the overthrow of Franco and the return of his government to Euskadi were the principal concerns of Aguirre in these years, he also dedicated much time and energy to European affairs, including especially the federalist European movement. Under the leadership of such post-war European figures as Konrad Adenauer of Germany and Alcide de Gasperi of Italy, the European movement was officially formed at a meeting at The Hague in May 1947. Aguirre, who attended that meeting, was named to its Committee of Honor, along with British prime minister Winston Churchill and other European leaders. From the resistance workers in Spain, rumblings of dissatisfaction were heard; many of the underground activists doubted the usefulness of these international gatherings that seemed to have little to do with the daily demands of their struggle. But Aguirre persisted, believing that in the long run the fate of Euskadi lay in a federated "Europe of the Peoples."

One of the principal impulses to the European movement came from Christian democracy, which had survived the war determined to restore democracy to Europe founded on the principles of the Catholic faith, including freedom of religion and the protection of other fundamental human rights. Despite the strength of Catholicism in Spain, at the beginning and for many years thereafter the only Spanish groups that would be admitted into the movement were the Basque Nationalist party and its Catalan counterpart, the Democratic Union of Catalonia. José Antonio de Aguirre was to play a significant role in the founding and nurturing of this movement and thus in the development of the movement toward European unification that took shape during the 1950s.

In an effort to recover some of the lost momentum of his government following the failure of the policy of collaborating with, and depending on, the United States to bring down the Franco regime, Aguirre launched what would prove to be his final great undertaking. In his traditional Christmas message of 1954, he announced the convening in Paris of a World Basque Congress, which would bring together political leaders, scholars, intellectuals, artists, and other Basque figures from around the world in a celebration of Basque culture and a renewal of the Basque struggle for survival. Eventually, some 363 persons would attend the congress, which opened in Paris on September 23, 1956. Basques of all political leanings were invited, except the Communists, who were excluded. Costs of the congress were paid by wealthy Basques still in exile in America. It was said that never before in history had there been such a gathering of the Basque intellectual and political elite. The high point of the meeting was a speech by Aguirre, in which he reported on the activities and policies of his government since the end of the war.

Some seven months before the World Basque Congress, in February 1956, General Franco had reorganized his cabinet, introducing the liberal technocrats from Opus Dei into the Spanish government for the first time. By the late 1950s, the influence of these men had begun to make itself felt, as Spain began its great socioeconomic transformation from an autarchic dictatorship to an authoritarian regime in control of a gradually opening and liberalizing economy. As this transformation steadily deepened its roots into Spanish society, the prospects of overthrowing Franco disappeared farther and farther beyond the horizon.

These changes did not mean, of course, that Basques would now give up their struggle. On the contrary, by 1959 the Ekin group had abandoned any hope of moving the Basque government and the PNV toward a more aggressive policy; so on July 31, a new organization was born—Euzkadi ta Askatasuna (ETA). Although the organization would not engage in armed struggle for nearly another decade, eventually they would become the most violent and feared insurgent group on the European Continent.

To those around him in late 1959, President Aguirre was already beginning to show the signs of exhaustion after nearly three decades of tireless service to the cause of Basque freedom. A friend who interviewed him in Caracas in April that year found him tired and hesitant in his speech. A persistent cough betrayed some lingering health problems. A photograph taken of the president in early 1960 shows a surprisingly aged man, with the appearance of someone much older than his fifty-six years. At least one of his advisors suggested later that he was slowly dying of a broken heart, principally because of the betrayal of the United States.

The beginning of the end came on March 18, 1960, when he began to feel ill while working at his office in Paris. His physician sent him home and to bed; but his situation worsened steadily until the twenty-second when, at about 6:00 P.M., he died of a heart ailment. After a Mass and funeral ceremony in Paris, his body was taken to its final resting place, in St.-Jean-de-Luz in the French Basque Country. He was buried on March 27, 1960. José Antonio de Aguirre y Lecube was taken from the Basques after thirty years of unselfish and noble service to the cause of human freedom. It is not likely that they will ever again see someone who so completely embodies all that is honorable and praiseworthy in their land. His final words to the Basque people, his annual Christmas message in December 1959, ended with these lines: "A people comes to know itself in adversity, and there is only one answer to our misfortune of the moment: the ironclad union of all the Basques. Is there a better way to win our struggle? One people, one flag, one government, and, as I have repeated to you more than once, and do not doubt it, freedom will crown our efforts."

In preparing this brief introduction, I have consulted several historical works that contain biographical information about José Antonio de Aguirre. The most important of these is by Martin de Ugalde, *Biografía de Tres Figuras Nacionales Vascas: Arana-Goiri, Agirre, Leizaola* (San Sebastián: Sendoa, 1984). Other important sources included Koldo San Sebastián, *El Exilio Vasco en América: 1936/1946—Acción del Gobierno* (San Sebastián: Txertoa, 1988); J. M. Romaña Arteaga, *La Segunda Guerra Mundial y los Vascos* (Bilbao: Ediciones Mensajero, 1988); Emilio López Adán "Beltza," *El Nacionalismo Vasco en el Exilio, 1937–1960* (San Sebastián: Txertoa, 1977); and Koldo San Sebastián, *Historia del Partido Nacionalista Vasco* (San Sebastián: Txertoa, 1984).

In addition, I have found very useful a number of important newspaper articles written by one of the leading historians of this recent period, Koldo San Sebastián, and published in the Bilbao daily newspaper, *Deia*. For the period prior to and including the Spanish civil war, the most useful articles were those that appeared on July 19, 1981 ("Euzkadi Peregrina"); July 25, 1981 ("José Antonio Aguirre y la Política del Gobierno Vasco, 1937–1940"); May 1, 1983 ("Trucíos"); May 8, 1983 ("Santander, Principio del Fin"); May 15, 1983 ("Aguirre y el 'Pacto de Santoña'"); May 22, 1983 ("La Delegación Vasca en Barcelona"); May 29, 1983 ("Política de Prestigio"); June 5, 1983 ("En Busca de la Paz"); June 12, 1983 ("La Dimisión de Irujo"); June 26, 1983 ("El Documento Aznar"); and July 3, 1983 ("La Epopeya del Lehendakari Aguirre"). For the period following the civil war, these have been most helpful: March 22, 1981 ("La Resistencia, 1937–1947"); March 29, 1981 ("El Pacto de Bayona"); May 3, 1981 ("El Partido Nacionalista Vasco, 1948–1949"); May 24, 1981 ("Política Vasca"); February 21 and March 7, 1982 ("Los Vascos y las Relaciones Internacionales"); September 19, 1982 ("El Reconocimiento de la Dictadura"); October 17, 1982 ("La Huelga General de 1951"); November 7, 1982 ("Polémica en torno a una huelga"); November 14, 1982 ("Los Vascos, los Americanos y Franco"); January 23, 1983 ("Superar la Crisis"); March 13, 1983 ("La Muerte del Lehendakari Aguirre"); March 22, 1985 ("José Antonio Aguirre, Testimonio de Dignidad"); and June 29, 1985 ("En el Congreso Mundial Vasco del 56 participaron todos los sectores"). I also found of interest the article by Ronald Koven, "Grudge Left from World War II May Cloud Basque–U.S. Ties," *Washington Post*, November 11, 1979.

Finally, I would bring to the attention of the interested reader a fascinating collection of several hundred photographs of President Aguirre from his infancy to his final days. The title of the collection is *José Antonio de Aguirre, retrato de un Lehendakari,* and it was published in 1990 by the Fundación Sabino Arana in Bilbao on the occasion of the thirtieth anniversary of his death.

A GUIDE TO READING

THE ANNOTATED EDITION

Annotations that contain historical, political, or other background information have been incorporated into the text. These annotations are preceded by an asterisk (*), begin with the words "*Editor's note,*" and are enclosed in square brackets. An asterisk marks those passages in the text to which the annotations refer.

Numbered endnotes can be found at the back of the book. Superscript numbers in the text usually identify places in the American edition where material from the earlier Spanish version was deleted entirely. The missing material is usually paraphrased in the accompanying note. Occasionally, a superscript number will identify material found in both versions but substantially changed from the Spanish edition, in which case the original (Spanish) material will be paraphrased in the accompanying endnote.

The author included a few footnotes in his original text. These notes have been incorporated into the endnotes at the end of the book, and are followed by the words "Author's note" in square brackets.

Square brackets enclose material that first appeared in the English translation but was not found at all in the Spanish version.

All references to the "Spanish edition" or the "Spanish version" are to José Antonio de Aguirre, *De Guernica a Nueva York Pasando por Berlin,* second edition (Buenos Aires: Editorial Ekin, 1944).

ESCAPE VIA BERLIN

I

WHERE ARE WE

TO GO?

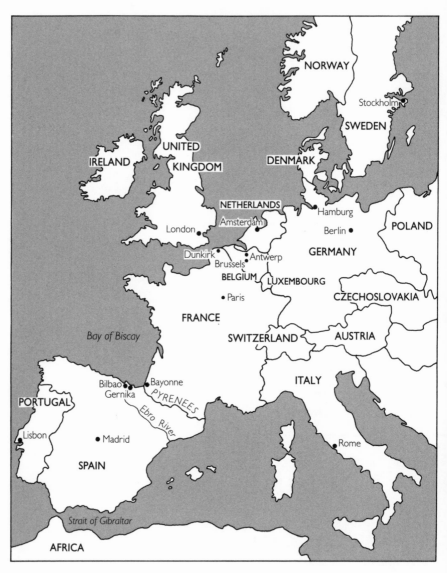

Western Europe in 1939

CHAPTER I 1

In the early morning of May 8, 1940, my wife and I with our two small children left Paris for the last time, although we did not realize it then.

On the face of it we were a simple young family with everything to live for. My little boy was full of health and high spirits, and his older sister, who looks like her mother, was also in holiday mood. But there were few who would have changed places with us had they known our story and how our journey was to end.

We were a happy family until then despite our exile, because Paris had been for nearly three years a hospitable if temporary seat of the Basque Government-in-exile where we had been able to preserve some vestige of our normal life. I had been President of the Basques since 1936, so there, as the ones to whom the two hundred thousand Basques in exile with us had looked for leadership and protection, our government had found the safety in which to carry on.*

*[Editor's note: The government to which Aguirre refers here is the government created in October 1936 by the Spanish parliament. By the time the home-rule regime was created, most of the Basque Country had been overrun by the forces of General Franco and their allies. There remained only the province of Vizcaya in which the Basque government could exercise its control. Even this sliver of land was lost when the government went into exile in June 1937, first to Santander province, then to France. During the war, while Aguirre's location was unknown, the government functioned in London; after he reached New York, it was situated there. In 1945 Aguirre returned to France and brought the government with him. The government remained in France until 1979, when the president, Jesús María Leizaola, returned to Bilbao and officially turned over home-rule authority to the Basque Autonomous Government created under the Spanish Constitution of 1978. That government now resides in the city of Vitoria, capital of Alava province.]

Our trip had started out this May morning to be a short reunion in Belgium with my wife's mother and my own mother who had rented a house at La Panne, a small town ten miles from Dunkirk on the Belgian coast. It ended, however, in a new exile—if you like—since our personal and official effects, all of the necessary equipment of both a family and a Presidency, still are where we left them, and we have been wanderers on the face of the earth ever since.

Nor did we realize that this simple family reunion would take place in a lion's den from which we would witness the carnage of Dunkirk and see the collapse of an army before our eyes, caught as we were in the sudden German invasion.

In those days, everyone thought La Panne was the safest place. In the previous war it was the last position held by the Belgian Army, and King Albert had spent a great deal of time there. Moreover, the current rumors in Paris were that the next German offensive would take place in Yugoslavia. The rumors, of course, were false. Rumors . . . rumors . . . rumors. Had I been an ordinary citizen they would not, perhaps, have been so important to us as they were.

This happy little family of ours knew that our happiness and our safety could be interrupted again at any moment, and that this interruption would be a fatal one.

My wife, Mari, and I knew that to be in the path of a German invasion would be the prelude to my finding myself before General Franco's firing squad, which I had until now escaped.

It went without saying that once the Gestapo found me, I should be recognized as a juicy political plum, for execution.

When this moment came I knew that I had reached a dead end. It was useless to attempt to run away from the Gestapo, since there was, in the short space of our holidays at La Panne, no longer any place to which to run.

I, therefore, was prompted to take the only course open to me— that was to brave the lion's mouth itself, and see what happened. In other words, to escape from Nazi-occupied Europe into Nazi Germany itself and live under Hitler's very nose while leaving behind me a trail of rumors as to my whereabouts. It was by these means that I eventually reached safety—but there, I am getting ahead of my story.

2

To cross the Franco-Belgian frontier in the spring of 1940, when France was already at war, it was necessary to have a special document, a safe-conduct from the French Government. I went to considerable trouble in Paris to obtain this document in order that my wife and children and I might visit our families, and be able to reenter France. This document proved to be of considerable value, as we shall see.

In the train to Dunkirk I felt a strange sense of foreboding. Several French officers traveled in the same car with us. They belonged to different branches of the Army, and some were of high rank. At first they were silent. Then, as I began talking in Basque with my children, Joseba Andoni and his sister Aintzane, about the beauty of the landscape, they spoke freely. They talked of the difficulties involved in the mobilization of the Army. Suddenly, a major in the Medical Corps raised his voice and, addressing the whole group, exclaimed:

"Anyway, what are we fighting for? Do you believe we'll get anywhere with this *sale gouvernement?*"

This "filthy" government happened to be Reynaud's. Some of the officers agreed, the others kept silent.

I looked with astonishment at the major and went out to the corridor for a smoke. I thought, here was France fighting for its very life, and this one French officer didn't seem to realize it. I remembered the time when we had visited the President of the French Parliament, M. Herriot. He was Honorary President, with Cardinal Verdier, of the International League of Friends of the Basques. We had discussed the final misfortune of the Spanish war.*

*[*Editor's note:* The reference here is to the final days of the Spanish civil war, which ended in March 1939, and to the final defense of Catalonia by the Catalan and Spanish republican troops. Aguirre uses this opportunity to introduce one of the book's important themes: the need to resist the evil of aggression and fascism by first clearing away much confusion and misunderstanding about the true nature of the enemy. He was throughout the book quite concerned with clarifying for the American reader the real reasons for the Spanish civil war and for the plight of the Basques in the early 1940s.]

"But what happened at the front to Catalonia?" M. Herriot asked. "The spirit was lacking there." We argued against this point and succeeded in convincing him of the magnificent struggle which was made by the Catalan and Spanish Republican troops at the Ebro River. President Herriot compared the story with the Basque fight. "You resisted for three months on the last forty kilometers," he said. He had followed our war in detail, and in spite of our arguments he thought that the Republican Front had lacked spirit. When I heard that major on the train to Dunkirk, I could not forget President Herriot and his words. "The spirit was lacking."

A country and an Army, it is the same: when the country is confused, its armed forces are also confused.

The fate of France was the matter of immediate importance, but my chief personal preoccupation was, of course, with the way in which its defeat would affect our people.

We Basques had lost the soil of our country, *Euzkadi*, and a year and a half later the Spanish Republic had also succumbed, defeated by the aid given by the Axis Powers to Franco.* The policy of the embargo and the Munich Pact had resulted in the first disaster to the Democracies.

*[Editor's note: "Euzkadi" is the name given by Basque nationalists to their ethno-nation, the homeland of the Basque people. Today it is usually written "Euskadi." In principle, Euskadi includes all seven Basque territories, including four in Spain and three in France. In practice, Basques from the Spanish side of the Spanish-French border customarily use the term to refer to that portion of the Basque Country south of the international border.]

The men of the Basque Army who had survived the war found themselves in the prisons and concentration camps set up by General Franco's dictatorial regime.

As President of the Autonomous Basque Government, I was absorbed, during those days, in the fate of my exiled compatriots. The strong colonies of Basques in America, especially South America, little by little sent their assistance, which helped to prevent many misfortunes.

We had to take care of thousands of children and their mothers, old folks, and hundreds of maimed war victims, besides the great mass of men thrown out of their country, deprived of any savings they might have and their normal occupations. They were unemployed and in exile. Homes and hospitals took them in, schools and sanatoriums looked after the children; and while in the end you might say that our people in exile lived poorly, they lived with dignity.

In Belgium alone, benevolent societies took in close to five thousand Basque children. There were over fifty Basque priests accompanying them in exile. Also a group of students, among them my brothers and brothers-in-law. My mother and mother-in-law lived with them in Louvain, where the younger ones continued their studies at the University. It was two years since we had seen each other and some of our relatives had not yet seen my little boy, Joseba Andoni.

Instincts of family life are strong in us. The whole Basque tradition of government is based on the sanctity and importance of the home and family life. It seemed we must overcome all difficulties and get to our families in Belgium, and the prospect of this reunion must have blinded us to the dangers in our course.

We reached La Panne at noon on the 8th. There was a small party to celebrate the family reunion. My brother Juan told Joseba Andoni and Aintzane that he would take them over to the wide sand beaches in the morning. We went to bed early—tired after our journey. My wife, Mari, and I were happy; both our families were well and everyone was pleased with our children.

At four o'clock on the morning of May 10th we awakened to the sound of bombs exploding. I remember thinking at first that it was a torment in my own mind: the noise I heard was not real; it was the memory of a bombardment. I dressed quickly and hurried next door to get my brother. We went out into the street. The skies were thick with black billowing smoke. Gasoline reservoirs just outside of Dunkirk had been bombed.

At about nine o'clock we saw the arrival of the first French troops. They had crossed the boundary that same morning and their advance was disorganized. Military trucks came first—later motorcycles, then officers in small cars and finally even some of the Navy.

The marching was continuous—but there was no impression of strength or unity. The soldiers were obeying orders hastily given, and the air was alive with quick and untried optimism. People on the streets cheered until they were hoarse, as if with one voice. It was like tremendous music heard too closely. I carried my two-year-old son Joseba Andoni high on my shoulder. Women emptied the stores of chocolates, crackers, cigarettes and gave them to the soldiers. Flowers, pennants—streamers of the Allied Countries were thrown or fastened to the trucks as they passed along. Some soldiers wept as they marched. We returned to the house—my little boy cheering with the rest, as if his lungs would burst.

[Every night at their bedtime, I tell my children a story. All over the world there are fathers who share this habit with me. It makes the invisible bonds between a father and his children stronger although the reason for the added strength is hard to describe. In much the same way a man who has worked for his country (carrying a gun, manufacturing the ammunition, or on the ideological front) feels more definitely the ties which will make his feet turn toward home at the first opportunity. This night with a new hope singing through my heart, I told them of all the other exiled children of Euzkadi who would again see their home. "Today is the beginning," I told them. "As these soldiers go to meet the Germans, they will make your country free. The peasants, the sailors, the mine workers, the rich, the poor, will all speak freely again—as I speak to you now—without fear. Perhaps it will take time and travel before we return home, but we will return."]

Instead of good news, bad news rolled back—gathering momentum and power with its incredible speed. German troops crossing Luxembourg had flung themselves toward the interior of France and were nearing Sedan, while they broke through the Belgian defenses by the Liége front.

We let the first tremendous caravan of refugees pass. I received word that several of the Basque exiles in Belgium wanted to join us and make the journey back into France under my protection . . . and as we waited we saw the surging flood of humanity choke the roads and grow ever larger and more surging. Thousands were marching along the coastal highways, the whiplash of fear driving them on and the Nazi planes spattering them with death and desolation. . . . We were calmer only because we had more experience. This same air power had made the Basque roads during our war a mockery to civilization as it had afterwards on the mountain pass from Catalonia to the French border.

Our parents' home in La Panne became, for the Basques in Belgium during those few days, the symbol and substance of our homeland. We grew into a small army of refugees—forty-six in all—

whose main commandment was: never lose yourself from the unit. Each one was dependent on another and responsible for someone else.

[First of all, however, you must know all the people who were with us—but especially the dead. Let our dead greet you first. Look well at them; explore their faces; remember their names. There were only two—but they made us feel the universal death around us more deeply. Now coming to meet you is my sister Encarna. She is full of life. Up to the moment of the wound which proved fatal, she would say, "Don't worry—for all this, the Allies are going to come through victorious . . ." In the middle of a bombardment, she would talk of victory—not as a distant possibility beyond realization in her lifetime, but as if each bomb that the Nazis unloaded was a bomb which made more certain their ultimate defeat.

This is Encarna. The journey is before us, and she is going to die. I am thankful we are ignorant of the future as we start out.

For a moment Encarna talks with our friend, Cesareo Asporosa. He is a very vital man and big, but no one has ever lived more gentle in heart than Asporosa. He has been one of the heads of the Basque Commercial Delegation in Belgium. From Antwerp he had helped to provision Euzkadi during our chapter in the war.

Before we started out, we made Asporosa treasurer. All the money in the group was turned over to him. He would see that everyone received the same care and the same benefits—if such could be found. The treasurer, on such a journey, must be someone trusted and respected by all in the group, someone who was accessible as well. Asporosa was such a man. The smallest child, the shyest girl had never been afraid to speak with him.

There are nine children, several young girls, a caravan of students, four priests, four old people—some of them have nothing. They can say quietly to Asporosa, "I have no money," or can tell him of some other need. He never fails them.

During the bombardment of Dunkirk, many would pray to die; but none would die, except two who wanted most to live—my sister Encarna and our friend Asporosa, who there in the beginning, as they talked together, were the most optimistic of us all.]

I decided at last that we could wait no longer for any of the others. We left a letter for them on the door of our house, in case they should get there—written in Basque, and giving them what I hoped would appear to be an official document. To a reader who has not had the problem of frontiers and frontier officials to cope with, this attempt at documentation may seem a little pompous or unnecessary. It is difficult enough in times of peace to pass a frontier without a document—but in times of war, it is impossible . . . If you have some official scrap of paper, at least you can present an argument to the frontier official, and you may eventually exhaust him or persuade him by financial means to let you pass.

May 17th, we started out. Where to? Only God knew the answer. . . . Safety was the name of a place which perhaps we should never find. The younger men carried the luggage on their shoulders. Cesareo Asporosa was helping some of the younger children. My son Joseba Andoni was the most contented one of all, as Sabin carried him on his bicycle, which also bore the two heaviest valises.

"I thought I was lucky," Sabin said with good humor as he took on a second suitcase, "that I had this bicycle. Now I am not sure."

The rest of the children, from four years upward, walked. Asporosa had a child on his shoulder, and a piece of luggage in his hand.

Before we had come to the outskirts of La Panne, there was a terrific bombardment. Just ahead of us streets were torn open wide—and before our children's eyes other children were blown into bits or crushed beneath a building which crumpled sadly, in a dejected fashion like a house made of cards . . . It was terrible: the sound and the smell; the awful noise of the suddenly wounded. We were at first frozen to the ground where we stood, and then the planes began circling and swooping down with their machine guns singing out their merciless pursuit of anything that lived—however small . . . We had seen all of it before. It was such an old story to us now, we were not so afraid as some others. But our women were terrified. Some of the children became quite ill, vomiting in the street from what they had seen. We had to make them get under a tree and we had to encircle them so they would not try to escape. The noise and the sight of a bombardment make the power of reason leave quickly. Since it was impossible to take refuge from the bombs, at least to keep under the trees was to keep from being a target for the machine-gunning pursuit planes. The firing grew more intense. A German pilot, whose plane had been downed by anti-aircraft guns, descended suddenly in a parachute. Everyone, with a gun, shot at him. He was killed there in the square a thousand times—riddled over and over again. Asporosa, watching with me, said, "It's too bad, you know, that now they are wasting so many bullets."[2]

I could only think of how frugally and cautiously our men and our citizens had been trained to use those precious bullets.

It was five in the afternoon before the German planes, which had bombarded La Panne almost with impunity, without answer from their enemy, vanished.

We gathered our luggage and bundles together, counted our children, and reorganized. We gave final orders that no one should be separated from the whole group, for any reason whatsoever . . . and we went ahead.

It was slow. The older women had to rest often, and the children of course had to be carried half the time. We saw the frontier, in the distance, at about eight in the evening, and the sight was most disheartening. A terrified crowd, anxious to escape, congregated near the barricade. We were finally able to get to it, but the border was closed. A powerful string of gendarmes and one policeman not in uniform were guarding the pass.

What were we to do? Return to La Panne? There was only a small house, probably belonging to road workers, and it was closed.

I asked a guard, "When will the border be open?"

He answered, "At four or five o'clock tomorrow morning."

My brother Juan said at once, "I think we should stay here, José Antonio."

I agreed. "There will be more people coming, and then we will have to wait in line again." We were all together and in agreement that it was best to stay where we were for the night. But as food was quite scarce we were worried about the children. My brother Juan and his friends decided they should return to La Panne and get food from the house we had left. There were four bicycles with carrying baskets, and so the boys took them. In the meantime, we established our small camp at the edge of the drive. The clear night was cold. . . . The hundreds of people around us began to make themselves as comfortable as they could on the ground and in the fields which bordered the drive. Overpowered by weariness and tension, they had no intention of losing their place for passing the frontier the next day. Leaning back against one another, covered only with the coats we had brought, and huddled behind the protection of our valises from the chilling wind that rose, we tried to sleep. It was out of the question. The frontier guards told everyone that it was dangerous to remain on the border of the drive, as the night before it had been machine-gunned by enemy pursuit planes. People dispersed hastily, noisily. We preferred not to move. Our children slept soundly, and our places were to some extent protected by the walls of the road workers' house.

We could hear the vibration of airplane motors and the rattling sound of machine guns—but we had heard them so many times in our own country, we realized they were far away. Once in a while reconnoitering planes would throw Bengal lights into the night which descended like brilliant and mysterious meteors. They were looking for the prey of the bombardiers. The lights were the forerunners of death, and they chilled your senses—even more than the distant noise of the machine guns.

Some people tried to slip by the guards. They were knocked back—thrown on the ground. A moment's silence, and then the sudden noise of the guards' swearing. There was one civilian guard who carried a thick club. He walked like a man gone completely insane, brandishing the club and calling dreadful names to the poor people who, agitated by fear and exhaustion, practically fastened themselves to the wire fences. To compel them to withdraw, this man would rain barbarous blows upon them. There was a loud clamor of indignation. He swaggered all night. With the club as his alter ego, he became a symbol to me of all dictators.

But at last the moon had gone and the darkness before the sun's beginning had passed, and there on the road into France thousands of us scrambled for our places. At five o'clock the barrier opened. One by one we passed through an opening in the wire fence. The examination of credentials was done so rigorously and slowly it was a macabre contrast with the rapidity of military events which caused us to be there.

At last our turn came. I was at the head, imagining that my "privileged" document from the French Government would enable us all to pass through. All the people with me carried passports of the Spanish Republic, which had been expedited by the Basque Autonomous Government.

But Franco had since been recognized by France, and although everyone knew that he was pro-Hitler, our passports had no official recognition. They could only ascertain the fact that we were being persecuted for having fought in the first trenches of democracy. In spite of our friendship for France we were worth less than a scrap of paper with a seal. We were, in those moments, nothing but a group of exiles with no acceptable documents. Since we carried no Franco passport, our attempt to enter France was "illegal." We were rejected. Had we carried Franco passports, they might have looked at us suspiciously, but their barriers would have opened before us. The gendarme at the border could not understand that there are moments in life when people should be judged by their beliefs and their history and not by their documents. Who is more carefully documented than a spy?

"Your papers are in order," said the gendarme to me, "but the passports of the others no longer have any value."

"I had expected you to tell me that," I replied. "But doesn't our fight against those who now attack you, as they attacked us, mean anything? Before you, we saw the planes of Hitler; before you, we suffered those cruel bombardments. Are you to leave this group of exiles to the mercy of the enemy, based on an unjust legal evaluation of the passports?"

The gendarme looked at me in some confusion. Realizing the fairness and justice of my words, he called his superior, a subofficer, who came and repeated the same thing. Our passports were void, and he added: "Now, even you cannot pass, because we have received an order by which only Belgians, Dutch, French and English may pass. The rest will pass when all of these have done so."

[It was useless to argue. Thousands of us were forced back. A kind of chant arose in protest. It was called out and sung in many different languages, but the meaning was clear. Open—open the gate! German troops are advancing at full speed! Why do you bother with passports and regulations? It will soon be too late.

"What are we to do?"—from the more despairing ones.

"Where are we to go?"—from the frightened.

But the order was fulfilled. The man was doing his duty, and duty was more important than intelligence or consideration. All day long we watched people passing through to the other side of the frontier: lucky people who did not belong to a country already under the shadow of the Nazi swastika. And the unlucky ones joined us. By the late afternoon you could scarcely see the fields by the road, for the people were so packed together.]

Towards six o'clock a group of gendarmes began to drive stakes into the ground and to join them with wire netting, closing in a great expanse of ground. Horrified we saw erected before us what was obviously to become our own concentration camp. At first we refused to believe our eyes, but commanding, relentless voices banish any doubts:

"Everyone inside the fence . . ."

"Hurry—hurry! Get along there . . . Inside the fence . . ."

And one by one we entered—shoved, pushed, shouted at— women, children, clergymen, all of us. We were exiled from our own country because we had defended freedom. And now we were being imprisoned by the official order of a French administration whose soldiers fought, whose guns resounded, whose planes flew overhead—to defend freedom. More contradictions, more confusion. By betraying the purest and simplest ideals, Europe was being vanquished.

There was no adequate food for the children, no water, no roof over our heads. We surrounded our children, and we prayed. Praying to God is a comfort when men are deaf to the pleas of the helpless.

[Many people in other groups, who had walked for days and nights on end, exhausted with fatigue and hunger, began to weaken. Near us a woman fainted. She did not cry out; or, if she did, her voice was too small to be heard over the din of the thousand mumbling, chattering voices. Suddenly we saw her fall forward. My sister, Encarna, and my sister-in-law, Margari, went to her aid, and they were joined by the woman's husband. In the rush and milling of people, the couple had been separated. When finally the woman was brought out of her faint, she became quite hysterical on finding her husband with her at last. The two girls said that the couple were Czechs, and that they could not understand what they said. It was a form of thank you—and a moment's tremendous happiness, despite the circumstances, at their reunion.]

Other people lay on the ground burning with fever and delirium. Quite a few died. The place was sandy and dirty. There was no water. Among other things we prayed for a warm rain. When there is no water, even your skin becomes thirsty.

There were more than three thousand Jews in our concentration camp; Austrians, Poles, Czechs, a few Scandinavians, and even a few Americans. Since they were citizens of neutral countries, the Americans and Scandinavians went back to La Panne. And of all the people enclosed within those fences, these poor Jews were the most panic-stricken. I had never before seen such typical Israelites together in such great number. Many of them wore long beards which showed that they came from the Slavic countries. These people, upon whom the hatred of Nazi propaganda was concentrated, inspired in my heart and mind a most profound pity: brutally persecuted, treated with such cruel rudeness on the frontier, despised even by many who were suffering there with them. I could not forget that particularly in misfortune man should be looked upon only as man. I saw their women and children as I saw my own. I was their companion in sorrow. And I wondered how, as Christians, so called, those who turned away their faces could forget the origin of Christ and his doctrine.[3]

3

The night passed in relative peace, as the bombardment was heard only from a distance and the pursuit planes did not machine-gun us. The snoring of one of our clergymen who slept peacefully on the ground made much more noise. Surely to good Father Domingo that hard bed, with all its discomforts, had more delight than the cot he slept on one of the last nights he had spent in Belgian territory. This exiled Basque priest lived secluded in the Benedictine Monastery in Louvain. When invasion in Belgium started, the Prior gave the benediction to his monks, and with one hundred francs each they started on foot towards France, Father Domingo among them. He was sixty-four years old and a heavy man. Worn out and tired, he had separated from his companions, believing that he could find a shorter way by a fork in the road, when he was detained by a picket of Belgian soldiers. He was an expert in agricultural matters, and had in his small valise advertisements of some agricultural books written in German, which they found. With no more evidence, those confused army men accused him of being a German parachutist, put him in the death house, and that same night advised him he was going to be executed. They had been advised "on good authority" that the Germans descended in parachutes disguised as the clergy, and because of his agricultural advertisements they thought that Father Domingo was a German parachutist in spite of his years and his proportions.

Fortunately, the Prior realized that Father Domingo was missing and found him just as he was about to be executed. It was not difficult for the Prior to guarantee Father Domingo's identification, and absolute innocence. For this reason, as he snored beatifically in the concentration camp, I am sure our good priest could not notice the noise of the bullets or the airplanes.

We remained prisoners within those fences for three days, guarded by soldiers. We were hungry and thirsty and exhausted.

It was not surprising that at the end of three days there were people already dying all around us—or in the agony of death and sickness from hunger and thirst. No one had been concerned about supplying the citizens of our concentration camp with food or water. During the day the heat became unbearable. The sand beneath our feet was red-hot from the sun's rays. But it was the contrasting cold of night which extracted the heaviest toll of victims. Our children started to weaken. The uncertainty of the future was no comfort to the mothers, already deep in anxiety. But we all watched over the nine children. If a drop of milk came, it went to their small emaciated lips. How grateful I am to my countrymen who sacrificed themselves, and did not permit the inhumanity which surrounded us to corrupt them!

A Dutch clergyman, with a bicycle, had arrived at the boundary barrier. He showed his passport.

"Hollander?" inquired the gendarme sullenly.

"Yes, sir," answered the clergyman.

The gendarme, out of his wits, shouted, "The Dutch are firing against our troops. . . . Go back, traitor!"

The priest answered calmly: "If I were a traitor, I would not be here. I protest against this unqualified indignity."

A clamor arose on all sides, the most indignant cries coming from the concentration camp. The imprisoned men flung themselves against the fences, trying to break them down. Panic, indignation, exhaustion, excitement, agitated by hunger and the sight of the continuous marching through the frontier, produced that movement of angered protest. Alarmed, the French officers finally promised to solve the situation immediately.

On May 20th at seven o'clock in the evening, a half-hour before the frontier was closed for the night, all the imprisoned crossed the border. But two hundred yards ahead we found another barrier had been closed, which would not be opened until the next day. We had to sleep another night outdoors, leaning against some deserted houses, the first in the suburbs of Bray-Dunes. My mother-in-law and her grandchild, my little Joseba, spent the night inside a pigsty. Some Belgian peasants made room for my mother in a stable. It was her birthday. In the happy days in our home in Euzkadi, we would never have believed that one day she would celebrate her birthday sleeping in a stable while her children and grandchildren slept outdoors.

Towards four in the morning, we were again before the second frontier barrier.* While we waited for its opening, I carried my young son in my arms, so as to save him from the jostling of the crowd. A Belgian couple, of distinguished bearing, laughed at the efforts of the little one, whose only worry was to see that his cap would not be knocked off. This had a Basque coat of arms on its visor. The couple became curious and asked what it was. On being informed that we were Basques, and seeing the clergymen with us, the lady inquired in surprise, "But you must have been with Franco!"

"No, madam," I replied, "we find ourselves here for just the opposite reason. We fought Franco."

"But you are not Catholics?"

*[Editor's note: What follows appears to be one of those instances in which Aguirre uses a conversation with someone he meets along the way to drive home one of the book's important themes. In this particular case, he addresses what to Basques must have been an extremely vexing situation: the inability of many Americans to understand how Catholic Basques could have sided with the Spanish Republic (seen by many to be anti-Catholic and anti-clerical) and against Franco (thought by many American Catholics to be a staunch defender of the faith).]

Again this confusion is placed before me—I explain to her carefully. "We *are* Catholics, madam, who have defended the freedom of our people against aggression. Just as you are now leaving your country before the aggression of Hitler, we had to leave ours. Perhaps you do not realize that Hitler is an old acquaintance of the Basques, just as he was and is a good friend of Franco's."

"Ah, then they are cut from the same piece," answered the Belgian lady.

My little son could at least sit in the small hole that some Dutch nuns had made for him. They were also waiting to cross the frontier. One of them, with beautiful features, caressed my boy—wondering at finding in her path such a small exile. I beheld that scene in silence, and thought, "If you only knew whose child you are caressing, you would surely be surprised, for they must have told you that Franco is the Rescuer of the Faith and the Defender of Order."

They probably did not dare tell her the same about Hitler; but they must have presented the mirage of Franco, who continues to be the central point of confusion. There are many who vilify Hitler, mourn the errors of Mussolini, but fall into the snare of Franco, not knowing that he is the bridge which leads to Hitler. There is no element of confusion more disturbing to modern ideology than the dictatorship which abusively uses and compromises the Christian faith to accomplish its propaganda. It muddles everything like an inkfish in clear water.

We crossed the frontier at last. There was an officer who finally understood our case and gave the order.

CHAPTER 11

Six o'clock in the morning, and the dew still lay wet upon the ground. We were all tired, but not yet willing to admit even to ourselves that the journey was long and the road before us endless. We reached the church in Bray-Dunes, but nearly passed it by without notice. Trees surrounded it, and ivy guarded it, peaceful and timeless. We entered, and our priests said Mass. Right after, we started for Dunkirk. The women and children in our group showed distressing signs of complete fatigue, and so we approached every wagon and cart, every automobile and truck. At last a kind old man listened to our pleas and agreed to take the women and young folk in his truck to the other side of the city, where they would wait for us.

We paid him for this service and waved goodbye to them, thankful that they should have even this measure of rest in the journey.

Soon they were out of sight. Those of us who were left—the young men and boys, the priests, the older men—continued the weary trudge down the road. When we reached the outskirts of Dunkirk, a policeman directing traffic shouted:

"To Calais—and fast! Otherwise you'll be taken prisoner."

We didn't listen; so many policemen told conflicting things, you had to follow your own nose. In the distance we could see the smoke of Dunkirk billowing in the sky. Walking along, we would suddenly have to throw ourselves down close to the road's edge. Up and down, up and down, we made progress slowly. All day long, German planes seemed always to sweep nearer, closer to the earth.

We had walked since early morning; nothing to eat, a thimbleful of wine at noontime for our parched lips. We had given our noon ration of food to our women and children. Now as I walked along in the late afternoon all kinds of anxieties attacked me. We should have caught up with the women before this, I wanted to say to my companions; something might have happened. Perhaps they had become terrified at the enemy's aviation. Since the Nazis had machine-gunned us along the road throughout the whole day, they could not have spared anyone. I had that queer lightheaded, almost spiritual clarity that can possess the weary mind and the hungry body: First come senseless worries which nag and torment, and then a separation, and somehow, without definition, the whole picture of events becomes clear and the ultimate destination more assured.

We were silent now as we walked; perhaps a kind of group communion of thought and feeling was taking place which not one of us would speak about to the other. Like long-distance runners, we were getting our second wind.

At a curve in the road we saw Mari coming out of a farmhouse. Waiting beneath some trees were the rest of the women and the children. I breathed a prayer of thanks to God that they were all safe. Mari said as we joined them: "These people told me we cannot stay here. They have too many refugees under their roof now. There is no room for any more." She laughed shortly. "What could I say?" She looked at us as if somehow we must find the solution.

There was nothing to do but go on. It was growing dark. Where would we spend the night? My little son, in my arms, was going to sleep, but the other children—the older ones—were also tired. Asporosa picked up my little daughter and carried her. Soon all the children were riding on our shoulders. At last we saw an old barn, huge and sprawling.

"Look at that palace," Encarna cried out.

"There will be straw to sleep on, surely," Mari said.

Tired as we were, we all hastened forward. After so many nights spent out in the open and on the hard ground, just the thought of a roof over our heads was like a blessing from heaven.

When we first opened the barn door, the darkness was impenetrable.[1] We could not see that it was already full of refugees. They could see us, however.

"Close the door," a voice called out to us.

Another said, "There is no room here for all of you."

"Go on—go on there . . ."

"There is another barn a mile down the road. . . . Go to it. . . . There will be more room for you."

The last was almost a pleading voice—but nevertheless I felt that, if this barn was full, the next one would be also. We crowded in against a clamor of protest. When the others saw they could not get rid of us, they soon became friendly. They were mostly Austrian refugees with a few Belgian and Dutch soldiers.

My wife and our children, my mother-in-law, my sister-in-law, and I were able to make ourselves quite comfortable in a cart filled with hay that was under a shed outside the barn. Soon they were fast asleep. Overhead the planes roared constantly, but gradually our whispered conversations ceased. Around me I could hear the steady breathing of those deep in exhausted slumber. I envied them. I could not sleep. It was not the planes' roar, nor the sound of distant guns . . . I think I had gone beyond the point of sleep.

The barn was situated at one corner of an eighty-acre field. From the air, it might well have resembled a landing field. Waves of German planes were passing over us now, over and over, encircling us. The noise of their motors kept me awake. Everyone around me still slept, when suddenly one noise rose high above the roaring of the engines. It grew louder, singing as it approached us and reached a high, whining roar with a tremendous glare of light which awakened people into terror. The children clutched their mother. At first I thought it must be a bomb. The deafening noise had misled me. They were throwing Bengal lights upon the field and incendiary bombs. One fell on the very cart where we were lying. It hit a corner and bounced off. I stood up and shouted: "Don't be scared. They are incendiary bombs. . . ." I went outside to look over the ground. The sight of the field was harrowing and at the same time beautiful. Several hundred incendiary bombs burned on the ground. They had been thrown in pattern bombing with a particular skill over the target. Only two, however, burned near the house. I walked all around the barn, and it was intact. There was nothing near the outer shed. One bomb would have burned everything quickly, and the catastrophe which might have occurred was too horrible to contemplate. The burning bombs in the field produced a dangerous visibility. With some bricks and earth I extinguished the bombs whose flames menaced the barn, and isolated the ones which were nearer. While I was working, some soldiers and a Dutch sergeant came out into the night. I looked up, thinking they would help me, but instead they stared at me fearfully, a mixture of suspicion and horror reflected in their glances.

"What are you doing standing there?" I asked them impatiently. "Don't you know yet that incendiary bombs are not dangerous when they are isolated in time?" Not one of them moved. "They don't explode," I said. "Come help me. See—this one is already out. Don't worry."

Little by little the countryside resumed a normal aspect. The illumination was extinguished, and the bombs went out, aided by the dew of the night.

The other refugees in the interior of the barn slept so soundly that in spite of all this excitement only two woke up and came out to help us. We let the others sleep. The following day they could scarcely believe that several hundred incendiary bombs had surrounded the barn where, on dry hay, more than a hundred people slept. I shall not forget easily the night of May 21, 1940.[2]

2

The next morning, at six o'clock, one of the priests in our group started out with me for Dunkirk. Father Alberto was an eminent member of the Jesuits in Euzkadi.* He was exiled in Antwerp because he had loved his Basque country and he was an authority on social problems. We went to Dunkirk to try to see the Admiral of the base and obtain passage for our group to any French port farther south. We did not think then of England. We did not know the situation. We lived only between the earth and the sky.

*[Editor's note: The "Father Alberto" referred to here is Alberto Onaindia, a leading figure in the Basque clergy and a prominent spokesman for the Basque nationalist cause in the 1930s.]

At the entrance of Dunkirk, we were detained by a picket of soldiers. After some explanations, we were allowed to go on. It was seven o'clock. The city was dead. Military forces had taken over completely. Bombs had caused incredible destruction. Streets were piled with rubbish, littered with debris. All the shops were closed. A light pall of smoke, like a murky fog, covered everything. Very few soldiers patrolled the streets. We saw English troops on guard with the French. Once in a while a face would appear in a window or a door, and eyes would stare at us as if we were strange creatures. For what earthly reason, they seemed to ask, have a priest and a civilian come to Dunkirk?

"I want to say Mass," Father Alberto said to me; "and if we go to the cathedral one of the priests there will be able to help us get our bearings."

The church was practically deserted, and the emptiness seemed heavier because of the silence of the city itself. There was not the normal contrast of entering a quiet place from a noisy, bustling city street. There was an atmosphere of dread expectancy in the city of Dunkirk, and this had penetrated into the church so that there was no real feeling of peace before the sacred altars. The lone woman in a corner, undefinably sad in her aloneness, and the man with his head held between his hands were pictures of desperation born

from things lost in the spirit and in the mind. These people were
looking for strength to bear the anguish of their city's silence. A
priest was saying Mass at one of the many altars. The others were
empty. Beneath the sacred vestments we saw the tips of his military
boots.

We entered the vestry and were met by a young priest. We explained who we were and why we had come here.

"As you are Basques," he said, pointing to the priest with puttees,
"it is lucky that you have come to this cathedral. Do you see that
priest saying Mass at that altar? Well, he is a good friend of yours. I
know, because I have heard him speak often of the Basques. Wait for
him, and he'll help you."

When at last he came into the vestry, we introduced ourselves.
When he heard my name, he exclaimed: "Aguirre! But, if you are
Aguirre, don't you realize they are looking for you and they will
shoot you on sight? Don't you know yet that we are cut off?"

"What do you mean, *cut off*?" Father Alberto and I spoke almost at
once.

"Practically cut off from everywhere. Since the 17th they have had
us backed up against the sea, and only God knows how many will be
able to escape that way."

I felt helplessly sick, and, looking at Father Alberto, I saw that like
myself he did not know which way to turn now. The French priest
made us sit down with him, and we told him our story and what we
had hoped to accomplish on this visit to Dunkirk. The priest was a
member of the French military police. He had spent three years in
Madrid, he told us; but when Franco's regime was installed he as a
Frenchman could remain there no longer, so he left Spain.

"Everything I can do to help you," said the priest, "I will do; but
you must understand how badly events are going for us. Affairs of
the city are so disorganized it will be difficult to accomplish anything.
Also, I can only be with you until twelve, when I must go on duty."

We made our way toward the port, hoping to get to the Admiral in
his office there. The French priest, wanting the latest information on
the enemy's advance, asked us to stop off at police headquarters. The
Chief of Police didn't know much more. While we were with him the
siren wailed out, and we had to go down into the cellar, which had

been converted into an air-raid shelter. At one of the little docks in front of the headquarters, several small ships were sunk in the bombardment. The cellar was half-filled with gendarmes: some rested on cots and covered themselves with blankets; others sat on the floor, on tables, lounged against the foundations. They were re-signed, even relaxed, and they listened to the explosions calmly. At last the raid was over, and we went on to the Admiralty. We found the doors there closed to us. Only naval and military men could enter. We went back into the street, which was packed now with people moving like a slow, winding river. They did not know where they were going, and they were ignorant of the fact that they were already cut off. How could we hope for help from our people when we saw the helpless-ness of others? Twice we had to return to the air-raid shelter. German planes flew low and unloaded bombs accurately with no opposition at all. Everywhere we heard people complaining about the lack of Allied aviation. The French priest had to leave us, and once more Father Alberto and I were alone, discouraged and terribly thirsty. We asked for water, but no one would give us any. The water mains had been destroyed by bombs. Restaurants and hotels were closed. We rang at one in the central square, and a group of English soldiers told us it would be useless. On the march since before six o'clock that morning, with no food in my stomach nor a drop of water, my thirst made me feel almost savage; I did not know about my companion. For several days we had eaten nothing but crackers and chocolate. We had slept in the open. None of it seemed as bad as the thirst which was now with us and was immediate. We went into a little tavern which looked as if it might be doing business, and at last a woman took pity on us. She gave us each a swallow of white wine in liqueur glasses. Once we drank these few drops, we started on our way back to the farm—another five miles to walk.

3

Back at the barn, my brother gave us food at once. They had walked for miles to get it. As we had accomplished nothing in Dunkirk, we could only tell them that we were grateful to be back safely. They told us the women had gone on with the children toward Bergues, a small inland town. "From there they are going to take the highroad toward Calais. The coastal highways are closed now to all civilians," my brother said.

I looked at Father Alberto, and his eyes met mine. We finished our food in silence. None of them knew that the enemy surrounded us. . . . We were like wooden puppets in a vise, and the terrible tools of the Nazis were being sharpened for us.

One of the younger students was sitting on the ground beneath a tree, away from us, and I could tell there was something that bothered him. He called to Juan, "Why don't you tell your brother about Sabin and Deunoro?"

I turned to my brother. "What about them?"

Juan shrugged. "It is nothing serious. It is only that they have been gone a long time now."

"Where did they go?" Father Alberto asked.

They had followed shortly on our heels in the early morning and were going, they had told the others, to the outskirts for provisions. It was late afternoon, and they had not yet returned. But as we spoke we saw them coming down the road, accompanied by a town official and two French soldiers. They had been arrested as spies and detained for two hours. Finally they had persuaded the official to come back with them and interview me, and of course everything turned out all right. These incidents were minor enough, in themselves, but they added always to the tension under which we lived. Sabin and Deunoro were "cleared" of any guilt. Who would be next? We walked the ten miles to Bergues, and there we found that the next person to rescue was my own wife. The other women and the children were either in tears, or they were angry. Mari had been held incommunicado for several hours; no one would listen to her or examine her documents. As my brother Juan and I were starting for the village center they brought her back. At last she had been able to make herself heard, and she was free.

The women told us that everyone was acting insanely uncontrolled in the village of Bergues. My wife said: "People are flying about, bumping into each other—sobbing. When someone careens into you, instead of saying, 'Excuse me,' they say: 'The Nazi tanks are entering the town. Get out of their way! You'll be killed!'"

The truth, we soon found, was that the German motorized units, penetrating one of the breaks in the Allied lines, had reached the suburbs on the other side of the town. The whole night was terrible. Each noise we heard was the noise of entering tanks. We kept the knowledge of our trapped position from the women, and by silent agreement did not speak of it once. We found refuge in a small farmhouse whose gentle and kind owners took pity on us. We must have made a sorry picture, holding our children, the women tired— the older women so tired there was pain in their exhaustion.

"We can make room somehow for the women and the children in the house," the good people told us, "and then there is the old pigsty." The sty had several compartments, each one five feet in diameter; and four men slept in each compartment.

Without knowing it, I was living through moments of extraordinary danger.[3] In fact we all were. A French Basque, M. Ibarnegaray, who belonged to the *Partie Social Français* and who from the beginning of the conflict on the Iberian Peninsula had played Franco's cards, had become a member of the French Government. Once in this position of authority, he promised General Franco, according to an interview published in the *Paris-Soir*, that all Basque refugees would be thrown immediately into concentration camps, and said literally that Aguirre "saved himself by flying into Belgium and surely to Germany"—trying to insinuate that I followed the road to the Nazis in order to betray France.

M. Ibarnegaray, who was always more than willing to cooperate with Franco, was Minister in the first Pétain Government. This Basque Quisling, who had so glibly accused me of being a traitor, was one of the members of that government who went begging for the shameful Armistice that delivered his country to Hitler.

But M. Ibarnegaray saw to it that seven thousand Basques who had been working in war industries for France were gathered up at night, together with all the Basque priests who were refugees and the rest of the men, and herded into trucks like sheep for the concentration camp of Gurs. The police, following orders, respected no one. They would have taken the old Basque Bishop, Dr. Mujica, who was also in exile, but he was sick in bed. And this incarceration was the most important work which M. Ibarnegaray performed while he was a member of the government.

[Nor did I know, in these dark hours, the fate of my dear friend President Companys of Catalonia. While we were losing and finding one another, tramping for miles, thrown into concentration camps and beseeching pigheaded officials to listen to reason, Companys was thrown into the La Santé prison in Paris; and later he was mercilessly turned over to Franco. He was shot in the Montjuich Fortress of Barcelona, where he died a Christian and valiantly, with his feet bare so that he might feel in his last moments the Catalan earth, whose people had freely elected him their President.]

4

We spent a few days in Bergues resting. The kind family who opened their home to us, divided what little they had of food as well. They gave us milk for our children, and bread. They gave us eggs and some cheese, and they let us cook our food in their kitchen. Our children played with their children. The hours were healing as they passed. When we said farewell, our children left their dolls as a parting gift for the farm children. It was not an easy sacrifice for them to part with their dolls, which they had carried in their arms through the whole journey. A few tears were shed over them, but afterwards the children seemed content. They had paid what to them was all, and they seemed to realize it was worth more than the few francs we could spare.

On the road once more, we had to give up the idea of going to Calais. Great swarms of refugees who were coming from that direction told us that the Germans were already in possession of the city. We did not know where to go. We were trapped. We decided to make our way toward the coast and go again to La Panne, if possible. La Panne was the only place left where we could hope to find passage to somewhere. My brother, my brothers-in-law, the students, the priests—everyone in the group—kept hounding me to be careful. As if in those hours anyone was free from danger. "They are not going to shoot us," they would say to me, "but they certainly will shoot you."

We carried our suitcases and our children. The others would surround me as we marched. "If we are stopped, you don't have to be the one they question always. We are going to have Germans to deal with soon, and you know they will detain you and deliver you to Franco."

I thought the whole idea was absurd. "Right now," I told them, "the danger from the enemy's airplanes is more acute, and it is a danger we share equally." We were under constant attack by the German flyers, who seemed overanxious to clear the roads lethally of any traffic. There were times, however, when we paid no attention to them, but moved along as if by a collective instinct of insanity. The open road stretched before us, flooded with sunlight.

We arrived at the entrance of Bray-Dunes, a French coastal town. One of the sentries guarding the bridge which goes through the town to Dunkirk stopped us and said: "Do not go forward. Bray-Dunes is the most dangerous place. Troops have begun to withdraw toward Dunkirk, and the road is under heavy punishment. And in any case they will not let you through."

Desperately we asked, "Where shall we go then?"

The soldier was touched. "You are right. There is nothing I can advise." He shrugged. "Do as you please."

It is impossible to describe the condition of the roads: they were filled with refugees . . . The road before us became alive, choked, blocked—with an aliveness which was heightened by death, making it no longer a thoroughfare. Women and children would drop exhausted at the road's edge, while the caravan passed insensible of them because of so much suffering everywhere. No one cared about the danger. If an airplane's machine gun wiped out a whole unit of people before you, you would have to walk around them. Our priests stopped to administer last rites to a few. We spared a few drops of water to others; but had we gone on doing this we should have suffered for our generosity, in the end. You had to ignore any normal instinct of kindness . . . you had to walk without seeing . . . when parts of your body became tired you had to treat them as if they were separate things. Your feet must obey the mind's command to keep on and on—forever if it proved necessary. You must rise above the need for sleep. The few days with our good family in Bergues must not only serve as a memory of rest, but continue to refresh us—for how long, we could not be sure. Ahead the concentration camp loomed as perhaps the most gentle end of our journey.

Outside Bray-Dunes, we decided to find again, if we could, the little house where we had bathed our feet some days before, after crossing the border. The family let us stay there for four days. During those four days we saw the collapse of an army. This was the Dunkirk disaster which was heard around the world.

Troops were retreating in complete disorder. There were no squadron leaders, no officers . . . There was no command at all. Only the English preserved discipline along the roads. I went down to the beaches, where I found order excellently maintained by both the British and the French. There were approximately twenty thousand soldiers on the beaches. Transports were beginning to arrive, and the soldiers were building small narrow bridges of wood on the beach which would serve as gangplanks for their embarkation.

The second time I went down there, I found the military commander. It was 6:30 in the morning on May 29th. The colonel was very polite, but when I told him our story he said: "I understand your position, but you must understand mine. I can't promise you anything." His hand gestured over the whole beach. "You see, I am responsible for all of these boys. At the end, I'll try to help you."

I thanked him and went back to our temporary home. There was complete madness all along the road. Barrels of precious oil were open and spouting their black contents everywhere. Trucks full of food were being looted. Soldiers, giving up in their despair to drink, were everywhere—some completely unconscious in the ditches beside the road. Cars and trucks had been abandoned, causing further congestion of the road. I have seen several such movements in their last and most critical moments, but Dunkirk exceeded them all in dramatic disorder.

We were staying in the stable of the small house. There were several other groups with us, and I had scarcely returned when the doors of the stable were opened violently by two officials and a patrol of French soldiers. The soldiers pointed their machine gun at our group and ordered all the men to segregate themselves and to keep their hands raised over their heads. The women and children, who were resting, were ordered rudely to stand up. They asked us for our papers: "Come on now: out with your papers. Where are they?" At first we didn't know what it was all about. And then we recognized the old procedure. Once more we were accused of being spies.

One of the officials approached Father Alberto and said, harshly, "You are not a priest."

"Then I am not a priest," replied the venerable Jesuit.

"We are going to find this out at once," added the official, and he called his companion who was also a priest.

"Recite the words of the absolution," the French priest commanded him. Father Alberto began to recite them in Latin, but the official-priest stopped him curtly. "Slowly! I cannot understand you. You have said it wrong."

I could stand it no longer, and from the wall where we were all herded together I said: "I protest against this rudeness to our priest. We have worked too hard for France to permit this treatment." I went over to him, with my papers held out. "You were at the border and approved our passing. Here are my papers. Look at them and pay special attention to this document." It was the last permit I had obtained at the police station of Bray-Dunes, which explained our situation. The paper was signed by the police authorities. The officials were confused and ordered that the guns be lowered. They ended the whole conversation by asking our pardon for their attitude. Later we found that some farm neighbors had envied the small money we were paying for our lodgings and had reported us to the authorities, saying that we were spies.

5

As we still had hope of a possible passage, our visits to the beach were constant—the distance from our home was scarcely half a mile. On the afternoon of May 30th, I counted about forty boats which had come to take the troops. I could see as far as Dunkirk, and from every direction soldiers were streaming toward the beach. As soon as the Stukas roared overhead the commander ordered everyone to lie down, and at once the beaches were still, covered with soldiers pinned to the ground. The planes passed close to our heads, and seconds later the wave of their bombardment took its toll of the defeated troops.

Two French officials and two French soldiers were with me; but we could find no one of authority to talk with, and in any case I was convinced that there would be no room for us. I let the others stay and made my way back with a feeling of desolation. We were all of us hanging around the beaches, I thought, like hungry children who stand longingly before a restaurant window; but I could not permit myself to have these thoughts or these feelings. . . . On the way home I passed an empty military truck . . . there was a complete French soldier's uniform abandoned. I took it with me, thinking perhaps it might help to get one of us out. I had hardly reached home when the two French officials caught up with me.[4] Their faces were completely out of kilter. Never before nor since have I seen men so unstrung. They had absolutely no control over their facial muscles, and they were violently sick. They had seen one of the Nazi bombs explode on a ship full of soldiers.

"It was horrible," one of them babbled. "Everything flew into the air like a bursting fountain of arms and legs and blood."

After they had gained some composure they started out for Dunkirk on bicycles. They had not gone a mile when one of them was killed by bullets from a machine gun in a low-flying Nazi airplane.

We slept in the stables. During the day we sat in a little courtyard between the farmhouse and the barns. Each day we saw the Stukas fly over our heads en route to the beach, where they bombed the transports and destroyers which were at anchor some distance off the coast line. When the German planes appeared the deafening noise of machine guns, cannons, pistols welcomed them, with no practical result. During the four days we were at Bray-Dunes, we did not see a single plane shot down.

That night we saw Allied troops burning their motorized units. Tanks and trucks were scattered through the fields before us and burned so that they should prove of no value to the enemy. The bonfires flared lugubriously, and the faces of the men who watched them showed up sad and incredibly tired in the flames. Bengal lights of the enemy aircraft made everything an unearthly white.

Fatigue and demoralization are the most dangerous elements in the last phases of combat. Some soldiers took possession of our stable. "First the troops, afterwards the refugees," they said, unable to realize that people near the battle scene suffer even more than men in the army because they are defenseless. The same night a group of officers came.

"You must all be out of here by tomorrow morning," they ordered. And so at daybreak we were marching again. We had to leave most of our luggage behind. We just had no strength left to carry anything but the absolute essentials. We were going back to La Panne. Perhaps we might find there some fishermen who would take us to England. We had traveled now for two weeks in a circle without taking off our clothes. The humor of our children was exhausted, and their young patience was worn threadbare. At the French-Belgian border there were no barriers, no gendarmes nor wire fences. Evidence of our concentration camp was nowhere to be seen. A little farther on we saw some light campaign fortifications, in which a few soldiers were entrenched. A French colonel came toward us. "Where are you going?" he asked.

"To La Panne," we answered.

"But don't you know that the Germans are nearing La Panne, and that communication with the other part of France has been reestablished through Calais?"

"What you are saying is difficult for us to believe," I answered, "since this very night we have seen artillery shells exploding two miles from Bray-Dunes, and from the south of Dunkirk the Germans are nearing the square."

"You'll be taken prisoner," the colonel told us.

"In any case," my brother Juan interrupted, "we would rather go on to La Panne. We are exhausted, and it would be impossible for us to turn back now. In La Panne we hope to find some way to get to England."

"Well," the colonel shrugged, "do whatever seems best to you. I wish you much luck."

A few minutes after we left him, two Nazi fighter planes dived at us. We threw ourselves, with one accord, into the ditch on the side of the road under some trees. They dived to three hundred feet over our heads, but their bombs exploded, praise God, in a field seventy-five yards away from us where a few horses grazing were killed in our stead.

6

We reached La Panne at one o'clock in the afternoon, just as the first shelling from the Nazi artillery began. We lay on the broad highway which leads into the town, our women and children crying in terror. My brother Juan and several others went ahead to the house our families had rented for our vacation. When we met again they could only tell us that our house was already full of refugees. Shells were continuing to burst around us. We gathered our children into our arms, and crossing the avenue we forced open the doors of a strange house. There were several people waiting inside already.

"Where have you come from?" they asked us.

We answered as briefly as we could, telling them we were Basques, and a man who was in his late thirties looked at us speculatively. He was sitting on the floor and his arms were crossed over his chest.

"I have come back from Ostend," he said, "where the Germans are now. They are obliging and correct with everyone, but I learned there that those who fought in the Spanish war with Franco will be sent back to their country, but those who fought against him will be sent to the Königsberg concentration camp."

This rumor monger couldn't have chosen a worse moment to make such an announcement. Our women gave up completely and sobbed bitterly in despair.

During a pause in the bombardment, several of the students went out to find a place where we could stay by ourselves. One went to the house next door to our family's and found it empty. It was a very small house of five or six rooms, but all forty-six of us hid there. As we crossed the street, we passed troops retreating. They were English infantry. Some rode on trucks, others marched, all were in correct formation, with their officers. They were taking the road to Dunkirk.

When we reached the house, I said, "I am going to go out and talk with one of the officers."

My wife stood up. "Why?" she asked tensely.

"One of them may be able to tell me how to get in touch with the British authorities. Our Delegation in London must be taking steps for our evacuation."* Later on I was to learn that they worked unceasingly for us. British destroyers had received orders to take us on at Ostend or Bayonne.

*[*Editor's note:* As early as 1939, the Basque government in Paris had begun to send delegations abroad—to London, Buenos Aires, and New York—to look after the interests of Basque refugees, especially the tens of thousands of children who had been evacuated from Bilbao during the civil war. When World War II broke out, with President Aguirre's whereabouts still uncertain, political leadership of the Basques devolved eventually on a group of men who constituted the Basque delegation in London. For more on this, see Koldo San Sebastián, *El Exilio Vasco en América: 1936/1946—Acción del Gobierno* (San Sebastián: Txertoa, 1988).]

Mari tied a kerchief over her hair. "I am going with you," she said, and with us also came Sabin, a brave officer of the Basque Police.

"There is no sense for you both to go alone," he said.

We went out to the street and a young officer told me that the General Staff would probably be in Dunkirk since Ostend, where it was before, was already taken by the Nazis. We made our way to the dunes because he told us perhaps we should find some higher ranking officer who could help us. Just as we reached there, a furious bombardment by German artillery units began. We threw ourselves down, holding tightly to each other, not for a minute letting go, while around us shells were bursting. I had no thought of anything then but my wife and the terrible noise and the small space of vulnerable earth which we covered.

[I thought: "Here is a circle drawn on a detail map. Here is a target: these dunes, these buildings are the places to be destroyed . . . And this circle also covers the place where two human beings clutch each other for a hope of security and strength." My wife's breath was soft upon my hand and more endearing than the first glance she had given me. . . . Here in this sudden terror I was glad that at least we were together.

I felt Sabin's hand touch my shoulder. "We must get away from here," he shouted.]

We went close to the walls. Mari was unable to walk. She spoke quite calmly: "My legs won't walk right. There is something wrong with them. I don't know. Maybe they are hurt."

They were all right, I told her. All the way home I reassured her that her legs were not hurt, and that we would come out all right. Home, she went at once to her children. Comforting them, she found strength for herself. My two sisters, my sister-in-law, and Cesareo Asporosa were missing. They had also gone looking for a boat. We sat at the window waiting for them. At last we saw the three women rushing toward the house. Their faces were livid. When they entered the house, they were unable to speak. At once we saw that my sister Encarna was wounded in the shoulder. Blood matted her clothing.

"Asporosa?" everyone asked. "Where is he? Where is Asporosa?"

We learned, in all finality. On their way home during the bombardment which still persisted, one of the shells fell near them, and a piece of shrapnel had penetrated Asporosa's heart. Father Alberto and I went out at once to find him. The tragedy had occurred only two city blocks from the house: he had been so near to us. We took him immediately to an emergency hospital post where he died. He never spoke to us, but I believe he knew we were with him.

As we went through the main street of La Panne, a British infantry battalion was coming toward us. In spite of the shells bursting and the zoom of dive bombers everywhere, those men marched in correct formation, with their officers leading them, and they were singing. I have always believed in the eventual liberation of the world from totalitarian forces, but at that moment I was more than ever sure that the strength of democracy could not diminish. People who can sing in the middle of such gunfire cannot be vanquished.

The bombardment did not stop for a single moment until six o'clock in the evening. Some French patrols and the rest of the British troops passed through the deserted streets on their way to Dunkirk. They were protected by light British batteries that shot from the entrance of La Panne. We hid in the basement, about two feet below the street. The small house was lightly built and there was no water or light. Forty-five of us crowded together in complete darkness; the whistle of the shells seemed to grow louder with each passing minute, and each shell we were sure would end in our midst. As the Germans were shooting in batteries, we heard four or five whistling at almost the same time. One of the shells took away part of an upper story of the house, and seconds later another stopped at the basement door, filling the room with dust, smoke, and splinters. Several persons were wounded by the shrapnel, and among them my sister Encarna was wounded again in the shoulder and also in the chest—a few days later she would die in the hospital. The noise was incredible. It was like a mass lament. Encarna was moaning in pain and agony. Asporosa's sister was mourning his death while the rest of the women, especially the older ones, were praying aloud for protection. And over it all the shell's whistle, the cannon's roar, the sound of plane and machine gun, the marching feet, and the shrill screams of the suddenly wounded. One of our priests spoke out almost sternly to us: "The danger of death is imminent. I beg you all to cease your lamentations and prepare your souls. It would seem as though the good Lord had decided that our last hour has arrived." We all knelt there in the impenetrable darkness and received the collective absolution *in extremis*.

After this my brother Juan spoke to me alone. "It is very well," he said, "if we are going to die. But this is nothing we can assume. And now do you realize we are all penniless? With Asporosa went our treasury."

This was quite true. Naturally when Father Alberto and I had been with our friend in his last hours, we had not thought of the money he carried for our group. We were too stricken with grief at his dying.

I said to my brother, "Well, there is nothing we can do now, Juan."

But he insisted. "I have spoken with Sabin, and he is willing to go with me to look for the money. After all it is our money, and we will need it . . ."

Finally, I agreed.

"But go with care," I told them. "It is enough that Asporosa has died. Let no harm come to either one of you." They left quietly. It was no easy task which they had to perform.

In the darkness of the streets, half crawling at times to avoid the shrapnel, they made their way to the La Panne Mortuary, carrying candles and matches in their pockets.

"We had better take them," Juan had said before they left. "It will make the searching less difficult."

There were more than eight hundred dead. The mortal remains of a small town were thrown together, stripped of their poor clothes, of all identity, nothing now but a confused mass of heads, arms, legs, so lately stilled forever, so new to the anonymity of the massacred. It must have been a terrible sight for them. The finite mind comprehends with difficulty the sight of so many dead crowded together in one small mortuary. They had to look at hundreds of the dead faces before they found our friend—the unclosed eyes . . . After a long hour, the flickering candlelight revealed the face they sought. Our dear friend was deprived of everything but his coat. It was too old and worn for those who stole from them, and who had probably thought, "Well, it's an old coat—no wear left in it at all. Let the poor man be buried in it. He'll have nothing else."

Inside the lining of the old coat was the little money belonging to our group: the precious dollar bills which, if we were to live through this hell, would keep us alive.

They had to take the coat from him. Juan left his own in its place, and exhausted, they made their way back to the house. About four o'clock in the morning, the bombardment began to cease. At dawn,

British tanks were retreating. At eight o'clock in the morning, the first German cyclist patrols entered, and an hour later, the first German troops marched through the littered and torn-up streets.

We were in their hands—and there were two possibilities which lay ahead for me. The first was prison; the second, execution.

CHAPTER III

To understand my own dangerous situation in the face of the Nazi invasion in 1940, it is well, I believe, first to get a picture of the position of the Basques in Europe throughout the centuries. Gernika was chosen, not without reason, by the Franco-Hitler coalition in 1937 as the first civilian town to be wiped from the face of the earth. Why?

Gernika, centuries-old cradle of democracy, was sacred to a race of people who, the totalitarians had been taught, must be eliminated.

[Houston Chamberlain, an Englishman, became a German citizen during the last war.* He was the first man to hail Hitler as the savior of the German nation. He was the forerunner of the persecution of the Jews in Europe. In his published works Mr. Chamberlain warns his adopted countrymen repeatedly against the Basques. In *The Foundations of the Nineteenth Century* Mr. Chamberlain ascertains that we not only are an "un-Germanic race" but also are distinct from what he calls the "whole Indo-European group." We are more dangerous, he states, than the Jews to the sacred "Aryan culture."

[Editor's note: The following two and a half paragraphs were inserted in the English version apparently to stress for the American reader the racial nature of the Basque struggle, as well as to help the reader draw the connection between the Basques and the Jews as two persecuted races in Europe. This material does not appear in the Spanish version at all.]

He is particularly emphatic in his condemnation of Ignatius Loyola and Francis Xavier de Jaso, "the Basque champions of anti-Germanism," along with the rest of their race. But it would have been well for Chamberlain to remember, going back a little farther in history, that although the Basques were the only occidental European race to resist the Germanic tribes who swept down on and destroyed the Roman Empire, before that they had also resisted all attempts at Romanization. When the German Visigoths of Spain fell before the invasion of the Arabs from the south, the Basques in their mountain fastnesses in the Pyrenees continued an unconquered nation. Charlemagne, that great representative of Latinized Germanism, met with a similar surprise when his armies were defeated by the Basques in Roncesvalles. They would have been perfectly willing to accept him as a friend but would never submit to his domination.

At the time of the Arab domination of Spain, some of the Arab chronicles call the Basques a race "as dumb as the beasts." Naturally they are referring to the Basque language, which was so completely different from those of the "Aryanized" peoples under their domination but was the same as that heard by the legions of the Roman Caesars and is still spoken by the Basques to their children today.] Neither Romans, Germans, nor Arabs succeeded in altering one whit the face of the Basque nation which they were never able to dominate. From the most remote times of history, Basques were educated in a school of liberty and succeeded in maintaining their independence through countless bloody battles. But this constant struggle did not prevent them from absorbing the best of occidental civilization, whose fundamentally Christian and liberty-loving characteristics so permeated the Basque national spirit that they are today, as centuries before, the most outstanding traits of the Basque people.

Our history is a simple one. It is based on the belief that men and peoples are capable of governing themselves, and that, in the eyes of God, each man is as worthy as his neighbor. These ideas were carried over into the laws and political practices of the country, and made up a real civilization of liberty.

During the ages when it was necessary for a man to be of the nobility in order to enjoy personal liberty, the Basques declared all Basques were noblemen, although no Basque was permitted to claim dominion over the soil of his country or the soul of another man. I do not believe that there has ever existed in any country such an original method of defending individual liberty and democratic equality in an age so full of social inequalities and lack of respect for the individual. Beneath the branches of the Tree of Gernika, the Basque peasant or fisherman would sit in equality with the Basque landowner to make the laws of our country.

Today we do not know when the first *batzar* took place. *Batzar* is the Basque word for parliament, congress, government by representation. But from the earliest times when our forefathers were summoned together by the sound of silver trumpets and the burning of bonfires on the mountain heights, until today, the Basques have never accepted any form of government but a democracy. Long before France and Spain existed as states, centuries before Christopher Columbus discovered America, the Basques, beneath the Tree of Gernika, were recording for posterity those laws of equality and justice which they had heretofore known only among themselves.

After a trip in the Basque country, the Earl of Carnarvon wrote in 1836:

> The house of the Biscayan is his castle in the most emphatic sense of the word. No magistrate can violate that sanctuary; nor can exertion be put on him, nor can his arms or his horse be

seized; he cannot be arrested for debt, or subjected to imprisonment upon any pretext whatever, without a previous summons
to appear under the old Tree of Gernika, where he is made
acquainted with the offence imputed to him, and called upon
for his defence; he is then discharged on the spot, or bailed, or
committed, according to the nature of the crime and the evidence adduced against him. This, the most glorious privilege
that free men can possess—this, the most effectual safeguard
against the wanton abuse of power—this, a custom more deter-
minately in favour of the subject than even our own cherished
Habeas Corpus—was enjoyed by the Biscayans for centuries
before the far-famed guarantee of British liberty had an existence in our islands.[2]

[John Adams, second President of the United States and one of
the founders of its independence, in his defense of the American
Constitution, said of the Basques:

. . . While their neighbors have long since resigned all their
pretensions into the hands of Kings and priests, this extraordinary people have preserved their ancient language, genius,
laws, government and manners, without innovation, longer
than any other nation of Europe. . . .

Active, vigilant, generous, brave, hardy, inclined to war and
navigation, they have enjoyed, for two thousand years, the reputation of being the best soldiers and sailors in Spain, and even
the best courtiers, many of them having, by their wit and manners, raised themselves into offices of consequence under the
court of Madrid. Their valuable qualities have recommended
them to the esteem of the Kings of Spain, who have hitherto left
them in possession of those great immunities of which they are
so jealous. . . .

Many writers ascribe their flourishing commerce to their situation; but, as this is not better than that of Ferrol or Corunna,
that advantage is more probably due to their liberty.[3]

The prohibition of torture, established by law in the fifteenth
century following an immemorial custom, the regulation of prop-

erty to prevent social abuse, commercial liberty, and how many other provisions that seem modern even today, all constituted the basis for Basque life and secular independence.

In the beginning of modern times, when the big empires were dominating Europe and crushing out the independence of the smaller nations, the Basques were threatened by the growing power of the Imperial Spanish Crown.* To meet this threat they made a pact between equals, keeping their own national sovereignty and their laws and united with Spain only under the monarch, as Norway did later with Sweden and Hungary with Austria. "Any act or provision by the King against liberty," was pronounced null and void by the Basque laws, and the death penalty was established for any person obtaining dispositions from the King against liberty. Through this pact with the Spanish Crown, the Basques lived under a system of confederation with Spain from the beginning of modern times up to 1839. The King of Spain was accepted as King, or rather Lord, of the Basques only after taking an oath to respect the Constitution and liberties established by the Basque people. A fair parallel could be drawn between that system and the relations gradually evolved between the British Dominions and the English Crown.

*[Editor's note: Throughout these passages, as elsewhere, Aguirre, like a good Basque nationalist, refers to "the Basques" as if they were already a unified people with identifiable interests and aims. In reality, the relevant political actors throughout the period referred to here were the provinces and the cities and townships. In the absence of a unifying political unit such as the Basque nation, the several provinces claimed their rights and privileges solely for themselves, and only occasionally perceived their relationship with the crown in other than strictly local terms. This parochialism continues to plague efforts today to create a unified Basque ethno-nation, or even a single autonomous region under the terms of the 1978 Spanish Constitution.]

In the year 1833 the first civil war broke out in Spain, and the Basques were drawn into the conflict. The liberals and absolutists were not only fighting over the dynastic question of who should succeed to the throne, Isabel or Carlos, but over completely opposite conceptions of life. The Spanish absolutists had promised to respect the historic liberties of the Basques. The liberals—strange contradiction of history—believed that the Basques should renounce their political sovereignty in favor of what they called the constitutional unity of the Spanish Monarchy and the guarantee of individual rights which the Spaniards only attained a century later. The Basques fought on the side of the absolutist monarch—who was to them the constitutional monarch—for their national liberty.

In defending their attacked national liberty, the Basques were defending a just cause; at the same time they were fighting against another movement in the name of liberty, that of the progressive Spaniards. But the latter, in turn, were also committing a historical mistake in attempting to assimilate the Basques through violence.

The Basques laid down their arms only after receiving a solemn promise that their liberty—the Basque Fueros, or Constitution— would be respected. This promise was never kept by the victorious liberal Spanish Crown. Once the Basques were disarmed, the Spanish Parliament treacherously voted to deprive them of their right to self-government on October 25, 1839. Until 1876, however, they were able to retain certain important liberties—such as exemption from military service in the Spanish Army, financial autonomy, and some measure of freedom in local administration.

On July 21, 1876, the last remnants of Basque liberties were annulled, and the Basques were simply incorporated into the Spanish state after more years of fighting. The Basques never accepted the *de facto* situation imposed by superior forces. For us the fact remained that the traditional pact between the Crown and our country had been broken.*

*[Editor's note: Again, one might take issue with the historical accuracy of Aguirre's statement that "the Basques never accepted" the legitimacy of the situation imposed on them by "superior forces." In fact, many Basques not only accepted the situation (i.e., the integration of the Basque provinces into a unified Spanish state), but actually welcomed it. And one might also legitimately ask whether historically Aguirre's party, the Basque Nationalist Party, did not also at least implicitly accept

the situation by virtue of their contesting elections for Spanish offices, participating (as Aguirre himself did) in Spanish institutions and defending with their own blood a Spanish republic that offered them in return nothing more than regional autonomy, less than what a state might enjoy in a federal system such as that of the United States.]

This was a signal for the beginning of the Basque struggle to regain their national liberty. We were not alone during this period, for the Catalans in the northeast of the Iberian Peninsula were also working for their national liberty. The Spanish Monarchy never understood these problems. It simply denied their existence, and by this denial thought it had found the solution. Basque and Catalan patriots were persecuted. Everything possible was done to stamp out our language and culture.

The fall of the Spanish Monarchy in April, 1931, and the coming of the Republic, opened up a new period of hope for us. The Republican Government promised reparation of the old injustices and a grant of autonomy to those peoples who showed, by a clear majority of votes, that they were in favor of it.

At this time I was elected Mayor of Guecho, a city near Bilbao where I had lived.

Two months later, on the 14th of June, 1931, in Estella, a city of the Basque province of Navarre, a meeting of the mayors of all the Basque municipalities, who were at this time the only popularly elected representatives of the people, by an overwhelming majority of 90 per cent proclaimed the Statute of Autonomy of the Basque Country. Yet the Republican Government, still influenced by the centralist tendencies common to certain parts of Spain, refused to recognize the validity of this statute and set up a long procedure for the granting of recognition. This required the approval of Basque home rule by a majority of all Basque municipalities, the approval of every one of the four Basque provinces, and a plebiscite of the whole Basque country. After these conditions had been fulfilled, the Spanish Parliament still reserved the right to accept or reject the decision.

All of the conditions dependent on the Basque people were fulfilled. To give one example, the plebiscite, in order to succeed, had to have a quorum of 66 per cent of the electoral census; in the Basque plebiscite held on November 5, 1933, 88 per cent voted in favor of home rule.

Unfortunately, the Spanish Republican Parliament still delayed; and it was only after the Civil War began on October 1, 1936, that Basque autonomy was finally granted. Thus we resumed once more, though in somewhat qualified form, our long history of liberty which had only been interrupted for a hundred years in our entire history.

I was elected President, and on October 7, 1936, with the inauguration of the Euzkadi Government in Gernika and beneath its historic tree, I took the oath to remain faithful to the soil of our ancestors:

Jaungoikuaren aurrean apalik,	Humble before God,
	On the Basque soil, standing
Euzko-lur ganian zutunik,	In memory of our ancestors,
Asabearen gomutaz,	Under the Tree of Gernika,
Gernika'ko zuaizpian	I swear faithfully
Nere aginduba ondo betetzia	To fulfill my trust.
Zin dagit.	

I decided to form a national coalition government which would represent all shades of Basque democratic public opinion. This government conducted the war, and organized the emigration when it, like so many of its people, was compelled within a year to flee from its homeland. And this government has remained unchanged and still is the recognized head of the Basques, whether exiled or at home.[4]

G. L. Steer, correspondent for the *Times* (London) and the *New York Times* in the Spanish Civil War, wrote:

The Basque is proud of the year in which he governed himself; of how he kept order and the true Church's peace, gave freedom to all consciences, fed the poor, cured the wounded and ran all the services of government without a single quarrel. Alone in all Spain he showed that he was fit to rule; where others murdered and butchered, terrorized the working class

and sold their country to foreigners, the Basque bound together his little nation in strong bonds of human solidarity. . . .
He may hope, as I do, that it will be more successful; but he can
scarcely expect that it will be more honourable.[5]

This little nation situated between Spain and France, about the
size of Belgium or Massachusetts, with a population of no more than
two million, was hurled into unequal conflict with General Franco
and his totalitarian allies, Germany and Italy, who showed especially
cruel malice toward the Basques.

Once more the Basques as individuals and as a nation rose in
defense of their national liberty so gravely menaced by the modern
Caesars and their acolytes. They were only following the course
of their history. Neither abandonment by the civilized world—the
hour of trial for the big nations had not yet come—nor the misunderstanding of many, nor the outright attacks of others could move
them from the path of honor. And in defending their own liberty
they knew that they were also defending liberty for the rest of the
world.

2

We had eleven months of fighting. After the fall of
Irún the land frontier with the rest of the world was shut off for us.
We were surrounded on all sides just as those brave men of Bataan
were surrounded. Our only possible outlet was the closely guarded
sea and the air already dominated by Hitler. The last three months
were spent defending the thirty miles that separated Bilbao from
the initial front of the Franco attack.

One day, the 26th of April, 1937, the sacred, defenseless and open
city of Gernika was destroyed by the Nazi aviation, which the press
of the world in all seriousness called "Franco's air strength."*

*[Editor's note: The bombing of Guernica (the English version uses the
Basque language spelling, Gernika) is without doubt the most powerful
and driving symbol in the entire Basque political culture. For an Ameri-

can, it would be Pearl Harbor, the Alamo, and Bunker Hill all combined in a single, searing metaphor. Actually, Aguirre's description in the Spanish edition goes into much greater detail than the version presented here. The reader of the Spanish version learns, for example, of the specific types of aircraft used by the German attackers, the specific parts of town damaged by the bombs, and so forth.

One part of the Guernica mythology survives in Aguirre's account but does not square with at least one later description. Aguirre, like many other chroniclers of the bombing, leaves us with the impression that the town's population had grown that fateful day because it was a traditional market day, and the village was filled with simple peasants and farmers vending their produce. A later account—*Guernica: The Crucible of World War II*, by Gordon Thomas and Max Morgan Witts (New York: Ballantine Books, 1975)—says that in fact the farmers in the surrounding countryside stayed away from Guernica that day out of fear that the war—only a few kilometers away—would reach the town. The swollen population was due, rather, to the flood of refugees and retreating soldiers who had to pass through on their way back to Bilbao from the front. This difference does not, of course, diminish the tragedy suffered by those who were in the town that day.]

Gernika, a village of about seven thousand inhabitants, was the first totalitarian experiment in destruction. It meant striking at the very heart of the small Basque nation. As in all Basque towns, the most important buildings were: the church, representative of the religious spirit of the people; the town hall, symbol of its civilian spirit; and the pelota court (traditional Basque handball), proof of its strength.

The town proper was in the lower part of the valley; forming part of it, on a small green slope, stood the Biscayan Parliament and in its gardens, the famous Tree of Gernika, softly blown by the breeze, always silent, as if longing for the days of its national splendor.

Every Monday in the year, from the highest peaks of the mountains which surround Gernika, the Basque family settlements send all the products of their orchards and households to be exhibited in the plaza of the town. While goods are bought and sold, friendships between families are renewed, and off under the trees the donkeys and oxen wait for the journey back home. Once the business of the fair is finished, people fill the cafés and taverns and, after lunch, the pelota court. Laughter and talk are accentuated by the sound of the swift-moving game of the Basque ball players. Outside in the square, the chords of the *txistu* and the *tamboril* claim many dancers; but when the chimes of the churches announce the Angelus the venders begin to pack up; the Angelus is a traditional custom in our country. When the sun is setting, the church bells announce the *otoyak* (prayers). The fair is over. So, gradually, Gernika is quiet again.

This was the stage chosen by Franco and Germany for presenting to the world on Monday April 26, 1937, the first experiment of total war. Gernika was bombarded unceasingly for three and a half hours. Churches, homes, hospitals with the sick and the wounded were not exempt. Everything exploded into bits, and then there was the fire, which wiped out completely the last traces of the town so sacred to us. More than two thousand died. The majority were poor Basque peasants, who toiled on the farms from sunrise to sunset, and who said a prayer to God on commencing and finishing their tasks.

At night the skies above the Tree of Gernika—which alone remained unscathed—were still brilliant with the red light of fire. The few remaining survivors sat at the road's edge, dazed, frozen with grief. It was as if they had suddenly become insane. It was so quiet. There was only the sound of the licking flames, and the faint rustling of the wind, and the weird cries of the animals in their panic, while from high in the mountains little empty homes echoed the silence.

As President of the Basque people, I appealed to the world: "I maintain firmly before God and History who will judge us, that during three and a half hours German planes have bombarded the defenseless civilian population of the historic town of Gernika, pursuing women and children with machine guns, and reducing the town itself to ashes. I ask the civilized world whether it can permit the extermination of a people who have always deemed it their duty to defend their liberty as well as the ideal of self-government which Gernika, with its thousand-year-old Tree, has symbolized throughout the centuries."

General Franco pronounced at once: "Aguirre lies. We have re-spected Gernika, just as we respect all that is Spanish."

However, a few days later, to dispute him, Cardinal Gomá, the Primate of Spain, wrote a letter to the Basque Canon, Dr. Onaindia, telling him that the destruction of Gernika was "an announcement of what will happen to the great city." He was referring to Bilbao.

The catastrophe should not have surprised us. General Mola, who led the attacking forces, had fulfilled his threat. "We shall destroy Biscay," he had written to us on leaflets dropped from his planes; "and its bare and desolate territory will deprive the English of their wish to support the Bolshevik Basques against us. It is necessary to destroy the capital of a perverted people who dare to oppose the irresistible cause of the national idea."

But the English had not sent us a single cartridge. On the con-trary, with their policy of nonintervention, they impeded others in doing so.

It is only fitting to note here that we were not completely without support. The League of Nations "condemned" the bombardment of Gernika. In the United States, Senator Borah of Idaho, where 30,000 Basques live, was better able to understand the situation, and said:

"Here fascism presents to the world its masterpiece. It has hung upon the walls of civilization a painting that will never come down, never fade out of the memories of men . . ."

3

The destruction of Gernika constituted a symbolic act in the eyes of those who cherished freedom. At the same time, it was a cause for worry to those who abominated it, as they listened to the clamor to which that hideous crime had given rise in the world.[6]

Towards the middle of May, 1937, two weeks after the bombard-ment and destruction of Gernika, a Basque friend arrived in Bilbao by plane, by the one-machine air-line service which was our only link of communication with the outside world.

My friend was carrying out on that occasion a delicate and compromising commission. An Italian diplomat, Count Cavaletti de Sabina, had arrived in the South of France, perhaps with the excuse of resting in one of those delightful places so coveted by the Italians, but truly with a request from Count Ciano to me, as President of the Basque Government. It was a proposal that came from Mussolini himself, expressed in a "verbal note" and in some amplifications which were to be ratified later—also verbally.

The "note" expressed at the beginning the Duce's desire to arrive at a separate peace with the Basques, through the surrender—it literally said so—of Bilbao to his troops, after which Italy would guarantee the fulfilling of some very humane clauses tending towards the peace of the Basque country, and a guarantee for the members of its government and political and military Basque leaders. The note ended by pointing out the procedure which was to be followed in order to initiate negotiations: I, as the Basque President, would send Mussolini a telegram asking his intervention, basing this act on purely humanitarian motives. The official Italian secret code was offered me, to use freely.

"What's happening in Rome?" I asked myself, perplexed. And my perplexity would have been greater had I known at the time what I learned later.

The Basque friend said to me, "The Count requests an answer as soon as possible."

It surprised me that a diplomat should want haste in such a delicate matter, but nevertheless I replied to my friend immediately: "Answer the gentleman that the Basques do not accept any proposal in which the word 'surrender' exists."

My friend went back in "the plane," and returned in a few days by the same route. He came to visit me at the Presidency and said, "Count Cavaletti asked me if he could be received here by you."

"In Bilbao?" I asked in surprise.

"He would come in an Italian plane, but without colors or identification signs of any kind."

"No, please," I interrupted. "We have enough Italian planes which bombard us every day. If the Count thinks it necessary, let him come with you, and in our plane. I guarantee his safety."

It may be that a few would be surprised at this condescension on my part to an envoy of Mussolini, but my rule has always been not to reject a discussion when in it there might be something interesting. On more than one occasion this has brought me useful information.

"The Italian proposal," said my compatriot, "is more important than the note implies."

"More important than an offer of separate peace?" I argued.

"Yes," added the emissary. "The Count himself has told me that, once you have sent the telegram to the Duce, negotiations will start in which the studying of a possibility of an Italian protectorate over Euzkadi will be included."

"But that not even the Rome of Augustus could get," I interrupted with a smile.

"Well, the Duce intends to do it," went on my friend, "and the Basque experiment will serve to precipitate an identical situation with the Catalonians, and from there to peace with the Republic. They are well acquainted with national problems, and they can distinguish them from other war matters. The rest will be easy, once this is obtained."

I chose to answer him as seriously as I possibly could: "Tell the Count for me that my previous answer stands, and, should he persist in his idea of coming to Bilbao, that I maintain with the same firmness the guarantees of his safety."

But nothing took place. Cavaletti de Sabina assured the Basque intermediary that he was impressed with the sincerity of our guarantee, although he "*would not have been able to guarantee us the same thing.*" I was deprived of my whim of hearing from the lips of the disciple of Machiavelli—I suppose he was one—the explanation of the picturesque proposal of an Italian protectorate over the Basques.

The destruction of Gernika caused horror in the universal conscience, to which must be added the aversion which every honest person felt on hearing of the monstrous calumny which supposedly and mercilessly attributed to the innocent victims themselves the horrible carnage in which they had perished. It was by all means necessary to hide such disaster, which was to bring ill reputation not only to the false "crusaders" but to those who by their help became the accomplices of this crime. How to avoid it? This could be accomplished in two ways: exterminating the Basque people, or separating them from the fight.

The Vatican, in its noble endeavor at pacification, attempted the second solution: Cardinal Pacelli drew up an extensive telegraphic message. To judge from the form of its address, it was meant for me, as the Basque President.

The document invoked the convenience of bringing the fight to an end for the benefit of the high spiritual interests which were endangered in the cruel struggle. The peace proposal that was being made to me—alluded to in the document as generous and humane—took explicitly into account in its opening clause the acquiescence of Generals Franco and Mola. It demanded our surrender of Bilbao and the rest of Basque territory to Franco, without any destruction. In return, security of life and property was promised to the Basque people, and the safe-conduct to foreign countries of the political and military leaders. "The Basque provinces," said the document, "will enjoy the administrative regime equal to that of 'the most privileged province of Spain'" (*sic*). It reflected, as did the whole document, terms of kindness and a desire for peace.

To the Catholic leader of a country such as the Basque country, Catholic almost in its totality, such a test would have been a hard one, although the justice of our cause, and our firmness and loyalty, would have been the winners in the end. And I say "would have been," because the existence of such a telegraphic document did not come to my knowledge until a long time later—no less than three years later—when I was in exile in Paris. A violent article, full of misinformation, against the Basques, and concretely against me, by the Jesuit Father J. de Bivort de la Saudée, appearing in the *Revue des Deux Mondes* of February 10, 1940, brought its existence to our knowledge, as well as other facts absolutely unknown to us.

The article mentioned related the following:

> Monseigneur Valerio Valeri, Apostolic Nuncio in Paris, was entrusted by the Vatican with an "extraordinarily delicate" mis-

sion: that of "helping with peace negotiations between General Franco and the Euzkadi Government." "The Quai d'Orsay, as well as several members of the Diplomatic Corps and many Parisian personalities, lent their kind assistance. Among them an old government leader (the ex-President of Mexico, Señor de la Barra) had an important role." This took place "by the end of February and during the month of March, 1937," at the time Cardinal Gomá was officially the Nuncio to General Franco. Some weeks later (by that time Gernika had been razed), the Primate of Spain did all he could to get the Generalissimo of the Spanish Armies to propose to the Basque Government some conditions which might be accepted. He worked out a project with General Mola, which was submitted to General Franco.

It contained three conditions, destined to make Monsieur Aguirre accept the peace:

1. The respect of the lives and property of those laying down arms was promised.

2. The departure of the leaders would be permitted, aiding them in their flight.

3. Only the authors of crimes within civil law would be submitted to the Ordinary Military Tribunals.

General Franco not only agreed that these conditions be proposed to the Basque Government, but in a magnanimous gesture added another two:

1. The Basque Provinces would enjoy the same economic, political, and juridical privileges as Navarre, which is the most privileged province of Spain.

2. The economical and social betterment of the Basque Provinces would be maintained and developed following the trend of the Encyclical *Rerum Novarum* as Spain's financial situation permitted it.

Should these conditions not be accepted before the breaking of the *Iron Belt* of Bilbao, the national army would enter this town as conqueror.

This project was officially communicated to Monsieur Aguirre. A high Spanish ecclesiastical personage departed immediately to Saint-Jean-de-Luz and Biarritz, with the intention of getting in touch with Canon Onaindia, whose influence could have been great in obtaining the acceptance of the proposition from the Basque Government. After fifteen days, he [*sic*] asked that two clauses be added to General Franco's proposition:

1. That the President of the Euzkadi Government be not considered as a traitor, and

2. That the diplomatic secrecy of these negotiations and conditions of surrender be maintained.

General Franco answered that he was dealing only with general conditions of surrender and not with personal interests. On the other hand, he had promised actively to aid the flight of the leaders. In answer to the second petition, he made a pledge to keep it secret.

M. Aguirre demanded yet another condition. That by which all clauses be officially guaranteed by a foreign power. This condition was rejected by the national leaders as dishonorable to them. By this time it was already the month of May, 1937 . . .

The above is a story that left us all petrified. It was already February, 1940, and I, the principal actor in the supposed negotiations, did not know a thing about them. I called Canon Onaindia; neither did he know about it. What persons or groups were committing the impropriety of forging my authority? Who authorized them to send shameful counter proposals at variance with my dignity and my honor? Or, on the contrary, what cunning was being developed in the dark, or who had invented such a farfetched and clumsy story?

But in it there was something more important—a telegram from Cardinal Pacelli directly addressed to me, in view of the "failure" of the previous "negotiations." In order to clarify the truth of such a confused matter, I called Canon Onaindia again. I asked him to visit the Nuncio in my name and ask him for an interview with me. I had an earnest desire to dig out the truth in this mystery. The Nuncio answered that, as I "was a political personality semiofficially recognized in Paris," he would have to consult with the Vatican before accepting my visit. The Nuncio announced from the very first moment that I should be informed that he believed me absolutely ignorant of such an important matter. He then showed Canon Onaindia the text of the telegram sent to me by Cardinal Pacelli in the first days of May, 1937, a copy of which he did not wish to give Onaindia who memorized it almost in its entirety.

How was it that I had not received that telegram? We made all the inquiries we could, and at last we found the explanation. Such a telegram was sent by the Vatican via Rome to Barcelona, where the telegraphic service operated under the Spanish Republic, instead of being sent—as I suppose it was intended—by cablegram via London-Bilbao. Moreover, it was an open message, with no code, which could be easily understood by the first one to come across it. When after three years this came to our knowledge, it could not but surprise us that so little precaution should be taken in such an important and serious matter. We must not forget the fact that the Quirinal diplomacy had offered its secret code.

And so the inevitable happened. When the message reached Barcelona, the telegraph operator who received it knew that he must bring a text of such great importance to the knowledge of the Government of the Spanish Republic, then in Valencia. There were conferences, reserve, and even sworn secrecy among the members of the Cabinet who knew of the telegram from the Cardinal, Secretary of State of the Vatican. The Republican Government met secretly without summoning the Basque Minister Irujo, the Catalonian Minister Ayguade and, perhaps, one other.* They all agreed to keep the receipt of the telegram a secret, to hide it from me without sending me a transcription of it.

*[Editor's note: The reference here is to Manuel Irujo, a prominent Basque nationalist leader from Navarre, who was one of Aguirre's most trusted friends and allies. In a move that had proved extremely controversial because it seemed to signal that the Basque Nationalist Party was collaborating with the Spanish republican government, Irujo had been allowed to accept an offer to join the republican cabinet, at first without portfolio and later as minister of justice. In the latter post, he was responsible for numerous exchanges of political prisoners that

saved countless numbers of innocent lives. Irujo later seized control of
the Basque delegation in London during the early chaotic days of
World War II, and probably more than any other single person was
responsible for holding the Basque government together until Aguirre
could reach New York in late 1941.]

Their attitude was reprehensible not only by their abuse of power
in keeping me in ignorance, but also because it placed me in a very
awkward position in the eyes of the Vatican. "The silence of Monsieur Aguirre was looked upon as strange"—so the Nuncio told
Canon Onaindia. Thus it happened that between the effrontery of
those who on one side assumed my authority, and on the other the
intolerable impropriety of those who withheld important telegrams,
the Basques and I appeared for three years before the eyes of the
Vatican as a rude people, who did not even know enough to answer a
message, if only to give thanks for the intervention and decline the
offer being made.

The Nuncio, Monseigneur Valerio Valeri, who, on several instances of great tribulation to the Basque people, had shown them
gentle demonstrations of affection, accepted the truth of our asser-
tions, which were later completely substantiated.

Deeply wounded, I drew up a long message addressed to Cardinal
Maglione, Secretary of State of the Vatican for His Holiness Pius
XII. In it I made a documentary history of all the facts, calling to
mind the traditional integrity of the Basque people, asking at the
same time to be given the names of those persons who had had the
audacity to forge my name, defile my honor as a man and as a
Basque. This message was delivered to the Nunciature in Paris on
May 7, 1940, the eve of my departure for Belgium. The catastrophe
of France took place a few days later, and with it my supposed
disappearance from the world of the living. If there was a reply, I did
not know of it.

I have brought to comparison the two above-mentioned facts in
which the two Romes intervened, the Christian and the pagan, in
order to show that both in competition had tried to arrive at a peace
agreement with the Basques. The moving cause behind these proposals was the same: the profound impression that the destruction

of Gernika had caused. Each differed in method: caution on the part of Fascist Rome; an open message through a closed duct on the part of Christian Rome. The motives were also fundamentally different: on one side, a pacification that came as a mercy from the Duce; on the other, a clear perception of the universal significance of the actions of a Christian people who defended their freedom and the freedom of others, because they were attacked by violence, even though such aggression was being made in the name of Christian civilization.

4

There was one simple method which the diplomats anxious to have us withdraw from the struggle never thought of trying. It was that of forcing those who had unjustly attacked us to withdraw from our territory.

But the attack was continuous and violent, and the Basques stood firm in the defense of honor and liberty. The totalitarian forces had been temporarily stopped in the mountains of Elgueta, an important position in the system of defense of the Basque capital, Bilbao. It is twenty miles from Gernika to Elgueta. It is about thirty miles from Elgueta to Bilbao. We held them off for two months. The fight was desperate.[7]

During the last fifteen days a Basque brigade under the command of a young officer who had formerly been a mechanic in a factory in Bilbao defended this important position with true heroism, staving off the attacks of motorized columns and Italo-Spanish tanks. General Franco, growing alarmed at the failure of this frontal attack and the tremendous losses he suffered, ordered an encircling movement around the mountainous position, with greatly increased forces and the aid of Nazi aviation. Elgueta was burning like a volcano, but the defenders stuck grimly to their posts until it became evident that they were in danger of being completely cut off. They finally withdrew only after receiving orders to that effect from the Basque high command.

The road from Elgueta to Bilbao was bloody indeed and was

defended inch by inch against Franco's Moroccan and Italian troops. Hitler generously loaned Franco seven hundred airplanes against which we had five at the beginning of this last attack. A few days and we had none at all.

While our *gudaris* (Basque soldiers) were fighting so heroically on land, our sailors were writing a glorious chapter on the sea.

The Basques were totally defenseless on the sea at first, and therefore we organized our Auxiliary Navy, getting hold of whatever we could. In this way, a few fragile vessels of less than one thousand tons each, which up to that moment had been used for catching codfish in Newfoundland, were raised to the category of warships. Thus were born the Gipuzkoa, the Bizkaya, the Araba, and the Nabarra (named after four Basque provinces). To these units the Donostia, the Iruña, the Goizeko-Izarra, the Iparreko-Izarra, and the Mari Toya were later added.

The Donostia was originally the Virgen del Carmen, an enemy fishing vessel which arrived in Bilbao after a revolt on board; and the Iruña originally the Mari Begoña, a French revenue cutter which had been part of the coastal patrols in the First World War and for some years now had belonged to Bilbao's mariners' register. All the rest were vessels of even smaller tonnage, simple fishing boats assigned the task of picking up mines.

The characteristics of the mounting of these vessels are worth specifying, in order to show their deficiencies for the kind of work which they had to do. The Goizeko-Izarra was the least protected of them all. It was not even mounted, a few machine guns constituting all its defense. It took part in guarding the coast, but on the night of January 17, 1937, it struck a mine and exploded, losing almost all of its crew. The Iparreko-Izarra had two cannons—one of fifty-two millimeters in the bow, and another of forty-seven in the stern. The Araba, Bizkaya, Nabarra, and Gipuzkoa had crews of fifty-two men each. The caliber of their two cannons, one at the bow and another at the stern, was 101.2 millimeters, although they were quite old. The Volunteer Sea Contingent, in which more than one thousand Basque seamen had registered, supplied the necessary crews for all these vessels.

Our "war fleet" admirably fulfilled its task of protecting fishing, watching the coasts, patrolling, preventing the formation of mined zones, exploding or picking up the mines that were found, and watching for the safety of our merchant marine. In the work of picking up mines alone they cleared the sea of more than three hundred, each containing 300 kilograms of explosives.

Let me tell you however of the naval combat in which our humble navy was covered with glory. Part of this battle I was able to follow from our coastal battery of Punta Galea.

On the night of March 4 the Bizkaya, Gipuzkoa, Nabarra, and Donostia sailed in the direction of Bayonne. They had orders to convoy from this port the Galdames, an old tramp ship which now, as we had nothing else, carried the mail, passengers, etc., between Bayonne and Bilbao (a distance of 120 miles) and served as our only contact with the world by water. This journey was extremely dangerous, as the sea was controlled by the warships of Franco—the armored ship España, the modern cruiser Canarias, and the torpedo boat Velasco. Besides, Franco agents practiced espionage with absolute impunity within the French border, so that the departures of the Galdames were made secretly on unexpected dates.

On this occasion the Galdames was carrying back hundreds of passengers (the majority, Basques who had fled to France at the time the frontier province of Gipuzkoa had fallen into Franco's hands), some machinery parts, and nickel currency which had been coined in Belgium for the Basque Government. Among the passengers were the Catalonian Deputy Carrasco Formiguera, appointed by the Catalonian President as his representative to the Basque Government, with his wife and children. He was apprehended on the Galdames and, later on, executed in Burgos in spite of the fact that he was the head of the Catalonian Catholic Party.

At eight-thirty in the morning the Basque vessels left Bayonne escorting the Galdames. About the middle of the morning, the battery from Punta Galea announced to Basque Naval Headquarters that an enemy cruiser accompanied by a captured merchant ship was in sight. A short time later, the same battery sent this message: "The merchant ship carries the flag of Estonia. The warship is the rebel cruiser Canarias." The battery of Punta Galea opened fire, but the Canarias withdrew from the range of the coastal guns.

It was a day characteristic of the Bay of Biscay at that time of year—heavy seas, violent squalls, little visibility. Amid the dense fog that enveloped the sea, appeared the tiny Bizkaya and Gipuzkoa, which with unequalled boldness opened fire on the Canarias with their cannons of 101.2. The eight-inch guns of the Canarias immediately answered with all their might. It would be well to note that the Canarias and the Baleares were the most modern ships of the Spanish fleet.

A while later the Nabarra and the Donostia appeared, escorting the Galdames, which on account of the fog and damage suffered in her helm lost her course and found herself unexpectedly under the gunfire of the Canarias. The latter fired four times at the Galdames, on which a horrible panic was produced, especially among the women and children. The people, maddened by terror, threw themselves into the water, fourteen perishing. The Galdames was not sunk, through some miracle, but was captured by the Canarias and delivered to the torpedo boat Velasco, which took it to the port of Pasajes next to San Sebastian—both in possession of the rebel forces. The Gipuzkoa and the Nabarra attacked the Canarias with their poor cannons, getting under the fire of the enemy battery which fired furiously.

They had carried on more than one hour when the Bizkaya, accomplishing a skillful maneuver, placed itself at the side of the Estonian vessel and, covered by it, compelled it to enter the port of Bermeo, which was in our hands, evading the mighty Canarias. Seeing her failure, this ship went after the Basque vessels with growing fierceness. Soon afterwards, the Gipuzkoa burst into flames. The Nabarra was left alone fighting against the Canarias. It was David fighting against Goliath.

I had arrived a short time before at the battery of Punta Galea, attracted by the extraordinary combat taking place scarcely ten miles away from the coast, whose progress I had followed through the official communications sent to the Department of Defense. But I was eager to witness with my own eyes the heroic chapter that was being written by our seamen—and so went to the battery. A mass of smoke and flames was slowly moving in the direction of Bilbao. It was the Gipuzkoa, withdrawing while it burnt, carrying on board one-third of its crew dead.

The Nabarra kept firing constantly. It was burning at bow and stern, but would not withdraw from the battle. At four in the afternoon a boat was lowered. Its crew rowed painfully near the small Donostia, which at that moment was getting ready to enter the battle with its cannon of 75 millimeters. When the captain of the Donostia saw that the men in the boat were wounded and covered with blood, he thought they were the only survivors of the Nabarra. He lowered the ladder, saying, "Come on board and we shall get to Bermeo."

"No, no," was the answer. "We have to go back to the Nabarra immediately. We need buckets to put out the fire and bandages for our wounded. Our captain orders that you go back to safety, as this 'round of the pelota game' shall be finished by us."

The captain of the Donostia insisted, but those in the boat answered: "You go back home. If we are to lose a boat, let it be ours. Withdraw immediately. We shall defend your withdrawal. Good luck!"

The captain of the Donostia gave them all he had, and raising his beret, with tears in his eyes, cried to those brave men: "*Agur mutillak! . . . Gora Euzkadi Askatuta!*" (Goodbye, boys! . . . Long live Euzkadi free!)

"Gora!" answered the boys, and they were gone.

The Nabarra battled against the Canarias for two long hours after this.

"But how could you resist?" we asked one of the heroes of this episode.

"Because of the magnificent morale of the crew, we had started the battle with mad enthusiasm. Yet, what could we do against such a ship? We discharged between ninety and one hundred cannon shots, and only God knows how many the Canarias must have aimed at us. Our poor Nabarra was pierced by gunshots and in flames.

"Once the engineer Cajigas came up to tell the captain that he had already complied with his orders to open the bottom in order that we all go down with the vessel; but the captain answered, 'Close them again, for we yet have to show them who we are.' At another time the pennant at the steerage could not be seen very well as it had gotten entangled with the pole, and the captain ordered one of the sailors, 'Go to the bow, lower the Basque flag, and after you have unfolded it, hoist it again. . . . Let them take a good look at it. . . . Floating freely in the air, it shall go down with the Nabarra. It was not made to be trampled by traitors.'

"The last moments were horrible. I was wounded, and so was the telegraph operator. One shot hit the feed tube of the boilers, killing the three engineers and several of the firemen and oilers. The rest went up on deck with terrible burns. They looked as if they had come out of hell. The cannon at the bow had been damaged, but we kept firing with the one at the stern. The boat was in flames. We couldn't stand it any longer and started to throw ourselves in the water. The sea was rough, and as we were all exhausted, only a few of us could reach a boat that had been lowered from the Nabarra, which was still floating. A few of us could get into it, others drowned right before our eyes. We saw the Nabarra go down in flames. With it went the captain and the first officer, who preferred to die rather than surrender to the enemy.

"The Canarias did not get hit during the whole battle except for one shot from us which killed a midshipman. The missile did not explode, for if it had, it would have killed some 140 men who were in the hold, through which it had entered. I was told of this afterwards.

"We were picked up by the Canarias. The commander asked us about the captain. We told him that he had remained on board."

"How did they treat you on the Canarias?" we asked.

"First of all the commander told us that we were despicable because we were separatists. Then he changed his tone and praised us for our behavior in the battle. Certainly, we were half naked and dying with cold. On seeing that we were shivering, the commander said, 'Don't tremble, for we are not like the Reds, who assassinate people.' I answered, 'We are not trembling with fear but because we are cold.' They gave us clothes and coffee, and as we were all wounded they took us to the infirmary. There was our second officer Olabeaga, gravely wounded, with many others."

"How many of you were saved?"

"Twenty. Thirty-two had died. The next day they treated our wounds again and at three in the afternoon they put us in the torpedo room awaiting the Velasco which was to take us to Pasajes, and from there to the Ondarreta jail. As we stood in line, the commander followed by the staff passed in front of us, accompanying the body of the midshipman. The commander said, pointing to the dead man, 'There goes a Spanish soldier who knew how to die for his country, and not traitors like you.'"

"And how have you come up here?"

"On March 26 they passed a brief judgment on us and condemned five of us to die. On June 13 they passed another judgment and condemned us all to die. This is the justice of the Francoists. But on November 28, 1938, that is, a year and a half later, they set us free. Appearing at the revision of the process, the commander of the Canarias asked our freedom and said, 'These men are heroes, and heroes deserve to live!'"

Here ended the narration of that brave seaman, in a serene and simple manner.

Thus, these Basque seamen wrote one more page of glory, without ships and without guns, but with such firm courage and devotion to their cause that Walsingham might well-nigh have been writing of them when in his English history he recalled the naval battles between Basques and English in 1350: "They preferred, because of the rudeness of their heart, to die rather than to surrender."

To the honor and glory of the Nabarra the English poet C. Day-Lewis dedicated the following poem in which he states:

They bore not a charmed life. They went into battle
    foreseeing
Probable loss, and they lost. The tides of Biscay flow
Over obstinate bones of many, the winds are sighing
Round prison walls where the rest are doomed like their ship
    to rust—
Men of the Basque country, the Mar Cantabrico.

Simple men who asked of their life no mythical splendour,
They loved its familiar ways so well that they preferred

In the rudeness of their heart to die rather than to
   surrender. . . .
Mortal these words and the deed they remember, but cast a
   seed
Shall flower for an age when freedom is man's creative word.

Freedom was more than a word, more than the base coinage
Of politicians who, hiding behind the skirts of peace
They had defiled, gave up that country to rack and carnage:
For whom, indelibly stamped with history's contempt,
Remains but to haunt the blackened shell of their policies.

For these I have told of, freedom was flesh and blood—a
   mortal
Body, the gun-breech hot to its touch; yet the battle's height
Raised it to love's meridian and held it awhile immortal;
And its light through time still flashes like a star's that has
   turned to ashes,
Long after Nabarra's passion was quenched in the sea's heart.[8]

5

Bilbao is surrounded by small mountains. It is rolling
country like parts of New England, and the roads curve around the
mountains' edge so that as you travel you look down into the cultivated valleys.

Three days before the fall of Bilbao I was in my office, which faced
the Artxanda Mountain. Two ministers of the government were
with me. We were planning the evacuation of the civilian population. Three or four shots splintered the window close to my desk.
The Italians were shooting at us from the Artxanda.

Directly behind us, Mount Pagasarri was falling into the hands of
Franco's troops. Soon Bilbao would be surrounded. The highway
which follows the Nervión River to Santander was the only way out,
and over it the enemy machine guns and artillery crossed fire.

We decided that I should speak to our *gudaris* at the front by radio, requesting that one last attempt be made to detain the enemy's advance, so that the civilians—the old men, the women, and the children—might leave the city. There was no water, no light, no gas. For several days the people had slept in cellars.

That night, after I had spoken, three battalions, chosen among themselves for this final sacrifice, ascended the mountain, singing the hymn of the *gudaris:*

Euzko-gudariak gara	We are Basque soldiers
Euzkadi azkatzeko,	To liberate Euzkadi,
Gerturik daukagu odola	Our blood is ready
Bere aldez emoteko.	To be shed for her.

An English author, witness of those crucial moments, says:

As night fell over the smoke and flames and unbroken row of battle, three of the flower of the Basque National Infantry Battalions were sent out for the final effort. The Kirikiño, the Itxasalde, the Itxarkundia. In the history of the sacrifice of human blood for democracy, may their names live for ever. . . . As long as laurels spring out of the generous ground there will be leaves to crown their memory. Heroes salute! A forlorn hope, and knowing it, they went up the line singing the solemn songs of Basques, songs like the Gaelic laments of prehistory to be accompanied upon the bagpipe and the *txistu.* Their deep voices were lost in the dark.

They hurled themselves recklessly upon the enemy lines with grenades in their hands. They had nothing but their rifles, perhaps a few had machine guns—but the Artxanda was recaptured and remained in our possession for more than twenty-four hours.

There were two ships, the Bobie, a French vessel, and the English Seven Seas Spray, which the Basque Government had chartered a few months before for civilian evacuation. In these last weeks, more than 50,000 persons were ferried to Bayonne. Others walked to Santander, and some rode in an odd assortment of vehicles. The noise of the carts groaning through the streets of Bilbao was like the sound of the earth breaking to release a deep-rooted tree. But order was complete. Our *gudaris* watched. No act of violence was committed. The sound of the refugee steps could be heard over the constant rattling of the enemy pursuit planes.

Members of the government met, and we thought at first of surrendering ourselves in order to save the people. It would mean our certain death—which was no solution. Our task was not finished. There were already nearly 100,000 Basques in France. More were emigrating. And in Catalonia other thousands of Basque refugees would need whatever help a government-in-exile could give them.

Three members of the government went with me to Trucios, which is one of the last towns in Basque territory en route to Santander, to organize the evacuation. Two other ministers were sent to France, and were beginning to carry out our plans for housing, the distribution of food, education, hospitalization, and employment services for our people. Two others had gone to Catalonia.

As we left, our *gudaris* on the Artxanda were no longer able to hold out against the intensive artillery and air bombardment of the Italians and the Francoist troops. We ordered that they should retreat to the opposite bank of the Nervión River. They were ordered also to open the prisons in Bilbao. Nearly 2,000 political prisoners were permitted to reach enemy lines in perfect formation during a momentary cessation of firing. We were criticized for this action by those who were heartless, the enemy laughed at us, but we never regretted it.

Our Minister of Justice, Jesus Leizaola, with Santiago Aznar, the Minister of Labor and Industry, and Juan Astigarrabia, Minister of Public Works, stayed in Bilbao with the General of the Basque Army until the last moments, when the Italians were marching in the streets toward the government offices. A section of our police also waited for their entrance. They surrendered themselves, cheering Euzkadi and the men of our government to show their steadfast loyalty even as our flag was lowered.

We had lost our country. In the words of François Mauriac, "Some day it shall be known that this small nation sacrificed itself for us, because, like Christ, it was crucified and then slandered."

6

Out of that army of 100,000 men only 30,000 were left, reorganized in four divisions, with little artillery and few machine guns. The rest had died, were wounded, or had been taken prisoner. These four divisions, who kept their souls invincible, as well as their courage to continue fighting, constituted a force of great value because of their experience in the battle, and the endurance acquired in such an unequal and sacrificial fight. These remnants of the Basque army were formed in line within the province of Santander, a territory of the old kingdom of Castille, from the coast to about one hundred kilometers in the interior.

We were certain that the next attack would be directed, not against the front defended by the Basques, which faced the Basque country, but at the rear, through the lines that bordered the province of Burgos.

The purpose of this attack through the southern front was to surprise the Basque army, put it out of combat, destroy the Republican troops, and divide Santander from Asturias. The scarcity of ammunition, the loss of the industrial zone of Bilbao, which had supported with its production the most urgent needs of those fronts, showed clearly the seriousness of the situation. The concentration of Italian divisions at the boundary of Burgos, having been recalled from the Basque front, indicated preparations for the next attack.

For the first time I left my emigrant people and my troops, and flew to Valencia where I arrived one afternoon in July, 1937. The object of my visit was daring. I was going to propose the immediate shipment of the Basque divisions, transferring them to the front in Catalonia. For that we should have to obtain the means of transportation, the money to charter the boats and the permit to cross France. The Spanish Republican Government could fulfill the first two requirements. The third would have to be obtained in Paris.

I had a long interview with President Azaña, to whom I explained my project.* I recall one of his answers: "To understand you, one needs only to know geography." And, really, it was so, because our troops were encircled with no means of help. I had another meeting with the Prime Minister, Negrin, who asked me to interview Prieto, Minister of War, who was then in Madrid. Zugazagoitia, the Minister of the Interior, later shot by the Franco authorities after he had been delivered by the Gestapo from France, was also present at that meeting.

> *[Editor's note: The references in this paragraph are to leading officials of the Spanish republican government: president, Manuel Azaña; prime minister, Juan Negrin; minister of war, Indalecio Prieto; and minister of interior, Julián Zugazagoitia.]

I then went to Madrid where I met Minister Prieto, busy with the Brunete offensive. We had a four-hour conversation, in which I asked for the transfer of the troops.

I then went to Barcelona, where I was moved by the warmth of the Catalonians' reception. I exchanged ideas with President Companys, who understood my project, which had a greater meaning than the simple departure of the troops—and I repeated the same pleas I had made to President Azaña.

What was my purpose? The cause of democracy in Spain had been received abroad with some reluctance, even in strong democratic countries—because of the enemy's skillful, damaging propaganda. Unfortunately, some of it was true. The burning of churches and convents (not unusual in the history of Spanish revolts), the taking over of enterprises, including foreign ones, by certain syndicates, the showy syndicate placards, abundance of extremist emblems, in the first moment of confusion and disorder—these things cooled friendly feeling in foreign countries toward the Republican cause.

We Basques, who had prevented these excesses in our territory, and who at every instant preserved a respected authority, with churches open, clergymen walking freely through the streets, with no syndicate seizure of property, felt deeply the unfriendly foreign attitude which labeled us with names that were not just nor reasonable.

In Catalonia the Basque divisions could have served as a nucleus for many Catalonian patriots, and together they would have constituted an element that could have restored the features of the Republican territory, with which it was necessary to face Europe.

The army of the Spanish Republic was being organized but really did not yet exist. In Catalonia both the confusion and the indignation of the patriots increased every minute. Extremist organizations were smaller in number, but bigger in audacity. The Catalonian authorities lacked coercive means, of which military rebellion had deprived them. The arrival of the Basque divisions would have saved the true Catalonia, and changed the course of things. Many have forgotten that, just as the Basques were fighting to defend their threatened nationality, the true Catalonians, in greater numbers, were fighting for the same end—for freedom, as against totalitarian violence.

Was my proposal understood, or was it not? Was it too well understood? This is no place to investigate it. I visited M. Delbos, then Minister of Foreign Affairs in Paris. Ossorio Gallardo, then Ambassador of the Spanish Republic in Paris, accompanied me. I explained the object of my trip to Valencia and asked the Minister whether it was possible for the Basque troops to pass through France on their way to Catalonia as though they were "expeditions of wounded," in case this was permitted.

The Minister showed personal sympathy, but admitted that in a case of such importance his government had to be consulted. But the French decision was now of little interest as Prieto notified me from Valencia that the case had been submitted twice to the Superior Council of War, and my petition had been rejected because of "political and military motives," as the communiqué literally read.

I relinquished all further responsibility in a telegram to President Azaña, and returned to Santander to join my troops and my people scarcely eight days before the fall of Santander, ready to do what would best save the greater number of men.

We arrived miraculously after flying 150 miles over the enemy coast. The bombing and pursuit planes overtook us, and we had only enough time to abandon our plane as it landed at the Santander Airdrome and get into a shelter, while a load of bombs filled the field with craters, not a single one hitting our plane. Thank God, as it was the only one we had.

This audacious plane had its history. It had belonged to Emperor Haile Selassie during the Abyssinian War. The Basque Government had acquired it from the Negus for five thousand pounds. It was a pursuit plane, Curtiss type, fitted out for rapid trips, and without armament. It had its back painted with coats of arms and emblems of the countries where it had served. I recall those of several of the states of the U.S.A., the Lion of Judah, and finally the coat of arms of Euzkadi. The French pilot Lebaud flew it. The plane was baptized by the people with the name of "The Negus," and as "The Negus" we all knew it.

In spite of Lebaud's complete trustworthiness, no one—not even he—knew of our departure until we left the airdrome of Parme in Biarritz. We have had to act thus ever since the disloyalty of a Spanish pilot who delivered Dr. Espinosa Oribe, Minister of Public Health of the Basque Government, and Lieutenant Commander Aguirre, chief of our Artillery, to Franco when they were returning from France performing the duties of their posts. They were the victims of treachery, as the despicable flyer, bought by the Franco agents, descended upon a beach occupied by Franco's forces. Both were executed for the only possible crime of those worthy men—the defense of the freedom of their people against the attack of totalitarianism. The Basque Government also had its executed martyrs.

As we had foreseen, the advance through the south of Santander of the Italo-Francoist troops was rapid. The Santander front was easily broken, and in ten days the Fascist troops were reaching the capital and broke through to the coast, leaving no outlet, and surprising the Basque divisions—although they were not attacked. Our premonitions were fulfilled.

After this, Italians again became the principal actors in the great Basque tragedy. General Mancini, chief of the Litorio Division, promised the Basques—surrounded on the rocky cliff of Santoña and Laredo in a terrain of less than ten square miles—an honorable surrender. Our *gudaris* had only enough ammunition and food to last about a week. Basque envoys crossed the line of firing and met with the Italian General, and made an agreement known as the "Pact of Santoña," on condition that the firing be stopped. Meanwhile, the *gudaris* were expecting that the boats which came to take refugees to Santander would reach Santoña in order to take them to France.

The signed conditions were as follows, for the Basque army:

1. To surrender their arms to the Italians, who would occupy the region of Santoña without any resistance.
2. To maintain order in the occupied zone.
3. To insure the release of political prisoners who were in Laredo and the great Santoña Penitentiary.

The Basques faithfully fulfilled the three promised conditions. As for the Italians, they pledged:

1. To guarantee the lives of the Basque combatants.
2. To guarantee the lives and authorize the departure to foreign countries of all Basque political and military personalities who were in the territory of Santander.
3. To consider all Basque combatants subject to this capitulation free from all obligation of taking part in the civil war on the side of General Franco.
4. To guarantee that the civilian population loyal to the Government of Euzkadi would not be subject to reprisals.

Under these conditions the Basques were ready to surrender their arms to the Italian division of Blackshirts. And with them they dealt, for they had fought against them and the Germans.

At dusk on the 25th of August the Italians started to enter Laredo, and a lieutenant colonel, who preceded them, on reaching the square, read publicly the conditions of the Armistice, and posted them on street corners under the Italian flag, to demonstrate that that which was written there was sacred. On the 26th the Italians entered Santoña, and immediately afterwards the Basque Defense Council surrendered the town to Colonel Fergosi. And on that same night the two ships, the Bobie and the Seven Seas Spray, which had been busy carrying refugees, anchored in the Bay of Laredo to take away all the *gudaris*.

The harbor was most animated. A large number of fighting boats were lying at anchor—full of people. On the quay there was a mass of people throwing all their weapons in heaps: rifles, revolvers, machine guns, cartridge belts, everything. Armed men, Basques, guarded the quay and its surroundings. Troops in fair order were coming along the roads which opened on the port. They disarmed and dispersed.

The captains of the boats went to the Town Hall, which was surrounded by a crowd of Basques without weapons. Inside, the stairs and corridors were packed with people. They had great difficulty pushing their way into the room where the leaders were. This room had also been invaded by the crowd, and the wounded were everywhere. An open door at the other end showed another room full of wounded.

The captains asked the Basque military chiefs for instructions about the embarkation of the *gudaris,* and were told that news was expected.

At six next morning, the Town Hall was surrounded by Italian soldiers.

At the same time, the Basques began to mass on the quay in good order, waiting for embarkation. At nine, the captains received orders to begin embarking all those in possession of a special ticket issued by the Basque leaders, or a passport of the Euzkadi Government. The officer-observer of the Nonintervention Committee on the Bobie, M. Costa e Silva, examined the papers with the captains, and the work went on in a business-like way on both ships.

At ten o'clock an officer in the uniform of the Italian army, but a Spaniard, and carrying the Falangist badge, came and gave orders to stop the embarkation and wait for new orders. He said it was an order from Colonel Fergosi, commanding Santoña.

At this moment—about ten-fifteen—sections of Italian soldiers appeared on the quay, closed around the crowd of Basques who were still waiting to embark, placed four machine guns in well-chosen positions and set a guard on the Bobie's gangway. All communication between ship and shore was forbidden.

At two that afternoon, the captains and Silva, the officer of the

Nonintervention Committee, escorted by four Italian soldiers, visited Colonel Fergosi at the Town Hall. None of the Basque leaders were there now, and it was occupied entirely by Italians.

Colonel Fergosi informed them that he had received formal orders from the Generalissimo—Franco—that no one, Basque or foreign, was to leave Santoña. The captains drew his attention to the fact that all Basques on the two ships were now under the protection of the British and French flags, and that if no more Basques could come on board, they could nevertheless leave with those already in the Bobie and Seven Seas Spray. His answer was definite. "No one is allowed to leave Santoña, and the Almirante Cervera, which is outside, is already so informed."

That night the Spanish officers ordered all passengers to leave the Bobie. All was done in an orderly way, and the ship was then searched from top to bottom by four other Falangist officers. As daylight began to show, the men who had been disembarked that evening walked along the road to Laredo. There were others on lorries carrying the Italian flag, that went by another road.

The Italian guard was commanded by Lieutenant Colonel Farina. There were also Colonels Fergosi and Piesch, the latter in charge of concentration camps.

Two groups formed on the quay: on one side, the Basques who had fought in the war and had been disarmed; on the other, the political leaders.

The Nonintervention officer conversed with Colonels Piesch and Farina. The latter, in a frank moment, expressed his bitterness and anger for all that was going on. "It is disgraceful," said Farina, "to see that an Italian general cannot keep the promise which he has given," and "There is no case in all history of such a thing happening." Colonel Piesch added words of assent.

Toward eleven, Colonel Farina told the officers of the Bobie to anchor and await orders, and those of the Seven Seas Spray to dock at the quay and disembark the people aboard.

The captain of the Bobie asked Colonel Fergosi in the presence of Colonel Farina if the Basques were really prisoners of the Italian

Army, and only of the Italian Army. He was assured that such was the case, and that it was not the intention of General Mancini to deliver the Basques, whoever they were, to the Falangists.

At nine P.M. an Italian officer, accompanied by four Falangists, themselves officers, boarded the Bobie to give the captain orders to leave. Another search of the ship was made, and at ten P.M. she was headed out to the open sea. The Seven Seas Spray followed shortly after.

Thus, the Basques were forsaken by some and betrayed by others. History will judge those who were most responsible. Those brave boys who had given all to defend freedom and democracy were carried away in trucks, to captivity. Some were executed, others hanged, and all condemned to suffer hunger and misery in Franco's prisons.

Basque military and political leaders were confined to the Santoña Penitentiary. On the very square where they had been promised respect, several of them were executed. As for the *gudaris*—many were violently taken away from concentration camps and killed at night on beaches or deserted roads.

7

August 23rd, two days before these happenings, I was in Santander, where the Basque Government had taken refuge in the country home of a Philippine citizen. What days of anguish I spent there—those tragic hours are hard to forget, separated from my troops, the private guard of my own house for our only protection.

The first movements of revolt, in charge of the fifth column encouraged by the approach of the Italo-Francoist troops, started in the city. That night I spent with the two Basque ministers who stayed in Santander with me. The rest of the government members had left for France on my orders, to organize the more than 150,000 Basques who had already emigrated. We spent the night walking in the garden, expecting the assault any minute, either from the advance guard of the Franco army, or from the revolting elements whose intentions were to get hold of Santander. All defense means were exhausted; there was no army, and personal security had disappeared.

As dawn came we had just retired to rest a few hours, when General Gamir Ullibarri, an old leader of the Basque Army and then head of the Northern Loyalist Army, came to invite me to leave for Asturias in a submarine that remained in the port. The General Staff of the Northern Army and the Santander authorities were to leave in it. I declined the offer.

At midday the leaders of the Basque National Party arrived.

"We came here to beg and, if need be, to order that the President leave immediately. Our forces are surrounded without possible outlet, and Santander may fall in a few hours. The fifth column practically owns the city."

"I thank you for your visit. I know all this well enough. I had not hoped to see you again. We spent all last night in the garden with our pistols ready, expecting trouble any minute. But how do you think I can leave?"

"Won't the Negus arrive today?" they inquired.

"You know the plane always comes at dusk. Today, it will come around eight. It may be too late . . ."

"Well, departure is necessary, urgent. A way must be found."

"General Gamir Ullibarri has proposed my departure to Asturias in a submarine. I have not accepted it. . . . What am I to do there away from my troops?"

"Your departure is necessary because the Basque fight for freedom must be continued from abroad, and you are the President."

We all remained thoughtful. What was there to do? Only God knew the end that awaited us.

At that very moment, a small dot appeared on the horizon that got bigger and bigger. It was a plane. An enemy plane? No—it was the Negus! It landed as best it could between the gaps of the aviation field. Lebaud reached our house panting. He said quickly:

"Mr. President, there is not an instant to lose. The firing has already started, and the airfield could be totally destroyed if not occupied by the enemy within a few hours."

"But how did you come at such an early hour?" I asked.

"When I left for Biarritz yesterday," he answered, "I realized by the state of the town that this was the last day for Santander. It was something I felt deep in my heart. I was uneasy. That's why I came at one o'clock instead of at eight."

"And what will you do?" I asked the Basque leaders.

"Once our President is saved," they answered, "we will follow the destiny of our troops."

And those excellent men, wishing to duly celebrate my departure, brought from the cellar two champagne bottles which had been carefully preserved by the owner of the house. And while planes flew overhead and rifle shots were heard near by, they lifted their glasses in a toast to my safe arrival in France and the future happiness of our people. They knew very deep in their souls that very shortly they might find themselves facing a firing squad—as did happen to some of them—or in prisons. Ajuriaguerra, Arteche, Unzeta, Rezola—some day all will know the greatness of your sacrifice.

"They are flying over the airfield," said Lebaud. "We cannot lose one second."

We left in a car in the middle of a heavy bombardment. At the garden gate, my guard presented arms. It was the farewell salute which they made more firmly than ever, tears glistening in their eyes. I have wept very few times. This was one of them. There stood my colleagues and friends with their glasses still in their hands— here, the brave guards that always accompanied me with unfaltering loyalty, and hurrying me, the pilot Lebaud, who later, in 1940, died gloriously in France fighting against Hitler. Many may know what the feeling of loyalty means; but those hours of loyalty in which I lived among my people—those I know in the innermost recesses of my soul.

From the car we jumped to a shelter, from which we came out in spite of the bombardment, for we feared losing our only plane. We all pushed the Negus, and through the only free passage left on the field, we tore off with sudden speed, accompanied by my fellow men of the government—Monzon and Torre—taking to the sea, flying close to the cruiser Canarias, which was watching the port, getting ready to enter it.

An hour later we arrived in Biarritz.

My wife and my little daughter, Aintzane, who was then two years old, were living in a small house in Biarritz. They had been evacuated when the Basque Government decreed the departure from Euzkadi of women, children, and old people.

One day the Subprefect of Bayonne, M. Daguerre, had come to see my wife. "Madame," he said, "our secret police has been notified of a maneuver which is being plotted by a group of Franco followers. They are planning to kidnap your daughter. Although we are ready to prevent it, we advise you, for the moment, to go and live in a town in the interior." And my wife, with anguish in her mother's heart, left with her little daughter in her arms, to move away from the fiends who were being praised by so many as the new Crusaders.

I had not been notified of this. People who were close to me kept this nefarious plot from me until I had reached France, after the loss of my country. When I visited M. Daguerre to thank him for all the attentions he had given the Basque refugees, he confirmed this fact.

"I would not have believed," he ended his account, "that such procedures could be employed by persons who are considered civilized and call themselves Christians."9

"When a society becomes so deeply wanting in charity," I answered, "its sentiments and actions can well be worthy of any kind of qualifying name, but never that of Christian."10

La Roseraie was once a magnificent private hotel that the very famous financial adventurer, Staviski, had built in Ilbarritz, a few miles from Biarritz. Staviski had built gardens, swimming pools, cabarets, and incredibly luxurious gambling halls. In this setting, we installed our mutilated Basque veterans for treatment and rehabilitation. More than 800 young men with their legs and arms destroyed by shrapnel passed through that sumptuous summer home. Workshops were created where our poor crippled soldiers received education for the future. Also our immigrant people had free hospitalization and clinics there. Basque doctors attended them. The French doctors, at this example of patriotic fraternity, permitted our doctors to exercise their profession, although it broke the French regulations. The institution cost our government-in-exile more than 300,000 francs monthly, but the endurance of the men and the spirit of service were sufficient proofs of its worth.

On the day I visited the institution, a choir of crippled soldiers sang in my honor. Few times have I felt more profound emotion. Those men were singing with all their hearts. They couldn't hate. They had forgotten revenge. They were singing to their fatherland, which they had gladly served. As they rested on their crutches, some without legs, some without arms, some blind, they threw their whole souls into the valiant notes of the popular Basque songs. I only wished that the entire world could have been present face to face with those whom certain "friends of the order" called *la canaille*.

At my side the chaplain of the institution was telling me: "They are angels. What good people are the humble!" I have said "chaplain," because the Basque people emigrated with their beliefs and their priests. The priests were also people, and they followed the destiny of the persecuted the same in exile as in front of the platoon of executioners.

For the Basques, religion is a necessity of the soul, and in those moments was a source of consolation. For that reason the refugees went devotedly to the churches of the French towns where they were living. One day from the pulpit of the Church of Cambo a priest announced, "The masses for the people will be celebrated at the usual hours; for the refugees there will be a special mass at eight o'clock in the morning." They separated them as if they were undesirable. These simple people could not understand that the religion of Christ should declare some of her followers outcasts. And this is because the propaganda of the enemies of liberty had reached even to the altar. And the worst was that the Church had opened its doors to falsehood. Decidedly the crisis of charity that originated in Spain had passed the frontiers. But the mutilated young men continued singing, and they sang from town to town where the people received them with admiration and understood that those who were singing in this way carried something positive in their hearts. They sang of their homes, their dogs, their river, everything that had been taken from them, in those simple words of our poet Elissanburu which symbolize for the Basque all the poetry of the world:

Ikusten duzu goizean	Don't you see in the morning
Argia asten denean,	When the light begins
Menditxo baten gainean	On the peak of the mountain
Etxe txikitxo aitzin txuri bat,	A white little house,
Lau aitz ondoren artean,	Among four great boulders,
Iturriño bat aldean,	A little fountain near by,
Txakur txuri bat atean?	With a white dog at the door?
An bizi naiz ni bakean.	There I live in peace.

One day the separation in the churches was abolished. Another day the Cardinal of Paris, Monseigneur Verdier, blessed and encouraged the orphans of Gernika whose voices astonished the audiences of Paris and other French cities with their "Elai-Alai" (Happy Swallows), a group of children's chorals and dances.

"Emanda Zabalzazu" (Give and spread your seeds), one of the verses in the hymn of the Tree of Gernika, is a tradition with us. While the cannon roared very close to our house, three days before the fall of Santander, a director of the Basque choirs received my last instructions. "It is possible that we will remain here," I told him, "without being able to leave. But that is no reason to end the fight. I order you to leave immediately for France and to form among our refugees the best choir possible, which will carry to all the world, through our melodies, the memory of a people who die for liberty, because there are many who do not know yet that we are fighting for them. If we fall, you will remember us and continue singing."

The choir leader left in the Negus, and the chorus sang in Paris, London, Brussels, Amsterdam, and other cities of Europe. And it continued to bear fruit and change opinions. It was propaganda, yes; but it was a propaganda for liberty because, with singing, only spiritual seeds can be sown. And, singing, the Basques announced to the world that the same brutal force that had exiled those beautiful songs was capable of closing the lips of other people who believed themselves more secure.

Paris, that warm human city, received us graciously. I spent a

month in Paris and a month in Barcelona, where we had almost
100,000 refugees, organizing the emigration. The French authorities were most courteous and helpful, and the Basques were corre-
spondingly anxious to show their appreciation. In spite of this there
were still those who continued to attack us as they later attacked the
very soul of their own great liberty-loving country, France.

One day I went to a lecture which the Duchess of Atholl gave in
the Théâtre des Ambassadeurs of Paris. The subject was the Civil
War in Spain, and it was heavily documented. We followed all her
arguments, which did not admit reply. Some protests arose. A furious lady attacked the Duchess, some others laughed derisively. The
Duchess replied calmly, "The Spanish Republic represented the
right versus aggression," and in the case of a revolt against the
French institutions, aided, for example, by Hitler, she would never
doubt that her contradictors would defend France. "Rather Hitler
than Blum," cried the lady from the floor.

Another day M. Bonnet, Minister of Foreign Affairs, called me to
his office. It was the 8th of August, 1938, a month and a half before
the Munich Pact. He kept asking me anxiously whether I thought
the Spanish Republic, then engaged in the Battle of the Ebro River,
could hold out until the 1st of October. I answered that I was sure it
could, giving my reasons and calming his doubts in the hour-long
conversation which we held. The Loyalist troops were able to resist
even longer than the 1st of October, but the Pact of Munich was
signed on the 28th of September—among other consequences,
signing the death warrant of the Spanish Republic, which was already being slowly strangled by the increasing flow of men and
materials from Italy and Germany to Franco.

A few months later—February, 1939—the defeated Catalonian
and Spanish Republican troops were forced to withdraw toward the
Catalan-French border in the Pyrenees.

Early in the morning of the 4th of February, the President of
Catalonia, M. Companys, was leaving his country to follow the tragic
road of exile. I walked by his side, for I had promised to remain with
him to the end.

We did not leave until the last of the people had crossed the
French border. These enemies of the Axis were utterly forlorn. The

airplanes of Hitler, Mussolini, and Franco pursued them unceasingly.

Looking down the mountain pass, you could still see them coming, some of them almost barefoot, their sandals were worn so thin. For this immense caravan of people without country and without homes there was no hope of hospitality other than the concentration camp.

"Send them to the Colonies," said the French press friendly to Italy "the Latin sister," and enemy of England the arch imperialist. At the same time every kind of murder and evil deed was attributed to them when they deserved a more humane treatment, if only because they were so completely bereft. We at least had received aid from Basques all over the world. There were homes which always could make room for one more family. There was a loaf of bread which could be broken forty times more if necessary. Whatever we had, each Basque who went into France knew that he would share with us equally. It was our pledge. It was our creed.

Those defenders of democracy with all their defects and all their mistakes were still an advance guard of liberty. But there were the Nonintervention Committee, the Munich Pact, the arms embargo. In Paris, London, Washington, silence reigned.

Only seven months later France was at war. But France was torn apart internally before she even started to fight. To the confusion of the Rights was added the complete disorientation of the Lefts. The Hitler-Stalin Pact took the wind out of the French masses. To the cry of "Rather Hitler than Blum" was added another as disloyal and suicidal as the first: "Rather Stalin than Daladier."

Weakened from the Right and the Left, France entered the war reluctantly, her people bewildered and disunited. We saw here the same symptoms which had just forced us into exile. The Basques, however, felt the cause of France to be their own, and 50,000 Basque immigrants signed a pledge offering to serve either at the front or in the factories, in this new battle for freedom.

After the anguished times we had just lived through, we had no inkling that our innocent family visit to La Panne was to initiate a new series of trials and anxieties in the days to come.

CHAPTER IV

After this review in the preceding pages of recent Basque history, it should not be difficult to understand our tragic predicament at La Panne, where my story was interrupted at the end of Chapter II. It was June 1, 1940. The Germans were entering the town. Here was Santander over again except that, in repeating itself, history failed in one important detail—there was no Negus this time to take us out. The bombardments were just the same, the sight and sound of a village dying were not new to us. We all crowded at the windows. We could see the German soldiers marching through the streets.

["What are we going to do now?" my wife asked.

My mother-in-law spoke up. "I think José Antonio should get out. You and the children," she said to my wife, "are in more danger with your husband than without him. If they find him now, you are all doomed; if they find him alone, he could more easily escape."

I agreed with her at once, despite Mari's protesting glances. We went into the small dining room and sat around the table. Some of the students sat on the floor.

"If I get out," I explained to Mari, "I may be able to get you out. Your mother is quite right. If we are all caught together, we are like rats in a cage."

"Where will you go?" she asked. She was sitting very straight, and her hands were clasped.

"I don't know." Where should I go? Which road led to an open gate? "I don't know—but I have at least twenty-four hours. No army of occupation can search for civilians until their own machinery is set up. It takes them some time to do that."

"You must be someone else, and not yourself," Father Alberto said. "When you leave us, you must be prepared to meet anyone."

"He could be a South American," Sabin suggested.

"I could also come from South America." Mari leaned forward.

It was getting like a game. Everyone threw his ideas onto the table, and the ideas were picked up, examined, and thrown away or accepted. It might have been a real party except for the echoing of the marching Nazi troops, the sight we all still held in our retentive minds.

"I will be your traveling companion," Mari said to me, joking. "I will be the lady from—"

"And the children?"

"We will always say the children belong to my sister, and we are taking them home."

"No." Juan spoke from the floor. "Joseba looks too much like his father. You'll have to think of a better scheme."

"I still think that José Antonio should go at once and alone. You can stay with us." This time it was my mother who spoke.

Santi, my brother-in-law, said, "We will look after you, Mari."

"If you go back with us to Louvain," Juan said, "we will introduce you as our cousin from South America. I think it would be wisest for all of us to return to our present homes in Louvain as soon as possible. All of us—but José Antonio. He is the only one they would bother to kill. The rest of us are safe enough. We are unimportant. We have never done anything against them—that they know about. We will live quietly as best we can, and help to get each other out."

Mari was looking at me, level-eyed, composed. "What do you think?" she asked.

I answered that I thought our mothers were right and Juan was right. "You must change your identity as much as I must change mine," I said. "If you go on being Mari Aguirre, the Nazis might well turn you over to Franco."

At this moment it was too difficult for me to contemplate Mari in any other role than the one in which I had known her since childhood: first as a friend, since our families knew each other well, then as my fiancée, and from 1933 as my wife. To me she was Mari Aguirre, no matter who else I might myself become. Mari was tall, dark-haired, with very fair skin, and had been educated in England. Her father had lost his entire fortune merely because she happened to be my wife. All this, for our having been married. Now must she "divorce" herself from me and play the role of a Madame X to protect me?]

But the actual situation quickly awakened me from this reverie. We must separate now. "Where I should try to go, I am not sure," I said. "Perhaps back to Paris."

"Good heavens, don't go there!" my mother-in-law said. "Your home and the Basque Delegation office is probably surrounded by now with Spanish Falangists, waiting—just waiting for you to come back."

"Why don't you go to Berlin?" my brother Juan interrupted. "You would be safer in Berlin than any place. From Berlin you could go to a neutral country."

I stared at him. Everyone else jumped all over the poor boy. Was he crazy? What an idea! Berlin! Where the Falangists walked hand in hand with the Gestapo. Berlin!

I interrupted them. "I think what he says makes sense. Everyone else is running away from the Nazis, and right now that's impossible, since the Nazis are everywhere. If I am someone else, and not Aguirre, if I am a neutral South American, the German authorities will not interest themselves in me."

"José Antonio!" My wife drew in a sharp breath. "It will be too dangerous!"

"No more danger than we have already known—less danger."

Father Alberto stopped us short. He said there was no time to lose, and I agreed with him. I was still turning over in my mind the idea of Berlin as the way out. Whenever a flock of people go in one direction, you will find the Basque going in the opposite direction. We are good shepherds, but we make a bad flock. The more I thought of Berlin, the better it seemed. While the rest of my world ran away from their clutches, I would run between their legs.

Father Alberto was nodding in agreement. The rest of our group was once more enthusiastic about the plan.

On the first lap of the journey into Nazi territory, we were aided by a Catalan. He and his wife had lived in Brussels for several years. He was a loyalist who had occupied a high position in Belgium as a financial delegate of the Spanish Republic. I had met them on the 14th of May, just before we all started for the French border. He was making for it too, his car crowded with luggage. Now he wanted to go back—without his luggage but still in his car, a triumph for the times. He happened to meet Father Alberto, and from that moment clung to the good priest like a limpet.

"Father," he said, "I could take you to Brussels. It will be safer there. The orders are for the cars to go back with as many refugees as possible, and I have plenty of room. I was lucky to get some gas too." And he literally begged the priest to go with him. He was under the impression that the cassock would afford him a certain measure of protection on his trip—despite the fact that Father Alberto also was a refugee from the so-called "Savior of the Faith."

Father Alberto, however, thought of our plans and of me. "I am very grateful," he answered the Catalan, "for your invitation. I will accept it, but with one condition."

"What is it, Father?"

"That you take the president of my country with us, also."

"Impossible," replied the horrified Catalan. "That would get us all in trouble."

"All right. You think about it, because if you cannot take him you cannot take me."

They parted, and Father Alberto hastened home to tell us the new possibility. He had barely finished when we heard footsteps outside approaching our house.

"That's our friend, I'm sure," Father Alberto said as he went to the door.

It was the Catalan. "I accept, Father," we heard him say. "You may tell your president I am willing to take him with us."

I went out to greet and to try to calm him. "You needn't worry too much. I have torn up all my papers. I will carry no identification on my person whatsoever. I will insist to anyone who asks that I am a Basque student in Belgium."

One of my brothers who looked very much like me had given me his University identification card with his picture in it.

The Catalan looked at me dubiously. "Aren't you a little old to be a student, Mr. President?" he asked.

"Don't worry," I laughed. "We'll leave at dusk, and in the darkness I can pass as a student, in spite of my thirty-six years. Also by nighttime the soldiers who control the roads will be sleepy and tired. They won't pay much attention to us."

"We'll see, we'll see," said the Catalan, scratching his head. He left, saying he would return by six when we would start.

That evening the soft light seemed filled with anguish. I was leaving all I held dear in the world: my wife, my children, my mother, my brothers and sisters, among them Encarna, who died only a few days later. Joseba was eating his evening meal. I said goodbye to the little fellow, and then Aintzane, seeing her mother weeping, thought I was being taken away by force. Her grandmother had to carry the poor little girl out of the room.

"When will I see you again? When?" sobbed my wife.

"When God wills it," I answered, and cut short our goodbyes, for I could stand no more.

Having left my family in La Panne, I was tormented with doubts—not so much for my own safety as for theirs. There were no guards to stop us and ask for papers, and the German soldiers on the outskirts of the village shouted to us in arrogant voices to hurry along. I had not been wrong. The first few hours of the occupation were given over to dispersing the crowds of refugees and organizing their own police and military set-ups. Since they had us all in a net, the Germans could tend to anti-fascists later.

"It seems to me," I said to Father Alberto, "as though we were all entering a vast concentration camp—and there is no escape."

"It will not be easy for you," the priest replied, "but I believe that you will find your way out."

I could not be cheered. We had only just begun the journey, but already it seemed to me that I could feel the pressure of a heavy roof covering the earth. "It's as though we were in a tunnel," I said, "down which we were sliding toward some hermetically sealed place. We must say goodbye to the world, Father."

Very shortly we had to stop altogether. The road was completely jammed with cars. Wooden bridges had been hastily erected to replace those destroyed by Germans bombs or retreating Allied troops; so all the cars had to move slowly and cautiously. But fairly soon the Germans had the traffic under control. They had planned everything. Troops followed one route, and the civilian population another. There was no confusion. Crossroad signs directed all traffic. No military units passed us, only from time to time a horse-drawn cart filled with bags of food supplies, now and again a field kitchen. As we made ground, however slowly, we gained confidence; but when night fell orders were passed back that all traffic must stop until daybreak. Almost immediately I could feel myself praying for strength to remain calm, for the good Catalan's wife was nervous. I could read her thoughts. Would they ask for papers? One could not blame her. The journey had been long for her also. She turned around and said quite apprehensively to me: "Suppose they find you with us. Then what will we do?"

"No, we are all right with him," her husband assured her. "Don't worry."

Father Alberto calmed her further by saying, "If the worst happens, the fascists will only shoot Mr. Aguirre."

This was not quite true; but, while it did not soothe me at all, it kept me in a safer position, for the Catalan's wife grew quiet. She had hidden some food which she took out now and kindly shared with us; but we had hardly begun eating when the sirens in Nieuport sounded, and we had to take cover. I kept thinking of my family. I could tell that the German artillery was firing on Dunkirk from La Panne, and I knew the Allies would reply adequately with their own guns. I remembered the previous night: my sister's wounds, Asporosa's death. Were they going through it again? What of Mari and the children? Uncertainty tormented me. Decisions had never been difficult for me to make; but there at the road's edge near Nieuport, in Belgium, with the sound of the big guns making my head roar with noise and confusion, it seemed as if I must go forward and yet I must go back. Tracer bullets streaked the skies. Looking back, it seemed as if the light I saw was all of La Panne burning, and burning with it the house where my family lived. [Where were they? What protection had they sought, what had they received? It was worse than fighting a battle—far worse than the front-line trenches. There you have a job to do: battle plans to fulfill at any cost, a gun to shoot, a comrade to help—something. This was waiting for the end. I must go back. I knew that I must go back. I could remember my little daughter in Paris after we were first out of the Basque country. The elevator to our apartment made a weird and screeching noise. Aintzane would clutch at us, frightened, but Mari and I would explain to her again and again: "It is nothing. It is just the noise of the lift. It is not a bomb. You are all right. You are very safe."

How could she live through these terrible bombardments? Would she come out all right—and my son, Joseba Andoni? I was filled with the bitter longing of a prisoner who waits for the hour of freedom.] But if I went back what would happen when the Germans began rounding up prisoners: the concentration camp in Königsberg first, then Franco Spain, and at last the firing squad for all? I must remain alone.

At four o'clock in the morning, we began to move again slowly; but at least we were getting somewhere, and the noise of the bombardment was over, however temporarily. We arrived at Ghent at seven-thirty. Guards stood at the entrance of the town, but they were passing all the small vehicles without even asking for papers. They stopped only trucks and busses. We were let through so easily we felt very gay and decided to celebrate by breakfasting in Ghent. We were greatly surprised to find life going on as usual. At least there was food. The hot coffee and bread with butter made us think we were dreaming. Refreshed and almost happy, we started off for Brussels, arriving there at ten in the morning. The Germans were still allowing the small cars to pass freely. We had no trouble at all. Really, when we said goodbye to our Catalan friends in the middle of the Boulevard Anspach, we all had to agree that our trip had been quite uneventful.

I never saw my Catalan friend again, but I think of him almost daily. I hope that God has rewarded him in a better way than I have been able to do. If he ever sees himself in my book he will know that I call him my "providential friend" still.

2

Father Alberto took my arm. "We will go to the College of St. Francis Xavier," he said. "The Rector is an excellent person, and I am sure he will look after us and help us."

We went through the hilly section in the older part of Brussels. The streets were empty and sad-looking. We saw quite a few German officers eating breakfast in the cafés. They ignored us, and we ignored them. If they looked at all, they looked blankly. We were a priest of Brussels and a citizen—we carried no luggage. Neither the shirt nor the hat which I wore was my own. My whole capital consisted of 1,000 Belgian francs, which they had given me in La Panne from the family purse.

When we first reached the college Father Alberto talked with the Rector privately to explain my predicament. I was a former student of the Jesuits, and this was greatly in my favor. In a little while, the Rector received me.

"Father Alberto has told me everything," he said. He clasped my hand. "You may feel at home here. Stay as long as you need, but try to make your plans quickly. A prolonged visit might arouse suspicion. We never know when we may be searched by the Germans. Since your position is so grave and so dangerous, we will keep your identity secret. Say nothing."

I assured the good Rector that he could rely upon my discretion, and thanked him from the bottom of my heart for his generosity. He turned to my companion.

"Father Alberto, you may introduce him as an old student of ours who is getting his documents ready to leave Belgium."

Then the good Rector took me up to my room and got everything for me that I would need—even a razor, since I had brought nothing with me.

During my short stay at the college I did two very important and serious things. The first was the spiritual exercises of St. Ignatius of Loyola, the second was growing a mustache. The spiritual exercises calmed my soul and strengthened my faith: the mustache and the eyeglasses I acquired gave me a new personality, but the first gave blood and life to the second—of that I am convinced. During this time I followed the customs of the community. I went to bed with the sun and rose early. I helped Father Alberto with the Mass and spent the rest of the day in my room, reading and meditating. From my window I could watch the students playing in the yard, during their periods of recreation. They reminded me of my own school years and my own country.[1]

Meanwhile, Father Alberto went to see the Consul of Venezuela, Dr. Rómulo Araujo (at this writing, Dr. Araujo holds an appointment in the Department of the Interior at Caracas). Dr. Araujo understood my situation at once and was sympathetic. His diplomatic status, however, was not yet clear because he had just been appointed, and he feared any papers he might give me would do me more harm than good. He sent me a few shirts and some pajamas, for which I was grateful, and said I should keep in touch with him. Father Alberto also visited the Papal Nuncio, Monseigneur Micara. He was unable to help us. He had just received word from the

Germans to leave Belgian territory in two days, like all the foreign diplomats credited to the Belgian Government. He gave us good advice, however. "Tell Aguirre," he said to Father Alberto, "that he mustn't hide; he must lead a normal life, neither hiding nor showing himself too openly. This is the best advice I can give him. As for me, I shall inform the Vatican in case the worst should happen. But please tell him to try not to put us in such a critical situation."

Paris fell that very day. Father Alberto told us the sad news at the evening meal. We were all deeply moved. A few moments later, the Rector came in and announced that all religious houses were being searched. One of the Jesuit residences had been gone over from top to bottom. He warned me of the dangers which lay ahead for me. I had no papers, no consul, no ambassador, no guarantors of any kind. He was right. I knew also I was placing my protectors in jeopardy.

"I will leave at once," I said to the Father Rector. "Your kindness has already been great." And, turning to Father Alberto, I finished: "And this time, I will leave alone. I think it is better."

It was early evening when I left the College of St. Francis Xavier. My mustache had grown enough to disguise my features somewhat. As I made my way to the railroad station, I passed many German officers. Brussels was the same in the soft light as it had been the day Father Alberto and I had arrived with the Catalan; perhaps the shadows made one feel more acutely the city's sorrow, or perhaps it was because I was starting out alone and I was not entirely sure which way my feet would lead me. I took a train to Antwerp. Father Alberto had told me that Asporosa's sister Martha had returned there after our tragic pilgrimage and her brother's death. She might still be there, and she might not. When I arrived in Antwerp I went through many side streets and cautiously approached her house— making sure always that no one was following and no one watching when I knocked upon her door. She opened it herself. At first her eyes remained inquiring—a little puzzled. Who was this man at her door? That was a blessing to me. I smiled and spoke her name, "Martha!"

"Lendakari!" She opened the door wider, pulled me into the

house quickly, and shut the door. "It is lucky that you came here at this hour. No one is home. They are out looking for food. What are your plans?"

Asporosa's house was not a big one, and the living room where Martha led me was very small.

"Who else is living here?" I asked her.

She gestured. "Several refugees. I cannot turn any away. After our journey and those cruel nights in the open, I could not refuse; as long as there is a roof over our heads and the walls to protect us, I will let them in. Several have to sleep on the floor . . ."

"You are a good woman, Martha," I said. "Will you have room then for one more?"

She clasped my hand warmly. "Of course."

We agreed that I must be treated like the other refugees she was sheltering in her house, in order to raise no suspicions. I spent eight days in this house, keeping to myself, letting my mustache grow, and not going out at all. I slept on a mattress on the floor. I learned that my family were back in Louvain, and Father Alberto told them where I was. One night at a very late hour, Juan arrived in Antwerp. He was the bearer of sad news. My sister Encarna had died in the hospital at Knocke, near Ostend. Gangrene had set in as a result of lack of care when she was wounded. The doctors had succeeded in arresting the course of the disease, but the powerful injections they had used had stopped her heart, weakened already with so much suffering.

"And they were the happiest ones," I said to Juan, remembering the beginning of our journey. "Asporosa and Encarna had more optimism than any of us."

It was not possible for me to go home even at this time. Two of the compatriots who had been with us on the journey were acting as a small "intelligence service," and they had already reported that my parents' home was being watched. Sabin was not sure, but he thought even Asporosa's house was under surveillance. If the Gestapo should come to the house, I should be under immediate suspicion. I was the only one without papers of any kind except the University identification card of my brother.

In the meantime, Father Alberto was still working for my safety.

The Mexican Consul in Antwerp had told him once: "If ever you should find yourself in difficulty, go to see Mr. Guardia Jaen, the Consul of Panama, and say I sent you. He is one of the finest people I know, and I am sure he will help you."

Mr. Guardia Jaen listened sympathetically to the story of my predicament. He told Father Alberto to send me to his Consulate. One of the students delivered the message, and the next day I made my way to his office. I had only a brief interview with him, but two days later I held a most ingenious document in my hands. It was a provisional passport from Panama, to be used as such until the authorities "sent" permission to issue the final one. It stated that my old passport had been lost with my baggage in one of the numerous frontier incidents. We had combined names and initials so that my own initials and my new ones would coincide, and also so that my new name should be that of some well known family of Panama. I became a new citizen with a new country: José Andrés Alvarez Lastra, Doctor of Law and owner of properties. José Antonio Aguirre y Lekube made his temporary exit from the world.

3

The Basque Commercial Delegation in Antwerp, of which Cesareo Asporosa had been the chief, had employed a Belgian boy, Pierre. Aside from a few of my own countrymen, he was the only one who knew my secret. A few days after Dr. Alvarez was so efficiently papered at the Panama Consulate, Pierre took me to the Belgian Police Headquarters. The Belgian Police were still issuing identity cards to foreigners. The official was a friend of Pierre's, and when I gave my name as Dr. Alvarez his look seemed to say, "All right if you say so." He was angry with the Germans. He didn't believe that they were going to win the war nor that they should. He only asked me a few questions.

"Why did you come from France, when the Germans were advancing? Why didn't you go south?"

We had our story well fixed. The German invasion had caught Dr.

Alvarez on his way to Holland, where he was to embark for Venezuela on the 13th of May. We had made sure that there was a scheduled departure from Amsterdam. "I tried to go back through the border at La Panne," I told the official, "but they would not let me pass. I returned to Brussels, and there I decided I'd better see my consul in Antwerp." The official was examining my provisional passport, and he looked up at me. "My stay in Belgian will be very short, I believe," I told him. "I am only waiting for money to arrive from Panama."

He seemed satisfied with these explanations and then began grumbling more about the Germans. He could still talk against them because the Nazi Kommandantur had not yet descended upon the place. He asked about the doctor's degree, which impressed him not at all. When he saw in my passport that I was a landowner, he erased the word "doctor" from my card and wrote *Landerpachter*, the Flemish word for "renter." To our good police officer, *landerpachter* was something more positive. He handed me the card, which I still have in my possession.

Pierre and I left the police headquarters. "Well, Pierre," I said, "Dr. Alvarez is doing very well. Only two days in this world, and he now has two papers." But we were not feeling too safe. Sabin's suspicions about the Gestapo encircling us were well founded. Asporosa's house was being watched so carefully and so openly, we decided I should not return there. Pierre had spoken to a friend of his, saying that he had a Central American friend who must stay in Antwerp for a few weeks.

"She will most certainly let you stay," he told me as we approached her house. "She lost her husband only a short while ago, and her family is her complete life."

Madame Tirlemont received me with great kindness. "I had not expected to take guests in my house; but, since my friend Pierre has asked me, I will gladly oblige you."

Three of her daughters lived with her. They were very charming, but I could tell they had many doubts about Pierre's friend. I could hardly blame them. My mustache, my glasses were enough in themselves to shock conservative young ladies; but the clothes I wore—a yellow gabardine coat, a black, broad-brimmed hat! Wherever I went in Antwerp, I was determined people should remember the Central American. It was part of my own carefully planned psychological warfare. The more Dr. Alvarez was remembered, the more would President Aguirre be forgotten.

The two elder daughters, Thérèse and Renée, were teachers; the youngest one, Claudine, worked in the office where their father had worked when he was alive. Claudine was the prettiest, and quite flirtatious. She welcomed me more warmly than the other two. Several weeks later they confessed to me that their first opinion was not too flattering. Renée told me she said to her mother: "He looks like a confidence man. The clothes he wears—that raincoat! Mother, what kind of friends does Pierre have these days?"

"Do you realize that he had only one suitcase, Mother? How can you be sure he will pay for his lodging?" Thérèse asked.

"Pierre said he lost his luggage at the border," Madame answered; "and the way he dresses is his own affair."

But Claudine was the one, they told me, who defended me. "You are both making a fuss about nothing," she said to her sisters. "This man is no doubt a diplomat of some kind. He is on some secret mission, I am sure. Anyway, since Pierre has brought him to our house, we should be polite to him. He no doubt will keep to himself—which is a pity if you were only clever enough."

"What did you mean?" I asked Claudine when they were relating the story.

"Well, you are in a very safe and lucky position," she laughed. "When you leave here to go back to Panama—perhaps you might help us to get out. Myself, I have no love for Antwerp with German voices gabbling in the streets and the thought of the Gestapo's hands over my head all the time!"

The Gestapo's hands over *her* head! I could scarcely conceal my amusement. I looked at the young girl closely and wondered if she were telling me the story for a double purpose. Had she guessed my true identity? Her face looked entirely innocent.

"I'm sure I don't blame you," I answered fervently. "I consider myself a man of rare good fortune that I am a citizen of a neutral country."

4

One morning when I was breakfasting with the Tirle-
mont family, one of the girls said, "Today, Dr. Alvarez can meet our
friend Betty."

"And who is Betty?" I asked.

When I heard that she was a writer and a newspaperwoman, and
they finally told me her last name, my heart turned over. Scarcely a
year and a half ago, I had been invited by the Antwerp Chamber of
Commerce to visit the city. Accompanied by several Basque financial
experts, I had made the trip for the purpose of studying the possibilities of trade agreements, and questions of even larger import,
between the Basques and the Belgians. We were very well received.
An official dinner was given in our honor, and we received an invitation from the director of the Standard, an important firm which
published about six Flemish newspapers. The Standard people had
arranged a dinner for a small but select group. Mlle. Lagarde, a
young lady of a distinguished Flemish family and a very successful
newspaperwoman, was among the guests. She was a fervent admirer
of the Basques and a great friend of my brother Juan, who was in
exile then in Antwerp. Through this friendship and that of Pierre,
Juan was a frequent visitor at Madame Tirlemont's house. After the
dinner party she had asked me for an exclusive interview, and we
continued our conversation in the hotel lobby until very late in the
evening. The next morning at nine o'clock, this Flemish Dorothy
Thompson was again at the hotel, and we continued our talk of the
previous night.

The Tirlemonts' friend Betty Lagarde was this girl, and common
sense told me that a young woman not much over thirty, and single,
will not easily forget a masculine face. She was coming to lunch, they
said; and so in the middle of the morning I excused myself to
Madame. "I am so sorry, Madame Tirlemont, but I can't be at home
for luncheon today. I have an important engagement." She did not
seem to mind. She seemed to have forgotten that Betty was expected.

To get to the house where Sabin and Deunoro lived, I had to take a most tortuous route, retracing my steps countless times, in order to "lose" anyone who might be following me. They lived scarcely twenty minutes' walk from the Tirlemont house, and yet I would spend at least an hour in walking before I would approach their residence. Finally I was sitting in their room, exhausted.

"I certainly had a narrow escape that time," I said, and told them about Betty.

They burst out laughing. Sabin said, "Our President will always mix up his appointments, if it is at all possible." And I had to admit later that he spoke more truth than I realized at the time.

At seven-thirty that evening I returned to the Tirlemont home, confident that the danger had been avoided. To my horror, the first person I encountered in the front hall was Betty Lagarde herself. "I am certainly lost now," I thought to myself. I had mixed up luncheon with dinner—but now there was no way out.

Claudine, the young and pretty flirtatious Claudine, stood on the first step of the broad hallway staircase and seemed to be enjoying my apparent discomfort. I was formally introduced, "Our guest, Dr. Alvarez." We shook hands and went into the living room.

It was the latter part of June, extremely warm, and I had reached the house after a long and arduous walk—but the beads of perspiration which shone upon my forehead were there not from the summer heat, but because she was staring at me quizzically. Every gesture, smile, and glance must be giving me away. We went into the dining room, and I was placed next to Betty, with Claudine sitting opposite me and watching, very closely, it seemed to me, all the expressions of my face. Perhaps Claudine was thinking that being wealthy and single, as her own friend Pierre had led them to understand, I might fall in love with her friend Betty and remain in Belgium.

Betty broke the almost uncomfortable silence which pervaded the table and said very seriously: "I have just had the best news. Dr. Menard will permit me to enter her insane asylum if things become too dangerous for me."

Everyone at the table burst out laughing. "Betty! Betty!" Madame said. "What will you think of next!"

I joined in the laughter a little more heartily, for the contrast of my own panic with hers was too much for me. She was so worried she had not noticed the sharp lines of my nose and jaw. I was laughing really to myself, at my fierce mustache, at my ten-franc glasses, at the romantic notions of the young ladies who—with a war surrounding them—could still make happy dreams of a "prince" from America who could make their friend Betty his "princess." And Betty herself planning to enter, instead of matrimony, an insane asylum.

"You are laughing so heartily, Dr. Alvarez, because you don't believe me," said Betty.

"Certainly I believe you, Mlle. Lagarde," I replied; "but in these times, the craziest things happen. Some of them are really funny, in spite of being so serious. Don't you think so?"

"Yes, I guess so," she answered; "but when you are so close to the serious situations, it is not so easy to see the humor."

I could only shrug my shoulders in answer.

"You are safe, Dr. Alvarez. No one can harm you because you are an American."

"I hope you are right," I answered studiously, fixing my attention on the tablecloth.

"With me, though, it's quite different. I have written several anti-Nazi articles, really blistering them. I've lectured against them. Friends of mine well connected with the police have already warned me that they might arrest me any time now. I'm not afraid, you know—not awfully; but there's no reason why I shouldn't try to protect myself."

I was able to look up at her. "What have you done?" I asked. "Are you really going to enter this insane asylum?"

"Yes," she said, "certainly I am. I have all the papers ready. This is no joke, Dr. Alvarez. To slip by the Gestapo, one must be very clever."

I could only agree with her.

Coffee was served in the living room, and the conversation was centered around the war. "The hours seem dark now," I was saying, "but we must remember that the British will never give up. Their persistency will win in the end, make no mistake."

"But in the meantime," said one of the older girls, "there are so many suffering."

There was a small silence. I was sitting in my chair feeling very American and very comfortable, when suddenly Betty began telling the Tirlemont family the tragic circumstances of my own sister's death. Without being able to show it, I was very much touched by the comments and the sympathy in everyone.

"Where is Juan?" Betty asked. "I have thought of him so often. Have you seen him?"

[Claudine answered, "No, and Pierre has not seen him either." She threw her head back in a gesture of laughter. "When he comes back to Antwerp, he will come here. He likes to play tennis with Renée."

"What a player!" Renée said. "He is so furious."

"Do you play tennis, Dr. Alvarez?" Claudine asked.

"Yes, quite well," I answered, hoping this would be a chance for a change in conversation. As a matter of fact I had taught my brother Juan how to play the game.

"It would be good for this boy to play with you," Madame Tirlemont said. "Yours is such an easy-going nature—so different from the Basque."

"At least as you have known them, Mother," Thérèse put in. "I don't think Juan's furious game of tennis is typical of the Basques necessarily."

"Oh, yes, it is," Betty said. "You have not known them as I have. They are very strong."

Claudine was smiling at me. "What do you think, Dr. Alvarez? You are always so silent. Have you ever played tennis with a Basque?"

"There are many of Basque descent in my country," I answered carefully, "so I am sure I have at one time or another played tennis with them."

"What I meant," Madame Tirlemont said, "was that Dr. Alvarez would play an easy game of tennis, and yet he would most certainly beat Juan Aguirre."

I had to restrain myself from agreeing with her, for experience had long ago taught me that I could beat my brother at this game.

"I see what you mean, Mother," Renée said. "Juan would get more fun out of the game if he didn't work so violently at it. Well," she smiled at me, "if he returns we must surely arrange an afternoon of tennis."]

"What has happened to Juan's brother?" Thérèse asked. "The Basque President? Where is he?"

Betty answered, "I don't know, but I imagine he must have left Paris, where he was living."

"Remember last year," Claudine broke in, "when you had to interview Juan's brother? You should hear that story. How we teased her!" she said to me. "Tell him, Betty, tell Dr. Alvarez how you interviewed the Basque President. She stayed so late, even his brother teased her."

It was all a youngster's joke, but with this excuse Betty had to tell me—me, of all people—all the questions she had asked me, and all my answers: how I had given her an exclusive interview in the hotel lobby. Fortunately she told everything in a truthful and kindly way. As she spoke, each episode came to my mind. Once or twice Dr. Alvarez was on the point of adding some small detail, but he remained discreet.

I kept hoping Betty would go, and when finally she rose to leave I went with her to the door. At last she was gone. I was quite exhausted by the evening, but gave thanks to God for this test of my new personality which gave me strength to face whatever the future held in store for me. From that evening on, I became more Panamanian, not only for the Tirlemont family but for myself.

CHAPTER V

Madame Tirlemont and her three girls were cultured and charming. They were typical products of the highest type of family education, full of dignity and devotion to their home. The house was always full of Madame's grandchildren, whose fathers were serving their country, one of them a prisoner of the Germans. The grandchildren used to visit her by turns, and her home was a warm living center of the traditional Christian family life characteristic of the Flemish people.

After dinner several friends used to come to the house, and we gathered in the living room. These parties gave me a real opportunity to study the spirit and morale of the Belgian people, besides distracting me from my worries.

We used to talk about all kinds of subjects, but the conversation always turned in the end to the war. That night we discussed the behavior of the Germans in Belgium.

"The fact is that the Germans are well behaved," one of the young girls was saying. "I don't know how they acted in the last war, but in this one we cannot deny them that much. And believe me, Mother, everybody is delighted. The British destroyed bridges, broke into the houses and, what is worse, deceived us. The Germans came in, and look how they respect everybody. I am telling you, the people are very pleased with them."

"The same as in the last war, my dear daughter, exactly the same, except that you cannot remember because you were very little," answered the mother. "They committed a few isolated atrocities in the first rush, but in general there was not much cause for complaint at the start. As long as things go well for them it won't be so bad. But God help us when things begin to go badly. Then it will be the same as in the last war. First hunger, then the informers, and at last persecution and death. Unfortunately for you, you shall see it. Don't you think I am right, Dr. Alvarez?"

"I have no doubts, madame," I replied, "because you have the advantage of your experience. Personally I have also noticed that wherever the Germans go—in some cafés where I have seen them, on the street—their behavior is excellent; and it is a nice sight even if it is the result of discipline. But, like you, I know that this discipline means giving up entirely the right of thinking for themselves, and can lead them any day to obey the most brutal orders. Those who believe in force as the supreme power, and the only one to be used in bettering their own country, must first trample on their own consciences and learn to despise the rights and lives of others. Now they are only waiting for the right moment."

"My girls are too young to remember the last war," replied Madame. "Then I feared for my parents, now I fear for my children and grandchildren. Soon you will see how they will let us starve. They take everything with them. The reprisals will begin when anyone protests. Believe me, the Germans are a terrible people: I have known them very well. Young people are always impressed by appearances. A gallant gesture from a handsome German soldier captivates them, and they forget that this same soldier is an invader of their country. Unfortunately, you will very soon see that I am right."

"Perhaps you are, Mother," replied one of the daughters; "but at least up to now the behavior of the Germans has been irreproachable."

"I shouldn't go so far as to say that," I spoke up. "You must not forget the thousands of innocent people, whose only fault was that they disagreed with these men, herded into concentration camps and tortured, and the thousands of others whose guilt consisted only in their having fought to defend their own country. Look what has happened to the Poles and the Czechs, to mention only a few."

We had many such conversations from which I gathered, along with my personal observations, that the German policy was one of trying to win over the conquered people by a show of seeming good manners. And, in fact, they did make a very good impression. Whenever they gathered in cafés, one was struck by their neat appearance. They were always well dressed, well shaven, and clean, spoke with lowered voices and were extremely polite to the other café-goers.

I felt all the sorrier that a country which could educate its children, whether soldiers or not, to have such correct social manners, should so corrupt their souls that they could become the greatest menace that civilization has ever known. It seemed to me that the orders which these boys received every morning must ring like metal, and lacked all the spontaneity, freshness, and humor of the discipline of liberty-loving peoples.

At first, large portions of the Belgian public had succumbed willingly to the German conquerors, impressed and encouraged by their correct behavior. The reasons for this were many and diverse. German propaganda had sown the seeds of discontent especially among the Flemish young people, and this had contributed largely to the discredit in which the politicians were held. Also the German campaign to cultivate the belief that democracy was a decadent and corrupt form of government, and the attack on the government-in-exile as a bunch of traitors, had had a certain success among the people, making them welcome the New Order as a force which would sweep away all the ills and dead weight of the past. One of the chief aims of the fascist propaganda is to strike at the reputations and characters of public figures, and the Germans are very clever at it.

I remember the visitor the Tirlemont family received one day. She was a lady, Madame Martier, whose son had been drafted into a territorial battalion of the Belgian army. She was very happy that day because "my Marcel," as she called him, was coming home. He had not even been taken prisoner. He had escaped from the trenches as well as from the Germans. He was a marvel for escaping. He had followed his mother's advice well. She always told him, "*Mon Marcel*, rather than see yourself in danger, either give yourself up or escape." And she told us: "It seems to me that this war is none of our business. Let the politicians fight if they like. But of course they have all run away. Thank God the King acted like a man. Let the English do their own fighting."

Renée spoke up, saying, "Don't you think that if all mothers were to give the same advice to their sons we might as well give up all hope of liberty and resign ourselves to permanent slavery?"

"Not at all," replied the lady. "As a matter of fact, I think it's only a question of whether we shall be submitted to the English or the Germans, and I really don't know which is the worst. Moreover my Marcel is a special case . . ."

This woman's whole vision was bounded by her son. She was an almost fanatical mother, but what a confusion of ideas her words showed!

"And where is your son Paul?" she finally asked Madame Tirlemont.

"Unfortunately he was made prisoner near Ardennes. But at least I have the satisfaction of knowing he did his duty to the last," replied Madame Tirlemont with dignity.

The conversation then turned to the all-engrossing subject of food.

In the evening after supper, when the family was gathered together, there were comments on the attitude of the afternoon's visitor.

"Did you hear her, Dr. Alvarez?" asked Madame. "That is the way many Belgians think. With such lack of patriotism do you wonder the army didn't do any better? I was very glad"—she spoke to Renée now—"to hear you when you answered Madame Martier. But don't you think that you young people also help to contribute to this lack of faith in ourselves when you praise the invaders and criticize our old allies?"

"Madame," I spoke up, "it is very human to blind ourselves to our neighbor's suffering and shut our eyes when his house catches fire. It has been the fashion, lately, to look out solely for one's own welfare without paying the slightest attention to the welfare of others. What has happened among individuals has also occurred among nations. The comfortable egotism and lack of inner development among many people leads them to ignore the evils and the danger until it touches them personally. Some day you will see your friend Madame Martier protesting violently because of the food scarcity or because the Germans have bothered her precious Marcel. Then you will hear her talking about the German persecution and injustice and recalling with nostalgia the good old days of 'English oppression,' when there was plenty of freedom and butter, in spite of the 'knavery' of politicians. These people feel no solidarity with anything or anyone. The downfall of a free country does not disturb them, the death of millions of innocents leaves them cold, the persecution of conscience, the loss of freedom of speech, the disregard of all human dignity—all these leave them untouched. Their motto seems to be 'Let the world keep quiet about its troubles, let it cease to think and agitate, and leave me in peace.' But this egotistic way of life is due to disappear. The present struggle is so profound that not even Marcel can remain untouched by it."

The girls started laughing, but their mother said, "Where Dr. Alvarez said 'Marcel,' you can substitute any people here or elsewhere whose ideals have withered."

2

A few days later Madame Tirlemont brought us word that the Germans had emptied the warehouses at the Antwerp docks and carried off the huge reserves of food stored there. They had also taken all the butter, chickens, and eggs from the markets. The women complained, but that was all the satisfaction they got.

With all these events—practical tokens which rose from the stomach to the brain—life became daily more difficult. Prices doubled and tripled. Many people who had been asleep to their situation, or merely apathetic, began to wake up. And this was only the dark beginning of an even darker future.

"You see I was right," said Madame Tirlemont to me. "The first year of the last war we were not so badly off. Our food supplies lasted through that year, and the Germany of the Kaiser was better prepared than now. The second year was pretty bad, and the year of '16 was even worse; but, thanks to the American help which came through Holland, we just managed to get along. When America entered the war in '17 the help stopped, and our situation was truly horrible. Just think what is going to happen to us now. The Germans take all our food at the start, we don't receive anything from America, and there are millions more in Europe still to be fed."

Starting from that day the tone of the conversations changed materially. All Madame's visitors were becoming more and more anti-German. I followed these conversations with interest, as they were a true reflection of the mood of the different Belgian social strata. The good manners of the soldiers, so much admired during the early days, were now deemed to be hypocritical, a mere cover for their plundering. The food restrictions, the taking over of public buildings and factories, the requisitioning of private houses for the use of officers, and the many limitations to the freedom of citizens which grew more numerous daily, raised protests from everyone. This was the "intolerable tyranny of the Boches." The Germans had disappeared, and people now spoke only of "the Boches." Thus spoke all the Belgians still at liberty. Those others locked up behind prison bars felt the oppression in their bodies and in their spirits.

One day Paul, the brave lieutenant who had done his duty, came home. With great deliberation he recounted to us all that had happened. They had fought until they had been cut off. There had been many individual cases of heroism, but also a great many desertions.

"Dr. Alvarez," he told me, "they had us beaten before we fired the first shot. Their scheme to corrupt the Belgian spirit was well carried out. You don't realize how much I suffered to hear young men like myself proclaiming that democracy had failed and Germany's hour had arrived, just at the time when they should have united and stood their ground against the common foe. I used to answer them that, if Germany's hour had arrived, Belgium's hour had not yet passed, nor that of liberty. With such lack of patriotism, how could they fight well? But I had one consolation. The concentration camp acted like an electric shock to many of my misguided countrymen. Finding themselves suddenly deprived of liberty, they came to understand that their own country was in the same position. The Belgians became more and more united in thought and feeling, and I assure you that when I left the concentration camp there was only one desire among them all: to throw off the yoke of the invader. I used to be one of the early followers of Léon Degrelle. And believe me, there is much in Belgium that needs to be changed. But that is no reason for throwing away our freedom, and much less for asking our enemy's help and protection and giving ourselves up completely."

"I am very glad to hear all this, Paul," I replied. "And how did they treat you in the concentration camp?"

"A concentration camp is never a very pleasant place, but in general we weren't treated so badly: perhaps because they feared our unity, perhaps because they wanted to make us like them. Whatever the reason, we were treated better than the other prisoners. The English, for instance, were treated very harshly; also the French. The Frenchmen were certainly a sad case, Dr. Alvarez. They couldn't seem to come to any agreement among themselves. Continuing their old quarrels, they made a tragic spectacle and gave one a sensation of the completeness of the French collapse."

"Didn't the patriotic and courageous position of General de Gaulle raise their spirits?" I asked.

"Yes, during the first few days; but later they went back to their arguments over who was responsible for their plight. However, I think that in the end they will unite as we did, for, after all, we only appreciate liberty after we have lost it."

Several days later I was invited to the house of one of Madame Tirlemont's sons. There I made the acquaintance of "mon Marcel." He was there with his "mama" who was protesting vigorously against the situation "to which the Boches have led us." "The same as the last war," she added. Marcel was giving a vivid account of his escapes. In one of them he had almost reached Marseille. He told his story with such funny gestures that everyone burst out laughing: everyone except Paul, who started to leave the room, saying to me, "Don't you think, Dr. Alvarez, that when so many have died at their posts one shouldn't listen to such talk?"

And we left the room together for a smoke. Later they called me back, saying, "Madame Martier can't understand how you happened to be here, since you are an American." "Yes," added Madame, "when I first met you at Madame Tirlemont's I thought to myself: how can anyone remain here in this inferno when he can live comfortably in America?"

"Well, you see, madame, we Americans are like that. I enjoy studying all these new European systems, and so here I am."

"Do you call this a system? What a sense of humor you have, Dr. Alvarez!"

"No, no. I don't think that's the reason," answered one of the girls. "There is some mystery about you, Dr. Alvarez, because sometimes I am certain you are deceiving us and you have come here on some secret mission for your government—"

"Renée insists on thinking," I answered, "that I am some sort of diplomat."

"Yes, because you explain things so well it sounds as though you must have lived through them."

"No. It's simply that I have read a great deal and Europe is such an interesting subject for study—"

"And aren't you thinking of leaving?" asked Madame Martier.

"Yes, I am planning to leave; but I must prepare for the trip in a leisurely fashion because, as you know, everything is difficult nowadays, even to receive money—"

"Ah, but you are an American and your dollars can open any door. How lucky you are, Dr. Alvarez! Here we must stay, isolated from the world, and shortly we will be starving since the Boches take all our food to Germany. Have you noticed the price of butter? Three times what it used to be. And you simply can't buy potatoes. You must speak plainly and tell the truth when you return to America, and not let them be deceived by the Nazis."

"I shall comply with your wishes with great pleasure, madame. It will give me great satisfaction." It was with difficulty that I restrained a chuckle, for this was the same lady who not so long ago had complained of the "English oppression."

The conversation then turned to the pressing and ever present topic of food. It was the chief theme for many months. But I was more interested in the altered opinion of Madame Martier, because it demonstrated the changing atmosphere in Belgium and she was only one in hundreds.

3

[At last the day arrived for the tennis match with my brother Juan. I looked forward to it because an afternoon with him, whom I rarely saw and never openly, would be a real treat. But also I dreaded that afternoon because my brother and I would be taking part in a comic scene which could result in revealing my real identity through an unforeseen incident.

At the tennis court were Madame Tirlemont, her three daughters, Pierre, and a group of friends of the family. I must confess that I awaited my brother's arrival as if I were going to play against the champion of the world.

When Juan arrived, Madame Tirlemont introduced me to him. "Dr. Alvarez," the nice old lady said to me, "here is Mr. Juan Aguirre, a good friend of my daughters." And, addressing Juan, she added: "Dr. Alvarez is a very cultured and nice gentleman. I am sure that from now on you will be good friends."

My brother and I shook hands heartily, with smiles on our faces that threatened to develop into a burst of laughter.

Juan's partner was Claudine, while Thérèse was mine. The onlookers joked about who was going to win the match, whether the impetuous Basque or the calm Panamanian. The majority backed Juan, first because he was younger, and second because, as Pierre put it, "no one has ever seen a mustached gentleman win a tennis match against a shaven youth."

My brother has always been a sportsman with a great deal of *amour propre*. He started the game joking, but when he saw that I was playing better, perhaps because of my luck that afternoon, he put all his effort into the game. He even got angry when I made a point. We took advantage of changing courts to speak to each other in low voices as we passed near by.

"What a mustache!" Juan would say.

I answered, "Well, with mustache and all, I will win the match."

Other times when we jumped over the net he told me, "I will win," and I answered, "I'll bet you don't."

The last sets were fiercely contended, and the match ended with the victory of Thérèse and myself. When I shook hands with Juan over the net he said, laughing: "I congratulate you, Dr. Alvarez. I don't know why, but it seems to me that you must have some Basque blood in your veins!"

Everyone laughed, of course.

When we were in the shower we spoke at our ease. "Who would have told us when we were in Euzkadi," I observed, "that some day we would meet in Antwerp and I should have to deny that you were my brother?"

"This is very comical but also very sad," answered my brother.

"And I, camouflaged with this ridiculous mustache."

"Well, I must say that your mustache is a great success. I am going to tell you what happened the other day at home," added Juan. "Do you remember the picture you gave me of Dr. Alvarez?"

"Yes," I answered. "Certainly I remember it."

"Well, I had quite a joke with it when I returned to the family at Louvain. I did not mean to make a joke of it. I only wanted to make certain that Dr. Alvarez looked nothing like my brother José Antonio."

"What did you do?" I asked. "Did you show the picture to my children, and then they screamed?"

"No, no," Juan laughed, "the contrary. When I returned, your wife Mari said at once, 'How is he?'"

"'Very well,' I answered. 'He is very well.'

"Right away Mother was after me. 'What is he going to do? Has he a passport yet? Where is he going?'

"'Wait a minute,' I told them both. 'I will explain everything. José Antonio is all right. He is safe. He has a wonderful man for a consul who will protect him on everything.'

"'Who is this man?' Mari asked.

"'The Consul of Panama in Antwerp,' I replied, slowly drawing from my portfolio the photograph of Dr. Alvarez. 'Here is a picture of him.'

"They both looked at it. 'Oh, I don't like his face,' Mari said, slowly, 'I don't like it at all.'

"I said nothing. I was trying my best not to laugh. Mother had been staring for a long time at the photograph, and I was not sure whether or not she saw the face behind the tremendous mustache.

"'This man is a Falangist,' Mother said violently. 'You are a fool, Juan, to leave José Antonio with such a man. No good will come of it. This man will betray him.'

"'How do you know he is a Falangist?' I teased.

"'His eyes,' Mother answered.

"'But, Mother, you cannot see his eyes. They are covered with glasses.'

"'That's what I mean,' Mother said. 'This man has some reason to hide himself behind glasses. I don't like his face at all.'

"Mari reached for the photograph. 'Wait a minute,' she said. 'Let me look again.' I handed it to her, scarcely able to keep back the mirth.

"I don't know if your wife saw the expression on my face or not," Juan told me, "but anyway I could not keep the joke to myself for long because your little son came into the room, and when he saw his mother staring at a photograph of a man, he went over to look at it too. He put his face very close to the picture and then looked up at Mari and said in Basque, 'Aita!' [Daddy!] When he said that, of course, I was lost. I started laughing, and then they knew."

"You comfort me a great deal," I said, and then I told him about my evening with Betty.]

4

A few days after the wonderful party with my brother I was listening to the Berlin radio with Claudine and Renée. A Spanish voice suddenly announced: "The ex-President of the Basque Republic, José Antonio Aguirre, has taken refuge in the Chilean Embassy in Brussels. The Spanish authorities will probably ask for his extradition at once."[1]

["I heard the name Aguirre," Claudine broke in, as the announcer continued. "I don't know enough Spanish to understand him. What is he saying, Dr. Alvarez? It's probably about Juan's brother.

"Dr. Alvarez," Claudine insisted, "what has the announcer said about Juan's brother?"

"I didn't hear it all," I answered. "He said that the Spanish authorities understood that Aguirre was hiding in the Chilean Embassy in Brussels."

"Oh," Claudine gasped, "I wonder if he is there!" She jumped up. "I am going to see Pierre and tell him. He will know how to warn Juan. Come with me, Renée."

Renée put her knitting down. "Oh, dear, that girl is always in a hurry," she said. But presently the two young ladies were walking down the street, and I thanked God fervently that I was left alone to think clearly on this new development of my situation. They were on my trail. There could be no doubt of it, and it was childish to ignore the fact.]

Carefully I made my way to the place where Sabin and Deunoro and I met, in a small café on the outskirts of Antwerp fairly near their room. Many times when we had an appointment we could not join each other. We would sit tables apart from each other engrossed in our papers, waiting for the watching eyes which had followed either one of us to leave; and if they did not leave in time I would go. We would let many days go by before trying to plan another meeting. They would check up to make sure that the watching eyes we had feared were entirely innocent—and when they were sure we would laugh about it, laugh with the deep-reaching relief only the pursued can feel over a few moments more of liberty. They were there, but we were not sure of the safety. The second day we changed the hour of meeting. At any time when any one of us thought we were being observed, we had a prearranged system that I would come to the café three hours earlier or later the next day. One of them would be there in the morning and the other in the afternoon. The second day I met Sabin in the early morning, before lunch.

We were the only ones in the café, but this did not add to our feeling of safety. Perhaps someone was watching from outside. We decided to go to their room separately. We spoke of the radio announcement. It was decided that I would avoid all contact with my family. "The rumor must be circulated, thoroughly," I said, "that at the last moment I succeeded in escaping with my wife and children to England." It was agreed, and I went back to the Tirlemont house to chat with the young ladies, or to play with the grandchildren who visited often. They were a source of real consolation for the homesickness I felt for my own children.

In the days that followed, I led a very cautious life, but I had to leave the house occasionally. It was summertime, and the good Tirlemont family must be kept completely innocent. If I stayed inside all the time, they might wonder. I used to go to my "consulate" by a very roundabout route to avoid the more crowded streets. My mustache had grown out well by now, and my new thick tortoise-shell spectacles completed my disguise. I had good proof of this as one day in the street I passed close to two of my countrymen who thought I was in London. They did not recognize me. I continued occasionally to meet with Sabin and Deunoro, who brought me all the news: what they were saying in the Spanish Embassy and consulates, what was happening to the refugees, and the movements of the police.

In the latter part of July I was waiting for Sabin and Deunoro at the small café when they arrived with preoccupied and disturbed faces. They brought me bad news of Martin, a Basque who had worked with Cesareo Asporosa in Antwerp. "Martin has been arrested," Sabin said.

"They have entered the Delegation office and taken all the papers, and the place is closed now by police orders," Deunoro put in.

"The papers are unimportant," Sabin went on. "They will find nothing to help them in their search for you. Lucky for our peace of mind that only day before yesterday I saw Martin, and he was fully convinced that you were safe in London. The rumors we started had reached him, and he said he knew he was under surveillance, so he was destroying all the papers in his possession."

"When I heard that Martin had been taken," Deunoro replied, "I hurried to the office to see whether I could save anything; but the Gestapo was there before me. I watched cautiously from the street. Officials from the Spanish Consulate were with them, and as a matter of fact, they sealed up our office with strips of paper bearing the Spanish colors."

"You shouldn't leave the house," Sabin said to me, and I agreed.

"Things look very bad," I said. "I am worried for all of you. We must not meet again for some time. I think it would be wise if you both separated. If one is taken, the other is still free."

"It looks," said Sabin, "as if they had orders to arrest all of us until you are found. In spite of our efforts, yesterday in Brussels it was said that you couldn't escape because they had you in a trap."

"They thought he was in Paris though," Deunoro said.

Sabin shrugged. "How do we know that is what they really believe? If we can spread a rumor, so can they. Perhaps they want to catch as many of us as they can for Mr. Franco—and at the end, as the *pièce de résistance*, our President himself."

"It would be like them," I agreed. "We must all be careful."

We made arrangements whereby a picture postal card of a certain cathedral sent to any one of us would be the signal for a meeting. Otherwise we would not attempt to get in touch with each other. The crisis was definitely at hand, and the worst part of it was that we had no definite plan of action as yet for our escape. Since we were in the heart of enemy territory, we did not know when and how we should make the next move. There are times of danger when a man can be content with only patience and faith. This was such a time. More than a month passed, and poor Martin was still held incommunicado. No one could reach him—not even his wife and children; but, as we had suspected, the imprisonment of Martin was only the beginning.

One day in the early part of September, I was returning from a long walk with "my Consul." As usual we were avoiding the crowded thoroughfares; but as we finally approached the consulate a man rushed up to Guardia Jaen and spoke to him excitedly in German.

"Mr. Consul, did you know that the Gestapo has arrested Juan Aguirre?"

The Consul could not conceal his consternation. He continued speaking in German to this friend of my brother's in order to hide the news from me. The man was an employee of a shipping company whose ships carried the Panama flag. When he left, Guardia Jaen said:

"That's the last straw. Did you understand him?"

"Of course, for though I don't understand German the two words 'Gestapo' and 'Juan Aguirre' were enough for me."

"Yes, they have arrested your brother, and they are holding him incommunicado. Courage, my friend," said the good Consul. And he repeated his favorite phrase, " 'Life has inexhaustible resources.' It would have been worse if they had arrested you."

I was not to be comforted. "But when the Gestapo makes an arrest they hold them for such a long time. Look at Martin's case. Moreover, it is not only my brother I am worried about, but all the family. I can't go to them or help them, and now they are completely defenseless. Juan's arrest will be a terrible blow to them. More arrests are sure to follow, and what will the women and children do without help and without papers?"

The day after I left La Panne all foreigners received orders to go to the police and register their names. With so much destruction everywhere, it was understandable that many should have lost their papers. The police were not exacting in those days; so, when Juan took my wife to the headquarters and she gave a false name, the police issued an identity card to her without any question. They advised her to get in touch with her Consul as soon as possible. This she had not done yet, since the Consul must first be found.

I left Guardia Jaen full of sadness for my brother and family. That same day I had been advised that there was only seven thousand francs left in our fund, and that money had to pay for the food and lodging of more than forty people. When I paid for my trolley ticket, I realized that I had only twenty francs left myself, and now I didn't know when I should be able to pay the month's rent to Madame Tirlemont. By the time I reached the house I was in the depths of despondency.

"Here comes Dr. Alvarez! Here he comes," the Tirlemont grandchildren shouted.

If they saw me coming up the street they would wait for me at the door, or I would hear them clamoring in the hall after they had heard my usual double ring at the bell. I was popular with them because I played with them a great deal. They reminded me of my own and took my mind off my troubles. "For a bachelor," Madame Tirlemont would remark, "you seem very fond of children, Dr. Alvarez." "Yes, they remind me of my little nephew and niece whom I love dearly. Children amuse me anyway," I would answer. When they asked me what my nephew and niece were like, I always described my own children. And when they asked me what my sister-in-law was like, I described my wife.

This night when I returned, heavy in heart, they were all in good spirits. They had just been paid a large debt that they had thought would never be settled. Whenever there was occasion for any rejoicing Madame Tirlemont used to celebrate it by opening a bottle of excellent Burgundy, so common in the well stocked wine cellars of Belgian families.

"Is everything going well with you, Dr. Alvarez?" Madame Tirlemont inquired that night, as she always did.

"Oh, very well, madame," I answered, smiling, "very well."

"What a man of good fortune you are!" she said. "You are always happy, and everything turns out well for you. Today, we must drink a toast to Dr. Alvarez. May he have a good trip to America!"

"Oh, Dr. Alvarez!" cried Claudine. "Are you leaving us soon?"

"No, not yet, Claudine," I answered; "but it might happen that one day I shall decide to leave very suddenly."

"We shall hate to lose you," said Madame, "but I should certainly advise you to think of going home soon. Things are going to get much worse here. You would be much better off out of Europe. Isn't your family in America worried about you? Have you heard from them lately?"

Very seriously, I took a letter from my pocket and said: "Yes, they are worried; but I have told them nothing, as yet, of my plans. This letter from my brother scolds me for staying on, the family wants me to come home as soon as possible."

Feminine curiosity would not be satisfied until they all knew the letter's contents, so without smiling I read it aloud. For anyone in my position, foresight is of major importance. I had ordered some sheets of lightweight paper, used for air mail, with the name Antonio Alvarez Lastra printed on them. This was the name of my imaginary brother who wrote me from America and sent his letters in care of his consulate for greater safety. In the consulate I took some real envelopes, mailed in Panama, which had come through in the diplomatic pouch without censorship. On the envelopes I had typed "For Alvarez." The letter was written by myself, said whatever I wanted to put in and was signed by my "brother Antonio." Thus the good Tirlemont family heard that my family couldn't understand my folly in remaining in Europe any longer, and what steps they had taken in the Ministry of Foreign Relations to have me appointed to a diplomatic post in the East. "But we would rather have you give up these ideas and return to America," I read from my "brother's" letter. He spoke of my business in Venezuela and other countries, and gave many details which might possibly prove of value if Dr. Alvarez found himself at any time in difficulties.

"You see, Mother, I always said Dr. Alvarez was a diplomat," said Claudine.

"I really am not," I replied. "I wanted very much to study the

Orient, and I asked for this position as it would greatly facilitate my journey out there and my stay."

"How would you go?" Renée asked.

"Across Germany and Russia, and finally by the Trans-Siberian Railroad to Japan, seems the most likely route."

"Oh, how lucky to be able to make such a trip!" Claudine clapped her hands. "Couldn't you get us some visas so that we too could leave?"

They were asking *me* for visas! I had to stifle my anguish for my family with laughter, even with lies.

"Dr. Alvarez, you are one of the happiest people I have ever known"—Madame Tirlemont was repeating one of her favorite theories about me; "and yet you give the impression of having suffered greatly in this life."

"What happened, Dr. Alvarez?" Claudine asked. "I am sure it was an unhappy love affair. That's why you don't want to go home. Some beautiful girl in Panama has been forced to marry another man!"

"Claudine!" one of her elder sisters spoke. "You must not say such things."

"It is all right," I smiled. "These things can happen to all of us." It was wisest to let them believe these romantic ideas, and they afforded me certain amusement.

"Well, in any case," said Madame, "whatever sorrow you have had in the past, I think we must drink to your future—the lucky Dr. Alvarez!"

Condemned to death by the military tribunals of Franco—far from my family—with my brother, who had guided and looked after them, in prison—pursued by the police and with only twenty francs (then about sixty cents) left in my pocket—I raised my glass of Burgundy and drank, with the others, to the future of Dr. Alvarez, the "lucky" one! The feeling of nightmare I had was well concealed by my foolish glasses and my grotesque mustache, and I remembered that song of my country:

Begiak barrez barrez,   . . . eyes always laughing,
Biotza negarrez . . .   While the heart is crying . . .

5

The next day Guardia Jaen took me on one of our favorite walks, which was toward the harbor of Antwerp. Although entrance to the port itself was forbidden, we could make out pretty carefully how much work was at a standstill. There were scarcely any merchant ships. The few that arrived were German, come to carry off anything of value to Germany, leaving nothing for the Belgians. The paralysis of that great port made one infinitely sad, but the plundering of a whole country was enraging.

What interested us most were the preparations for the announced invasion of England. There were many barges all along the big Antwerp canal, and these had been taken over by the Nazis. Many of them had their prows cut off, and a metal door had been fitted on which could be lowered to allow tanks to roll out under their own power. The barges had also been equipped with powerful motors which gave them considerable speed.

"They are going to cross the Channel," my Consul said. "No doubt about it."

"They may cross the Channel," I answered, "but God help them when they get there. Anyway I don't believe they will be foolish enough, at the last hour, to attempt it. Do you realize the enormous number of barges needed for such an undertaking? They can't do it without the protection of a large fleet of warships, and the Germans have none."

"Don't put your faith in that," the Consul said. "I have lived in Germany for many years as a consul. When those people set out to do anything, they are really terrible. Moreover, think how many thousands of barges there are in Antwerp alone. The Channel is very narrow here. It would only take them a few hours of these dark autumn nights to make the crossing."

"That's all very well," I replied; "but I am sure they could never make a landing without the protection of a powerful sea escort. Aviation cannot protect them all the time, and alone they are lost. The English have always defended their island. Since William the Conqueror every attempt at invasion has met with defeat."

"Look," said Guardia Jaen. "That barge has an anti-aircraft gun."
The preparations continued, and almost every day that we walked by the port we saw groups of barges, fitted with anti-aircraft guns and with metal doors at their prows, moved down the Scheldt River toward the sea. I listened to the nightly English broadcasts, with great caution, as I did not wish to compromise the Tirlemont family: the punishment for listening to a foreign broadcast, especially the English, was very severe. In those days of September, 1940, the English gave very high figures for the planes they claimed to have shot down. The Germans also gave exaggerated figures. Sabin and Deunoro had some friends who worked in a factory, not far from Antwerp, which had been taken over by the Germans for repairing their airplanes. We learned through these people that the number of damaged planes brought in for repairs had increased tremendously. They told us further that work had also increased in the section for motor repair. In the enemy's camp itself, I had the impression that the German air arm was materially weakened by the aerial offensive against Great Britain. I concluded, therefore, that Nazi plane production never reached the enormous figures usually attributed to them. Later I was able to verify this conclusion. I also realized that the Nazi prolonged aerial offensive weakened and exhausted their air force more from damage done to the machines than from actual loss of planes in combat.

The month of October arrived. My brother Juan was still held incommunicado. My wife and children were staying with some relatives near Brussels. The consul and I continued our walks and our waiting. Under the pretext of visiting two Panamanian ships moored at the Antwerp docks, we were able to observe clearly the great number of barges piling up in the Flemish harbor. Many of them had already been dismantled of their cannon platforms and metal turrets. The Nazis had discovered for themselves that invasion was not an easy thing. With the failure of their aerial offensive, the undertaking was much more difficult than they had probably bargained for.

During those days I spent some pretty bad moments. The Tirlemont house was very near one of the Nazi air fields. In those days of the war, the loads of bombs were not as heavy as they are now, so we were in no particular danger from them. The Gestapo, however, began an investigation of all the houses near by. Fortunately I was out at the time they arrived, and the maid gave information about all the members of the family except me. All the foreigners living in the neighborhood were cross-examined, and several were taken to the police station for further investigation. The maid's fortunate lapse of memory spared me this trial, but I thought it advisable to see Sabin and Deunoro. My Consul was very worried about me and thought I should get away at once. Sabin had a fantastic scheme. "I have been in contact with the English Intelligence Service," he said. "If you agree, we can get you to England."

"How?" I asked.

"Very simple," Sabin answered. "A plane will come and pick you up. They will let you know only half an hour before the time. They are in touch with London. I presented your case, without giving your name, as one of an important political person who is in danger."

"All right," I said; "but in this kind of business the greatest caution must be used, and I shall have to ask proof of good faith. Will you ask this agent to send a message which I shall compose, to my friends in London? Once I receive an answer, I will give him a definite reply."

The message to London was in a code which combined certain Basque words with others in French. It gave news of my whereabouts and situation to the Basque Delegation in London and asked them to make inquiries about the feasibility and expedience of the proposed trip. The message was delivered to my countrymen in London, so the agents assured Sabin; but we never received an answer. We decided that I should not make the trip.

"Another way out will present itself," Sabin said. "I am sorry this one has not worked out. It would have been such an adventure!"

"Too adventurous, I'm afraid," I laughed. "I am not too anxious to take a joy ride in a Nazi airplane. I'm afraid there is something shady about your friend in the so-called British Intelligence Service. I would not trust him very far."

Sabin also knew where to stop.

As popular reaction against the Germans increased, the most fantastic tales and rumors of mysterious airplanes and wild adventures of English secret-service men began circulating around Antwerp. The tales grew as they passed from mouth to mouth. The story even went around that on Armistice day, R.A.F. pilots in their own uniforms boldly descended and placed wreaths at the foot of the statue of King Albert. Certain it is that many wreaths were placed there. The monument was surrounded with people when I passed it in the trolley. The Gestapo had many plain-clothes men busy that day tearing off the little Belgian flags and rosettes which many citizens wore in their lapels to commemorate the Armistice of the last war.

6

One day, shortly after this, my brother suddenly appeared at the house where Sabin and Deunoro lived. The Gestapo had freed him. His first question was about me: "Is José Antonio still here in Antwerp? Have they followed him at all? What has happened?" The boys told him there were no new developments. I was still here. I was still planning, with my Consul, the way out for myself and my family. Juan told his story. After being held incommunicado all this time, he was finally summoned to the Gestapo chief's office. One of the officers questioned him.

"Are you Juan de Aguirre?"

"Yes, sir."

"And you are not José Antonio de Aguirre?"

"No, sir."

"We have been able to check that. Where is your brother?"

"I can't tell you because I don't know myself."

"Haven't you heard from him since he left Paris and crossed the Belgian frontier?"

"Yes, sir. I was with him at the French border; but he left at the end of May, and I don't know where he is now."

"Don't you have any idea where he could be? Where do you think he is?"

"I don't know, but I am almost sure that he is in London."

"We thought as much. Tell me who is this man?"

The Gestapo official showed my brother a photograph of a man in shirt sleeves, with his hair all mussed up. It was a typical picture of anyone photographed in a street fight. My brother, who is very cool-headed, asked himself what reason they could have for showing him this picture of an unknown man, and answered categorically, "I don't know him."

"What do you mean, you don't know him? This is José Antonio de Aguirre."

"Well, if I know my own brother, this person is not José Antonio de Aguirre." And drawing out his billfold, which inexplicably they had let him keep since they had taken everything else from him, Juan said to the German officer, "Look, here is a picture of my brother."

It was a picture taken while on a visit to our troops at the Basque front. I had on a leather jacket, Sam Browne belt and bayonet blade, also our classical beret and high boots. There was a world of difference between that photograph and Dr. Alvarez.

The officer studied the picture carefully. "May I keep this?" he asked.

"Certainly," replied my brother, who was as carefully studying the face of the officer and noting his reactions.

"Your brother is thirty-four, isn't he?"

"No, sir, he is thirty-six." Juan was acting on the theory that it was wisest in this case to tell as much of the truth as possible. Since the life and success of Dr. Alvarez was based on fiction, the disappearance of Aguirre must be based on fact.

The Gestapo officer spoke to my brother in a friendlier tone but at the same time very seriously. "It is really too bad that you don't know where your brother is now. The authorities are very anxious to get in touch with him. It is an order from Berlin."

"I've already told you I'm sure he's in London."

"All right then, you are free to go," the Gestapo officer said; "but you must report to us twice a week. Moreover, you may not leave the city without our permission. If you try it, you will be punished severely—and remember that you will be under constant surveillance."

A week passed before Sabin and Deunoro felt it was safe to report my brother's experience to me. Deunoro said: "The whole plot is clear. The Gestapo want to use your brother as bait to catch you. They don't believe him, and hope that by keeping careful watch over Juan they may some day surprise you with him."

"I don't agree with you," Sabin interrupted. "I think the good old Gestapo is on the wrong track. Good Lord, they are not infallible! I tell you our rumor has taken root and spread. They are on someone else's trail, and I think it's your great chance to make a break. I advise you to cross the frontier and get to the French Basque country as quickly as possible."

"I don't think that would be wise at all," said Deunoro. "If you are careful, you are safer here. The only thing you must avoid is a chance meeting with your brother. Don't forget: if they are looking for you here, they are looking for you at all the frontiers—particularly the road to the south of France. They would suspect you of going there at once."

"True enough," I said; "but I think Sabin is right in one respect: the time has come for decisive action. I must begin to make an escape. One road is no more dangerous than another, for the traveler on that road will always be, from his soul to his skin, José Andrés Alvarez Lastra of Panama. If I remain here, I am afraid the Germans will eventually see through the disguise and psychological game I am playing. That would be fatal, for Franco's demands won't wait and I shall shortly be joining my ancestors in heaven!"

"The fact is," said Sabin, "I heard the other day that the Falange representative in the Antwerp Spanish Consulate admitted that you had escaped them. They didn't know where you were, this Falangist said; but they were certain that you were in occupied territory, and thought you could not possibly have escaped to England."

"I heard that story, too," Deunoro broke in. "The Falangist's name is Ruiz, isn't it?"

"Yes," Sabin answered, "that's the same man."

"Well," said Deunoro, "this Ruiz reported that they were not going to make the same mistake with you as they made when they shot Companys. There was too much noise and adverse criticism over that. This time, once you have been captured by the Gestapo, you will simply disappear without leaving a trace."

"What you tell me does not surprise me in the least," I said. "The Gestapo is looking for me. That in itself is a good reason for moving on. The thing for us to realize is that they may be looking for me for political reasons. The Gestapo agent may not have been incorrect when he told my brother that they had received orders from the higher authorities to find me, as they wanted to talk to me."

Only a few weeks ago, we had met a secretary of the Flemish Nationalist Party, a young man strangely duped by the propaganda of the Nazis. He knew that both the boys, Sabin and Deunoro, were Basques interested in the national liberty of their country. He did not know my identity, other than that I was a Spanish-American friend. He could not understand why the Basques had not made an alliance with Germany. "The leaders of your government really made a mistake there," he told the boys. "The Germans are the ones who appreciate the national aspirations of peoples, not the so-called democracies. Look at the Slovaks. All these nations have their own representatives in Berlin—the Ukrainians, the Croats, etc.; and all of them are very well treated."

"But what good," I countered a little gently to the young fanatic, "to have a representative in a country which denies its own citizens the right of representation?"[2]

Analyzing my predicament, the three of us recalled that conversation with the Flemish secretary.

"You mean they might try to make a deal with you?" Sabin asked.

"Certainly," I said. "Then, finding me uncooperative, there is nothing they are not capable of doing—not alone my execution. They are experts in forgery. They could publish any number of declarations, manifestos, and instructions to the Basque people on both sides of the Atlantic. Hitler, or at least his diplomatic service, understands very well the problem of the Basques, and knows of their friendship with the great numbers of Basque immigrants in the Americas."

"I would never have thought of such a possibility," Deunoro said; "and it's so logical."

I stood up to leave them. "It is so logical, it is what we must guard against most diligently." We said goodbye again, and I went to the Consulate, where I talked with Guardia Jaen for a long time.

"This place is getting too hot for you, and you are much too calm about it," he told me.

"I am not avoiding a decision, and I am certainly not calm," I answered. "I am willing to accept any reasonable plan."

In these days it was difficult to control my feeling of tremendous impatience; but, whichever way I went, I wanted to be sure my wife and children would follow. We were all well equipped with passports now. My own was from the Republic of Panama and was made out in the name of Dr. Alvarez Lastra. We were rather worried by the fact that the passport was dated after the entrance of the Germans in Belgium. It couldn't be made out in any other way, since the provisional passport which I had used to obtain the Belgian identity card was dated June, 1940.

My wife and children had Venezuelan passports. Dr. Araujo, the Consul in Belgium, had received a telegram from the Minister of Foreign Relations in Venezuela, Señor Gil Bornes. This telegram was very carefully worded but gave clear orders that visas be issued to both my wife and myself. Our Basque friends in America had apparently received news of us and were working to help us. The Colombian diplomat, Dr. Melguizo, had taken my message to the President of Colombia, Dr. Santos, a very good friend of ours. President Santos knew how to act discreetly and efficiently, transmitting the first news to our friends. This filled me with hope and optimism. "This is a comedy," Dr. Araujo said. "How can I visa your passport, if you haven't any? The only way I can interpret this order is to issue you a Venezuelan passport."

Guardia Jaen interrupted, "You may give his wife a passport, but since Alvarez is my own creation, at least let me have the satisfaction of finishing my work." He turned to me. "You shall have a passport from Panama. Let Dr. Araujo give your wife one from Venezuela."

"As a matter of fact," I said, "I think it is wiser that we do have different passports: we are different people, we are not related, we come from different countries—but, should it ever be necessary for us to be together again, there could be nothing thought of a Panamanian bachelor showering a little attention upon a Venezuelan widow."

We laughed quite a little over that joke, and then settled down to a serious discussion over the name for my wife in her new passport. We tried to think of every angle, but chiefly the danger of an unconscious indiscretion on the part of the children. My wife was given the name of María Arrigorriaga de Guerra (widow). In the mouths of the children, Aguirre and Guerra sound very similar, especially to foreigners. My little girl's real name is Aintzane, which is Basque for Gloria. We called the boy Joseba, which is Basque for Joseph. On the passport we named them Gloria and José. We told the children these names were a translation of their own names, and that they must use them always and never forget them, in order to be able to travel easily. In spite of being only five and two years old, they were models of discretion the whole time.

I did not see my wife and children on this trip to Dr. Araujo's office in Brussels. It was terrible to be so close to them, but Guardia Jaen said: "Patience, my friend. It is too dangerous now to risk anything. Remember, we cannot tell how much they know."

"Or how little," I finished. But I considered it best to take his advice, and we went back to Antwerp. At least we all had passports now.

CHAPTER VI

Only a few days later, Guardia Jaen telephoned me at the Tirlemont house. "Dr. Alvarez," he said, "I want you to come at once to the Consulate." He sounded quite excited, and I was really surprised to have him telephone me. One of the things he had cautioned me against was using the telephone. ("I am sure they are tapping all wires," he said. "Avoid the telephone as if it were plague-ridden." "That will be simple," I answered. "I don't like them any-way.")

Claudine was home from work that day, and so she had answered the phone. She was sitting in the living room off the hall, and I could tell that she felt very curious over my brief conversation. I had merely said, "Very good, I will be right there," and hung up. "My consul," I explained to her, "has news for me."

"Oh, Dr. Alvarez, you will be leaving us—now that we're so used to having you part of the family."

I laughed. "Well, it takes so much time, Claudine," I said, "to arrange a journey these days, perhaps I will be your guest for the duration in spite of my efforts."

"We wouldn't mind," she answered, while I was praying silently that such would not be the case. I left the house and hurried to the Consulate—for the first time avoiding my roundabout route. Guardia Jaen wanted me there quickly. Well, he was my consul, and I would hurry. In a way, I thought, we had been too cautious. The citizen of a neutral country would naturally keep in touch with his consul during a war.

As soon as Guardia Jaen saw me at his office, he said, "Do you want to go to Germany with me?"

"How?" I asked. "What reason are we going to give them?"

"I have to go to the doctor who treated me some years ago, and I shall let the authorities understand that this is the only chance I have to see him."

"Very good for you. But what about my permit? Why am I going?"

"We shall ask for a permit. I shall say, since you are my friend, I want you to accompany me. There is no reason why a Panamanian can't go into Germany."

"You are right. This is the adventure I have been waiting for, and I accept it. Of course we shall have to ask for my permit at the Kommandantur, and the Gestapo will have to approve it."

"But this is a chance we must take," Guardia replied.

"You are really a wonderful friend, Guardia," I smiled. "It would be a pity if you should suffer any annoyance for being overgenerous with me."

"Look, the most they can do to me is to kick me out of these countries—at that, perhaps they would be doing me a favor; but they will shoot you. And if we do not act soon I am afraid that some day they will find you right here. Tomorrow I shall go to Brussels and try to get you a permit. Give me your passport."

I gave it to him, and in the morning he left for Brussels. I remained behind and thanked God that men of such caliber still existed in the world. I had my consul—and what a consul!

He returned from Brussels, however, disappointed. I was waiting for him at his office. "You will have to appear personally at the Kommandantur," he told me. "It was not possible for me to obtain the permit."

I thought for a minute. "Really we should not be surprised at this outcome," I said finally. "It's quite natural. Why should the Germans give you such a permit for me? They are at war, and they are not going to disregard all rigorous formalities for anyone."

The Consul could not be cheered. "I am sorry. I wanted to avoid your appearing before them. These Nazis are dreadful when they become suspicious. They will cross-examine you in such minute detail that in the end you will be caught. They will ask you where your shirts were made, where you bought your hat—everything. I know them well. I have lived among them several years now. They are awful."

"I am not afraid," I smiled at him. "I have everything well prepared, including the shirts. There is not a single label in my clothes. The only way we will lose our battle of wits against the Gestapo is if we lose our sense of humor and become rattled by their ridiculous questioning."

"Don't underrate them," Guardia warned. "You have not faced them yet."

"I will not," I answered; "but it is as foolish to overestimate their powers. They are men. We are men. I choose to believe our intelligence is greater. I am not Aguirre, I am Alvarez—that is the one point we must remember always. Alvarez has no political history at all: the future he has depends upon us."

"Let us plan then," Guardia answered. "What has your story been, and how can you back it up? You have explained that the day before the German occupation you arrived in Brussels. Very well, then—where did you sleep that night?"

I drew a card from my wallet. "Here is my host's card."

The Consul read the card. "Who is this gentleman?"

"The Viscount de Bovigny de Salles is an old friend of ours. We advised him long ago that in case of any police investigation he should say that I spent the nights of May 9th and 10th in his house. He assured us that he would do so. In Paris, you know, everything is arranged so that at the Quentin-Bauchart No. 5 address they will say that Dr. Alvarez had lived there. And before this, the traces are lost, for Dr. Alvarez arrived in Cherbourg in the last days of the month of July of last year on the Empress of Britain, the records of which are on the other side of the ocean; and the ship is at the bottom of the sea."

"Do you have absolute confidence in this Viscount?"

"As much as I have in you."

"And the letters you have received from Panama"—his eyes were amused as he looked at me. "Do you keep them?"

"My brother Antonio's letters," I answered seriously, "are trial-proof."

We spent several hours examining in detail the whole history of Dr. Alvarez and prepared ourselves to appear before the Gestapo.

2

Our friend the Venezuelan Consul, Dr. Araujo, lived in Brussels. He always said we must stay at his apartment whenever we were in Brussels, and often he entertained us splendidly. This same evening he had invited us to dinner and to spend the night, which fitted in admirably with our plans. We arrived at his apartment a little early. When Dr. Araujo learned that we were to appear before the Gestapo in the morning to ask for a permit to enter Germany, he first looked at us to convince himself of our sanity, and then he began to laugh. "Well, since we shall probably all end in a concentration camp, I suggest that we make this evening a celebration." He told us that a young Venezuelan friend was coming to dinner. "The boy is studying engineering here in Belgium," Dr. Araujo said, "and I am afraid at the moment he is an ardent admirer of the Axis. So be careful how you speak in front of him."

The student turned out to be a rather frail-looking boy, but he was very funny. He had recently become acquainted with a group of Basque professional pelota players who had played in Brussels. "What appetites those men had!" he said. "I went to a supper with them. It was a tremendous meal—I could eat only a quarter of what they ate."

"You should play their game," Araujo said. "Then you would be able to eat with them."

"Another one drank twelve bottles of beer, and he felt fine. He was not even drunk," the Venezuelan boy said. "I had to be carried home just trying to keep up with them. I shall have to desert those Basques," he finished, "they will send me to my grave."

"Have you seen them recently?" Guardia Jaen asked.

"The last time I saw them, they were worried about the execution of the Catalonian President, Luis Companys, for they are afraid that the same thing may happen to theirs. And the truth is that, wherever he is, the Basque President must watch his step."

Dr. Araujo's smile grew each time he glanced at my mustache. In the end, he leaned back in his armchair and burst out laughing.

"But what are you laughing at?" the boy said.

"It is nothing—nothing," Dr. Araujo answered. "Your story of the pelota players still amuses me. I have known them also."

"At the Spanish Embassy and the Consulate, where do they say the Basque President is now?" Guardia asked.

"Well, some say in England, others in Mexico; and still others say that he may be moving about in France."

Guardia and I did not dare look at each other for fear of more laughter. During supper I spoke hardly at all. I did not wish my accent, which in spite of my efforts was different from a South American accent, to make the student suspicious.

When Dr. Araujo returned after taking him to the door, he said: "Do you know what the lad asked me? He said, 'Who is that fellow who only speaks in monosyllables?' I answered, 'I will tell you the story one day—and then perhaps you will have quite a laugh.'"

The apartment house where Araujo lived was modern, with six or seven floors, and was almost entirely occupied by German officers. A captain of the Gestapo lived on the next floor. While we were there that evening, after the student left, we discussed more details of our visit to the German police.

3

The next day Guardia and I went to the Office of Permits and Visas of the Kommandantur, which is in front of the Grand Hotel on a corner of the Avenue Louise.

We had a bad beginning. My good Consul Guardia Jaen had an argument with a German corporal, who tried to eject us from a room which we had entered without permission. I tapped Guardia on the shoulder. "Tell him you are the Consul of Panama."

"Let me act," Guardia answered. "I know very well how to handle these men. We must answer this rude fellow's language in the same way."

The noise of the argument brought another soldier who politely asked what was the matter. The Consul explained, and his card was taken to the commanding officer's desk.

"Don't you see? Everything has been fixed because I spoke harshly."

"There's no doubt about that," I answered; "but perhaps it is best that we do not continue to do so, as I feel that in our position it is more appropriate to speak gently."

"No," Guardia said, "you don't understand these people."

In a short while we were called to the desk of the officer in charge of visas. He was about fifty years old, a classical type of Prussian military man. He frowned deeply, and his whole face was silent and sullen-looking. He neither stood up nor asked us to sit down.

The Consul reminded him of his visit the day before, and introduced me as a citizen of his country, who needed a permit on his way through Germany to continue his trip to Switzerland. (Our intention was to have access to Switzerland as a neutral country.)

"To Switzerland?" asked the officer. "That cannot be granted here."

He carefully examined the passports and looked at me from head to foot. He kept silent while examining the application we had made in Antwerp, which had been signed by the Consul himself in my behalf during his last visit.

The officer took a red pencil and started to underline the application slowly and solemnly. The Consul and I looked at each other. I did not lose sight of the pencil point, and it was a great effort for me to remain apparently calm.

The officer broke the silence and said to the Consul: "Your passport will be approved because of its diplomatic character, and because it has the visas of the German Ministry of Foreign Affairs; but this gentleman's will have to go to the police for the regular investigation."

This was the Gestapo in action. Both the Consul and I had the same feeling of terror and danger.

"But why shouldn't you grant the visa when yesterday you told me that the only necessary thing was for this gentleman to appear before you?" Guardia spoke with some note of righteous indignation in his voice. "That is the only reason why he has come with me today."

The officer rose and replied coldly: "I have told you already that this case has to be investigated by the police. There is no use in your talking to me. I have to obey the rules which have been made."

"But yesterday you did not tell me any of that," answered the Consul with greater force, "which compels us to postpone our trip."

"You can go, but this gentleman's case must be investigated by the police," answered the officer. "Come back in three days."

And with no more explanation he sat down and continued his work.

As we went down the stairs to the street, Guardia said: "You are lost—in the hands of the Gestapo. . . . And, stupid of me, I am the one who has led you into this trap. Now they will not leave you in peace until they have found out everything. You have to get away at once. You see, I know these men very well."

"I don't think it's so bad," I said. "In the first place, they have let us go out into the street; then they have summoned us back in three days. If they have certain established rules for all these cases, as we surely know that they must have, what's strange about their applying them to me too? Besides, I assure you that in the investigation they will never find out my true identity—come what may. I am Alvarez, and I shall never depart from that. I will show letters, documents, whatever they may wish, and they will not be able to find out anything else."

"And in your house?"

"My kind landlady was the first to be deceived. She will say that I came as Alvarez, and that I am Alvarez. I find no other danger than the one I have always pointed out to you, the chance meeting with a person who might know me. Some Spanish official who works with the Gestapo could fix his attention on me, examine me carefully, and then recognize me. But these coincidences are not so frequent. Up to this minute they have not taken place. And as to your worries, please forget them, because I owe you all that has saved me, and your intentions of bringing me here could not have been more generous. We will run the risk together, my good friend Guardia."

"You are *not* to come back here on Sunday. Is it understood? I shall come alone. And I believe it best for you to hide, as they may appear at your house any minute."

As the Consul spoke, I saw he was nervous. He continued to blame himself for having brought me to the Gestapo.

"But haven't you given the Consulate's address as mine in case of a call?"

"That's true," he answered.

"Then they will go to the Consulate before going to any other place, for it would be quicker for them to do this than to make any other investigation. Don't you remember that, fortunately, there is no record on the application of my real address, and that I have not even signed it? There will always be enough time to sound the alarm signal."

"Yes, it is better, I guess, to think a bit about things and leave the solution for tomorrow," answered the Consul. "But you must plan immediately a quick way of complete concealment or of flight."

Our feet instinctively took us to a train. We did not even go to Dr.

Araujo's to tell him what had happened. Inside the coach, with the small blue lights shining faintly, we went on considering our problem.

The next day I went at once to the Consulate.

"Why did you come?" asked Guardia as soon as he saw me enter. "You are very unwise."

"Simply to let you know that I am going with you again to the Kommandantur. You saved me, and continue to help me, and it is my duty to run all the risks with you."

The Consul stood up and, reaching over, took my hand in his.

"I have decided that, if you appear before the police alone, it will be one more reason for suspicion," I added. "On the other hand, if we both go, they will at least think that we have nothing to hide."

4

Sunday morning we went again to the Kommandantur. We arrived there fearful but determined. We had documents, letters, papers; and even our friend the Viscount was prepared to testify.

We entered the building, showed our cards, and waited. We were called into the main hall, where the commanding officer of the department of visas appeared, and told us that we were to be taken care of that very moment. Two officers came in, and one of them, a captain, speaking correct French, was the first to greet us. The other remained silent and observing. The Prussian officer we had seen previously appeared, bringing my passport and the application. He saluted the two officers of higher rank, and left.

"This petition is very strange," said the captain. "Will you tell me why you are going to Germany?"

"It is simple, captain. I wish to get to Berlin in order to speak to the Minister of my country about a personal matter that is of great interest to me."

The captain had not expected such an answer.

"But you can do that by writing," he said. "Is it so important for you to go to Berlin?"

"Certainly, it is not a matter of life and death." I paused. "Well, I suppose I must be more explicit with you. It seems certain that my government intends to send me to a diplomatic post in the Far East. You can understand that sooner or later I shall have to go to Berlin, for our Minister there will receive the final orders. It is true that I could wait here to receive them, but as my friend, the Consul, is going"—I indicated Guardia who was at my side—"it is a wonderful opportunity to make the trip well escorted, as I do not have a good knowledge of German."

"Besides," joined in Guardia, "I cannot delay the trip, as I am going for my health, and my friend Alvarez would be an excellent companion."

"I understand," said the officer very slowly, somewhat confused by the unexpected trend that the conversation had taken; "but these things are so difficult. Besides—"

"Please excuse me, captain," I interrupted, feeling that our plan had not been preposterous. "The case is very simple. If you can grant me the favor, I shall be very thankful. If it is impossible for you to grant it, I am a man who can understand the position of a country at war, and these things are quite difficult. However, I shall have to appeal to the Minister if you cannot help me. I am certain he must have some notices on my appointment already."

The captain and his companion looked at each other, more and more confused.

"As it is an uncommon case—as you are mentioning the Minister . . . Well, perhaps it is not advisable to bother him. If it rested in our hands, we could arrange things quickly, but this is a case that must go to Berlin, as it is necessary to obtain a special permit from the Department of Foreign Relations."

"But the other day the officer who is in charge of applications told us that a police investigation would be sufficient," said the Consul, minimizing the importance of such a dreaded test. "Now you say the petition must go to Berlin. Why?"

"It is necessary, and we are very sorry."

"How many days will it take for the thing to be expedited in Berlin?" I asked.

"About twelve days," answered the captain.

"Oh! It's too long. To tell the truth, I am not interested in the trip unless I can make it with the Consul. I would prefer that the Minister, whom I did not wish to trouble with things of this kind, arrange the whole thing. I can only hope he will not be annoyed at having to ask for favors—but I am afraid it is necessary."

"It will take at least that much time for the Minister to obtain it," the captain almost pleaded. "Four days for our letter to get to Berlin, another four to get the answer, and let us say two or three to resolve the matter there. There are only twelve to fourteen days gone, and I am sure your Minister could not accomplish anything in less time."

The manner of the conversation had changed completely. There was a pause and a moment of silence.

"May I speak to my Consul in Spanish?" I asked the officer of the Gestapo.

"Certainly," he replied.

"It almost seems as if it would be better to drop the subject and let Dr. Villalaz know in Berlin. He would probably avoid the compulsory proceedings for us, despite the extreme politeness of these officers who seem only anxious to help us," I said to Guardia.

"I think it is quite all right," seriously replied the Consul, guessing my intention.

We were risking all and playing with fire, for certainly Dr. Villalaz was completely ignorant of Alvarez's existence.

"If you will permit me, I shall translate it for you," I said to the captain.

"Oh, no need to bother," he answered me with even more cordiality. "I know Spanish very well, and have understood all that you have said."

My suspicions had been correct. From that moment, the captain became our ally, trying to find an adequate solution for us.

"I beg you not to give up this plan," he said. "As it is necessary, I shall send the petition to Berlin. But it occurs to me that if you, on your part, get in touch with your Minister and ask him to send a note to the Department, rapid action on the permit will be more assured. In that way perhaps we can save a few days. What do you say?"

"It is a negotiation and a pact of alliance," I answered smilingly.

The officers both smiled back at me. With all the tension of the interview I could not help seeing its comic side as well.

"This simultaneous plan of action is well conceived, and I believe it is the best," Guardia Jaen said, and then he thanked these officers of the dreaded German Gestapo for their kind attentions.

The storm had been weathered. The Consul, with great skill and with the authority his knowledge of Germans and Germany gave him, went right on talking. He spoke of the doctors he was to visit, the health institutions, and other similar details. The plan of attack which was so carefully prepared had produced the psychological effect we had hoped to achieve.

5

In the street, Guardia and I wondered. They had been too kind. We almost preferred the rude and unpolished officer we had first seen. This was the theme of our conversation while we lunched, exhausting our ration stamps, as the tremendous step we had just taken seemed well worthy of a celebration. We were optimistic, and we were doubtful—but we were also hungry, so we ate well.

"I feel that this is taking a definite course. Ever since I knew you, I have said to myself, 'He is a man of good luck!' And I am myself," the Consul said to me.

"But don't you feel these Nazis have been extremely polite? Have they been playing with us, just as we have played with them? They may use the telegraph wires, which they possess and we do not, and ask the Minister of Panama in Berlin: Who is Alvarez? He would answer, of course, that my name does not sound familiar to him."

"These are critical days, my friend," Guardia answered. "We shall see it now. But, in any case, have everything ready so that they don't trap you."

"You have a permit, haven't you?" I asked. "Why don't you leave immediately for Berlin and warn the Minister?"

"I had already decided doing that before you mentioned it," he said.

Two days later the Consul arrived in Hamburg, and from there he went directly to Berlin. I remained alone in Antwerp. Sabin and Deunoro kept a watch on every move during those days.

Yet, why should the Gestapo suspect anything? I was a Panamanian accompanied by my Consul with documents, letters, references, and even could count on the friendship of the Minister in Berlin. There was nothing in the Belgian and German police records except information supplied by me and prepared conscientiously. With some other person, perhaps they might have continued the questioning, but having been faced with my Consul, and the threat of appealing to the Minister, they did not dare. It is remarkable the effect that these appeals have on officials belonging to a country whose leaders have scoffed at all kinds of hierarchy and authority. Mention the name of a diplomat, and they are filled with awe. Guardia had told me of this, and his advice was sound.

"They want to be obedient to some one," Guardia said. "That is the secret, I'm sure, of Hitler's success here."

I observed great caution while my Consul was away. As it was December—and cold—my staying in the house did not cause any suspicion.

Eight days later I received a letter from my Consul in which he let me know that the Minister had already been warned, and that he would help in whatever way he could.

On December 20th, fifteen days had elapsed since my interview. I was just finishing the annual Christmas message to my people which they were to understand had been written in London. Impossible as it seems, this message actually reached its destination in time by secret means and was read by many of our people.

I had barely finished when I received a summons from the Kommandant to come to his office for the permit to enter Germany. Would I ever send another Christmas message, and from where? Next day Christmas was far from my thoughts again.

I presented the summons at the Gestapo headquarters and was led to a small hall. It was the antechamber of the Prussian officer. Great anxiety filled me. I was alone. At last I heard the officer's voice inviting me to come in. He received me smilingly. He seemed transformed.

"Are you going to spend Christmas in Germany?" he asked in very bad French, after greeting me and even asking me to be seated.

"No, sir," I replied. "I will spend the holidays here saying goodbye to my friends."

"I have a leave now to spend the holidays home. I leave for Germany tomorrow," he said joyfully, and glanced at me with great satisfaction. "Let us see how much time you have asked to stay in Germany."

"A month," I told him.

"Bah! that's too little. Would you like me to make it two?"

"Much obliged," I answered casually.

And he gave me a permit to remain in Hamburg and Berlin until February 28, 1941.

"Here is your permit, and here's your passport."

I thanked him. We said farewell, and he accompanied me to the door of his office. Had he clapped me on the back, I would not have been surprised. I scarcely noticed the ridiculous clicking heels and salutes of the lower Gestapo agents as the Prussian officer led me to the door. It seemed completely like a fantasy. On reaching the street I cast a thankful glance to Heaven—it was as though God had arranged even the opportune vacation of that officer, who for so many days had been our worry and our torture.

What had happened? I do not know to this day. The Minister in Berlin was not called, nor was I asked for any more explanations. Our plan succeeded because the police report sent from Brussels by the captain had been, apparently, enough for Berlin.

As I walked on the street, I was proud of my German document. Surely I was now a thorough American citizen. I had even been "purified" by the waters of the German Gestapo.

I reached my house and showed the document. That wonderful Tirlemont family was happy for me and at the same time said that they were sorry to lose me, as they had come to regard me with deep affection. We celebrated my departure. I left them in total ignorance, convinced, more than ever, that Alvarez was a diplomat who at last would achieve his eager desire for adventure, his golden dream of making a study of the Orient, going through Russia via the Trans-Siberian Railroad.

"Remember us," Claudine called in goodbye. "We will remember you."

6

It was a long time since I had seen my family. With a permit that gave me no less a privilege than to enter Germany, I thought myself well protected. My absence now could be long—very long. Was it possible to say goodbye to my wife, my children, my mother, my brothers? . . .

It was Christmas afternoon. I took the train to Louvain, where they lived those days under the protection of their Venezuelan documentation and their false names.

With an emotion impossible to restrain and with the haste of one who, after having overcome so many grave obstacles, was liable to lose everything with the least indiscretion, I went through many streets, reaching the place by a devious route. Finally I knocked at the door of the house where my wife and children had taken refuge. The scene following, the reader can imagine. Surprise, happiness, tears, contentment, the sadness of separation, and the fear and doubt of the future were blended in the space of a few moments.

My son, who was then two years old, was afraid of me on account of my mustache. A while later he had more confidence and started pulling at it, as he could not believe it was real.

The whole family gathered around the table, celebrating Christmas. My poor sister Encarna was missing, but there was a place for her at the table.

We had suffered so much that we overflowed with happiness on that night. Since I possessed the documents which I had obtained with really incredible ease, there was a general feeling that everything would turn out all right.

I had to tell them the story of all our interviews.

Mari said, "I wish I could have seen José Antonio fooling the Gestapo." Everyone laughed. It was an occasion of great rejoicing.

In spite of the straitened economic circumstances, there was an ample meal, and even with rationing, between friends, two excellent courses could be put together, and there were wines and liqueurs.

After supper we danced. My brother-in-law Santi had a friend Max who belonged to a very good Flemish family in Louvain. He came to the house and joined the party, surprised at my presence, as he had never before seen me there. They introduced me as an American and an acquaintance of their Venezuelan cousin (as her own brothers called my wife). I had wished merely to spend the holidays with them. As the atmosphere was one of joy, there was no occasion for further questioning. But it puzzled the visitor that an American stranger should shower his attentions on and even monopolize the Venezuelan widow—and he even evidenced none too flattering suspicions.

One of my brothers-in-law said to him: "He is a fellow whom we don't like at all. He takes charge of our cousin, and, you see, it looks as if she belonged to him. He even let us know that he intends to stay in our house with us for a few days, putting us in an embarrassing position as we have no room for him."

In good Max's eyes I assumed the role of a "fresh guy," to judge by the glances he once in a while flung at me. But the merriment of the party increased and in the end we were good friends.

I spent a few happy days there until January 6, 1941. I had to say farewell again to my family, not knowing when or where we would next see each other. I had forgotten the number of our goodbyes. I only knew that each one was more painful than the one before.

And, as in La Panne, I repeated before the tears of my own family, "Until God wills." I left feeling as if my heart were surely broken, on my way to my new exile, and alone.

The night of January 6th I spent in the home of the kind Venezuelan Consul in Brussels. As always Dr. Araujo offered his hospitality, since the train was leaving at four-forty-five in the morning from Brussels.

At four-fifteen on the 7th of January, I was walking down the deserted avenues of Brussels to the station. Near by, a platoon of German soldiers crossed the street. They were going in the opposite direction—and the sight of their uniforms chilled me. I was leaving behind those who were my very own—subdued and depressed, facing grave difficulties in obtaining food. But if I did not leave them, they might never be saved. But I knew also that when I left the Continent my wife and my children would leave with me. I did not know how, but I knew that it would happen this way. The train began pulling out of the station. I was on my way to Germany.

THE DIARY OF

DR. ALVAREZ

CHAPTER VII

Many friends warned Dr. Alvarez above all not to keep a diary in Germany; otherwise, he might never have thought of doing it at all. Once he began, the temptation was so great that he cast all prudence aside. It was not that Dr. Alvarez had the temerity to be unafraid of the Gestapo. On the contrary, he had always regarded this famous police institution with certain respect. "But," he would think to himself, "they are men like me. If they were spirits, that would be another story."

He had become so thoroughly permeated by his new personality that he almost became convinced that he was who he was not. The papers he carried in his portfolio seemed to tell him, "You are Alvarez." His only weak spot was the glasses. Anyone could pull them off, and on seeing that they were made of ordinary crystal, could say, "You are not Alvarez." But, in spite of all that, the phenomenon of reincarnation had taken place so thoroughly that Dr. Alvarez became convinced that no one could confuse him with José Antonio de Aguirre.

This diary, which the reader will shortly read, was the inseparable companion of Dr. Alvarez's pilgrimage, and perhaps the one who best knew his sorrows and satisfactions, for with it he would converse in the solitude of his quarters, where the thorns in his soul flourished best.

The diary also had its adventures. It found itself inside pockets that knew not what they were carrying; it crossed frontiers and always had to go in hiding, as it was an eloquent witness of the metamorphosis, vicissitudes, and trickery of Dr. Alvarez. And that nothing should be lacking, it was lost one day, although, fortunately, it was recovered. But Dr. Alvarez will never forget the unpleasant moments he had to go through until he found it. From that moment on, he took more care of it than he would of a naughty child.

Here is the account of Dr. Alvarez's emotions and experiences in Germany, under the shadow of the Gestapo.

January 7, 1941

This morning as the train pulled out of the Brussels station, my scanty baggage was put in a compartment where three German officers were sprawled over all the seats, sleeping quite noisily. I had to wake them. I spoke in French. "Pardon—I am so sorry. I am afraid I must ask you to move a little." They all looked at me with ill humor and shuffled about until finally there was a small corner for me to squeeze into. As they gradually woke up, they became more polite. I offered them Belgian cigarettes. "I am so happy to be going into Germany," I said. "This is not the first trip for me. Before the war, I spent many happy vacations in Berlin."

One of the officers spoke French very well, and by the time we crossed the border at two-thirty in the afternoon we were all quite friendly, which was what I had been working for. It was worth the package of cigarettes they smoked because their attitude gave me a measure of self-confidence. The officer who checked documents at the border stared at me for a long time before he spoke. Was he thinking that my mustache was artificial—my glasses? (You are Alvarez, I began saying to myself, as the officer stared at my documents and then at me. Remember, you are Alvarez.)

"How much money do you have?" he finally asked.

"Three hundred marks," I answered. This was the maximum amount permitted to enter Germany, as well as the maximum my circumstances permitted me to have.

He was still doubtful of me. Perhaps by now the Gestapo was satisfied that I was not Alvarez at all and had already notified this very man: Hold the man who carries a Panamanian passport under the name of Alvarez. He is not Alvarez—he is Aguirre, wanted in Berlin.

"Why are you coming to Germany?" the officer interrupted my inner panic.

I looked at him calmly. "I have been called by the Minister of my country in Berlin," I answered.

Again he looked at my mustache, and again he examined my credentials. Then came the inspection of my worn-out shirts, shorts, and socks! Why would a man called by his Minister have such pathetic-looking personal belongings? In agony I was asking myself the questions which I felt must be running through the officer's mind. At long last he gave an order in German to an underling who put the seal for entrance on my papers. I could breathe easier. I must take this small experience as a lesson and not permit myself even slight inner misgivings. Had I been a fraction more nervous inside myself, it would have shown upon the surface. I did not like to contemplate the ensuing results. The border official was the type of man who would have welcomed the chance to show his authority. He would have detained me, if only to watch me grow more uneasy. But Germans have a reverential attitude toward social hierarchy, and with my reference to the Minister my own rank ascended, at least in the eyes of my traveling companions.

"So you are an American?" one of them said, as the train left the border.

I was putting my papers back into my wallet. "I am from Central America."

They showered me with a thousand questions: What are people thinking in America? Are they going to enter the war?

They seemed convinced that eventually the United States might enter the war, and this had them really worried.

We arrived in Cologne two hours late, and I had to hurry to catch the Hamburg train. The officers called goodbye to me quite affectionately. They were going to Berlin. While I ran for the Hamburg train, I tried to get the baggage boy at the station to understand that I wanted to send a telegram. He followed me into my compartment, and I wrote the name and address in Hamburg of my Consul, Guardia Jaen. I wanted to let him know of my arrival there, but I could accomplish nothing with the boy. Just as I was giving up, a tall and distinguished-looking German naval officer entered my compartment and kindly served as an interpreter.

The officer, a man about forty-five, seemed quite friendly. "Were you in Paris?" he asked, as he arranged his luggage and settled down in the seat.

I told him I had been in Brussels.

"I come from Brest," he said. He was a commanding officer and wore two war crosses.

"Are they from this war?" I asked.

"One of them, yes," he answered. "The other is from the last. The war!" he exclaimed, and then quickly continued, "How do *you* think this war is going?"

I hesitated before answering such a dangerous and unexpected question, and finally said, "I think that the world is astonished at the rapidity with which you finished France last summer."

"So are we," he said.

This surprised me. "Now everyone is waiting for the assault on England."

The German officer shook his head. "Ah—England! England is very powerful, sir, very powerful."

"But the German army is more so," I prompted.

"England is very powerful," he repeated, then with a disdainful gesture added: "Besides, look what allies we have. Those Italians!" He began reading a book, still shaking his head. I studied the serious and worried furrows on his forehead and thought how weird it was to find myself traveling with a German naval officer who praised his enemy's strength, underrated that of his allies, and asked me, a stranger, my opinion of the war.

A porter brought the officer a raisin roll and a cup of ersatz tea. He began eating. I was awfully hungry.

"Do you think I could get something?" I asked him.

"If you have ration stamps."

"But I don't have any."

"To get this dreadful concoction," he said, looking at the tea substitute, "you may not need them."

We called the porter. The officer spoke to him, and in a short while I was eating a roll and sipping that tea, which, as far as its authenticity went, reminded me of Dr. Alvarez.

The naval officer said goodbye at Bremen. I took advantage of being alone in the compartment to get a can of sardines from my valise. The roll had been decidedly lacking in nourishment. The saddest part of it all was that in order to get the sardines I had to take the lock off my valise, which was like the tea and Dr. Alvarez. It looked like leather, but was only pasteboard. Dr. Alvarez is absentminded and had lost the key.

A little later three civilians and a lieutenant colonel came into my compartment. They were all amused when I told them I was a Panamanian. "Panamanian, eh? Ha! ha! ha! ha!" they laughed, with Wagnerian rhythm. I also laughed. It was funnier to me than it was to them.

We pulled into Hamburg at nine-fifty this evening. The blackout was complete, in the train as well as in the station. I could scarcely see my hand before my face, and I wondered how I would ever find my Consul in such impenetrable darkness. But his voice called out suddenly, "Alvarez!"

I turned. "Here I am," I answered, and we greeted each other.

Guardia took me to a modest boarding house run by an old acquaintance of his, Frau Mikolei. "Here is a countryman of mine," the Consul said, "and a good friend. Treat him well."

The nice little old woman treated me to some sausage and beer, which I greatly appreciated as it was quite some time since I had eaten the roll and the sardines.

"I will come for you in the morning," my Consul said. "You know you have to register with the police."

I am going to bed now. I am too tired, after the first lap of my incredible journey, to think, and I cannot permit myself to worry about my wife, my children, my family, my friends. I must believe that God will take care of us. So far He has guarded us well. I am in Hamburg. I have a permit from the Gestapo. So far, so good.

January 8, 1941

Last night I slept well, and today did not even feel nervous going with Guardia to police headquarters. With polite indifference some policemen checked my papers and then placed a seal on the document which the Gestapo had given me in Brussels. They did not even look at me. Why should they? Dr. Alvarez was a full-fledged citizen, according to his papers, which are the only things considered in a world where all that is official is not always legitimate.

After our appearance before the police, we lunched fairly well at the Municipal Restaurant. After that black and inedible bread in Belgium, I could scarcely eat the little white rolls which they served us. I could only remember those empty and impoverished Antwerp docks. Each of those little rolls means more hunger for the Belgians, the Czechs, and the Dutch. In the "new order" the Germans eat, and their victims do not. At police headquarters they had given me ration stamps. Those for bread were abundant; those for meat, scarce; for butter, five grams a day; for margarine, a little more; eggs, none; milk, skimmed; pure water. "These rations will just barely keep you alive," the Consul said, and Dr. Alvarez agreed.

The "Baedeker" may rightly say that Hamburg is a beautiful city, but it impresses me badly. All that which makes life agreeable has disappeared; the atmosphere is a sorrowful one. Monotony reigns everywhere. Is it truly that way, or do I merely see it that way through my glasses?

Thursday January 9, 1941

Decidedly, with 300 marks I cannot permit myself any luxuries. "They will not last you long, as life here is very expensive," the Consul said to me.

I shall then have to perform miracles of thrift, for even though the Consul brought a few dollars here for me which my family and friends had collected, I must save them to continue my trip, wherever this may be.

"Yes, take good care of those dollars," said the Consul. "They are worth more than gold in Germany. Keep them, and do not show them, as they have great power of getting one anywhere, and for this reason those who possess them are fiercely persecuted."

I accompanied the Consul on his visit to a German family, who were neighbors and friends of his own family when he had a post in this capital. They treated us to a generous afternoon tea—pie, pudding, coffee, pastries, a bottle of cider, and even a glass of cherry liqueur to finish. They went to the table dressed in their best finery, but the cloth showed clearly its poor quality. They were apparently well dressed and satisfied, as if trying to perpetuate the memories of better times.

In the street I told the Consul of my surprise at the abundance of food. "Do not be surprised," he answered. "The German people are very generous in their family lives. This kind family, which is typically German, has made a great effort to entertain us. I am sure that this meal was their only dinner today."

"Well, so much more reason to thank them," said I. "It is truly pitiful that a people in whom such eagerness to live can be seen, and who continue to maintain an outward semblance of plenty, should be led into roads of privation and madness."

"And have you noticed their clothes? What poverty-stricken luxury! This you will see everywhere. This is an impoverished country—that tries to preserve its old rank!"

"But one cannot enter into war in this way," I answered.

Before going to bed I shall read Plutarch, whose Lives of courageous people bring me comfort for the future. For there is always something that can overcome everything. . . .

Friday the 10th

It is truly magnificent, this port of Hamburg, through which we have just walked. It is intensely cold, and the Elbe River is frozen. The port is completely paralyzed on account of the blockade. There is a sadness in this lifeless commercial emptiness. What I do not see is destruction, or even traces of the bombardments. Only slight damage to one of the houses which overlook the docks below the Hospital for Tropical Diseases. And there is the same impression when traveling through the city, which is intact. The R.A.F. bombardments are still weak. From what I can now judge, its visits are reduced to a few planes that drop their load and go away.

The smoke a bomb raises is so great it looks as if the destruction caused were of great proportions. But the illusion disappears like the smoke.

Today is a compulsory fish day. So is Tuesday. By way of these fasts of lay character, meat is saved. The fish is brought from the Baltic and, generally, is not good.

Sunday January 12, 1941

I had been in Hamburg since Tuesday night. Yesterday, the Minister of Panama, Dr. Villalaz, called to ask us to come to Berlin. We took an early train this morning and arrived in Berlin at one in the afternoon. We ate meagerly and at great cost, before going to the Panamanian Legation at three. The Minister received us with great kindness, but he was worried.

"I'll help you in every way I can," he said, "but be careful! These Nazis are terrible. Perhaps they are letting you walk and move around to arrest you when it suits them. They may even know who you are. It would be like them to be making fun of us. Remember you have involved us seriously. Be very cautious, and trust no one."

"I appreciate your advice," I answered, "but I feel that we should consider my case simply as that of any other American citizen. I am Dr. Alvarez. If we insist on thinking always of Aguirre, we alone will create difficulties. If the Germans had suspected me, I don't think I'd be here. I might be in Berlin—but in the custody of the Gestapo."

"But what can I do for you?" Dr. Villalaz asked. "I don't know what I can do. I think you had better go quickly back to Hamburg and apply for your departure from Germany there."

"Alvarez has permission to reside in Berlin," interrupted the Consul.

"Yes, but it is wiser for him to make his application in Hamburg," insisted the Minister. "He would be less noticed there than here. You don't know these fellows."

The Consul and I exchanged glances. The Minister did not wish to commit himself too much—but to go back to Hamburg! I leaned over his desk. "You see, Mr. Minister," I said, "it is not just a question of getting out myself; my wife and children are also waiting. I am sure, Mr. Minister, that you yourself would find it difficult to be patient under similar circumstances."

"This case of yours is certainly complicated," Dr. Villalaz answered. "I'm going to call the Minister from the Dominican Republic. He will know how to advise us." He telephoned Dr. Despradel and invited him over for the evening to see Guardia from Antwerp, and then when he was through he said to us, "Dr. Despradel will be here after dinner."

I stood up. "We have an appointment with Dr. Zerrega Fombona, the Venezuelan Minister, to talk over my wife's case," I said. "We will return later."

Dr. Zerrega lived at the fashionable Hotel Adlon. I had a letter of introduction from Dr. Araujo, the Venezuelan Consul in Brussels who is protecting my wife and children. Dr. Araujo's letter merely asked Dr. Zerrega to listen to my story.

"Please be seated, gentlemen," Dr. Zerrega said. "What may I do for you?"

"I am here only to speak of my wife and children," I answered, "and to ask your aid in getting them out of these countries. This man"—I indicated Guardia—"is helping me."

"But why are you so nervous? I don't understand this case," Dr. Zerrega said. "You are"—he looked at Araujo's letter—"Dr. Alvarez Lastra of Panama." He leaned back in his chair. "If you are from Panama, so is your wife. Why have you come here?"

"I am not Alvarez Lastra," I said. "I am José Antonio de Aguirre from Bilbao and—"

"Speak softer, please." Dr. Zerrega had sat up straight when he heard my name, and now he looked very worried. "They may be listening to us. This hotel is full of the Gestapo. They may have placed microphones right next to us—right here," he said, pointing to one of the corners of the room. "You don't seem to know the kind of things they do. You are a man of courage to be here in Berlin—but I also think you are very foolish."

I pulled my chair closer to his so I could tell him briefly what had happened to us and what I hoped he might do. I had the text of the telegram from the Minister of Foreign Relations of his country which had prompted good Dr. Araujo to issue the passports in Brussels. Dr. Zerrega read it. "Yes, yes," he said, "I know. Of course I have heard about you—but I didn't expect to see you here. It's so difficult. If it were only a case of going through Spain! The Nazi authorities will say that is the only natural way for her to go, and if we insist that she must not they will become suspicious. Why should she come through Germany? Why don't we ask for a visa through Spain? If the Spaniards discovered her true identity, what would they do to a woman and two children?"

"Dr. Zerrega, I know that it is almost impossible for you to realize—but, believe me, anything is possible. An old woman, the widow of a Basque patriot named Renteria, who died in exile, had just crossed the border from France into the Basque country. She was seventy years old and alone. She thought she would return to her home and somehow eke out an existence in the surroundings she loved and close to those neighbors who were still alive and whom she had known all her life. She was sent to prison. If they would do that to an old widow of seventy, whose husband's political position was merely that of a loyal Basque, think what they would do to my wife!"

"I had not known these things," Dr. Zerrega said. "Passage through Spain is certainly not advisable." He stood up. "I will do everything I can. As your own situation develops, keep in touch with me."

Guardia and I went back to the Panamanian Legation, and a short while later, Dr. Roberto Despradel, the Minister of the Dominican Republic, arrived. I was introduced to him. When he heard my name he stared at me.

"Are you the Basque President?" he asked.

"I am, Mr. Minister."

He crossed the room. "I must shake hands with you," he said enthusiastically. He turned to Guardia, who was standing next to me. "And you brought him here, Guardia? Really? You are a fine man." He clapped Guardia on the shoulder. "I congratulate you." He turned again to me. "Don't worry. You are going to get to America. There is a place for you there."

I was terribly moved by his sincerity and his emotion, and I could only say, "I am so comforted by all of you that I feel as if I were already free."

"Don't worry," Dr. Despradel repeated. "We shall plan a campaign—shan't we, Dr. Villalaz?"

The Panamanian Minister agreed, and I looked gratefully at Guardia Jaen, since he was the first man to help me. I felt wings on my feet and real hope at last. Dr. Despradel was a man of swift action.

"You shall go," he was saying. "America will get you out."

It was quite late, and it was decided that Guardia and I would lunch with Villalaz tomorrow to continue the planning.

January 13th

It has been quite an eventful day. This morning, Guardia Jaen and I went to the American Express on Unter den Linden to find out if I could travel through Russia.

"What is your nationality?" I was asked.

"Panamanian," I told them.

"Has Panama recognized the Soviet Government?"

"I don't believe so," the Consul answered.

"Well, in that case, you can't obtain a visa."

"How long does it take to get a visa?" I asked.

"About fifteen days; but if your country doesn't recognize the government they won't grant it at all."

We left the office terribly disappointed and went to the Legation. We were a little early, and the Panamanian Minister was busy. The woman in charge of the office is a German who speaks Spanish very well. She greeted Guardia when we entered, and he introduced me.

"Are you also Panamanian?" she asked.

"Yes, madam."

She studied my face. "But you don't look it. You are so different from the others who come here."

At this moment Dr. Villalaz entered the office. "What nationality does he look like then?" he asked the woman.

She looked at my face again, thoughtfully, "French," she said at last. "He looks much more French than American—maybe it's his mustache that makes him look so French."

We restrained ourselves from laughing, while the Minister deftly changed the subject. Now I know that if this incident had happened in front of the Venezuelan Minister, he would have been sure that the poor woman was a Gestapo agent.

Once we were alone at lunch, we discussed our disappointment over our proposed trip through Russia. Dr. Villalaz still felt apprehensive. "Look," he said, "you must listen to me. I am sure it is better for you to make the application for departure in Hamburg. They might surprise you here any day. These men are terrible."

"And through what country shall we ask to leave?" I inquired. "Would it be best to try to go through Switzerland or Sweden?"

"I think the way through Sweden is closed," he answered. "It may be necessary to apply through Switzerland. You would be safer waiting there."

Carefully I said that I would like to have time to consider the proposal. It filled me with a hopeless sense of prison and waiting.

Switzerland was too encircled. I must get to America—there must be a way out.

"Do not give up hope," Guardia said to me, when we had left Villalaz. "Life has inexhaustible resources. You will get to America in spite of their apprehensiveness."

Guardia had made an appointment with Dr. Olivera, the Ambassador of the Argentine Republic in Berlin. As we approached the Argentine Embassy, I said to my good friend: "You tell him the story, Guardia—I am tired of telling it. I will answer any of his questions; but you tell him in the first place." And indeed, it does get very monotonous—the same story, the same reaction from nearly everyone who must hear it: "You are Aguirre?"

"Yes, I am."

"What are you doing here in Berlin?"

"I want to get to America."

"But, my good fellow . . ."

Dr. Olivera listened politely when Guardia presented my case. To my surprise, he turned to me and said: "I imagined it might be you when they called me this morning for an appointment. In fact I have instructions from my government to the effect that you should be assisted. You Basques have good friends in Argentina. But why did you come here, to Berlin?"

I told him the story of our journey from La Panne to Dunkirk and back again to La Panne—of how my brother Juan had said perhaps the way out was via Berlin. I told him of my retreat with the good priests of the College of St. Francis Xavier, my stay with the Tirlemont family, my brother's arrest and his release, and my final triumphant entrance into Germany.

The Ambassador looked at me as if he thought he were confronting a madman. "You do not seem to realize where you are," he said, at last. "I warn you that you are in grave danger. When do you expect to leave?"

"As soon as I can. But it takes a long time to get visas, and I am afraid I shall have to stay at least fifteen days."

"Fifteen days in Berlin? You are insane. I beg you to leave now. Don't even wait until tomorrow."

"But how, Mr. Ambassador?"

"However you can. I assure you that your optimism will deliver you to your enemies in the end. So far you have met many good people; but the next one . . ."

"I should not be here now, Mr. Ambassador," I answered, "if there were not more good people in the world than bad. What happens is that we insist on judging them wrongly. I am young, but have lived more than many of my elders and have learned that among human beings the good is the normal. Had I seen an enemy in every man, I should not be here. You are another example. Before, there were the Ministers of Venezuela, Panama, and the Dominican Republic. Before that even, the German naval officer on the train to Hamburg, who helped me to get tea and food when I was hungry. And what can I say of this man?" I looked at Guardia. "Without his help, I should have been lost, and here he is near to me, just as if he were trying to save his own life."

"You are impossible," the Ambassador laughed. "But do not trust anybody. Be cautious. I fear for you. Don't forget that it is the least detail which might betray you. Beware of the unforeseen meeting, the servant who left your house many years ago, and who is here without your knowing it, in the enemy's camp. And do you suppose the members of the Spanish Embassy and the Falange have no eyes? And the Gestapo—do you know what the Gestapo is?"

Guardia told him how we had encountered the Gestapo, and when we said goodbye he warned me again to guard against my optimism and to trust no one. He was very kind and sympathetic. It was a consolation and gave me a feeling of strength and safety to know that all the American countries who know Dr. Alvarez's problem are anxious to help solve it.

We dined with Dr. Despradel at the Legation of the Dominican Republic. I had been thinking all day about how I might be able to get the Russian visa, despite rules and regulations, and I remembered that the Secretary of the British Embassy in Moscow, Mr. Stevenson, was a good friend of ours. He had been the British Consul in Bilbao when we were at war and had written to me before going to Moscow on his new assignment. I told Guardia and Dr. Despradel about him and suggested that we might get permission to send a letter to Mr. Stevenson via the American diplomatic mail. I could explain my precarious position to Mr. Stevenson and ask him to take steps in obtaining the visa, with the aid of his Embassy, in Moscow.

Dr. Despradel thought it was an excellent idea and telephoned immediately to Dr. Villalaz. "Alvarez has a friend in Moscow whom he wishes to write," he explained cautiously. "This friend may be able to expedite matters for him."

Villalaz was very interested. Now we are all going to meet at the Panamanian Legation tomorrow morning at ten.

January 14th

We met at the Legation, and after a short conference everyone agreed my idea was a good one. Dr. Despradel made an immediate appointment with the Chargé d'Affaires for the United States. It did not take him long to return. The United States has neither an Ambassador nor a Minister in Berlin now; but, according to Villalaz, the Chargé d'Affaires is the only representative of the American nations who is respected by the Nazis. Dr. Despradel's interview was very successful. The letter, which I have written, will be sent to Moscow tomorrow in the United States mailbag, accompanied by a letter from the Chargé d'Affaires here in Berlin, asking that the matter be expedited. Surely the answer will not be delayed.

But we are back in Hamburg now. Villalaz was too worried, having me in Berlin. "Wait in Hamburg for the answer from Moscow," he begged me. "There are not so many Spanish officials in Hamburg who might see through the heavy glasses and the bushy mustache." Guardia had business to do here, and so we took an afternoon train, arriving here at eight. The only trouble is, Guardia has to go to Antwerp and I shall have to stay here alone.

January 15th

Guardia left today for Antwerp to take charge of his post. I saw him off on the train. At least he will be able to take news to my family, who have heard nothing from me—but when the train pulled out a feeling of extreme sadness overwhelmed me. I could speak to no one. I could write to no one—not even my wife. There is such comfort in writing. It was intensely cold at the station, but I stood quite a while watching a group of men who were shoveling snow to clear a path for traffic. I envied them. At least when they finished work, they could go to the warmth of their own homes. Self-pity is good for no one, particularly a man fighting for his freedom; so I stopped in a church on my way back to Frau Mikolei's boarding house, where I am staying. My good landlady is not a Nazi, but she has great admiration for the Führer. She believes in astrology and has told me that triumphs await Hitler, but from July 4th of this year onward his star will begin to decline. She says that Hitler is destined to have a disastrous end. She also told me that I look like a man of much luck. As this, in a way, is partly true about me, I am hoping that Frau Mikolei's guesses concerning Hitler are even more accurate.

January 17th

The two lakes at Hamburg are frozen. They have driven a great number of small pines into the ice, which gives the impression of groves. Their purpose is to deprive English airmen of these two guiding spots.

January 22nd

I had a pleasant surprise today. The Consul suddenly arrived at the boarding house. He brought me news of my family: they are well and happy to know about my situation, but worried at the same time. All these circumstances have made this day an unforgettable one. How little it takes to cheer one up!

"Tell me what you have done, for I can assure you I have been worried all these days," the Consul said.

"You see, I have nothing else to do but to write a diary."

"A diary? It looks as if that little book is going to cost us both great unpleasantness. Do you remember the fright of the Venezuelan Minister when you took it out to read the text of the telegram to the Minister of Foreign Affairs of Venezuela? Well, I am also scared. Keep the diary, and tell me all about yourself."

I related the story of the monotonous life I had led, the books I had read, and my meditations, my walks around the lake in the afternoons observing everything, my long sessions at the movies, and my meals in a corner of the restaurant of the Hotel Esplanade, where I do not attract attention.

"You have come in time, as my rationing stamps are almost gone, and the waiters look at me queerly. As we already know, one of the waiters is an informer; so I have resorted to buying *Il Popolo d'Italia* and *Il Lavoro Fascista* and reading them while I eat. I have been able to make them laugh on the sly, instead of looking at me with suspicion. For the laugh Mussolini, and not I, is responsible."

"Is it possible that in such a beautiful city as Hamburg you have led such a boring life?" the Consul, who is in a very good mood today, asked.

"I have also had my little emotional moments. Yesterday I went to have a glass of beer at the Alster Pavilion, to kill time on one of these endless afternoons, and sat in an inconspicuous corner near the door. At that moment two gentlemen came in. One of them carried in his lapel the badge of the Spanish Falange. I was startled when all of a sudden he asked me in German whether the table next to me was free. I answered him in inarticulate sounds. As they started to sit down a friend called them from the other end of the restaurant, and they went there. I breathed easily again, and once more I believed in my mustache and the fact that Alvarez is a perfect creation."

"I am afraid of this kind of meeting. But some day—Listen, tell me. How would you like to come with me to Greece?" said the Consul suddenly.

"To Greece? Why? How?"

"This is a secret I had in store for you. It may be a solution. I shall have to go to Greece on account of some Panamanian ships. You could come as a legal advisor. What do you think?"

"The idea of going through Greece took me by surprise; but, as I have told you many times, I am ready for anything that will take me out of here, and not continue to put you all on a spot."

"I shall call the Minister in Berlin."

The latter answered that we must go to Berlin on Monday.

It is a curious fact that within Germany you can talk freely by telephone to anyone, but all communication is prohibited with foreign countries. On the other hand, in the occupied countries one cannot telephone within or without. In Antwerp, just before I left, one was permitted to telephone, but only inside the city. The occupied countries are nothing but great concentration camps, where people barely exist and die.

January 27th

At eight-thirty this morning we boarded the train for Berlin, where we arrived at three in the afternoon, instead of at twelve-forty. The equipment was old. It gave me the impression that Germany lacks sufficient transportation facilities for the huge movements of its troops. We have seen several military trains passing. In Hamburg we have been informed that they are taking troops to the Eastern front. Would it be to the Balkan countries? We thought of our trip to Greece.

In Berlin we visited the Minister who informed us of his fears. He feels that the trip to Greece must take place immediately. He has been informed that German demands on that country have started and that Greece is remaining firm.

The Minister accepted the suggestion that I go as a legal advisor. He wishes to see me far away, and I agree with him. But he sees many difficulties in obtaining the visa.

"With a note from you to the Greek Consulate, it will be granted," remarked Guardia.

"But why don't you go there without any note from me?"

"Because it will be more difficult," answered the Consul. "Besides, we are all interested in ridding ourselves of Aguirre, and the opportunity for doing so has already presented itself."

In order to erase with dignity the bad effect caused by his indecision, the Minister has invited us to dine at the Kranzler Restaurant, one of the best in Berlin.

To this restaurant go the privileged of fortune. I was astounded to see how our neighbors, two of them army men, ate. They had started with a dozen oysters each, and then devoured enormous lobsters. With this as an hors d'œuvre, accompanied with aqua vitae of good quality, they continued their meal with a consommé and two main dishes, and excellent French wines. My thoughts wandered to Belgium and to the German people, subject to rationing and salaries that do not keep pace with the extraordinarily high cost of living.

The waiter hinted that we avail ourselves of the opportunity, for oysters as well as lobsters were getting scarce. So we ate oysters, consommé, and excellent turkey. We did not lack good wines or French cognac.

"I see you are surprised," commented the Minister.

"I am. It doesn't seem true that in this impoverished Germany such abundance should exist. I knew Germany on two other previous occasions some years ago, and it impressed me as an austere country. Now the madness of war is being lived, or shall I say the fear of a future of want?"

"Here, with money, one can live as in no other place."

"That happens everywhere, Mr. Minister," I replied.

"Rightly so, but here, especially if one has dollars, with the exceptional rate of exchange, living is extremely cheap."

"I would think so with strangers. But do Germans also handle dollars?"

"Those who come to these places probably do. There is such a great quantity of dollars on the market that it is surprising. People probably go about it very carefully, because they are liable to punishment—but there are always favors for many, especially for those who are well placed."

"It is the case of all countries without freedom. When I discovered the fact that the dollar was being exchanged some days ago at the rate of twelve marks instead of 2.40 as marked by the official standard, I realized that those who are wealthy could live here splendidly."

"Twelve marks, and occasionally more. These people have lived well and cannot resign themselves to live badly. That is why I feel that what happened in the last war may repeat itself. As soon as the people felt hunger, no one, for instance, dared to enter the Tusculum Restaurant, which was watched by crowds with hungry eyes."

"In plain language, what a future is in store when the accumulated reserves, the results of having emptied the stocks of Europe, are ended!"

"I know very well this nation has great virtues, but I fear for it. As I have already watched it from the streets in 1918, I can imagine it again rebelling and desperate. Well, what do you have to tell me about the bombardments of Hamburg?" asked the Minister.

"Bombardments? An alarm sounded days ago. There were a few distant explosions, but that was all. Bombings, there were none, at least not in Hamburg."

"But here it was said that half of Hamburg was destroyed. You see? That's another thing—the hoax. And they themselves spread it. These people say the strangest things. Especially here in Berlin, there is much gossip, and the greatest exaggerations are spread. I can assure you that the morale of Berliners will not stand if heavy bombardments take place."

We left the restaurant at eleven. There is total darkness in the streets. We have a comfortable room at the Victoria boarding house in Kurfürsten-Damm, the Champs-Elysées of Berlin.

Tuesday January 28th

I am greatly worried. Today we visited the Venezuelan Minister. Dr. Araujo is leaving Brussels for Venezuela, by orders of the Government. What will my wife and children do in Belgium without their Consul? The Minister has assured me that a solution will be found. He considers them citizens of his country whom he will protect. I wish there were some way of letting Mari know this. She will be nervous when Dr. Araujo leaves. I am troubled for her.

January 29th

Today has been another one of adventure—of near recognition. A narrow escape. I also encountered a man who thought I might be a German spy!

We went to the Greek consulate. The Consul, a very young and kind man, rapidly visaed Guardia's passport because of its diplomatic character, and the binding reciprocity. Then it was my turn. Since he must receive authorization from the Minister of Foreign Relations in Greece, he questioned me thoroughly on the matter of the Panamanian ships. It was a good thing Guardia had told me all the details. But the young Consul regarded me doubtfully.

"With all the rumors that are being spread, a simple note would be necessary; just the seal of the Minister of your country would be enough. It's the present circumstances. Naturally I don't believe Germany has any interest in disturbing our peace; but, after all, so many methods are employed that our government is distrustful." There was no doubt left in my mind. The young man thought I was a Nazi spy! This was the only thing I had not gone through.

"Is there an impending danger of a German attack on Greece?" I counterattacked.

"I don't believe so," he answered. "Why should Germany attack us?"

"Excuse me, Mr. Consul, there are no reasons for any of these acts of aggression committed by Germany—only what suits her convenience. Just as she has attacked so many others, so she will attack you. These men have no moral standards."

I had convinced him. He looked at me with more confidence. "Well then," he said, "I must tell you these moments are extremely grave. But as you say this trip of yours is so necessary, I will send a telegram to Greece, urgently asking for the authorization."

We said goodbye until tomorrow when we will take the note from my Minister. I asked myself: Will the Grecian doors open? How will I get Mari and the children out this way? But we felt quite happy. Guardia said, when we reached the street: "This has been a good morning. We must lunch at the Hotel Eden to celebrate."

The restaurant at the Hotel Eden is very large and elaborate.

While Guardia was still checking his hat and coat, I stood in the doorway, waiting for him and looking over the room—at the people eating and chatting together. As always when we dine in these extravagant places, I am struck with the fantasy of another world, removed from the war, from all suffering or care or conscience; a kind of quick anger against them surges through me. As Guardia joined me, I saw the silhouette of a Spanish deputy, Señor Espinosa de los Monteros. I drew back.

"What's the matter?" Guardia asked.

"Let's take a table behind those columns," I replied.

"Why?"

We sat down. We were well protected by the columns, but at the same time I could see my old opponent. "One of the two men," I told Guardia, "lunching at that table is an old member of the Spanish Cortes, a Monarchist in the service of Franco and a friend of Señor Calvo Sotelo."

"Does he know you?"

"Naturally."

Guardia started to stand. "Let's get out," he said. "It's imprudent to stay here."

"No, I think it is far worse to be coming and going. We are well hidden, and they have not seen us."

Guardia settled in his chair again. "Would he recognize you?"

"I don't think so. The whole life of Alvarez has a psychological aspect which cannot be forgotten. If your own brother came in with big mustaches and heavy glasses, do you think you would recognize him? Probably not—even though you might be haunted by the likeness. You would think: 'Of course it's not my brother. What would my brother be doing in Berlin? How does he happen to be here?'"

"Nevertheless," said Guardia, "I feel we should cross the Eden off our list."

"Anyway it's too expensive," I agreed.

Just as we were being served, Señor Espinosa stood up and, as if attracted by a magnet, started coming toward our table.

"Don't turn around," I said. "But he is coming here."

"Here?"

"Yes." I took a drink of water. "Remember I am Alvarez. You will see also that I am a good actor, for, if he asks if I am anyone else, I am not going to know the gentleman's name."

I was not put to the test, however. Espinosa stopped at another table about fifteen feet away from us. He conversed a long time with the family who sat there—but finally left. We had been eating the rich and expensive food mechanically, as if it were hay or straw. At last he left, and we could breathe easier. We promised each other again never to return to the Eden.

We did not tell the Panamanian Minister of our adventure, since we were asking him for the note demanded by the Greek Consul for soliciting my visa. Both the Consul Guardia and I had to talk quite a while to convince Señor Villalaz of the absolute necessity of the note. At last he dictated it and, considering his fears of involving his country, his action commands my deepest gratitude. I wish I could write to my wife about this new hope.

January 30th

Hitler delivered a speech today. We went into a tea-room in Kurfürsten-Damm the instant he began. It was crowded, and the radio was going full blast. Every establishment is required by law to tune in on all speeches and all official communications. The Consul translated the most important points of the hour-and-a-half speech, but I was more interested in noticing the reactions of the people. There was not a rumor of applause or approbation, not a single enthusiastic gesture. With a cold indifference that only an eyewitness could believe, the public listened. Everyone seemed to say: "Good, that is good! We are agreed that the victories are many— but when will the last one come?"

January 31st

The greatest danger for me here is the Spanish element which goes about Berlin so freely. We took Villalaz's note to the

Greek Consulate. The telegram is being sent to Greece, and now I have only to wait again. But after we left the Consulate we took seats on top of the bus from Unter den Linden to Kurfürsten-Damm. And there was Espinosa, the Spanish Deputy, again, seated in the bus. He was sitting in the last row. We hurried past him to the front of the bus and stayed there until he alighted. Today it was Guardia who reminded me of the psychological aspects of this case. "Remember," he whispered, "you would not expect to find your brother in Berlin . . ."

Saturday February 1st

The restaurant in which we ate today, because it was cheap, is one in which waiters enter into conversation with the patrons.

"Did you listen to our Führer's speech?" the waiter asked us.

"Yes, sir," the Consul answered.

"You are not Germans, are you?" cautiously inquired the waiter.

"No, sir, we are Central Americans."

"Ah, Spanish Americans. . . . What do you think of the speech?"

"And you—how did it impress you?" countered the Consul.

"Very well, as everything our Führer says."

"And the war? . . . How do you believe this war will end?"

"The war is won. It will end this year; the Führer himself has promised it, and he never makes a mistake. These are not the times of the Kaiser. Now the German people are the ones who govern through our Führer."

"And do you believe the people still trust Hitler as they did three years ago?"

"Yes, sir, because Hitler has raised the level of the people. Now castes and inequalities have disappeared; we are all equal."

And getting closer to us, in a very low voice, he said, "Hitler is carrying on the social revolution we had wished for, and in a short time no values or fountains of richness will exist other than those of work. Germany, with its victory, will implant everywhere the benefits of our social revolution. You shall see."

The waiter spoke enthusiastically. He went away proud.

"Did you hear him?" asked the Consul.

"Yes, and it has not taken me by surprise. I knew that the workers, without spiritual resources and subject to ceaseless propaganda, speak that way. What I don't understand is that the cultivated elements should place their hopes in this regime. And I, naturally, don't mean the bourgeoisie and the capitalists, the selfish partisans of any regime of force."

"It is because of the fear of disorder and bolshevism. Also propaganda . . ."

"Of course," I answered, "that is the excuse or the deceit; but they don't realize this is something similar, although working through different channels. Remember what one of our Minister's chauffeurs said to us the other day when we asked him, 'When the war is ended, what do you think victory will achieve here?' 'Here? Communism.' Do not forget also that we have been warned of the fact that he, as well as many of his associates, has never ceased to belong to Communistic organizations."

"Perhaps the sense of order which this nation has will save it. And then, too, freedom."

"I also share the opinion that here, as in the rest of the world, human sentiment will impose itself, for it is not real evolution in the social structure which we must fear, but the disappearance of liberty from the face of the earth. Future social evolution is a reality whose extent we cannot yet foresee, as it is the aching cry of humanity which will not permit, one way or the other, the uncertainty of a future without work and without participation in social benefits, while there is plenty for the privileged ones. But this same natural sense makes humanity unwilling to endure the loss of freedom, for man is born with intelligence and knows that bread alone is not enough, if his spirit is enslaved. The realization of social reforms and the maintenance of freedom is the solution that 90 per cent of the people are eager for. It is for this reason that the German system is incapable of satisfying these desires, as it does not permit freedom to play its part. They do not know it."[2]

"It is a fact," retorted the Consul, "that it is precisely in the social structure that this regime has exerted itself in obtaining results, and has actually obtained them. Now then, in the political, in the human—"

"Naturally, dictatorships with their unbounded power and irresponsible methods can do many good things, actually do them. Otherwise, how could they explain their existence? But of course all this is done at the cost of that which is most precious to man, that which distinguishes him from the beasts—freedom. Don't you think that their desire to appear as the redeemers of society is incompatible with so much blood, so much suffering, and so many concentration camps?"

"You are right, a doctrine must be able to convince, not just impose itself by force."

As I record this conversation, I must say how fortunate I am to have some means of relieving my feelings—otherwise life would be intolerable here.

Sunday February 2nd

I go to Mass. The church is crowded with people. Composure, earnestness are noticeable. All sing with great devotion. It is the only thing they can do. Religious following has been noticeably reduced—very few young men can be seen. Youth is little by little being weaned away from the Church. This is taking place without great physical violence, but with stubborn methods and moral compulsion. The pulpit is being watched. Churches continue to exist, but have no freedom. In the streets priests or members of religious orders are not to be seen in their ecclesiastical garb.

February 3rd

This has been a good day and a bad day—a terrible disappointment and a new hope. Dr. Despradel called me right after he had talked with the Chargé d'Affaires of the United States. I went at once to his office.

"Bad news, Alvarez," he greeted me.

"What's happened?" I asked anxiously.

"The letter you wrote to your British friend Mr. Stevenson in Moscow has been returned. The Embassy of the United States in Moscow said it was too delicate a matter for them to handle without authorization of their government."[3]

I could not believe my ears. I had been waiting with so much hope. I sat down at his desk. There was nothing I could say, but my silence spoke for me.

"Don't torture yourself any more," the Dominican Minister said, "for the American Chargé d'Affaires is a man of great heart, and he said to me, 'Tell Dr. Alvarez that if he happens to have friends in the United States who could help him I will gladly send a letter to them in my mailbag.'"

"Thank God!" I looked up at him. "You have given me courage again. Please convey my extreme gratitude to this American gentleman."

"We agreed," the Minister continued, "that you should write freely. The letter will go in a sealed envelope addressed to the Legation of the Dominican Republic, where my good friend, Señor Pastoriza, our Minister in Washington, will send it to your friends."

I came back to my room. I felt as a man must feel on a raft in the middle of angry seas who suddenly knows that he has been sighted by a passing ship.

February 4th

I wrote the letter to my compatriots in America, addressed to my good friend, the protector of so many hapless ones, Manuel de Inchausti, and delivered it to the American Chargé d'Affaires, who promised to send it in the first mailbag.

February 5th

Guardia went to Hamburg today, since he must finish with his doctor before leaving for Greece—whether alone or with me. Villalaz goes to Switzerland tomorrow. I spent the afternoon in my regular hide-out, the movies. There, in the darkness, I am more comfortable. I have time to think about everything and everyone— Mari and my children, my parents, the problems of my country. I stayed there until evening, when I was due at the Dominican Legation for dinner. Dr. Despradel continues to be my good friend, and does not permit me to remain gloomy for long. I left the Legation at eleven. There is a full moon, and a visit of English planes seems probable.

February 7th

I have been reading Cicero for two days. Doctrines and happenings much alike—those of two thousand years ago and those of today. After lunch I took a stroll through Kurfürsten-Damm with the Dominican Minister. These strolls are a joke. The Minister takes them every day after lunch for about an hour. Being a habitual stroller, he is greeted even by the policemen; and they are starting to look at me, as his companion, with friendly feeling.

["Believe me, my friend Alvarez, that there is a lot of humor in your case. You better get away soon, as you cannot imagine how great is my desire to laugh," the Minister would tell me.

He was a friend of the head of the Spanish Falange in Berlin, who rated all the political men of the Republic as villains and criminals. He would say that the Presidents of the Basque and the Catalonian autonomous countries were two "gunmen with a record" or "thieves."

"Get away, Alvarez. Get away, because I'm biting my tongue. Just imagine when I tell the head of the Falange that I have strolled with you through no less a place than Kurfürsten-Damm. Then I shall ask him about the 'gunmen with a record,' and if he can tell me where they are, that I may shake hands with them."

The Minister would say jestingly that, after knowing the men who had fought in the Spanish War on both sides, he would not trust any one of them unless he were a "gunman with a record."

I shall never forget either the wit of this cultured and excellent friend, his generous heart, or his hospitality.]

February 8th

The Consul, Mr. Guardia, arrived from Hamburg. We ate at a Hungarian restaurant, where there was not a dish or a wine from that country to be found. This is a common thing in this country, where the show windows are filled with articles in which such establishments specialize. The show cases of the tobacco stores are filled with all kinds of tobacco—of grocery stores, with all kinds of provisions; there are shoe stores, luxurious department stores—but nothing can be bought, as all this only exists in the show windows. It impresses me as a nation which does not wish to lose its external grandeur. These people seem to me like children who can easily be caught in their lies. All that is needed is to walk into the stores.

February 9th

As a general rule one does not eat badly in the restaurants. That is, one can eat just enough to live. Food has very little grease. Naturally, German citizens cannot eat in the restaurants, as their ration stamps do not suffice except for eating meat only twice a week, and at very reduced rations. Thanks to the generosity of our Ministers, we can permit ourselves these luxuries. But the German people have for years been leading a life of privation, because they prefer cannons.

Today is the day for a "single course," one of those impositions the object of which is, so they say, to accustom the people to obedience and sacrifice in moral and disciplinary orders. But its practical end is the collection of a certain amount which is added to the charges of the bill, which takes the place of the course that was omitted—omitted against the consumer's will. For instance, today the "single course" in the restaurant in which we ate consisted of a plate of potato soup with a sausage. This soup, which in itself is not worth a mark, had cost us more than three marks each. It is the *plus* that is paid to the state. Just one of the many taxes imposed upon the German people.

After a walk we felt that with the cup of milk—which is not milk— which we had in the morning, and the midday "single course," we needed a little more refueling. When the Dominican Minister, who was strolling along with us, discovered this, he scolded me. "Take notice of the second Sunday of each month," he said to us. "As soon as you see it approaching, take the road that leads to my table, which Hitler has not yet commanded."

To right the wrong, he invited us to supper at the Tusculum Restaurant. It is the best restaurant in Berlin—very Parisian; and, that the imitation might be complete, the *maître* and even the waiters delight in speaking French.

We entered the restaurant with great solemnity to the chords of the Dominican anthem. For this, meals cost the diplomats twenty to thirty marks extra. This is the tip owed the orchestra pianist, who watches carefully for the entrance of the diplomats. He has them catalogued, and as soon as one of them appears at the door—the national anthem.

"Not bad, my dear Minister, from the concentration camp to the Tusculum, and entering to the chords of the Dominican Anthem. Don't you think I am a vivid instance of freshness and luck?"

"Hush, Alvarez, they will have to play the Basque Hymn for you right now. . . . Look here, *maître*—"

"Eh? Watch out, Minister, for I do not wish hymns that announce my death. Some day you will enter my country to the chords of your anthem and mine. But, for today, the Dominican is enough."

February 11th

I like to observe the real life of these people, worthy of a better fate in all its aspects. For contrast, I dined at the Tusculum two days ago, next to diplomacy and *haute bourgeoisie;* then today in a modest restaurant at 1.75 marks a cover. I sat next to humble employees and army men, silent and irreproachable, as a rule decently dressed, despite their clothes showing the cheapness of the material. My attention was called to the fact that, with the established restriction of "one suit a year," people were relatively well dressed, as they were using their best and last suit. This is quite possible, but I judge that they do so because of their natural disposition to decency. I am more in agreement with the one who made this observation to me: "Look, Dr. Alvarez, this is a people of decent poverty." It is obvious that this fact also has its limits. What is happening to my shoes must be happening to theirs. Because of walking so much, my shoes have started to show threatening shreds at their tips. I cannot have them resoled—strangers just stopping here have no right to this, and, should I do it, it would be worse, I was told, because of the very poor material used as a substitute for leather. It follows that what is happening to these Germans' suits will happen to my shoes! I shall have to substitute them with the best I can find. What is worse is that I have only two pairs, and both have ragged edges.

Wednesday February 12th

We spend the days going around. Mornings pass quickly in our room at the boarding house. Today it occurred to Consul Guardia and me to eat at a Chinese restaurant. We have made a promise not to go back there. Chinese food, disfigured with the imposed restrictions, seemed to us double ersatz. It pleased me to see the pictures of Sun Yat-sen and Chiang Kai-shek. There was quite a group of young Chinese gathered there.

During the meal I recalled to my Consul an episode of my exile in Paris which filled me with emotion. A Basque seminarist, exiled from our country for being a patriot, died at the Saint-Sulpice Seminary in Paris, where he had been continuing his studies for the priesthood. His fellow members watched over the dead body during part of the night, but one kept a watch over it all night. He was a Chinese seminarist student. When a group of Basques entered the death chamber they found themselves confronted by a strange and lonely spectacle—a Chinese watching over a dead Basque.

Prompted by curiosity, they asked the reason for such devotion and comradeship. The Chinese student answered: "My comrade was a saint. Besides, he was a Basque patriot who had defended his small country, which asks nothing but its freedom. I belong to a big country which also fights for freedom. The two of us have been attacked in quite opposite places, but by the same spirit of injustice and violence. It is for this that I wanted to do the last homage of admiration and respect to both my comrade and his country. We have understood each other so well! . . ."

[Some of the visitors could not control their emotion and wept. For this reason, recalling the episode of Saint-Sulpice, I have looked with respect and friendliness upon those Chinese students or public officials who ate rice with their chopsticks, lifting the bowl close to their mouths, under the pictures of their two renowned compatriots who some day shall save China—and perhaps civilization, one because he has uplifted his people's spirit, the other because he has placed his sword and intelligence at the service of good and justice.]

In the evening I went to the Opera and saw "Traviata." It was a good performance. Naturally, I had been invited, and went up to the theater accompanied by the Minister of Santo Domingo. In my worn-out shoes and my shiny suit listening to the *brindisi* from a box—no less—I could not but remember another *brindisi* of Iparraguirre, the adventurous Basque singer, also in exile because he aroused his people to freedom, when he sang these stanzas:

Egun batian txiro,	One day poor,
Beste baten jauna,	Another rich,
Onela ibiltzenda	Thus the Basque artist
Artista euzkalduna.	Is wont to live.

February 14th

I have been in Germany a month and a half, and I still don't know how or when I'm going to get out. The Greek visa does not come. I have no word from the United States. Have Inchausti and my friends received the letter, or has still another diplomat considered my case too delicate and returned it? I have heard nothing of my family. I cannot write to them for fear of arousing suspicions—but the worst thing of all is that the permit which the Gestapo granted me in Brussels expires the coming 28th. It terrifies me to think that I might have to return to Belgium. My minister is still in Switzerland. Guardia continues to delay his trip to Greece because of me, and now the news is definite that the war will extend to that zone. I explained all my anxieties to Dr. Despradel this afternoon and, as always, he has understood.

"Everything will be settled," he said, "and there is always my house. No one will take you from here. You have to get away, and you shall get away." He looked at me thoughtfully. "Why haven't we thought of Enrique?" he asked. "He can arrange everything."

"Enrique?"

This man is in the consular service. He was born in the Orient, of German parents, and speaks several languages.

"Yes," the Minister laughed. "I am not fooling you. He is a rascal; but knows every one of these Nazis, and he can accomplish anything. He has friends everywhere, and they always want to help Enrique. I don't know why. He is a friend of a lieutenant colonel, as well as of the Dean of the Cathedral. He will straighten out the whole mess." And Dr. Despradel called the man to his study.

Enrique is a tall and fairly handsome fellow. One can tell at a glance that he can be flattered easily. "Enrique, I have to ask you to do me a favor again," said Dr. Despradel. "You know everyone in Berlin. I want you to get Dr. Alvarez an extension of his permit for staying here. He's a great friend of mine and too occupied now to be bothered with the usual red tape. Should they ask you anything at headquarters, tell them his Minister, Dr. Villalaz, is out of town and it is my great desire that he be well taken care of, without the annoyance of going back and forth."

While my friend spoke, I was studying Enrique's face.

"That's easy, Mr. Minister," the man replied.

"You see, there's nothing impossible for Enrique," retorted Dr. Despradel.

"It's easy," added Enrique, "because the policemen who take care of these things are friends of mine."

"You see, Alvarez. They are friends of his besides. Just imagine the deals this fellow probably makes with the police."

Enrique laughed. He does not know, of course, my real identity. He asked me for my passport and promised that by the next day everything would be arranged. Every time my passport goes to the Gestapo headquarters, I tremble. Since it was drawn up after the Germans entered Belgium, it is subject to questioning at least.

An hour later, Enrique was back with my passport. In order to obtain the extension of time it was necessary to fill out an application form which he gave me.

"But aren't you going to leave Germany, Dr. Alvarez?" he asked.

"I hope that I may."

"Why don't you ask for your departure at the same time?"

I looked up at him. "Do you think I can?"

"Certainly, in the same application."

"But I don't have the visa from Greece yet."

"From Greece?"

"Yes, from Greece," Dr. Despradel answered for me. "Dr. Alvarez is going with Consul Guardia Jaen, on business."

"But I am sure his permit to leave can be obtained without a visa," said Enrique, "and then it will save him time and trouble if we get it now."

"Well," said the Minister, "get it if you can. It is a good idea—but I think you are attempting too much, Enrique."

"Oh, now," said Enrique, satisfied and flattered, "my friends can attend to all of this."

After he had gone, Dr. Despradel and I laughed quite heartily. "If the Gestapo don't ease you out of the country themselves," said the Minister, "their friend, Enrique, will do it for them. You can never tell who will help you, Alvarez. I only hope you leave before I laugh in their faces."

February 15th

Enrique came to my boarding house early this morning, bringing my passport. "We must get a simple document from your landlady, saying that you are to stay here four more weeks, before they will sign the permit for departure," he said. "I asked for the four weeks so that you may obtain the necessary visas. Everything is arranged, and next Tuesday or Wednesday they will expedite the order for departure."

I could scarcely believe my ears. We called the landlady, who wrote out the "simple document" without asking to be paid in advance.

Guardia is getting ready to go to Greece. He obtained the visas from Jugoslavia and Hungary today. There were none for me. Without a visa from Greece, Jugoslavia would not extend hers, and without the latter's there was none to be had from Hungary. My thoughts, my time, my full occupation are all concerned with the unraveling of this senseless red tape.

February 16th

Today the Minister from Venezuela returned from his trip through Switzerland and Italy. He invited us to lunch with him at the Bristol. He spoke a great deal of Italy, where he said the atmosphere is hostile to the regime which has sent them into war.

From Switzerland he brought us the news that King Alfonso XIII of Spain, due to his illness, has abdicated in favor of his son, Don Juan, who has accepted the crown without a throne. It looks as if the Spanish Monarchists cherish a hope.[4]

February 17th

In the morning we were informed that in order to obtain the Greek visa it is necessary to have that of the United States. On the other hand, they advise me to prepare my trip through Sweden, as it will be impossible to go by way of Greece.

The Dominican and Venezuelan Ministers have visited the American Chargé d'Affaires to obtain my visa as well as that of my wife, the latter through the American Consul in Antwerp or Brussels.

The Ministers have been successful in their action as far as I am concerned, for I must go tomorrow to the American Consulate, where I shall be given the visa. However, it is not possible to okay the passport of the Guerra widow—which is my wife's false name—as the Consulates in Belgium have had no authority to grant visas since the first of the year. It looks as though I shall have to leave my wife and children behind, and get away myself by whichever outlet I can. And the permit for leaving Germany? Enrique has not been around these last few days. A bad sign.

When I reached the boarding house, I stumbled upon a dozen young men in the entrance hall, who were waiting to be assigned to their rooms. I asked the servant the nationality of those young men, and I was told they were Russian aviators. Russian aviators? Russian aviators in Berlin?

"Here you have the Hitler-Stalin pact and its consequences," I said to the Consul. "Do you remember how much we had to endure when people insisted on calling us 'Reds,' Communists, and other such names? Here you have me still enduring the consequences, with false passports, with these glasses and mustache, that are already annoying me, and having to live by lies and deceit. Instead, these people have fixed it all with a simple pact. They have visas, the people who are no longer the 'Communist Monster,' nor the others the 'Fascist Beast.' What do you think of it?"[5]

What luck, that of the Soviet aviators! They go in and out of Germany with permits and visas. I must be a perfect idiot.

February 18th

Today at the United States Consulate I found myself confronted with a person who put me through the inquisition I had always expected would come from the Gestapo. The inquisitor was a lady, well along in years. In her desire to be efficient and thorough with her questioning, she succeeded only in making an extremely unpleasant impression on anyone who might meet her. She was thin, small, lean-faced, had iron-gray hair, and wore a look of perpetual disapproval.

All citizens of the American countries have the right to a visa for the United States once they have proved their identity. I did not need many proofs, as my Consul was with me, and anyway the Chargé d'Affaires is in on the secret; but this lady was in charge of questioning those who apply for visas. For Mlle. Inquisitor there were no regulations other than those which she had already received (from the President of her country she would have you believe by her attitude) or any rules she might add herself. The questioning she put me through lasted two and one-half hours. Guardia went into the private office of the Chargé d'Affaires and after an hour came out.

"Great heavens," he interrupted, "are you still at it?"

Mademoiselle looked up at him and said firmly, "It is necessary that I have complete information, and you may as well be patient for I still have many questions to ask this gentleman."

Apparently she had forgotten that she had asked me the same questions many times. "You had better not wait for me," I said to Guardia, in Spanish. "I am going to take care of this woman and answer every one of her questions a thousand times if necessary."

The inquisition went something like this:

MADEMOISELLE: Where have you come from?

ALVAREZ: Belgium.

MADEMOISELLE: Why do you want to go to the United States?

ALVAREZ (thinking to himself, The old fool—who doesn't want to go to the United States?): I am going there only on my way to Panama.

MADEMOISELLE: Why do you want to go to Panama?

ALVAREZ: That's a funny question, mademoiselle. I am going home.

I began to feel amused by the whole thing, and I wondered by what route this lady had reached Berlin. She went on and on, over and over:

"On what boat did you arrive from America? . . . On what date? . . . When did you arrive? . . . Where is the boat?"

Here she was defeated. My lesson for the Gestapo in Brussels had been thoroughly reviewed. I answered: "The boat? The boat is at the bottom of the sea." She stared at me somewhat angrily as if I had personally sunk the ship, and then went back again to the questioning, trying to find some contradictions. I shook my head as I looked at her, typing furiously on her machine. "You can't win, my good woman, you can't defeat me." She even asked me questions about my "business in America." I answered. Guardia and the United States Vice Consul came in. They were both annoyed with the old spinster and the Vice Consul said: "Haven't you finished yet? I beg you to end it soon." But Mademoiselle Inquisitor resented the intrusion into her little world and went right on questioning.

She asked me the names of my partners in America. I answered. When my Consul, Guardia, overheard me giving names and explaining my business, he became alarmed and said in Spanish to me: "You don't have to answer all those questions. Don't give her that information."

Mademoiselle was looking at us. We knew that she did not understand Spanish, so we were not being indiscreet to speak so freely in front of her.

"If I don't, I am afraid we will start all over again," I replied to Guardia. "I will exhaust her in the end—don't worry."

At that moment, she turned to her typewriter, put another sheet of paper in the machine and asked me crisply, "Which way are you leaving?"

"Sweden, but it is probable that I shall go through Greece."

"And why don't you go via Lisbon?"

"Because, mademoiselle, I have matters to take care of in those two countries."

"In Greece also?"

"Yes, mademoiselle. You may ask the Greek Consul. He has not yet received my visa, though I asked for it many days ago."

"Then you will leave by way of the north, by Petsamo?"

"Most surely."

"And on what date will the boat leave?"

"When the company gives the order. You know that there are no fixed sailing dates."

"But we must know."

"In that case, mademoiselle, please inquire, as I am not a prophet," I replied somewhat curtly, as we had been over all of it so many times. She was finally worn out. She led me to the room where they took my height and weight. The Vice Consul was waiting, somewhat impatiently.

"It's the times," he said to me, smiling while he signed the visa. I also smiled, and we said goodbye cordially. Mademoiselle Inquisitor glanced at me, still with suspicion and disapproval in her eyes. Pity him who might lose his temper with her!

February 19th

Guardia leaves for Greece today. He cannot wait for me any longer. We are still fighting for the visas. We go to the Swedish Consulate. They will not give us a visa there, unless we have one from Finland, as ships for the United States sail from Petsamo. We go to the Finnish Consulate. Here they tell me they must send the application to Helsinki. They all ask the same question: "Why don't you cross Spain and go via Lisbon? It's the simplest route and the least dangerous." Again I had to place the needle on the record and repeat the old song of "my affairs, my business."

As I have done on other occasions, I slowly walked over to cry on my good Dominican Minister's shoulder.

"My dear Alvarez, I want to introduce you to my wife, who has just arrived from Switzerland with my daughter," said the Minister, introducing me to his wife.

Naturally, the conversation revolved around my person, my family, my business. The Minister talked in my stead, as my accent showed, in spite of my efforts, that I was not a real Latin American.

"You speak like a Madrilenian or perhaps like an Andalusian," said the Minister's very kind wife.

"Yes, you see I was educated in Spain, and naturally, with the years, one loses a bit of the American accent."

"Ah, of course, now I understand."

"Alvarez is a great friend of mine," said the Minister. "He is a doctor, a big businessman, has a shipping business, owns lands. Well, he is a very important man."

"Not really, Mr. Minister, not really," I would answer, feigning bashfulness and even modesty.

When we were alone the Minister said to me: "My wife is a very good woman. I shall tell her the truth about you, and I am sure she will have the same affection for you that we all have."

February 20th

Enrique came today and told me that my permit to leave Germany will not be expedited until certain negotiations through the Ministry of the Interior are ended. As my actual permit is for entering Germany and returning to Belgium, it is necessary to get the approval of the Belgian authorities. In short, more days of waiting.

"And what if there is no answer from Brussels by the 28th?" I asked Enrique.

"You remain here, of course," he said. "I can arrange it for you— besides, you have your own Minister."

"Yes, but I would be grateful if you obtained the permit before the 28th. My Minister is in Switzerland now."

Enrique left somewhat bewildered by the fact that a man who was eating lunch and dinner almost daily at the Legations would have to resort to him for help.

I went for a long walk and then to a movie.[6]

February 25th

The walks I have taken on these lonely days have worn out my shoes. This morning I carefully trimmed them as their raveled edges might catch the eye of a policeman or a hotel waiter, who might then become suspicious of Dr. Alvarez. In the afternoon, as a contrast, I went with Dr. Despradel to his tailor, where he was fitted to a new dress coat. The Minister was in good humor and he asked the tailor if the cloth was made from wood. The tailor pledged his word that the material was excellent. "You can't buy material like this," the tailor said. "I use it only for my most exclusive clients."

The Dominican Minister replied that as spring was nearing, he would not like to attend a reception of Hitler's with shrubs and blossoms growing from his sleeves. The German did not get the joke until some time after, and then he laughed uproariously for a full half-hour. We left the tailor's and drove in the Minister's car back to the Legation.

"My friend Alvarez," Dr. Despradel said suddenly, "your shoes are completely worn."

"I am more worried over the extension of my stay here, which ends on the 28th, than I am about my shoes," I answered.

"Three days from now? I must get after Enrique. He must get that extension no matter how. Finally, Villalaz must ask for it—if not, I shall myself, even though my intervention may seem strange."

"A return to Belgium would be a terrible thing for me and for my family."

"That cannot be, and it shall not be," answered the Minister.

In spite of his assurances, I cannot get over the nightmare of a possible return. I cannot sleep. With the light turned off I immediately feel as if I were boarding the train, and, half awake and half asleep, I dream of crossing those borders again—this time going in the wrong direction; and in my ears I hear the laughter of those Germans on the train, who said: "Panamanian, eh? Ha! ha! ha! ha!"

February 27th

Notwithstanding his many occupations in these last days the Dominican Minister has not forgotten my difficult situation. He telephoned me this morning.

"Alvarez," he said, "the extension has been obtained for four more weeks. Therefore do not worry about tomorrow's date. Enrique is on the way there now with your passport duly sealed."

"A thousand thanks, Mr. Minister, a thousand thanks."

"I still have more news for you. The Minister from Venezuela, who has real affection for you all, has just told me that he has now written to the Consul Araujo, in order that he obtain without delay the exit permit from Belgium for the widow Mrs. Guerra and her two children. Are you satisfied?"

"Extremely satisfied, thank you."

I wanted to go into a church and thank God for his protection; but it was closed, just as it was yesterday: Ash Wednesday, the day on which I wished to comply with this pious rite, reminder of our misery—*pulvis eris,* as my shoes—and could not do it. How I missed those churches of my Basque country, always open for worship when we, the "undesirables," ruled! Amongst those who helped Franco, "defender of Christian civilization," I find they are closed almost every day.

March 2nd

When today I went to the Dominican Legation, the Minister's wife received me with demonstrations of true friendship.

"Well, hello, hello, Alvarez. That's right? Alvarez?"

"Yes, madam, Alvarez."

"Roberto has already told me everything. What things happen! But, don't worry, we shall do everything for you, everything we can. Only be careful with Rosario, who is very good but (being a woman, you know) a bit curious, and may wish to know more than she should. It wouldn't be advisable."

Rosario is a secretary at the Legation. She sits at the Minister's table and observes a lot. Today is the Minister's birthday, and I have been specially invited by his wife, after she had been informed of the whole story. The Minister told me a German friend of his, a high technician in an important firm engaged in the construction of traction vehicles, automobiles, and tanks, was coming also.

"He is a very interesting and competent fellow. You will see. We shall try to get his opinion on the trend of the war."

The technician arrived in the evening. He speaks several languages, among them Spanish. He is a very agreeable person—and a very polite one—who has traveled widely. A very special friendship exists between him and the Minister. I am introduced as an American, a trusted friend of the family. After the generalities prescribed by the rules of good manners, the conversation drifted to Italy, and Mussolini's recent speech.

"All the hopes of this man lie in Germany," commented the Minister. "A sad situation, that of Italy, to judge at least from Mussolini's last speech."

"If it were only that . . ." added the technician.

"Is Italy's situation bad?" asked the Minister.

"It is a country of deceit. It might have been better for us to be alone."

"But I know that they still eat well, that they still—"

"Yes, but I am not referring to food. That is not a matter on which I am well informed. But with regard to the construction of war matériel, which is the thing that interests me, the present Italian situation constitutes a grave burden for us."

"What a lack of foresight . . . In this way they enter the war?"

"Imagine the condition in which they must have entered, when, within a year, they have exhausted all their supply of steel. They have nothing. We had to send them matériel in moments of such intense need as are these. Would to God that they had remained quiet."

"Yes, but don't you believe that after all it is better that Italy be on your side than with your opponents?" I asked.

"To tell the truth, I don't know. That is a problem for military experts, but I feel that that would have been solved in a few days, as in the case of France."

"Ah, the case of France; that has been baffling."

"Colossal," answered the technician with great satisfaction.

We kept on talking of the German armies' victories. The conversation revolved around the future. "Do you believe this will be a long war?"

"No, very short."

"What do you call short? A year? Two?"

"No, nothing like that. The war must be ended this summer."

"This summer?" both the Minister and I cut in. "How can it be possible in so short a time?"

"Because it is absolutely necessary for all kinds of reasons."

"But do you believe that Great Britain—that is, the British Empire—and America, as a last resource, can fall so rapidly?"

"How, I don't know, but I am certain that our Führer will end the war this summer. Naturally, England has to be overpowered. You speak of America? We know that America is neither prepared nor will be in a long time. For this reason she will not arrive in time to impede the defeat of England."

"You said that it is necessary to win the war this summer, didn't you? For what reasons?"

The technician smiled and said, "You are very curious."

"And if the war does not end this summer?"

The technician glanced at us with a worried look. Then he said, "*If the Führer does not end the war this summer, we have definitely lost it.*"

The Minister and I exchanged glances of wonder and contentment. We had spoken so often about the impossibility of the Axis defeating the democracies with rapidity.

The conversation then drifted into a more intimate vein, about the Führer's person, the ability of the German people to endure their discipline, and about the attraction all military things have for them.

"I must tell you that I am not a partisan of National Socialism. I feel that it would be harmful to the German people. I admire the Führer because he has saved our honor, and is a man of great talent; but I fear him. Do you know why? Because Hitler has not traveled abroad. He does not know that in the other countries there are also good things, some of them superior to those of our nation. It is a pity he has not had the opportunity to know the countries which I have known."

"This admiration for the Führer in contrast to the fear of his future work is very queer," I said.

"It is something very much our own, which is difficult for you to understand," replied the German engineer. "You watch marching through one of these streets—military formations with their music ahead—and think of German militarism and, in these times, of Nazi domination. Well, I feel with such emotion that, in spite of not being a young man, I would follow the colors and that music. It is something that draws one. For this reason, do not be surprised to hear me speak of the Führer with enthusiasm, when in him I see the leader. When I start reflecting and repress my enthusiasm, then I think of the dangers which await us, and even of the adventure in which we are now engaged."

"Quaint contradiction not easy to understand until we realize the special education to which this nation is being subjected. Do you believe that this happens to every German?"

"To the majority. A flag and a marching formation attract us in such a way that few of us are capable of resisting its emotional influence. But I must tell you more, and it will seem stranger still. Military marching has such an influence on us that there is where the grave danger lies. You have seen many young men march off behind their flag. Well, if that flag is substituted by another, and the pace is continued, and the music plays, I am sure that the formation would continue its march."

"But that is incomprehensible—"

"To you, yes; to us, no. Here is rooted a great danger that worries many of us who have witnessed the queerest changes in this nation."

The engineer, worried, was looking down at the floor.

"This means that some day things may change radically, to judge from what you have just told us," we replied.

"I hope that the Führer finishes the war this summer. If he doesn't, anything is possible."

The conversation went on to other subjects, and in the end this man said goodbye to us—faithful to his trust, without giving us figures of production or any other interesting details, but saying enough to make me remark to the Minister: "This man's statements are grave. There is something in the inmost recesses of these people which can suddenly transform them."

"In my opinion," said the Minister, "these people meet with great difficulties in production. They see with fear the prolongation of the conflict."

"The doubts of intelligent men whom I keep coming across leave me perplexed. Do you recall the episode of the naval officer whom I met upon entering Germany? . . . A people whose leaders doubt is not a people destined for victory. . . ."

March 4th

The Minister from Panama invited me to coffee at his home. While I was there a gentleman came in, irreproachably dressed, a stranger to me. The Minister told me the secret of his identity. He was an Austrian clergyman whom the Apostolic Nuncio in Berlin had sent. After a long conversation he left, looking suspiciously on all sides.

"Can you imagine that? These Germans have gone crazy. This Austrian clergyman comes by order of the Nuncio to beg me to grant the greatest possible number of visas immediately," said the Minister.

"Who are the visas for?"

"For the most prominent heads of the party and of Catholic organizations. Also for several ecclesiastical ministers. They are taking these people to concentration camps for the least motive, and the situation is so grave that they ask me for these visas, for they are afraid they may not be able to save distinguished persons belonging to these organizations, who are waiting for their turn, in time."

"This shouldn't surprise anyone. Now it's the Catholics' turn as yesterday it was the Jews'. . . . Tomorrow—"

"Don't speak of the Jews."

"Why? What's happened?"

"This morning a prominent leader of the S.S. came to this office. He told me of the situation of the Jews in the sort of Ghetto which they have created in Warsaw, where they are living like beasts. They cast their food over the wall of the enclosure . . . Well, it's something disgraceful—so disgraceful that he said: 'As a German, I am ashamed. We are going to such extremes that it will bring a curse upon us.' "

March 6th

It's my birthday today. Thirty-seven years old. In the midst of the sadness which I feel on spending this day far from the ones I love and in such a dangerous situation, there is something that comforts me, brings me hope. In the beginning I thought of not letting my friends, the Ministers, know about today, but I finally decided to invite them for dinner tonight, as I am indebted to them for their repeated kindness. I have invited them to no less a place than the Tusculum. My purse has suffered a serious loss, but I feel satisfied, although when I paid the bill my friends looked at me with deep pity.

The one who unbalanced my calculations was the pianist who played the hymns. Three Ministers came with me, and the respective hymns had been played. The pianist even asked whether I also was a Minister. Judging from this, I must not have looked too ragged to him.

March 7th

Another narrow escape. I went down Kurfürsten-Damm around 11:30 in the morning with the Minister and Guardia, who were going to make reservations for their trip to Holland. We were talking about my wife and children when I saw him coming toward us—Jacinto Miquelarena, a man from my home city of Bilbao. He was walking slowly—how often I had seen that same walk before. He glanced at us as he passed, grazing my arm. I wanted to look back, but dared not. Finally I turned. He had not recognized me—or had he? My friends were still talking to me, and I did not hear what they said. I waited until we reached the small square where Kurfürsten-Damm ends, and then I told them, "I have just gone through the worst moment of my whole journey."

"What happened?" they both asked in one voice.

"Miquelarena, who I believe is now head editor of the Madrid *ABC*, has just walked by. His arm brushed my arm. I don't know if he studied my face as he passed or not. He looked at all of us."

"Does he know you?" inquired one Minister.

"Does he know me! He was editor of one of our Bilbao newspapers. He went with the others. He is now in Madrid serving Franco and the Falange. A year and a half ago this same Miquelarena wrote a shameful article for *La Nación* of Buenos Aires, in which he related a conversation I supposedly had with M. Ibarnegaray, a Minister in the first French Cabinet of Maréchal Pétain. You can guess the validity of his article when I tell you that I have never met Ibarnegaray or spoken to him in my whole life."

"If he recognized you, do you think he will go to the authorities? A fellow like that—"

I shook my head. "I don't know," I told them.

But I am worried. We reassured ourselves that the mustache and glasses of Dr. Alvarez would fool anyone—but I am not too sure. Miquelarena has looked into my face so many times. I must go about Berlin more carefully; and yet, if I think calmly, I am sure he could not have known me.

March 12th

When those few who know my true identity fail me because of their absence, my life fades away into a terrible loneliness.[7]

At one in the morning the siren with its sad call awakened us. "Well, thank God it seems that the English are here," I said, getting out of bed. The tenants are told by telephone that they must go down to the shelter. Disobedience is punished. Those found in the streets are obliged to go to the nearest shelter. I faithfully obeyed instructions and descended. There all the tenants in the house met. The one in command fulfilled his duty—he came in and out, showing the way in an authoritative manner. The shelters are generally an interesting place for observing things.

This one, as many others which I have seen, was a moral antidote against panic. Nearly all constructions protect, solid ones much more than others; but, unfortunately, the majority of private homes, including ours, are deficient. In all probability a time-bomb of more than one hundred pounds would have destroyed all our illusions of protection.

As always, here also came forth the "technician" who explained to the others the impossibility of the English reaching Berlin. The discharges of the anti-aircraft guns could be heard at quite some distance, at least twenty miles. He would say that this was of little importance. A man of good appearance, with his characteristically close haircut and red cheeks, he was the one who enlivened that inexperienced audience. The first half hour went by amid the jokes of the "technician" about the English which greatly amused the others.

Suddenly the harsh prolonged crack was heard, characteristic of the almost simultaneous explosions of a string of bombs. It may have been at a distance of a mile and a half. Immediately the anti-aircraft guns reported back, especially those of the battery situated at about one hundred meters from our house. The crashing of the anti-aircraft guns produced in my companions an electrifying effect which I had witnessed many times before.

Several companions at the shelter, among them the "technician," flung themselves on the floor. When the scare was over, his explanations had completely ceased, and several sarcastic smiles could be seen. The "technician" had lost his authority.

Between lost sleep, the failure of his predictions, and the reality of the Berlin bombardment, people left greatly worried, judging from their eyes, which showed fear. The fact was that there crumbled another of the fables of German propaganda: the impregnability of German skies. People started to realize that this time the war will develop over the Berlin rooftops also.

I do not share the common opinion that the day the democracies have double the amount of planes they will have won the war. *No— they and we all shall have to win by landing on the Continent.*[8]

Tonight's bombing was not intense, to tell the truth; but it nevertheless made a deep impression on my German companions in the shelter. And I believe on all the rest of the people.

March 13th

Villalaz has returned from Belgium, but was unable to bring my wife and children. In spite of their Venezuelan passports the German permit was not granted. Another wait, and I am in the depths of despair and loneliness.

March 14th

The funeral services for Alfonso XIII took place today at the Catholic Cathedral on Unter den Linden. The whole Diplomatic Corps was invited. The funeral was arranged by the Spanish Embassy.

"I'll bet you wouldn't dare go to the funeral tomorrow," the Dominican Minister said to me yesterday.

"No, I don't dare. Do you not see that there will be many people who could recognize me?"

"But who would ever imagine you could be in Berlin at the funeral services of Alfonso XIII? Besides, you would be able to see the leader of the Falange who will be there, the officials of the consulates and the Spanish Embassy, so that later on you could guard yourself from them, should you meet them on your way."

The Minister was laughing, thinking how funny my being there would be, but never imagining that it would occur to me to go.

After saying goodbye to the Minister I thought it over very carefully. In spite of the offenses received by my people from the exiled monarch, the seriousness of the religious act which was to be celebrated inspired great respect in me. But my curiosity to see so many persons, whom I wanted to know by sight, and also an inclination to play a joke on my friends, the Ministers, and perhaps give them a scare, made me decide to go.

Therefore, I went to the funeral services of Alfonso XIII. At the bus stop near my boarding house, a young girl came up wearing a red beret, the Basque beret.[9] Shortly after, another girl came. I discreetly withdrew until the bus arrived. We all got in it, and I sat in front of the girls on the top part of the bus. They soon started talking.

"This poor man has finally died," said one of the girls.

"Yes, and away from his country. Do you believe it is better that the King be restored?"

"I don't know—it doesn't matter much to me."

"That is what those of the Falange say who are not keen about the Monarchy. It doesn't matter much to me either."

"But people are not satisfied with the Falange either. They say so much against it—"

"That's just it, no one is satisfied. It looked as if after the war things would go better, but it's just the opposite."

"My dear, I don't understand much about these things, but everyone speaks unfavorably about what is going on."

"And many are so disgusted that they say they will start another war in order to implant in Spain that which should have triumphed."

"Monarchy?"

"I don't know. I don't know what they want."

"Neither do I, for each time I understand less about these things."

I thought to myself, "And for this Franco has carried out a rebellion which has cost more than one million lives and has ruined the whole country?"

I reached the Cathedral with great precautions. I saw that the two girls with the red berets joined another small group of young people of both sexes, who were waiting at the church door. From a discreet distance I observed the movements, and entered the church from a side door. The church is small, and the whole thing resembled a spacious rotunda of the structure of a decadent Byzantine basilica.

In the chancel was the Spanish Ambassador, General Espinosa de los Monteros, in his uniform of a Spanish general; behind him were two German prelates. In the pews of honor to the left sat a representative of the Führer in his uniform of a German general, and other high officials dressed in the uniforms of the diplomats in the service of von Ribbentrop. In the pews to the right appeared the Diplomatic

Corps in Berlin—among them, my friends. There were not more than fifty other people in the church. I sat in one of the last pews. Two Spanish policemen who serve at the Embassy were my neighbors. I wondered if they classified me as a Monarchist or a Falangist—or perhaps a suspicious element? They must have known the fifty others who were there.

Then the Berlin Falange force of five men and six women made an entrance in perfect formation and at a slow pace. The leader was the best dressed of them all, wearing a white military jacket. I ask myself why these little totalitarian leaders so dearly love to wear white military jackets. Today it was cold. The four Falangists who came in at the last stood at the sides of the casket, which was placed in the center of the church.

When the funeral services were over I went out quickly and stood at the door amid the group of curious onlookers, who came near as soon as they saw so many uniforms. I saw my friends, the Ministers, come out to their car. I did not step forward and speak to them because I was afraid they might be too startled at seeing me there. Later in the evening when I told them I was next to them at the funeral, they did not believe it—until I began giving them all the details. My namesake, José Aguirre, who was a good boy when I knew him in Madrid, passed me closely as he went to his car.

[But tonight, as I recall all the incidents of the day, the one thing I remember most clearly and bitterly is the dishonored Basque beret. The beret has always stood for freedom and democracy, and never oppression. With berets like these on their heads, thousands of young men have died defending liberty.]

March 16th

I spend many agreeable evenings listening to the radio at the Santo Domingo Legation. I am very much amused, for when the Minister, his wife, and I are alone her feelings as a wife and mother make her ask a thousand questions about my own wife and children.

"I assure you," she said to me this evening, "that, as I learn more of Franco's doings, I like him less—and above all what you are going through now. It's too terrible."

"You see," the Minister said, "I knew that some day I would hear you say that about Franco. You women were fooled so much!"

The sincerity of Doña Isabelita—as she is called—is on a par with her generosity; but when a person joins us who is not in on my secret the conversation and the scene changes deftly.

Just as Dr. Despradel finished his comment, Enrique came in to say that my permit will be expedited. I thanked him, and he left. "He has brought me the same news so many times," I said to my friends. And the Minister's wife promised me she will begin a novena to the miraculous Virgin of La Altagracia in Santo Domingo who is all-powerful. "You are very kind," I smiled at her.

"One novena is very little," the Minister continued, teasing his wife. "You have to make at least ten."

"Why ten?" she asked.

"In order to right the wrong done to the Virgin when you made the novenas in favor of Franco."

Doña Isabelita laughed. She has a wonderful disposition.

March 20th

Today the Police telephoned for me. I was really frightened and looked for a way out. I can tell the prolonged stay here has begun to take its toll on my nerves. The Legation phoned the police headquarters, and they say tomorrow will do just as well. Dr. Despradel has advised me not to go at all. Enrique will go for me.

March 21st

Enrique went to the Police. He came back and told me that my permit for leaving will be granted through any frontier but the Swedish or the Russian.

"The police say that the Spanish frontier is the best now, and the trip is better via Lisbon anyway. They will grant this permit immediately if you apply for it."

Looking at him, I wondered if this was the game they were determined to play with me. Do they know who I am, and are they waiting to exhaust me?

"That's all right," Despradel told Enrique; "but Dr. Alvarez has many matters to look after in Sweden, and he has no errand at all in Spain or Portugal. Here he is so near to Sweden where he must go: why can't he get there?"

Enrique looked adamant, almost like a member of the Gestapo—or was my imagination working overtime?

"At the police station I was told that no one leaves through the Swedish or Russian frontier—not even with the Führer's permission," Enrique finished dramatically.

"Why do you look as if you know so much?" asked the Minister. "What is going on then? What's the matter?"

As usual, Dr. Despradel knew when to flatter Enrique, who immediately assumed the manner of a person well connected and informed. "There are strong troop mobilizations near the Russian frontier," he said. "Exactly what is happening, I don't know; but it's serious. I believe that war with Russia is a matter of a few hours. But," he added, "it will be over within six weeks."

We had no answer for him, and he left us, completely self-possessed.

March 23rd

I have no patience left. Walking through the streets of Berlin is nothing more than pacing the floor of a prison cell. I feel myself at the breaking point when I know that I must remain intact and calm and clear-thinking.[10] Dr. Despradel has proposed my fleeing to Switzerland. I could do it hiding in his spacious automobile, which is never searched. Once in Switzerland things could be adjusted. I can see the flight to Switzerland, but once there—

where do I go? Dr. Despradel pointed out that I should be safer there, and, with this new feeling of uneasiness which I have almost constantly, I agreed with him. He is going to Switzerland in a few days, and he will see then how matters might be arranged. We said goodbye to Dr. Zerrega, who is flying to Spain. He will return within a week.

March 26th

After saying goodbye to that protecting shadow the Dominican Minister, who is now on his way to Switzerland, I boarded Bus No. 1, which took me to Unter den Linden. There I witnessed the preparations for the reception which was given the Japanese Minister Matsuoka this same afternoon. Thousands of yards of material in Nazi, Italian, and Japanese colors—an abundance of S.S. formations which filed off to their respective places—thousands of persons carrying the flags of these countries—and in general a spectacular mobilization *en masse* mark this day, which represents the completion of the *Anti-Komintern* Pact in full, behind Russia's back.

It looks as if the hour for decisions is nearing. We heard over the radio that Russia, according to American news, is to sign the Tripartite Pact.

Viewing in my solitary stroll such multitudes and so many unfurled flags—all for propaganda—I thought that truly the Germans are unique in these spectacular exhibitions.

March 27th

Again I am completely alone. All my friends are away. There are festivities in Berlin in honor of the Japanese Minister's arrival. Instinctively, I headed toward the avenues where the Monument to Victory is located. Later on I returned to Unter den Linden, and a short time after taking this direction I saw the Japanese Minister preceded and followed by a big retinue. He rode with

General Oshima, a friend of the Axis. They were headed toward the new Chancellery, residence of the Führer, for an interview with the latter. I did not wish to miss such an opportunity, and feeling myself a part of this crowd of men and women of the populace who went running in that direction, I intermingled with them and reached the streets that overlook the Chancellery.

I had to push my way through steadily, and managed to place myself at a distance of less than thirty yards away from the famous balcony at which Hitler shows himself when he receives the homage of his followers. I was in the first row. The great square in front of the Chancellery was reserved and occupied by the Assault Formations, made up of men in shirt sleeves. I mention this detail, as it was terribly cold. I admired those young men who for several hours stood steadfastly, even though their faces showed the cold which they were enduring for their Führer—or is it by their own choice?

More than two and one-half hours I waited, jammed in that crowd—there were many thousands there—for the Führer and Matsuoka to come out on the balcony as was announced from time to time. Meanwhile—the conference was getting to be very long—the assembled troops sang in order to try to keep warm; and so that we would duly show our enthusiasm some S.S. motorists were distributing small banners with the swastika and the rising sun displayed on them. Noticing that everybody was carrying the two flags, I did not wish to seem "unpatriotic," so I received the two small banners from a corpulent S.S.

I had never dreamed to find myself in such a spectacle, for right where I was were to be found fanatics of the Party, to judge from the shouts with which they answered the demonstrations. Here I was ignorant of Nazi customs, a thing which must have been noticed, as several of my neighbors glanced at me many times, undoubtedly because of the difference with which the sounds were uttered. Finally, I also shouted (which is not a difficult thing to do) and lifted the two banners energetically. They looked at me with pleasure. It was thrilling to be there, as I happen to have a very powerful voice.

At last the Führer and Matsuoka came out on the balcony. Göring and Oshima were accompanying them. It was difficult to see von Ribbentrop, who was standing back a bit.

I had never before received such a comical impression. I was remembering that one American diplomat said that this meeting was between the Bukovine gypsy and the "Asiatic monkey." The contrast was so great between this short and ugly-looking man and his companions, that I cannot understand the shouts and cheers of these racial champions, who pride themselves on animal selection. Scrutinizing facts, it seemed more logical that they should have sacrificed him instead on that very balcony.

March 29th

The small restaurant where I have lunch and supper when I am alone—as I am now—is very secluded. It is for this reason that I chose it. But on Saturday nights it boasts a little orchestra, and then it is full of people. There is also dancing in some of the upper floors on these nights. It is a wonderful observation place, full of loving couples. From seven-thirty to ten-thirty I do not stop reading the papers or looking at this youth full of the desire to live and to pretend. Everyone smokes, everyone drinks, but everything is ersatz. Whenever tobacco can be found—now if they give any at all it is only a pack of ten cigarettes—it is anything but tobacco. But one smokes. Cocktails are being drunk, which are not cocktails, but people have the illusion that they are drinking cocktails. This consumption is as a general rule modest. What is not lacking is beer, even though connoisseurs say that its quality is not what it used to be. We had a surprise today. A collector for the Winter Relief Fund came in suddenly and compelled everyone to keep silent. She practically whistled instead of speaking, as quite a few of her teeth were missing, but she had spoken her first words so energetically that the hall was silent. Then she delivered a violent speech against those who waste their time in such places, squandering money that might well go to the Winter Relief Fund. Out came the restaurant owners, but dared not oppose such a spirited speaker. On the contrary, she pompously announced that she was to give three loud "Heil Hitlers" and then pass around her money box from table to table. We all chorused the three "Heils" and gave her a "voluntary" donation. No one failed to comply with the "request," fearing that the speech be repeated at each table. I spent quite an amusing time thinking of how far a nation can go in which everyone could believe himself a Hitler, or at least an emanation of his spirit.

March 31st

I strolled for about three and a half hours today through the outskirts of Berlin where workers live. The same spectacle was to be found here as in any other place—unfriendly faces. I had an opportunity to listen to the deep opposition to the regime among strong groups of the working classes, but I am not a man who believes in affirmations that are void of proof. I feel that these people who are good, as all peoples are at heart, may be led very easily. Hitler knew how to link two fundamental ideas in his effort: one, the necessity of revindicating German national honor internationally; and the other, the implantation of socialism in the name of the German people. To call the Hitlerian regime bourgeois is one great error which only stupid propaganda can carry through. Hence, I could believe what I have heard from persons who know the German people, and also from personal observation, that Hitler's popularity has been great, and that even now more than half of the people are on his side. There is where danger lies, for a people who are aroused by doctrines that deny human dignity and fail to recognize other people's rights, and come to the point of accepting these doctrines as natural on account of a confusing and deforming spiritual process, constitute a greater problem than the futile motives of a misleading propaganda.

The moment these people realize that a force superior to theirs will reach Berlin with decision and energy to announce to them that the advocates of freedom—the worthiest thing for men and society—are superior to those who wish to crush it, then the hour will have sounded for common sense on the part of the German people. For one hundred years of antisocial philosophy and teachings cannot be destroyed with speeches or promises. Realities are needed, such realities as can actually be seen.

April 2nd

I am sitting on top of the world today.[11] My friends in America received the letter which the generous American Chargé d'Affaires here in Berlin sent to Washington in his private mailbag. The Dominican Minister in Washington, Señor Pastoriza, has addressed a letter to Dr. Despradel, acknowledging receipt of my letter and stating that my instructions will be followed. At last I am in touch with my own people; and, being in touch with them, I know that we will get free. Dr. Despradel invited me to dine at the Legation; and, to celebrate the good news, a bottle of Burgundy was opened. I came home happy and laughing to myself, thinking of my friends' astonishment when they started reading my letter: "Although it may surprise you," I had begun that letter, "I am writing to you from Berlin . . ."

April 3rd

Whenever I am too happy on one day, something unforeseen happens the next. Today I went to an ear specialist to have him open my ear, which has been bothering me these last days. He asked what was my nationality, and I answered that I was a Panamanian.

"Repeat whatever I say," he instructed me, as he began testing to see if my deafness had disappeared. "Barcelona."

"Barcelona," I repeated very suspiciously.

"Bilbao," he then said.

I jumped and repeated, "Bilbao."

"What's the matter with you?" the doctor asked.

"Nothing, doctor, just a slight contraction."

Who was this doctor? Was I seeing the Gestapo through my glasses?

When I reached the Legation, Dr. Despradel laughed. "Oh, he's a good fellow," he said. "He's attended the American Legations quite a few years now and he's really a fine doctor." Then he added, "For all your nervousness, you are in a better mood than we are."

"What's happened?" I asked.

"All the American Ministers are going crazy with the notes we must present to the Department of Foreign Relations because of all the sabotage German Navy men are doing to their ships stationed at our ports."

I beamed at him. "And you are angry because of that?"

"No—no, we are not angry. We are apprehensive. This road leads to the concentration camp."

April 4th

This afternoon Dr. Despradel asked me to ride with him to pick up his daughter at school. We were talking inside his car, waiting for the child at the school door, when a man put his arm through the window and said, in perfect Spanish, "My dear Minister, what have you been doing all this time that we haven't seen you?"

I did not recognize the man's face. Dr. Despradel was caught off guard for a moment. He stuttered a bit about his work and then, well poised again, he introduced us: "Dr. Alvarez from Panama, meet Dr. Navarro, the Consul of Spain in Berlin."

"I am highly honored to meet you, Mr. Consul," said Dr. Alvarez.

"Are you returning soon to America, doctor?" the Consul inquired.

"I hope so," answered Dr. Alvarez, not too anxiously, "as soon as possible."

Dr. Despradel took the conversation in hand at this point and asked the Consul, "Did you enjoy your trip home?"

"Oh, very much," the Consul answered. "You know I went to get my children." He shook his head. "The shortage of food in Spain is very acute. These are difficult times—difficult."

Luckily at that moment the children began coming out of the school. Franco's Consul shook hands with us and went away. As soon as he was out of sight, Despradel burst out laughing. "Alvarez, one day you are going to meet Franco or von Ribbentrop. There is no doubt of that." And I joined in his laughter.

April 10th

I went to Holy Thursday services. Poor services, these. Religious rites are impaired in the present situation. If only this were all . . .

When my friend the Minister and I took our regular walk through the "retreat of Kurfürsten-Damm Keep," as we call our hour of conversation after lunch, he proposed going to see the effects caused by last night's bombardment, which, he had been assured, were considerable. We got to the vicinity of the Opera House, near the old Chancellery, and found that the whole zone had been enclosed by a rope. The Minister took out his diplomatic pass, and I do not know for what reason that good guard let him pass.

"What about this gentleman?"

"He is my secretary."

"Ah, it's all right."

Thus we reached Unter den Linden strolling alone, save for a few persons probably in charge of watching the destroyed buildings.

This time the R.A.F. hit its mark. Few times before had I seen a better-aimed shot than that which hit the Opera House. There where I had just recently heard "Traviata," nothing was left except the four walls of the edifice. To judge from the walls which were intact, it was a case of incendiary bombs dropped with such skill that they had consumed the whole interior of the theater. This impression was confirmed by looking at the top of the University Library, the fire of which had already been extinguished, but where abundant smoke could yet be seen. We were told that the water had ruined many books and valuable manuscripts.

On the other hand, the bomb which totally destroyed the Commercial Bank had been of good caliber and well aimed. The impression left by this bombardment, which lasted two and one-half hours, had been deeper than those of past days. For it had not taken place in the suburbs alone, but in the capital itself, and at several points at one time.

Good Friday, April 11th

When I heard the "Agios o Theos" being sung this morning, I directed my thoughts to my poor country, which also is going through passion pains, and lifts its eyes to God asking Him to stop such confusion and disorder.[12]

Easter Sunday, April 13th

We Basques observe today the anniversary of our country.* I am sure that many have commemorated this day in the midst of sorrow, others in prison, others in concentration camps, others in exile. But all must have remembered it. Many many have thought of me, as I am thinking of all of them. Very few may have realized that it has been my fate to spend this anniversary of hope for future freedom, completely alone, in exile, far from my loved ones. But I feel confident that some day, when chains and visas are broken, we will all gather together in the real anniversary of our country in liberty—for we are suffering in order to achieve that end.

*[Editor's note: The "anniversary" referred to here is Aberri Eguna, literally "The Day of the Fatherland." The day is not really an anniversary, but rather a celebration of the Basques' existence as a distinctive people who deserved their own political institutions. The day selected for this celebration was always Easter Sunday, to reaffirm the strength of the Basques' Catholic faith. The celebration was first observed in Bilbao in 1932, and every year thereafter until the civil war. During the Franco era, the celebration was held clandestinely, but

it still attracted many thousands of persons despite police measures to suppress it. In the post-Franco period, celebration of the day has been highly politicized, with each major political party holding its own celebration, which each claims is the true and authentic Aberri Eguna.]

April 17th

Today the Minister from Panama arrived from Switzerland. There has been nothing done about my Swiss visa. He is determined that I leave as his chauffeur. I am ready for anything— either for managing the steering wheel or for carrying the valises.

News came again from America about the Soviet entering the Tripartite Pact. Meanwhile, the Swedish and Russian frontiers remain closed. Who can unravel this? Are these the last German "invitations" to Russia, courteously made with armored divisions at the frontier?

Berlin has been bombed again today, but it was not a heavy bombardment.

April 18th

A distinguished professor of international law visited the Dominican Minister today. He said he wished to go away.

"I, who have been von Ribbentrop's teacher, who have taught several generations of diplomats the patterns on which relations should be based, not alone of individuals, but of nations, I, who have dedicated my whole life to studying, find myself now deprived of my post—my life's illusion, to teach."

His accent was touching, which together with his age and venerable look moved one to deep sympathy. The Minister and I listened to him with respect, and in silence.

"They did not dare cast me away as they did the others. They have given me 750 marks a month as a retirement salary, so it should not be said that Professor ——— has been left destitute. And all because among my people, among those who gave me my being, there is to be found a Jew. . . . Give me the visa without delay, Mr. Minister. I wish to go."

"You know, professor, that there is no inconvenience on my part. But have you the permit for leaving Germany?" asked the Minister.

"Not yet. Do you believe they would deny it to me after removing me from my chair?" The professor could not continue. He finally added, "I must get away, it does not matter how—I cannot stand this dishonor."

April 19th

Once in a while a German lawyer, who lives in the vicinity, comes to the social gatherings of the Legation. Today he came in, all excited.

"I am afraid I shall be denounced by the concierge, Mr. Minister."

"Why?"

"I could no longer tolerate his unreasonableness, and answered him back adequately."

"And what is he to denounce you for?"

"Anything at all. As opposed to the regime—well, I don't know, anything he may think of."

"Don't you worry, he wouldn't dare."

The Minister turned to me since I had remained silent. "Have you heard that? The concierge of this house; and such things may be happening in other places. They are engaged in a most loathsome mission of policing and espionage. As he knows I am a diplomat, he regards me with considerations which I think are slavish, but with the rest of the tenants he assumes an irritating despotism. Do you know some old women tenants who live on one of the lower floors? Well, the other day I was ready to tell this concierge something he would have always remembered, because of the inconsiderate manner in which he treated them."

"It is a terrible situation to have to live under these conditions," the lawyer said. "They give authority to anyone at all, and we are all trembling with the fear that any day they may get us in trouble in their eagerness to ingratiate themselves."

"With me he is very courteous," I remarked.

"Naturally, because he sees you coming to the Legation frequently, and he considers you a diplomat."

"How well you live in America!" commented the lawyer as he left.

When he was gone, the Minister said: "It is really disgusting, this organized denunciation. Here, the concierge; there, the employee; and in the bosom of the family, the son. . . . This is a sound people," added the Minister, "but this regime is making it mean and despicable."

April 20th

Today is Hitler's birthday. Also my little Aintzane's, who is six. There are drapes and banners. Everything is ordained and prescribed by law. On the other hand, pain is real in many hearts which are clothed with black crepe. But why should children also suffer who cannot even spend their birthdays with their parents? or the parents who have defended honorably the freedom of their homeland?

I imagine having my children next to me, as when at other more peaceful times I would draw pictures for them and tell them of our *ipuñak* (folk stories), so simple and full of teachings. Their mother must have reminded them of their absent father.[13]

April 21st

Tonight the gathering at the Dominican Legation was quite entertaining, for we listened to a story of a Rumanian couple who have been able to leave that territory, thanks to the good offices of Dr. Despradel. He is a Rumanian diplomat, and she the daughter of a German, a big industrial man established in Holland, who has been one of the leaders of the fifth column operating in Dutch territory. In spite of his Nazi opinions, he is married to a Jewish lady belonging to an old family, whom the Minister describes with special praise because of her kindness. The one who cannot remain in Rumania is the daughter (her father a fifth columnist, her mother Jewish).

I witnessed a very significant episode. The diplomat's wife asked the Dominican Minister if he would permit her to telephone to Holland to say goodbye to her mother and sisters. She had not mentioned the father as they were not on very good terms. The Minister replied that he would gladly accede to her request, but it was not possible to get a telephone connection through to Holland, as it was forbidden. The lady, who seemed intelligent, smiled and insisted, saying to the Minister, "Will you permit me to try?"

"With much pleasure," answered the Minister.

The lady returned, saying: "You are right—communications are not permitted; but I have given my father's name in case it's possible."

No more than a few minutes had elapsed when the telephone service announced that the connection was to be put through. Shortly afterwards, the diplomat's wife was talking with her mother and sisters, while she was preparing to migrate to America.

The Minister and I exchanged glances while we discussed the morally twisted times in which we are now living, that triumph, influence, and even the telephone belong to those who are ready at any moment to break the pledged word and the loyalty owed. It is the era of fifth columnism, boldly and unfortunately rampant.

The conversation included the present situation in Rumania. The diplomat, who had a post in Paris, went to his country when mobilization was decreed there, because of the German and Russian attacks. He was inducted into a cavalry regiment, which never entered the campaign. The *coup d'état,* the country's new political order, and the resulting humiliation of the Rumanian people sent them back.

"What is Rumania's actual situation?" asked the Minister.

"One of deep restlessness. Who could ever agree with what has happened? We live practically in a civil war. You yourselves are witnesses of the slaughter committed by the Codreanu Iron Guard.

Now these excesses have been checked because it so suits the Nazis' interests, as the Iron Guard is not to be trusted by them. But I am sure we are finding ourselves in difficult days, and in the face of new bloody stages. We have been divided and annihilated. Do you believe that under such conditions energy for anything could still exist?"

"And since the entrance of German troops, what is the situation of Rumania?" I asked.

"Rumania," went on the diplomat, "was a country in which life was full—so full that I doubt whether in Europe there was another country of such an easy way of life. The first result of the entrance of German troops was the rise in living expenses. Now everything is twice or three times as expensive as before, and we have only started."

"It is remarkable how history is repeated," I answered. "We are going through, as far as economics are concerned, a period similar to that of Napoleon. I recall Chateaubriand's writings of 1814, in which he announced the fall of the colossus through the constant accumulation of ruins. A nation where the Emperor entered was a ruined nation. On the other hand, commerce flourished in the rest of the world. Something similar is happening in what pertains to the ruin of the nations which Hitler is occupying."

"The comparison is accurate," replied the Rumanian diplomat. "But the reality of the present time is yet more terrible, for with the present means of transportation and the rapidity of the services which are sometimes hypocritically called 'services of recuperation,' two months are enough to leave a nation of plenty in the most rigorous want."

"I remember the case of Belgium, when I had been assured there was enough food for more than four years of war, or necessity on account of the war. As you have just said, two months were enough for the Belgian people to realize that their deposits had been depleted."

"Would you believe that in Rumania, which is one of the granaries of Europe, bread has already become scarce?"

"That is terrible," said the Minister. "All this craftiness will have to fall through. They lie with propaganda, they pretend kindness with external formalities; but when necessity comes no one can avoid catastrophe. . . . This will happen once again—do not doubt it."

The Rumanian couple are headed for Santo Domingo to rebuild their lives far from their invaded and impoverished country. The Minister looked at them, touched and sympathetic. I looked at them with envy, for they had visas and permits to embark in Lisbon, going through Madrid.

April 22nd

The Dominican Minister's social gatherings are remarkable places for observation of all kinds of reactions. There come from other Legations other diplomats, pleasant and agreeable, from whom my identity is concealed. Among others, two young men also come, a Central American and a South American, both medical doctors who are specializing in their studies in Germany.

In general, among the young people studying in Germany, a current of enthusiasm for the Nazi cause is produced. Be it through conviction or impressionism, or perhaps through influence of the usual sweetheart of the student, who is the most insinuating propagandist, the truth is that these two young doctors are enthusiastic for the Nazi cause, more so in its spectacular war aspect than in the inward aspect of the new doctrine's system.

Owing to the victories in Greece and Africa, they are proud and even irritating. Every day, as they entered the small room where the Minister and I were poring over a few maps, they would say: "Again today? Forget about maps and fronts; Hitler will erase all that soon."

"Youth mustn't get excited or illusioned," the Minister would say, whose wonderful character, full of graciousness, enlivened those pleasant gatherings.

"But that no one can avoid, as it is already done. The German army is invincible," one of the young doctors would reply.

"And do you believe such a thing?" the Minister would retort. "I thought you were an intelligent man. Listen to me calmly, for I am going to tell you a secret. Don't forget it. I am staying here—do you understand—here, because I don't want to miss the spectacle of the Allied troops marching down Unter den Linden. And your German girl friends mustn't protest much, for we shall send them some Negroes to give them a scare."*

*[*Editor's note:* In the Spanish version, the Dominican minister refers to "un batallón de negros," recognizing the fact that during World War II American military units were still largely segregated by race. However, it is puzzling to the reader how a diplomat from the Dominican Republic thought that he might have some influence over such matters. In any case, the comment reveals the depth and extent of such racial stereotypes and prejudices of the day—that blacks might be considered especially frightening to Europeans, and especially European women; that a Latin American diplomat might express such a belief; that Aguirre might report such a comment; and that his American translators might allow such an observation to slip through into the English version, especially since they were so careful to screen out other casual comments that could have been considered offensive to one group or another.]

"What dreams you democrats have!" said one. "That is all past history: it is in the streets of London that Hitler's troops will march."

"It is possible," the Minister replied. "But listen to me well. I know not how, but the Allies marching through Unter den Linden is what we are to see this time, and I shall not miss such a sight. I have even prepared a chair in order not to get tired, as it will be long, very long . . ."

"You, Dr. Alvarez, who are keeping so silent—what is your opinion of the Minister's optimism?"

"My opinion is that you should take a look at the map in order to realize the size of the world. You will see, in spite of all that Germany is gobbling up, how small it is compared to the rest of the world."

"You always tell us to look at the map; but the truth is that each time the Allied territory will become smaller, and Hitler's larger. For, this time, there is no one to stop the Germans."

"It is possible that you may be right for some time—for a long time, if you wish—but everything ends. Humanity as a whole has yet to enter the war; therefore, we can say that the war has not yet started. So, do not hurry, for we are yet to witness extraordinary things."

"Dr. Alvarez is right," joined in the Minister. "Supposing the British Isles are lost, there still remains the Empire and then America. . . . It's too much flesh for Hitler. He would simply burst with indigestion."

"You are always thinking of America. That is far away, and I don't know whether she would get mixed up in these adventures if she sees England lost. . . . You now see they are contemplating an attack on Suez. What if Suez should fall?"

"I admit that Suez might fall—do you hear me?" I said to the young doctor. "But there remains Africa. And listen carefully: I expect to see the Americans fighting in Africa some day. If necessary, a gigantic African front shall be constituted in which Hitler will have to busy his troops. For fronts are not invented; they are created by circumstances. And here lies the great danger for Hitler; for, as his troops advance, his needs increase, and new fronts are created which have to be covered by his men. Do not forget that Hitler is confronted with an enormous human mass which has to be equipped as no other warrior human mass has ever been equipped. It is a process which will take more or less time, but an unavoidable one, as this war will be a long war, because it is a struggle of civilizations, it is a struggle for existence, where there is no place for neutrality, nor can one sleep as the cannon shots are too loud—"

At that moment the Berlin radio in its Spanish program of propaganda meant for Spain blared out: "The radio audience must know—about this time—of the establishment in London of a National Basque Council.* Here is another instance of English maneuvering, while they offer hypocritical friendship to the Spain of Franco."

*[Editor's note: The Basque National Council was created in London by Manuel Irujo shortly after the outbreak of the war. As the senior Basque official still living in a free country, Irujo seized the initiative to form the council as a way of maintaining continuity in the Basque gov-

ernment, and to coordinate resistance activities with the Free French government of Charles de Gaulle. The council entered into an agreement with de Gaulle in May 1941 that led to the establishment of an all-Basque military unit within the Free French armed forces. For more on the council, see Robert Clark, *The Basques: The Franco Years and Beyond* (Reno, Nevada: University of Nevada Press, 1979), pp. 89–90.]

The Minister and I could not restrain a smile.

"What Council has been established?" someone asked.

"The National Basque Council," replied the Minister.

"The National Basque Council?"

"Yes," said the Minister. "It is an organization which represents the Basque people, who are fundamentally a democratic people, and most surely the oldest of Europe, which has been most furiously attacked by Franco. Do you recall Gernika? It seems that the Basques fight for their freedom and organize themselves, and the English have respect for them. . . . Have you not heard of Aguirre during the Spanish Civil War? Well, he is the President."

The Minister gave me a wicked wink as if to say, "I can say whatever I please, enjoy it, and you have to keep quiet."

When the doctors went away, I said: "Laugh as much as you please, for I like to see you in that good humor. But listen to me. You cannot imagine the impression which I felt on hearing of the activities of my compatriots. Do you realize what it means to a people like mine to live under such circumstances, after having been expelled in all directions? My people live, and they are working. Think what my emotion is at these moments."

April 23rd

The day started according to my wishes. The Venezuelan Minister sent me the original telegram he received from the Minister of Foreign Affairs of his country, urgently ordering him to obtain the permit for the Guerra widow to leave Brussels, via Berlin-Sweden. This means that my friends in America have been successful in their efforts.

"This matter is settled," Dr. Zerrega said to me, quite satisfied by the interest taken by his superior.

But happiness is never complete. The Swedish frontier is still closed.[14]

April 26th

The Minister from Venezuela today sent an energetic note to Wilhelm-Strasse, demanding the passage of the Guerra widow and her children through Germany. He did it in compliance with the orders of the Minister of Foreign Affairs of his country, and, according to what he has told me, even threatening reciprocal treatment of German citizens in his country. This is the irony of destiny—an energetic note from Nazi Germany demanding the passage of my own wife.

April 27th

I have been notified today that the Finnish port of Petsamo is now open for navigation. Therefore, the Swedish frontier has also been opened. Has the conflict with the Soviet been settled?

All these doubts were the subject of our conversation during the dinner to which I was invited by the Dominican Minister, where I met an American diplomat with his wife, who is a German. The conversation afterwards concerned the economic and social situation of Germany.

"To judge this matter, you have only to hear my father-in-law. If the matter rested in his hands, he would finish off Hitler."

"But I understand that your father-in-law is a vehement Hitlerite," argued the Dominican Minister.

"He was, and so vehement and enthusiastic that he even convinced me in many respects, persuading me with his arguments. But now—now he is an avowed enemy of the regime."

"What is the reason for the change?"

"You know, Mr. Minister, my father-in-law is a big manufacturer. Moved as many others by the anti-Communistic propaganda and a sense of pride of the race, he enthusiastically supported Nazism. Now he believes that the inevitable ruin of German economy is owed to the ominous Nazi political doctrine. Besides, it affects him so closely. Imagine, a few days ago he was telling us that from all his manufacturing efforts, practically all that was left to him was his personal salary. Between taxes, compulsory donations, and other like obligations, he is deprived of the few benefits that come to him. In this way there is neither stimulus nor the possibility of betterment."

"But this," answered the Minister, "he should have realized before, as it is clear that his enthusiasm cooled down only when he felt quite keenly the effects of a doctrine which he had gladly accepted."

"So it is. He says this is the general background among men of enterprise, who are now disillusioned with a regime that is leading them to a completely static condition, and without having the right to protest."

"That is the most disagreeable part of these doctrines," I answered, "for we can understand the smaller or greater grade of socialization of a society or a State, if with it social evil would be avoided. But the lack of freedom, the fact of not being able to protest against injustice—which is the gravest thing—cannot be conceived, excepting in debased or tyrannized societies."

"I heard something to this effect when my father-in-law spoke about the workers' delegates in the manufacturing business. He said he had no complaints about its introduction if, with this, harmony between production workers and the prosperity of the business was achieved. But the case really is that instead of being the delegates of an economical social function they are the delegates of a political function, in the name of the Party, of the regime, or anything at all which they feel is opportune, and in this way their mission becomes only an extension of the Gestapo in the factories."

"All that is loathsome," said the Minister. "But how many start to realize it only too late, when the water is soaking their pockets, heedless of the fact that the best solution would be to stop the fountain, whence the water spouts!"

A German lady, the wife of a German manufacturer, and friend of the Dominican couple, came shortly after to say goodbye to the Minister's wife, who was leaving tomorrow for Switzerland. The conversation followed the same course, and after the visiting lady had listened attentively for some time, she said:

"All that you say is true. My husband is also extremely worried. But I as a mother am worried with another problem besides the economic one, as one can live with much, or one can live with less. What worries me is our children's education. You have asked me about my son"—she addressed the Minister's wife. "Well, tonight there is a meeting of the Youth of the Party, and he will not be back until late."

"But when do these children rest?" inquired the Minister's wife.

"I asked my son today, 'When shall we be able to have you with the family for one day?' 'Mother,' he answered, 'we have the duty of fidelity to the Party, and to be present whenever it may call us.' 'That's all right,' I replied, 'but bear in mind that you also belong to your family, and at least one—' 'We belong to the State,' he retorted. 'To the State. . . . But don't you think your parents are worthy of having something of you, or are we nothing to you any more?' 'Look, mother,' he replied. 'You belong to other times. You could not understand us.' And he left. 'To the State. . . . You belong to other times.' Believe me, I cannot forget those words pronounced by a sixteen-year-old boy. This is a graver problem than that of the industries to which you were referring. Money! Our children are worth more than that."

The German lady spoke with deep emotion, and we all remained silent for a moment, sharing the sorrow of that mother—who belonged to other times.

April 28th

I returned to Hamburg, as my Consul came back from Antwerp bringing me news of my family. I went accompanying my Minister, who was also making the trip.

The Consul tells me that my family's economic situation is very bad. They have no money or ways of getting it. They had given me all that they had in order to get back my freedom. On the first return trip of my Consul he will take them whatever resources are left in my pockets, shrunken already because of my prolonged stay in Germany. I shall adjust myself in whatever way I can. As everyone else who is worried about my situation, I have placed my hopes in my friends in America. And as if this were not enough, the Consul tells me that it is almost impossible to obtain a permit to leave for my wife and children.

When the Minister heard Guardia's sad story he was moved and promised that tomorrow we should go to the travel agency, in order to inquire whether the Swedish frontier is open, and if so, to request the permit to leave immediately, as it has been forbidden for quite some time.

"Your family's situation moves me, and your own tortures me," said the Minister. "Don't you have possessions abroad?"

"How could we have them, if all those belonging to my family, without any exception, have been confiscated by General Franco's regime?"

"Haven't they left you anything?"

"Nothing at all, Mr. Minister. Even my poor mother was fined three million pesetas, so that not one cent was left after the fine."

"Of what could they accuse your mother?"

"Simply of being my mother."

"That truly is a monstrosity."

"In this way live millions of beings in Europe who enjoyed legitimate comfort, and who are now reduced to want through procedures that are not used even with criminals. It is for this reason that my departure is urgent, not only because time is passing, but because I must return to my family the money which I now have."

In spite of my worries, I was able to notice that English planes had left quite a few traces of their visits in the most central streets in Hamburg. Their action is now making itself felt.

April 29th

We are informed at the American Express that the Swedish frontier has been opened, and a service has been organized, the first boat of which will leave Sweden, going to New York in the first days of June. We are told that from May 6th we can reserve our passages, but it is necessary to have American and Swedish visas, and a German permit to leave, in correct form. The first item I already have; the others I do not.

April 30th

I was again before the police at their headquarters. The Minister and the Consul accompanied me. Therefore I couldn't complain of my entourage. We reached Section Eleven of the Berlin Police Department around ten o'clock in the morning. The Minister explained my case—gave my name and said that two months ago a petition was made for a permit to leave by way of Sweden, which had not been expedited on account of the closing of the Swedish frontier. We are now informed that this frontier has again been opened, and we ask that a permit be extended to me.

The Police Chief looked steadily at me and answered: "It is not possible to go through Sweden. If you so desire, we shall give him a permit to go via Lisbon, which is the route most frequently used."

The Minister insisted firmly that the Swedish frontier had been opened. The policeman insisted that that permit could not be given. The Minister then begged him to inquire further. The Police Chief went away, and we were left alone in a room which was quite dirty. He took a long time in coming back, and we started to feel uneasy.

"It would be funny should we be caught at the last minute, and the three of us here. This would certainly be the best way to make fun of us," commented the Minister.

"Banish such thoughts," said Guardia. "If you ask for the permit firmly, they will give it to us."

"We shall see now," I joined in. "This is the real test. I find no reason why they should suspect me now after all that has happened."

"I have not gone through all of that," replied the Minister.

I shall never be able to forget this difficult moment so hard to describe, in which we were seized by such emotion. The Chief did not appear, and on that simple decision my freedom depended. The Chief finally returned.

"You are the Minister of Panama?"

"Yes, sir."

He asked for my passport, and left again. New uneasiness. He finally returned with the passport and asked how many days I needed to get ready to leave Germany, as they see I have no Swedish visa. We answered fifteen days.

"But the permit has been granted, hasn't it?" asked the Minister.

"Yes, sir, it has been granted."

The three of us simultaneously took a breath. At last. I paid eight marks and was given the passport with the great seal to leave and a permit for staying in Germany until the 25th of May. The police, knowing what obtaining visas meant, had added ten days more.

Once in the street, while I pressed my passport against my bosom, I embraced my two good friends and saviors with a feeling of liberation which I had not experienced in a long time. I felt as if in that moment the rooftop of this enormous concentration camp had collapsed, and that a little crack opened, big enough for me to slide through. It even felt as if the air which I breathed was different, that it was no longer foul air, for I had started to breathe through the crack the atmosphere that envelops the lands of liberty.

Today Berlin was again bombarded. It was of little importance.

May 4th

We went to the Swedish Consulate today. We cannot get the visa until we have a passage paid for, and of course I have no money. We decided to telephone Dr. Despradel, who is in Switzerland, asking him to send a telegram to the Dominican Minister in

Washington. My friends in New York can then be advised of my present position and they will be able to get the money to Sweden. I am only afraid that with this delay all the passages will be taken by the time my friends can settle the matter from New York.

May 5th

Last evening I spent the most amusing and at the same time dangerous hours of my life. With the permit to leave and affairs straightening themselves the way they should, we all suddenly felt a little reckless, even my Minister. Or perhaps it is more truthful to say especially my Minister. Last evening he gave a dinner party which he insisted I attend. The party was in honor of the Francoist diplomat Señor Mendez, who had formerly been in the service of the Republican government. When I was a representative of the Basque National Party in Madrid I had never met Señor Mendez. Whether he had ever seen my photograph or not, I do not know. I knew that he had been on Franco's side from the beginning of the rebellion.

When the Minister told me of his plan, I was flabbergasted but at the same time struck with the humor of the situation.

"I should like to meet Señor Mendez," I said. "But do you think I ought to risk it?"

"My dear Alvarez, you will never be recognized," he said, and with his eyes twinkling my Minister taunted me with the old story I had first suggested when he was more fearful than I. "Would you recognize your own brother in Berlin?"

He had to say no more. I stood up and smiled at him. "The dinner is at eight, isn't it? I shall not be late."

Dr. Villalaz asked me to come early, so I went to his Legation at 7:30. A short while later Señor Mendez arrived.

"Come in, my dear Mendez," Dr. Villalaz greeted him, and gestured toward me. "This is my countryman, Dr. Alvarez, who is having supper with us."

We shook hands and greeted each other cordially. We talked for a while on generalities and then went to dinner. As I watched him walking a little ahead of me, I wondered if I would be able to maintain a solemn face all evening. When we sat at the table Señor Mendez said very politely to me, "Your Minister says that you are leaving soon."

"That's true," I answered. "I am waiting for a Swedish visa."

"Swedish visa?" Franco's diplomat was astonished. "Why on earth do you go through Sweden? Why don't you go through Spain?"

"I wish I could, Señor Mendez," I answered, not daring to look at Dr. Villalaz, "but business has made me change my original plans."

"What a pity!" he answered. "Can't you get your Minister to arrange your business in Sweden? Then you could see my beautiful country."

"My Minister," I answered, "has done all he can. I am afraid I must go to Sweden myself. It makes me very sad because I know Spain very well. You see, I lived in Madrid, Barcelona, Sevilla . . ."

As I talked the expression on Señor Mendez's face became more and more friendly.

"Dr. Villalaz"—he addressed my Minister—"you didn't tell me Dr. Alvarez had been to Spain." And, turning to me, he added, "Were you ever in Saragossa?"

"Oh, yes, I lived there too."

"I come from there," Señor Mendez commented enthusiastically. "What country! It's so beautiful, isn't it?"

"Unforgettable," I replied.

The double meaning of my side of the conversation in violent contrast to the innocence of Franco's diplomat almost made Dr. Villalaz burst out laughing. I suddenly could tell his efforts in holding back were reaching the breaking point. As for myself, I had become so engrossed with the part I was playing that I didn't think about laughing; but for a moment I wanted to join Villalaz in his rather pleasant discomfort.

Dr. Villalaz abruptly changed the tone of the conversation to a more serious one by saying, "But life there cannot be too agreeable now, what with the Falange having so much power."

"Don't believe rumors like that," said Mendez quickly. "The Falange do not have so much power. They obey Franco's orders. And don't forget we owe Franco the order, quiet, and peace which we now enjoy."

"That is," interrupted my Minister, "if you are not involved in the war."

Señor Mendez drew back and, frowning, answered: "Oh, that is a terrible question. If it depended only upon us . . ."

I leaned forward. "But you already have your place," I said. "How can you remain neutral in the midst of a conflict between an authoritative order and democratic disorder? And what about Communism? Franco has the fraternal support of the Axis against these extremists which should make his place in the conflict obvious."

Señor Mendez glanced at me suspiciously. Fraternal support? Anti-Communism? What did I mean? "Señor Mendez," I said soothingly to put him at his ease, "don't you worry. You people must keep yourselves clear-thinking and strong. You must strike hard at the Reds. It will be better in the long run."

Mendez looked at me kindly. I had fooled him. He said: "Of course, it's our duty. Think of how they made us suffer . . ."

We went into the Minister's study, where we were served coffee. The smile on Dr. Villalaz's face was ironical and satisfied. Everything was going better than he had planned, but I could tell he wanted the joke to continue.

"But, Mendez," he said, "when are you people going to stop the shooting? Only a few days ago I read in the papers that several people have been executed."

"But, Mr. Minister, those people were assassins and thieves!"

"Maybe some of them were," answered the Minister, "but what about Companys? Why did you execute him?"

"Companys? But don't you know that he had a prison record? He was a gunman, a bandit, a racketeer—"

"Whatever you may want to say," interrupted Villalaz; "but nevertheless he was the elected President of the Catalan people and I don't think they would have chosen such a desperado."

"Oh, the elections!" said Mendez in disgust. "My dear Minister, they were a lie, a scandal. Don't believe anything else. Votes were bought and sold. If you only knew—"

CHAPTER VII 251

"Never mind," answered the Minister feelingly. "I still feel that President Companys' execution has been an act which you may well regret some day."

"Don't worry," Señor Mendez said emphatically. "I tell you they were all dishonest, completely crooked."

"What happened to the other one, the Basque President?" asked Dr. Villalaz, self-possessed for the moment.

I kept silent, repressing the laughter and wondering how the "well-informed" Señor Mendez would answer.

"To whom? Aguirre?"

"Was that his name?"

"Yes," answered Mendez. "He is another scoundrel. He was even more clever than the others."

"Why?" asked the Minister. "Why do you say that?"

"Because he escaped in time."

"Where is he now?"

"I don't know exactly. I believe in Mexico or the United States. I don't know where. But I have definite information that he is living splendidly with all that he has stolen."

"Stolen? What did he steal?"

"What did he steal? Well, he took all the money, gold and silver— naturally all stolen."

The Minister could no longer restrain himself and, rising suddenly, left the room. I saw that he was ready to roar with laughter.

"What's the matter, Dr. Villalaz?" Mendez asked.

"Nothing, nothing. I shall be right back."

I picked up the conversation, trying to keep calm. "That fellow Aguirre seems perfectly shameless," I said.

"Indeed he is, my dear Dr. Alvarez. You Americans were too sympathetic with these people. You do not know any of them well enough."

"He took all that money with him?" I questioned again.

"Certainly," he answered. "You don't know what we had to go through."

"I can understand now, Señor Mendez," I answered gravely.

Dr. Villalaz came back into the room with a bottle of Spanish cognac.

"Ah, cognac from my country!" Mendez exclaimed. "What good things we have there, haven't we?" He smiled at me.

"Magnificent," I answered, and Mendez looked at me with great satisfaction. We were good friends. When I left the Legation he asked if he might walk with me to the door of his boarding house.

"Goodbye, Señor Mendez," I said to him. "It has been a great pleasure to meet you."

"The pleasure has been mine," he answered. "We must have lunch together."

"Yes, soon," I answered. And now as I finish writing these notes I am still laughing.

May 6th

Dr. Despradel felt very disappointed that my Minister did not invite him to the dinner with Mendez. "It's just as well," he laughed, "for I'm sure I could not have kept myself quiet. What a story! Wait until Mendez knows the desperado he dined with." But I had been depressed even by the humor of the whole episode—for the humor was based on the success of false propaganda. I think I resented more the libelous things which were being said about my friend Companys, since he was a martyr and had been shot. He could not defend himself. As Alvarez, I had been unable to answer the false accusations hurled at Aguirre; but the time will arrive when I will combat these lies with the truth. Companys is dead. He cannot speak for himself. While my friends were laughing at the joke we had played on Mendez, I could only remember the journey I had made with Companys over the mountains of Catalonia into France, watching the endless line of homeless, hungry people, waiting for them—and Companys' deep dejection on the train ride to Paris. I interrupted my friends' laughter and told them of that journey.

On the ride to Paris I tried my best to comfort Companys. I reminded him that nations do not die like men, and that the hour of victory would sound for our countries.

"It is not that, José Antonio," he said. "I am worried about the people back there who have just crossed the border into France. They are my countrymen. What are they going to do? How will they be fed? Where will they stay? They are completely unprotected . . . and then my son . . ."

He then confided to me that all the money he could save, during the exercise of his office as President of Catalonia, was seventy-five thousand francs (about two thousand dollars at the rate of exchange at that time). "This money is not for me," he said. "I took it outside the country in order to pay for the treatment of my poor son who is in a sanatorium in Belgium." Companys was crying. He said to me, "I shall starve if need be, but not my son. No! No!"

I was deeply moved. This feeling I took along with me to Paris.

We Basques were organized in exile because we had been out of our country since 1937, and the Basques from all over the world and especially South America sent us financial help as we needed it. The exiled Basque Government agreed to attend to the needs of the President of Catalonia from the very beginning as we could, for he was a hero—and his death was a hero's death. And he died as a good Catholic after receiving the Holy Sacraments.[15]

"All of this will have tremendous repercussions in the future," one of the Ministers tried to comfort me. "They cannot resort to calumny, cannot lie knowingly, deceive people, execute the man whom the people freely chose as their leader, without their own kettle of water boiling over eventually to scald them for their treachery."[16]

May 8th

Today marks a year since that day of May, 1940, on which I left for Belgium. Since then the task of rescuing me has advanced day by day. A telegram came to the Dominican Legation in which we are advised from Washington that my friend Inchausti of New York has deposited money enough for four passages at the Nordisk Resebyra of Göteborg. Even for my wife and children.

This afternoon when I arrived at the agreeable American diplomatic gathering, I realized that my day had been perfect. The conversation interested me, as it dealt with one of the matters that were most appealing to me—the facts about German production.

The discussion was a heated one. The diplomats, those of Ministerial category, were in general partisans of the Allies; some young diplomats and the pleasant young medical men were enthusiastic for the Axis. There I stood as a mediator, as the young doctors, for instance, would say that it was not possible to argue with the Dominican Minister as he would destroy the argument with jokes.

"Germany builds three thousand machines a month," one of the diplomats said.[17] "I know this from a good source."

This expression of a "good source" is a common one that at least satisfies those who use it.

"Should German production not reach three thousand machines a month, it is not less than twenty-five hundred machines. It must be so, for otherwise how could such overwhelming superiority on all fronts be understood?" said one of the young men.

"Not on all fronts," replied one of the Ministers, "as those horrible bombardments of England of last summer are not taking place any more."

"All right; but the fight is now in the Balkans and, besides, the question of Russia is not yet clear. Do you ever think of the possible number of planes they must have on the Russian front? It is said that there are nearly two million men at the border."

"Whatever the reason may be," said the Minister, "the truth is that the Germans cannot attend to all the fronts."

"Why not?" (Here all the young men started to raise their voices.)

"According to what I was told, the Germans have about forty thousand planes, as in peacetime they only built half of what they do now," said one of the doctors.

"That does not correspond to the building of three thousand a month, but to much less," answered the Minister.

"The Minister is right," I joined in. "These matters are being exaggerated in a childish way. Let us make a calculation. Let us suppose that instead of three thousand they build two thousand a month. You just said that in peacetime half of the present amount were built. Well then, multiply the years 1934 to 1939, that is, six years, not counting '33, and considering all of '39 as a peace year, by the figure of twelve thousand planes (one thousand a month, half of the supposed present production). How many would result?"

"Seventy-two thousand. . . . Yes, that is quite a good many," said one of the young friends of the Axis.

"But we have not finished the operation yet, for we still have to add those built in sixteen months of the years 1940 and 1941 at a rate of two thousand a month; that is, thirty-two thousand, which, added to the seventy-two thousand of normal years, are exactly one hundred and four thousand planes. You can easily understand that this number of planes would have permitted Germany to attack at once on all fronts of the world, and would not have permitted the world to learn of Italy's total unpreparedness, while she was still out of the fight and trying to frighten everybody with noise, figures, and speeches."

"That is a fact," said one of the diplomats to the young man of the figures. "Besides, if, as they have told you, Germany has an air fleet of forty thousand machines, we would have to reduce Dr. Alvarez' estimate by more than half."

"I feel that even that is exaggerated: forty thousand planes are a lot of planes," I added.

I was thinking of our war, of the difficulties of building one single machine, difficulties for us as well as for the Germans. I then noticed that my friend the diplomat, who had such good connections in German affairs, was nodding to me affirmatively. He then called me near him.

"You see, my friends," said one of the Ministers, "that it is not so easy to deceive."

"I believe," I said, "that Great Britain's monthly production does not exceed five hundred planes."

"That's not possible," they replied. "She must be building many more. If not, how is she able to resist German attacks?"

"Simply because neither do the Germans produce what people think they do. Do you believe that planes are built like bricks?"

The discussion passed on to pilots. I was sitting next to my friend the diplomat, who said to me in a low voice, getting close to my ear: "I have at last been informed of German production. General ———— told me yesterday in an intimate gathering. He, as you know, accompanies Hitler, and forms part of his Chancellery."

"And what is it?" I asked in the same tone of voice.

"Eight hundred and twenty planes a month, and that now, built in all the plants of the occupied countries; before, it was much less."

"That's another story: it had to be so."

"Keep it a secret. Don't tell it to anyone here."

"All right. Thank you for the information."

When the gathering ended and I went to my room, I made my calculations and concluded that an air fleet, which in my opinion did not surpass twenty thousand planes, and perhaps less, was insufficient to strike on two fronts, even if British aviation on the Isles were one-fourth of that number. At the same time I wondered at the folly of those who insisted on not hearing the noise of those planes in construction since 1933, in spite of the open declaration by their builders that they were being made to kill.

May 12th

The Minister's secretary at the Dominican Legation has informed me that the Swedish company has advised the authorities that our passages are paid for, so that our visas may be expedited. But why doesn't the Swedish Consulate let us know?

May 13th

I shall not be able to sleep at all tonight—my happiness is so great and I am so anxious for tomorrow morning to arrive. I will wait for the sun, watching from my window for the streets of Berlin and the shapes of men and houses gradually to come alive.[18] Early this morning the Minister from Venezuela called me: "Alvarez, I think you will like the news I have for you," he said. "Tomorrow morning Señora Guerra and her two children will arrive in Berlin." I could scarcely believe my ears. I can scarcely believe it now. He invited me to lunch for a celebration. After I had the telephone conversation I could not move for a long moment. Was it possible?

Because of Holy Week, Dr. Despradel lent me Cipriano de Valera's translation of the Holy Scriptures. I read it as a duty every day, and today, before I joined the Venezuelan Minister at lunch, I found it was my turn to read Psalm 107:[19]

Give glory to the Lord, for He is good: for His mercy en-dureth for ever.

Let them say *so* that have been redeemed by the Lord, whom He hath redeemed from the hand of the enemy: and gathered out of the countries.

From the rising and from the setting of the sun, from the north and from the sea.

They wandered in a wilderness, in a place without water: they found not the way of a city for their habitation.

They were hungry and thirsty: their soul fainted in them.

And they cried to the Lord in their tribulation: and He deliv-ered them out of their distresses.

And He led them into the right way, that they might go to a city of habitation. . . .

Still meditating, I walked to the Hotel Majestic, which Dr. De-spradel had recommended for Mari and the children. It was small but seemed quite comfortable. I reserved two rooms. It is difficult for me to write this—that my wife and my children are coming here tomorrow. There are two rooms waiting for them. I went to the station to find out what time the train arrived, and to get my bear-ings for the morning. Finally I met Dr. Zerrega, feeling as if I were living in an unreal world.

"I suppose you are happy now," he said to me, smiling.

"Put yourself in my place, Mr. Minister," I answered, "and you know how happy I am."

May 14th

At 6:30 in the morning I was dressed. At 7:30 I was at Friedrich-Strasse Station. The train was late. I should have known it would be late. I walked back and forth on the platform; it was a kind of happy torture, this waiting. The train pulled in after nine o'clock. We saw each other at once. There were no words we could say—only an incredible gladness which engulfed us in silence. Mari and my two children: the simplest words of greeting in the language of our ancestors held more endearment in the sound than anything else. We spoke softly together and heard none of the noise of our surroundings. The children were well and full of spirit despite the long eighteen-hour train ride. In the taxi to the hotel, questions and answers began, rushing one on top of another. The vigorous and expressive phrases of our language had a special accent for me this morning. We were together in Berlin. We were speaking the Basque language, which Hitler's protégé had banished from our homeland.

"The children slept during the trip," said my wife, "but I couldn't. Crossing the German frontier tortured me. I was so nervous. Besides, when the little one was awake he would not stop talking, and I was so afraid someone would realize he was speaking *Euzkera.*"

"Did you have a difficult time at the frontier?" I asked.

"No. Fortunately I had recovered my composure somewhat. When we reached the frontier, customhouse officers and several policemen came in the train. They made all the passengers get out. I said to myself: "Well, I am not going to move. I have the children and too much luggage." I explained my situation to the officers.

" 'It is compulsory,' they told me in French. 'You have to get out and come to the customhouse.'

" 'But how can I with all these packages and the two children?'

"They paid no attention to me and left. I decided not to move unless they sent a baggageman to help me. Then a German officer came in. 'Why don't you get out, madame?' he asked.

" 'How can I, with so many valises and the children?'

" 'Wait a moment,' he answered. He went away and returned with a customhouse officer who examined the baggage. The officer stamped a seal on my passport, and I was the only one on the train who did not have to leave."

"It was very polite of that German officer," I reflected.

"I thanked him profusely," she said.

The rooms for my wife and the children are very pleasant, but the children could not understand why I had to leave them. "Very soon now," we told them, "we are going to be together. We will be on a boat—a great big ship; and we are going to America." When I told Mari that our passages were already paid in Sweden, she said: "I have been so worried about that, I couldn't even ask. I have only twenty marks, and our families contributed all the money they had for our trip. You can imagine—franc by franc—and finally we had the tickets. Your brother Juan came with me to the station in Brussels, and I had to buy his return ticket to Antwerp, for he had nothing."

"I have sent money to them with Consul Guardia, who left a few days ago for Antwerp," I told Mari. "I kept only enough for our expenses here, tickets to Sweden, and the first expenses which we may have there. After that, God knows."

We had breakfast at my wife's hotel. The children could not get over the white bread. Conditions in Belgium have grown much worse, Mari told me, and lack of food is getting to be a very serious problem. Discontent with the Nazis is widespread.

May 15th

My wife—that is, Señora Guerra—and her two children went to the Venezuelan Legation today. She was met by the Minister, Dr. Zerrega, who was the only one at the Legation who knew her true identity. My two small children had to remember their new names. We had told them from the beginning that their new names were a Spanish translation of the Basque: Gloria for Aintzane, and José for Joseba. The little ones did not get mixed up once, but the Minister did. I had to stay outside, because the Chancellor at the Legation knew me as Alvarez from Panama and he might wonder if he saw me so concerned about the fate of the young Venezuelan widow.

The Chancellor examined Señora Guerra's passport. "Ah!" he exclaimed, "you are from Mérida." We had picked the city of Mérida from a Venezuelan map in Belgium to be Mari's native city. What bad luck! The Chancellor had been born in Mérida. As soon as he told her this, Mari answered quite calmly, before he could question her further for details which she would not be able to answer: "I was only born in that town by chance. My family was going to Europe, where I lived until I was quite grown up."

The Chancellor then asked about her husband and Dr. Zerrega, wanting to forestall more questions, forgot that she appeared as a widow and answered, "In Caracas, man—he is in Caracas." The Chancellor chose to keep quiet, and so did my wife, while the Minister, realizing his slip, quickly and ably finished the interview.

At the Consulate of the United States everything was made easy by the kind Vice Consul, who immediately gave Mari her visa. But there was Mademoiselle Inquisitor. She questioned Señora Guerra for a full hour. When Mari showed her the Vice Consul's visa, she was highly indignant. "That isn't valid without these formalities." The old spinster was happy to tell us that individual photographs of the children were required, and so the rest of the formalities have to be left for the morning. This delay makes us very anxious, for we cannot obtain the Swedish visa until everything is settled at the United States Consulate.

May 16th

At the last hour everything begins to go wrong, and now I must minimize all the difficulties which we may encounter. Today I have learned that the travel agency, Nordisk Resebyra, sent two thousand dollars to the Swedish Legation, instead of a notice that our passages are paid. I asked why—what is the matter now? We do not want the money. We want passage to America. They phoned that the passages have not been paid for because the boat is full, and anyway its sailing date is uncertain. Temporarily I kept this news from Mari. We went back to the American Consulate, taking the children's pictures. Another questioning. I kept the children outside, and we had to wait for an hour and a half. When Mari finally came out she said the woman had merely repeated yesterday's questions. I could only sympathize.

May 17th

Dr. Despradel and Dr. Zerrega asked the Swedish Minister to please expedite our visas. At five the Swedish Legation confirmed yesterday's pessimistic news. There are no passages, and the sailing date has not been settled, and we can't get the visas until the passages are paid. My permit for staying in Berlin is up on the 25th, and my wife's, in transit, on the 30th. Our anxiety grows. What has not happened in all of these months is bound to happen in the last hours. Some of Dr. Alvarez's friends have seen him accompanying a lady with two children. I know they are wondering, and I do not like the situation at all. My Ministers have promised that Monday they will speak confidentially to the Swedish Minister. I have authorized them to tell him the truth about Alvarez, but they feel it will not be necessary.

Sunday May 18th

It is impossible to ask a mischievous child, who is not yet three years old, to be discreet. In the morning I had to take my son out of church because he began mimicking the preacher—in a loud voice and in *Euzkera*. We cannot leave the children in the hotel for the same reason. On the way back to the hotel from church we passed a group of children who were being instructed by an adult on how to isolate an incendiary bomb. The minute our children saw the bomb, they became hysterical. Passers-by and a policeman wondered what was the matter with them, and it was some time before we could calm them. I wonder how many months of real peace and security they will need in order to gain again the solid composure that is the birthright of all children.

In the afternoon we went to the zoological park. We had some refreshments in a beer garden. There were German soldiers there on leave, and many of them were wounded.

Dr. Despradel had invited us to supper. Laughing, he told us how his secretary had asked him: "What language do those Guerra children speak among themselves? I don't understand it!" The Minister gave a picturesque explanation of the dialect spoken by a servant in France, from whom the children had learned it. But this did not intrigue her as much as the unexpected appearance of a young widow, who was to be accompanied to America by the serious Dr. Alvarez. Despradel invented a passionate love story.[20]

May 20th

It was exactly a year ago that my mother spent her birthday within sight of Dunkirk. I wish I could have told her today that our visas are at the Swedish Consulate, ready for us. We are to get them tomorrow.

May 21st

We have the visas, and Guardia, "my Consul," has arrived in Berlin. He who created Dr. Alvarez had to be here for the farewell. He dined with us.

May 22nd

Customhouse, money exchange, train and boat tickets to Göteborg, all have woven themselves into the exciting, nerve-racking pattern of the day before the day of departure. Enrique has advised us to make the trip in an automobile. He has offered to take us to the border, as he has "influential" friends there too. We have accepted.

In the evening all our friends came to be with us. We said goodbye—until we meet again in America, and then some day in our Basque country, when we can welcome them. I wrote many letters, one for our countrymen suffering in the prison of Burgos.

May 23rd

At last we have left Berlin. At eight o'clock in the morning my Consul stood near the car door—the last warm handclasp, with which I tried to convey to him the gratitude neither time nor distance will ever erase. We made the trip from Berlin to Sassnitz, on our way to the Baltic. There was scarcely any traffic on the highway. The children enjoyed the ride. At three-thirty in the afternoon we arrived at the German customhouse. Enrique went ahead and, still ignorant of my true identity, told the customhouse officers and policemen that we were Spanish-Americans who must be well attended. My diary notes were put inside my little girl's doll, which, of course, never left her arms. A German officer noticed her and caressed her, recalling his own child who is far away. The officials complimented Señora Guerra on the charming manners of her small daughter. But it was mainly Enrique's efforts which got us through quickly: Enrique, who has friends everywhere—even in the Gestapo. We said goodbye to him and thanked him. Within a quarter of an hour we were on board the Swedish boat which was to bring us in four hours to Trälleborg, the first Swedish outpost.

When we left Germany, we could only remain silent and stare at each other, unbelieving. The strength to react was gone from us. We were on a Swedish boat—the shadow of the Gestapo, of the Falange was growing lighter and lighter over our heads. Soon it would disappear completely.

Documents and baggage were examined rapidly at Trälleborg. They were surprised that a citizen of Panama should be traveling through Sweden. "Panama?" they said, with a short laugh—a broader smile.

"Yes," I said, "Panama." And I had to smile once again. I had done it so many times before, but this time I did it breathing freely.[21]

TOWARD LANDS

OF FREEDOM

CHAPTER VIII

[The relief which we felt to find ourselves on Swedish soil was coupled with a kind of spiritual exhaustion. We tried to talk ourselves out—and we couldn't; for anyone who has lived through days of constant danger knows that eventually the danger becomes a repressed and a static thing which has occasional sharp moments. We were the same as if we had lived in constant pain and suddenly been relieved of it—or as people cured of insomnia. We could sleep at last, resting deeply through the long night hours.]

We were in Göteborg, the advance post of communication between the unhappy countries of Europe and the free nations of the Americas.

When we reached the Hotel Kung Karl, near the station, I presented my documents at the office. Being tired of so much deception, I wrote down "Married" in the hotel registry, thus performing with the stroke of a pen the marriage of Alvarez to the widow of Guerra. But while my wife was once more my wife, my children ceased to be my children, as our passports stated that Señora Guerra was a widow in 1940 and Alvarez had been a bachelor until this day. Documents and trouble go hand in hand.

Once we were in our room, the telephone rang. It was the manager.

"I would like to ask whether you are married."

"We are, sir," I answered.

"But your passports are of different nationality."

"Naturally. In America, each married person keeps his own nationality."

"Of course, but the children have a different name from yours."

"Of course. I only married their mother last year."

"Have you a certificate to prove this?"

"No, sir, the German customs officials kept all my papers. But if you wish to write to Berlin for confirmation . . ."

"Our apologies for what might seem to be an impertinence, but you understand the police are stricter every day, especially in these times."

I did not have the papers they wanted, but they might easily have disappeared in the customhouse in Berlin, for when we checked our luggage through to Göteborg, the police kept all my papers and books. Their naïveté amused me since they were so suspicious of the papers I had in my suitcases and paid no attention to anything we carried on our persons.

In Germany it was easy to find the same administrative laziness which one can observe in any bureaucracy which is either worn out or excessively complicated. In no other country in the world are the regulations for foreigners so simple as in Nazi Germany. In all the papers I used to enter, remain or leave the country, there is not one picture or one fingerprint of mine. The permit which the Gestapo gave me in Belgium could have been used by any one who said his name was Dr. Alvarez.[1]

We had spent only a few days in Göteborg when we learned through the travel bureau that our departure from Sweden had to be approved by both the English and the German authorities. This news worried us as there had been several cases of refugees who were denied this permission. Also they told us that all ships to America were stopped and searched at the first Norwegian port, probably Kristiansund. I could not forget the words of my Minister: "They are capable of waiting till the last moment, just to make fun of us."

The last boat for America had left just three days before our arrival, and no one knew how long we should have to wait for another. The only money we had left was eighty dollars, but at least we were able to communicate with our friends in the United States, though this had to be done via Berlin. However, we had a prompt answer and enough money was sent to last out our stay in Sweden and to replenish our wardrobes. Our clothes might have had a sentimental value for us, as they were the ones we had worn since our memorable trip from Dunkirk—but they also might have betrayed us. There is no better way to disguise oneself than by putting on a new suit of clothes and showing the world that one has plenty of money. When we were in Berlin, the Swedish Minister didn't want to grant us the visas because our friends had only sent two thousand dollars. When my Minister answered, "Where it says two thousand you can count on twenty thousand," the Swedish Minister answered, "Ah, then that is quite different." Apparently our respectability depended entirely on an extra zero.

We were completely alone in Göteborg, and time seemed to pass too swiftly, with nothing accomplished. One becomes impatient. When we were in Berlin I had to suppress my impatience constantly. Now there was only one thing for me to do—and that was to find someone I could trust implicitly. There was one employee in the travel agency who had the kind of open and generous face I was sure I could trust. I told him our full story. Lucky for us, he had been deeply concerned over the fate of the Basques in the war, and the razing of Gernika had made a terrific impression upon him.[2]

"From now on," Mr. Petterson said, "you may count on me as your friend, and I will help you."

He confided in me that there were some fifty thousand refugees in Sweden, all clamoring to get out to America. "Not more than one boat leaves every month," he said to me, "and as that is a merchant vessel there are not more than ten or twelve places; but I think we will manage all right."

We had several pleasant evenings with Petterson. We found the people in Göteborg were anti-Nazi—though we were told that there was a small minority group who were friendly to Hitler either because they had lived in Germany or because they were afraid of Communism.

Everyone in the hotel listened to the news from London: the elevator boys, the room clerks, the guests, all crowded close to the radio to find out what was happening. They warned me against one man who was known to be friendly to the Hitler regime and suspected of being a member of the Gestapo. Conversations overheard in the streets, articles in the newspapers, everywhere one found a strong anti-Nazi atmosphere. But side by side with this profound feeling of hostility toward Hitlerism, I observed during my long two months' stay in Sweden that there was also a strong feeling of hostility and suspicion of Russia. There were two different reasons for this, according to the working people with whom I talked. The first reason was that the workers of Sweden thought the position of the worker in the Soviet Union was poor and his standard of life infinitely inferior to that of the Swedish worker.[3] The other reason for the hostility toward Russia was the Russian attitude toward Finland and the Baltic States, Esthonia, Lithuania, and Latvia.

In order to measure their reactions I used to argue with them, "But isn't it possible that they have occupied these countries for strategical reasons in case of a war with Germany?"

Their answer was always the same: "What is bad is always bad."

The firmness of convictions among the workers in Sweden was one of the most interesting things that I was able to observe in this country where so many social advances had been carried out successfully. However, their feeling of revulsion toward the Hitler regime was really much stronger than their lack of sympathy for the Soviet Union.

2

Our friend Petterson informed us that our boat could not sail before the 5th of July. He advised us to go to Båstad, where we could enjoy the beach and, he said, live much more economically than in Göteborg. We had three surprises when we reached Båstad. The first was the splendor and magnificence of the Hotel Skåne-gården and its beautiful location on the sea.

My wife's first remark was: "José Antonio, I am sure Petterson has made a mistake. This hotel could not possibly be cheaper than the one in Göteborg."

"But the price he quoted was less than what we were paying in Göteborg," I answered. And so the second surprise came from a young lady who warned us that the price we paid covered only our rooms and not the cost of our meals—which made our stay in Båstad much more expensive, of course. The third surprise was to find that most of the other guests at the hotel were Protestant ministers of the Swedish Church who were attending a convention.

One evening after dinner one of the ministers came over to our table and started talking in perfect Spanish.[4] He had lived for several years in Chile, working for an English company, before becoming a minister. As he understood that we were "Latin Americans" he felt he must speak to us. After discussing America with that self-assurance which I had learned from my lessons in Berlin, and which, I could tell, made my wife feel like laughing, we began to discuss the question of the war.

"There is really a strong anti-Nazi feeling in this country," I said.

"Why shouldn't there be?" the Protestant minister answered. "We have the sad examples of the nations occupied by Hitler too near at hand, so much persecution—"

"And not even the ecclesiastics escape from it," I put in.

"If Hitler invades Sweden," the minister answered, "our Church would be the first to suffer. There would be many Niemöllers here. We would never submit to any spiritual slavery."

As he talked I could only agree with him enthusiastically.

"Here in Sweden," he said, "we know and can recognize the

neopagan policies of Hitlerism. When they try to make the churches submit to their authority they try at the same time to discredit them and make people lose confidence in them. You already know their campaign in Germany. First they alienate the young people, and then whomever they can. This is the most serious problem of modern times. Up until today the churches have been able to defend themselves, for they live under free governments; but if Hitler succeeds in dominating Europe by force, Christianity will have the worst setback of its history. We could never allow such an anti-evangelical doctrine as the Nazis' to filter into our seminaries. Their cult of reason, their adoration of force, the Hitlerian concept of justice and law, their scorn of Christianity for its Judaic origin, and all other similar ideas would be attacked by us and never accepted. And that would be immediately followed by the closing of our churches. That is one reason why Hitler wants to form a German Church, as he is trying to do now in Norway."

"But he has made a great failure in Germany."

"Absolutely. But there are always Judases ready to fall in with the plans of their powerful masters. The harm which they do is incalculable. Moreover, they accuse the priests and ministers who refuse to preach their absurd inventions of unpatriotism. Grave conflicts with young people grow out of such accusations."

"Do you think the Swedish people realize the danger?" I asked.

"Perfectly. That is why they are so opposed to Hitler."

"What about Russia?" I asked the good minister, since I had already heard so many reactions to the Soviet. "It looks as though she will get into the war soon."

He thought for a minute before answering. "Russia is another danger, but in a different way. There is another ideology with universal pretensions, but we are all apt to forget that it is more or less indigenous to Russia and can hardly be transplanted. I believe the Communist movements of the world are destined to disappear. In spite of the fact that our Scandinavian countries are so socially advanced, Communism has never been able to get a foothold here, because it doesn't fit in at all with our way of life. We have had Socialist governments for years, supported by everyone, because these governments have known how to respect our democratic liberties. In Russia they have been able to maintain a system of dictatorship and negation of liberty, because in Russia the masses are not prepared for democracy."

"Do you believe that the Soviet regime will be able to apply the materialistic conception of true Marxism to the full, or on the other hand that the mystic conception of Holy Russia and the revolutionary spirituality of the nineteenth century will rise to the surface again and even triumph over the other?" I asked.

"The phenomenon of Russia is unique," the minister answered. "In Russia there have been only two great forces: the tsar and the people. Between these two forces, the nobility, the orthodox clergy, and during the nineteenth century all the revolutionaries of the 'intelligentsia' have played their role. But between these classes and the people there was an impassable gulf. The people looked to the tsar as their liberator, but he either did not know how or was unable to liberate them, since he was the first prisoner. To a certain extent, the socialist revolution which has shaped the Soviet regime has liberated the people. But here again we have a conflict between the beliefs and age-long traditions of this conglomeration of countries, which make up the Soviet Union, and the new Bolshevik mysticism, which tries to implant an entirely new concept of life in its peoples. I believe that the regime will have to yield—and there are indications of it now—to the immense spiritual pressure of the Russian people."

"I think you are right," I said. "History tends to repeat itself with monotonous regularity. Remember the attempts of Peter the Great, and later Catherine, who both tried to change the mentality of their country. It is true that they did it in the name of 'enlightenment' and in an attempt to westernize Russia, but it is no less true that they failed miserably and aroused considerable hostility in the process." I asked the minister if he thought that the influence of a mystic communism had had a much greater influence on the Russian people than all that encyclopedic philosophy of the eighteenth century.

"I think so," replied the minister. "It's very difficult for people to comprehend a doctrine which *talks* a great deal *about* liberty but leaves them enslaved. Freedom of thought could not interest the masses of Russian people, while the fruits of their labors were enjoyed by others. The Soviet regime, on the other hand, has freed them from this physical slavery, in spite of all its other defects. The country has been relieved of a tremendous burden, mainly that imposed by the nobility, which took possession of all the land. But in spite of being oppressed for so many years the Russian people have often experienced a feeling of liberation; so it is not strange that they should patiently follow doctrines which they don't understand and are not even interested in. They have seen the results, and that is enough for them, and although they are perfectly satisfied with their social liberation the spiritual influence of the past centuries is so great that their beliefs stand up under all the attacks of propaganda. I know that the atheistic campaigns have failed. A new revolutionary period is beginning which will bring about the liberation of the spirit. Did you know that today they are permitting the great thinkers of the nineteenth century to be published?"

"Yes, and in the universities they are beginning, however timidly, to lecture on human rights," I said. "This is an advance toward westernization and in a certain sense a return to the Christian conception of social relations."

"I wouldn't go so far as to say that it was a new tendency toward westernization—but at least toward spiritualization. The Marxist doctrine has failed in its materialist conception. It has succeeded in incorporating its social concept and the practical consequences of it in the framework of modern societies."

"Which of these two tendencies will triumph?" I asked.

"That will depend a great deal on the position of Russia in the present conflict. If she draws near the western world in her struggle against Germany, the process of westernization will be accelerated and the whole world will benefit. If she remains isolated, the struggle between the bureaucracy, which represents the Bolshevik tendencies, and the immense spiritual power of the people, accumulated through the centuries, will remain internal. But if Russia compromises with Germany, then we shall witness the greatest human tragedy of modern times or of all times, for the enormous population of Russia will succumb to Nazi power which respects nothing; and this will lead to an epoch of physical and spiritual prostration which humanity has never known before."

"Then you believe that, in these times, Nazism is much more dangerous than the Soviets?"

"Without a doubt. The Nazi doctrine was born in the West and is directed against western civilization. It is a new powerful, materialistic force which is sweeping forward too impetuously. As it aspires to universality, a Nazi victory would mean a sweeping application of its law, while if Russia leans toward the democracies (as it appears she will) and triumphs with them, she will find herself under the influence of her allies—England and the United States—who since they are more powerful will have the final say. We may almost have confidence that Russia will become a Christian bulwark in the future."

Mari had long since gone upstairs to be with the children, and the hour was very late; but I had spent one of the most interesting evenings of my journey, and I was determined to make notes of our conversation as soon as I went to my room.

"I admire the interest you take in these important problems," I told the Protestant, "and, more than anything, I admire your knowledge of them."

"It's not unusual for us," he answered; "because of our country's geographical position, we are at the crossroads of all these ideologies."

"But I am glad to know that all of you are resisting so strongly any attempts to introduce these doctrines," I answered.

"When a country has lived in freedom," the minister said, "and has known how to develop this freedom without too much friction, it stays healthy and has no need to seek salvation through despotism or tyranny."

"You are right," I said, and stood up to bid him good night. And I could not help commenting, "Only when one loses one's liberty does one become aware of the fact that it has no possible substitute."

3

The tension between Germany and Russia became constantly greater, and as it grew so did the anxiety of the Swedish guests at the hotel. Again we had to hear how lucky we were to be Americans.

A Swedish diplomat was spending his vacation at our hotel. He was a very kind man and was fond of our children. He gave my little boy a magnificent rubber fish, and from that moment on he became the child's idol. One day he came over to us at lunch and said:

"As you are not Europeans, I am wondering if you understand the risks you are running?"

"Why?" we asked ingenuously.

"Because war between Germany and Russia is very near. Once hostilities begin, they will surely close all the frontiers; and I'm afraid they'll stop all boats sailing for America."

"That would be terrible. What should we do?"

"Go to London," the diplomat answered.

"To London? How?"

"By plane. You ought to start making arrangements immediately with the American and English Ministers and leave as soon as possible. I can give you some introductions in Stockholm."

It would be a wonderful plan for getting out, if it were not for the children. I suggested that because of them it might be difficult, and the man spoke very feelingly: "Poor little children! They are so nervous. I am very fond of them and of you, for their sakes. That's why I want to see you get out safely."

We decided, after this conversation, to return to Göteborg. I felt awfully sad and worried. I did not know a single influential person who could help us, and then—as if to remind us of our precarious position—a large German troop train passed us, symbolic of the tribute Sweden was forced to pay for her neutrality. My little daughter quickly noticed the swastika on the coaches and said:

"But, Aita [daddy], you said that there were no Germans here!"

"There are none," I answered. "They live in Germany."

"But that train had their flag on it."

"You didn't notice the colors. The colors were different."

"Oh!" exclaimed Aintzane. But she was not completely convinced.

On our return to Göteborg I got in touch with my friends in New York. There were so many cables and long-distance telephone calls that Petterson warned me they might arouse suspicion, especially all the phone calls that had to go through Berlin.[5]

The 22nd of June, Mr. Petterson telephoned me, "Dr. Alvarez, the war between Germany and Russia has begun."

Two instinctive reactions shook me to the core. One was of joy, "Hitler is definitely lost now," and the other of agonized grief: "Dear God, how can we get out now? Must we see the Kommandantur here also?"

I went out that afternoon with my wife and children to walk in the park. It was Sunday, and there were throngs of people; loudspeakers from bordering restaurants gave out war news every few minutes. Every face was grave, and people spoke in hushed tones. Newspapers were snatched from the hands of the venders as soon as they appeared. Not even the children played that afternoon.

When we returned to the hotel, the clerk on duty seemed very excited. "So the anti-Communist fight is beginning," I remarked, wanting to test him.

"Anti-Communist fight?" he demanded. "Nobody believes Hitler in Sweden. We have lost neither our memory nor our decency here."

Three days went by. A laconic dispatch from Stockholm announced that Sweden would permit the passage of German troops through the north. Everyone was terribly upset by this news. My friends in America sent word that they could no longer send any money, for the Government of the United States had forbidden it. Without money, with fictitious names, with no protection . . . But the 26th of June was my little son's birthday. We went to the park and even rode on the merry-go-round and the mechanical automobiles. That day we had to live in the world of childhood, where wars and worries are prohibited.

When we returned to the hotel there was word that Mr. Petterson had asked me to call at his office. He told me the good news that within three weeks a boat would sail for Rio de Janeiro.

"Do you think Sweden will remain neutral for that time?" I asked him.

"I don't know, Dr. Alvarez. I don't know. What I do know is that the country is terribly indignant over Parliament's decision to allow the passage of German troops. They would rather fight than permit this dishonor."[6]

"I realize that," I answered, "but it's an ill wind which blows nobody good; and, thanks to the sad situation here, my chances to escape to America are better."

4

Theoretically Sweden was a neutral country; in fact, the ugly shadow of German fascism had descended upon her. Göteborg gave the same impression of inaction and sadness as Antwerp or Hamburg. There is something of the quietness of death in all of them. The numberless ships and ocean liners tied up to the wharfs made Göteborg look like a cemetery of petrified monsters.

Depression in the shipping industry affects the whole population. Restaurants are almost empty, the hotels see their clientele vanishing, and the stores sell less and less every day. The increased taxation needed to preserve "neutrality" with half a million men under arms adds to the economic crisis. Moreover, Sweden, a country whose economy is based on a flourishing foreign trade, had to export exclusively to Germany and accept in payment Hitler's depreciated currency. Small cargoes going from time to time to South America could scarcely be a remedy to the general collapse. It is the fate of all Europe, victim of the great adventure of the tragic mysticism of the Germans.

In the afternoons we used to walk through the harbor. Only two ships seemed to give an appearance of life. Thin columns of smoke arose from their funnels.

"Look," we would tell our children, "they are painting them so we may leave."

There were many other refugees taking these watchful walks— looking at those ships as their only means of salvation.[7]

One day in July we decided to go and see a horse race, which turned out to be quite different from an afternoon at Ascot or Chantilly. The race track in Göteborg was one of the most democratic sights I have ever seen. Sailors with tattooed arms mingled with the sons of the first families of the town, the young girl of a rich family sat close to one who cares for children at the botanic garden. Our hotel clerk, who had suggested the outing, was not missing, and to complete the democratic picture King Gustav also arrived—very quietly and with no fanfare at all; but the audience soon recognized him and stood up to clap with respect and affection.

We had hardly returned from our pleasant afternoon when Mr. Petterson called to give us bad news. "The company won't admit the children," he said. "On the last trip they took two children and two sailors had to take care of them. The children were so seasick, and the parents still more. So, you and your wife may leave—but alone."

"I have never heard such a ridiculous proposition," I said. "What on earth does this amazing company think we are going to do— leave our children behind?"

"They say that because the ships don't have a doctor or a nurse."

"I think it is an excuse to give our tickets to some more influential refugees," I answered, and I was also determined not to give in.

Next day the company notified us a boat would be leaving for New York the 15th of August, that it had a doctor and a nurse, and that they would reserve passage for us; and then the boat was not going to New York but to Rio de Janeiro, and the sailing date was not in August but some time in October. The more I learned, the more my suspicions were confirmed.[8]

Mr. Petterson told me that no one could understand why an American should have to get out. All day long, our good friend said, he had to listen to such questions as:

"Who is this Dr. Alvarez?"

"After all, what can happen to him—an American!"

"A Panamanian has nothing to lose."

"Dr. Alvarez will have to understand . . ."

"My dear Petterson," I said, "I think the moment has arrived to make it known that Dr. Alvarez is a poor fool of whom all the world is making fun.[9] Will you go with me to Stockholm where Aguirre will

again make his appearance? Then there will be three of us to continue the struggle. You, Alvarez, and Aguirre. There are times, I
think, when one must act with decision. Do you agree with me?"

"I am at your service," he answered, and "Alvarez," Petterson, and
I left for Stockholm on the night of June 25th.

We arrived early the next morning and went straight to the Brazilian Legation. When we told the secretary we wanted to get a visa
and showed him our passports, he made quite a fuss—but finally
made an appointment for us to see the Minister that afternoon.
Perhaps—just perhaps—something might be arranged. While we
were at the Legation we were able to confirm the fact that none of
the eight passengers who had reservations on the boat had received
the Brazilian visa, as they had not yet heard from Rio. Dr. Alvarez
immediately flew to the nearest telegraph office, where he cabled his
friends in New York asking them to arrange it so that no visas should
be granted to anyone before they were granted to Americans "such
as himself"; then he telephoned his friend Dr. Despradel in Berlin.

"What!" said the Dominican Minister. "You haven't your visa yet?
We can't allow an American to be pushed aside for anyone. I will
speak to the Brazilian Minister here, and you will see some action
there."

We had a good start. The Brazilian Ambassadors of Washington
and Berlin were telegraphing their colleague in Stockholm, and the
Swedish Minister was telegraphing the steamship company and the
Brazilian Minister.

Then came Aguirre's turn. Mr. Petterson took me to the central
offices of the Social Democratic Party in Stockholm, where he had
many friends. We were received by one of the secretaries of the
party, and I introduced myself to him in my true personality.

The secretary immediately stood up and came toward me with his
hand outstretched. "Are you Mr. Aguirre? I shouldn't have recognized you; but I visited you in Barcelona with a group of Swedish
Parliament members."

This was good luck for us. I explained my precarious position and
asked him if we could reach a person of sufficient influence in the
government who could speak in our behalf to the company so that

my wife, my children, and I might obtain passage on the boat leaving the 31st. The secretary made an appointment with the Prime Minister for the following day.

"I can't tell you how happy I am to be able to serve and help you," the secretary told me. He said that none of Sweden's Social Democrats would ever forget the way the Basques had fought for liberty and democracy, and that the destruction of Gernika had thrown the true light on Franco's false crusade. It made me very happy, of course, to know that so many people in Sweden had followed our fight. "After the destruction of Gernika," he said, "many people, formerly antagonistic, began to open their eyes; and after the Republican government in Spain succeeded in overcoming the initial disorder, still more people were convinced. Later on it was Franco's regime, with its totalitarian ideas and brutal reprisals, which disillusioned even its earliest friends."

"What you tell me does not surprise me in the least," I answered. "Totalitarian propaganda follows a policy of confusion, and in the first moments many people are deceived. The attack had to reach Czechoslovakia, Poland, and many other countries before some people could begin to understand that the uprising of the Spanish militarists had an identical aim: the imposition of a regime by force and, as far as we are concerned, the desire to wipe out a country which wished to live in freedom and govern itself as it had a right to do."

"The fact that the Basques—a religious and orderly people—were fighting side by side with the legitimate Republican government was the most decisive argument against all the adverse totalitarian propaganda," the secretary said. "You people have won the right to liberty. Nobody can dispute that, when the war is over. I envy you in spite of your present sufferings. You have known how to fight."

I thanked him again, and then he asked me quickly, "What do you think of Sweden's present policy?"

"It is difficult for me to answer that question," I said, "since I am ignorant of the motives which determined Sweden's position in the face of German demands; but it seems to me that since the failure of the Scandinavian Pact, the occupation of Norway, and the Finnish war, your position is understandable—although it might be wondered at."

"Yes, but I don't know whether they will interpret it the same way abroad—especially in America. We had become accustomed to the benefits of almost perpetual peace, and when a country becomes too comfortable it goes to all kinds of extremes to preserve material peace. You can tell them in America not to forget what kind of a country we are. Sweden is and will remain democratic. At times we get into situations which might give rise to criticism, but here both the government and the people are on the side of liberty. That is not so in the case of France and Spain—don't you agree? In those countries an anti-democratic group has gained control of the countries and totalitarianism has full sway, because that is what the present leaders believe in; and because of this they constitute a real danger to democracy. But Sweden is a democratic reserve like the rest of the Scandinavian countries, in spite of the Quislings in Norway and Finland's unfortunate war."

"I agree with you," I answered. "After the war is finished, there will be nothing to change here, for you have not changed the regime, nor have the democratic powers recognized any other regime than the democratic. On the other hand, in those other countries—"

"You have explained much of the small countries' discouragement—these recognitions of the enemy's violence. Add to this the inexplicable complicity which has followed the course of Nazi expansion, and it is easy to understand that you cannot expect heroism of the smaller countries when the large ones come to terms with the enemy or with the friends of the enemies of liberty."

We parted great friends, and more than once I have recalled his words "If the big countries come to terms with the enemies of liberty, why expect heroism of the little ones?"

On the 28th of July we visited the Director of the Nordisk Resebyra (travel company). He was quite young, a member of one of the most wealthy families in Sweden. As soon as we were alone with him, I explained my case. At first he looked at me rather suspiciously; but as I told my story his stern and unbelieving expression changed to one of sympathy and understanding.

"I am very glad you have confided in me," he said. "Now I begin to understand many things. Our chief difficulty is the fact that we have promised all the places on the ship, and we don't like to go back on our word. The one solution which occurs to me is that you might get some Swedish authority to request the company to reserve the first four places for you. You might ask the Brazilian Minister to ask this favor of us, also, as it is a question of Americans."

We told him that we had an appointment with the Prime Minister and promised to try and persuade the Brazilian Minister to do us this favor, and we went at once to the Brazilian Legation. The Minister was still invisible. He had many appointments. As it was a case of Americans (here Dr. Alvarez spoke), we hoped that the Minister would recommend us to the company. The secretary told us that the Minister might possibly receive us that afternoon.

We went back to see the secretary of the Social Democratic Party, who told us that the Prime Minister was informed about everything and was deeply interested in helping me. He had asked us to telephone him, and Mr. Petterson did so. All of this time—beneath the rushing around to see one person after another—I was thinking of my wife's anxiety and hoping that when I saw her again I should have good news.

Mr. Petterson turned from the telephone. "The Prime Minister asks us to inform the company in his name that it is his express desire that you and your family leave on the boat sailing the 31st," he reported. "If this direct intervention is not enough, he will receive us tomorrow in the Presidential office. He asks me to greet you for him and express his wish to meet you personally."

"We have won," the secretary said, and we all shook hands again. Petterson and I returned to the travel company, and the Director told us that the Prime Minister's intervention settled everything— but we must have the Brazilian visa.

Dr. Alvarez and Mr. Petterson then hastened to the Brazilian Legation for our appointment. The secretary warned us, as soon as he saw us, that the Minister was very angry. All the high officials, including the Chancellor, of the Legation entered the Minister's office with us. It looked like some sort of grand ceremony.

The Minister, a short, rather fat man with an angry face, asked us to be seated. After putting us through a kind of cross-examination to find out who we both were, he said:

"So, Mr. Petterson, you are asking, in the name of the Nordisk Resebyra, that I take steps with the company to assure this gentleman's passage because he is an American. Do you know that, as there is Swedish honor, there is Brazilian honor? And to ask such a thing only shows your complete ignorance of a Foreign Minister's obligations. Tell your superior that a Brazilian Minister knows what should be done in each case, and that it is not correct to ask for these interventions."

Poor Mr. Petterson did not know what to say. The Minister then turned to me. "As an American, Dr. Alvarez, you have the right to a visa, and I have given orders that you be issued one tomorrow morning in Göteborg—but that is all."

"May I speak a moment, Mr. Minister?" I requested formally.

"Yes, sir," he answered.

"There has been some misunderstanding, Mr. Minister. The most that either Mr. Petterson or I did was to ask you, through your secretary, if you could recommend me as an American—if you considered it wise—to the company, so that they in turn could have the pretext of some authority to give me preference in the places on the boat. I don't believe there could be anything incorrect about that, which is why I wanted to meet you and talk with you personally, as my friends, the South American Ministers, in Berlin, advised in their telegram. Would you like to see it?"

The Minister said that was not necessary as he had received telegrams from my friends himself. He accepted my explanation, and we parted amicably enough.

It was, of course, the Prime Minister's recommendation to the company which clinched everything. It was the 28th of July; the boat sailed on the 31st. Any passenger wishing to reserve passage had to pay the full fare and have all his papers in order. Any one who failed to fulfill all these conditions by the day of departure would lose his passage money. I was the first to accept these conditions and was awarded the first four places.

The only thing which we needed now was the permission of the German and English authorities to cross their respective zones. Mr.

Petterson and Dr. Alvarez went to the German Legation first, where a species of Göring granted our request after talking on the telephone with the German Consul in Göteborg. As a matter of fact, he was a Naval Attaché, who was quite polite to us. He told us that Berlin had called the Consulate twice to ask if permission had been granted yet to Madame de Guerra.

We went to the British Legation, where a very friendly good-looking young Naval Attaché received us. The moment I saw him I knew I could trust him and decided to introduce him to Aguirre—if the need arose.

"But why do you leave these things to the last minute?" he asked us. "We will have to send word to the Admiralty—the boat leaves in three days. . . . I would like very much to help you, but I don't know whether there will be time."

I revealed my true identity to him, and told him my story—all of it in bare outline. When I had finished, he congratulated me on my escape and said:

"You have our permission now. We will do everything necessary to help you. Don't worry any more."

Then he wanted to know more details of our adventures, and we spent a pleasant half-hour. He was very anxious to have me meet the Minister next day, but it was impossible. We had to get back to Göteborg.

To leave, to escape, to reach America. America—that continent which in these years of misery in which we are living has attained a marvelous personality.[10] But it is not so easy to reach this country of salvation. How many unfortunate people have been taken from the docks, almost from the very decks that were to have carried them to freedom, to concentration camps. Perhaps because of me, because of my victory over my competitors for a place in the boat, one of these poor people will end up in prison. But what would have been my own fate had I lost out in that contest? A feeling of infinite compassion weighed on my soul, thinking of them.

When we were already on board the *Vasaholm,* Mr. Petterson, with tears in his eyes, said, "Good luck, a great deal of luck and safe passage to you."

Another of the company's boats had left Göteborg only a few

months before with twelve passengers. They passed the Faeroe Islands and sent their last message. Nothing more was ever heard of the crew or the passengers. This is what was worrying Mr. Petterson, filling him with anxiety for us. What wonderful friends we found everywhere!

Finally on the morning of the 31st of July, the day the Basques celebrate the fiesta of their patron saint, St. Ignatius de Loyola, we embarked on our journey to America. Before leaving I had written a few letters of farewell "until we meet again" to the compatriots whom we left suffering and hoping. One of them even reached the prison in Burgos where my assistants in Santander, whom I had not seen since they said goodbye to me with their glasses high in a toast to our enslaved country, had been imprisoned since 1937. Others never received their letter because they had been shot.

My children, fortunate little ones, realized nothing of all this. For them everything was a pleasant novelty, and from the moment that they entered the boat they were filled with delight with everything they saw. Their high spirits and their laughter attracted the attention of a commander of the Swedish Navy who was coming with us to Rio.

"Are these children traveling with us?" he asked.

"Yes, sir," answered one of the officers.

"Then they will be our salvation. These little ones shall be our mascots."

And that is how my little Joseba, barely three years old, became the pet of the ship.

5

It was a 6,700-ton boat, carrying general cargo for South America and only eight passengers, of whom we were four. The others were three men and a lady, all of Polish nationality but Jewish race. They were people of high position, polite and cultivated, and made pleasant traveling companions during our twenty-eight-day trip to Rio.

We were going to sail in a convoy. Besides that a Swedish destroyer was to escort us to the limits of territorial waters. In the outer harbor we met two beautiful Swedish tankers, of more than 15,000 tons each, and a small boat of 2,000 tons, who were to be our companions on the trip across. The service on board our ship was excellent. Everything was sparkling and clean, which was unusual on a merchant ship. The officers were friendly and polite. But then it was a Swedish boat.

At nightfall all the lights were lighted. Two big searchlights played on the big Swedish flags painted on both sides of the boat. A German seaplane, flying low overhead, saluted us when it was only twenty meters above our funnel. The muffled sound of our engines, going at half-speed, the mysterious and solemn looks on the faces of the captain and officers, the silent progress of the ships following us in the convoy, all gave the impression of some one tiptoeing quietly, hoping to pass unnoticed without waking the neighbors.

"We will sail close to the coast until we reach the German port of control at Kristiansund, Norway," the captain informed us. "Have all your papers ready, for it is possible that the Germans will want to examine them all."

A chill passed through us. Again the Germans . . . Always some doubt remains in our hearts. Any small indiscretion of any of the people who knew of our fortunes, believing us safe because we had escaped from Germany, any small careless detail which might furnish the police with a clue to our whereabouts, and the suspicion of "my Minister" in Berlin that "they are capable of leaving it to the last minute"—all this was so serious that we could not help worrying.

But we arrived at Kristiansund early in the morning, and the Germans entered the boat while we were sleeping. When we awoke, we were again on the high seas making for the English control in the Faeroe Islands. Our fears of the Gestapo were ended, for they did not control the seas.

During that first day at sea, our dreaded adversaries, the mines, made their appearance. Two of them, with their menacing tentacles, passed close by our ship. Immediately they began signaling with flags from stern to prow of the boats in our convoy, giving the exact position of the mines. We continued to see mines during the next two days, at least ten of them (that is the number I counted)—but

considerably more, to judge from the captain's smile when he heard
the figure I gave. The captain did not go to bed during the first ten
days. Nighttime was, of course, the most dangerous time for the
boat. We spoke a great deal about submarines to the Polish lady and
my wife. We wanted to get the idea of the mines out of their heads.
For submarines can see and mines cannot, and we were a neutral
vessel. These infernal contrivances which passed us in broad daylight at less than a hundred yards—how could they possibly be
located at night in that stormy sea?

On the 3rd of August we saw our first English planes. They circled
around our convoy, flying so low that they barely cleared our masts
in order to salute us. This sight had a deeper significance. It meant
that we were starting to travel through latitudes where liberty ruled.
And after only three days of sailing. Truly, when one thinks of the
great size of the earth and especially of the immensity of the seas it is
easy to realize how really puny is the power of the Germans in spite
of the fear which their war machine still inspires. I always used to tell
those South American students in Berlin to look at their maps, for
then they could see at a glance who the victor must be, unless it
should happen that those who ought to win preferred to lose. Then
it would be a question of will or lack of it.

On the morning of the 4th of August we drew near the Faeroe
Islands (owned by Denmark but occupied by the English), passing
between them and Iceland. When we reached the Faeroes a little
Norwegian pilot boat met us and guided us into the harbor, where
we dropped anchor for an hour and a half. Although it was August it
was quite cold. The summits of the small mountains were covered
with fog. The sadness of the atmosphere, the barrenness of nature,
the harshness of the climate were a natural setting for one of those
beautiful Norse legends, and the mystery which always surrounds
an island fortress far out to sea added color to the strange impression.

British officials appeared shortly on deck. While some of the
sailors with their enormous waterproof coats went about their inspection of the hold of the ship, the officer went over the list of
passengers and their passports. He didn't even look at my face; but

perhaps he knew who I was. They went through the whole thing very seriously and decorously.

We were allowed to leave. This permission granted us in the Faeroe Islands, the natural boundary between the old world and the new, had an important meaning. It was like a license to enter into the world of freedom. There was even a door in the shape of a little strait formed by two of the islands, through which we had to pass before continuing our Atlantic voyage. There was quite a gale blowing when we made the passage. The waves swept over the deck and even reached the bridge. But the faces of the passengers were happy and satisfied.

That night the captain said to me, "Don't say anything to anyone, but we are entering a very dangerous zone, at least for the next forty-eight hours." My little ones were sleeping tranquilly. Danger did not exist for them. After ten days of sailing they told us that we were finally out of danger.

We were sailing in a heavy fog. The foghorns of the convoy sounded constantly. That mournful sound in the middle of the ocean gave one a very strange feeling. It was as though in the middle of that silence they were calling the sleeping submarines.

[On the 9th of August the convoy separated. In the middle of a storm those magnificent tankers, all lighted up, passed close by us, making a beautiful spectacle. That night, after saying goodbye to the convoy, would be the first night that the captain had taken off his clothes to go to bed. The lifeboats and rafts were no longer in their position for danger. The lifebelts were put away, all but the two little ones the officers had made for the children; these they left out for the youngsters to play with.]

It was the 14th of August. At this same time the lone figures of President Roosevelt and Churchill were sailing in unknown waters of the Atlantic. The warships that carried them had met in open ocean in order to lay down the eight points of the Atlantic Charter, a charter of freedom for the world, of hope and alleviation for those who are suffering persecution for having defended justice. The day was almost over. I was in the cabin with my children, telling them one of the old Basque tales. They were listening attentively as they did each night after they had said their bedtime prayers. The story was interrupted by one of our companions who knocked at the door of the cabin, calling:

"Dr. Alvarez, come to the radio quickly. There has just been an important announcement. Roosevelt and Churchill have met in the middle of the Atlantic."

The radio was giving the news. It gave us a very special emotion to listen to that agreement and the conclusions arrived at for the good of the world, made on the same ocean we were sailing. Moreover, for the persecuted, for those of us who had come from beloved lands now subjected to oppression, it was like a special welcome sent to us in open ocean telling us to go our way in peace, that our hopes were not in vain. With our ears glued to the loud-speaker we followed word by word. The English and the Americans were speaking:

[They did not seek territorial aggrandizement.

They did not wish to make any territorial changes that did not respond to the wishes of the people.

They respected the rights of all countries to choose freely their form of government and wish to see restored the sovereignties and self-government taken away by force . . .

Big and little countries will have access to the raw material of the world.

All countries should collaborate economically to better the standard of work, the economic progress and the social security of all.

When the Nazi tyranny has disappeared a peace will be established among the nations so that man can live without fear and without want.

The peace will give the right to sail freely on all the seas and oceans of the world.

A system of collective security will abolish force and arrange for disarmament.]

We listened in silence. Each one recalled his own past tragedies. My Polish companions and I were citizens of countries both of which had been overrun by an enemy, countries with governments in exile, whose families had been despoiled and were in ruins, witnesses of horrible repressions and cruelties. The eight points sounded in our ears like the promise of reparation, of justice, and of peace.

"It was time they made such a declaration!" one of my companions exclaimed with enthusiasm.

"A magnificent declaration," I replied. "It has a universality which could only be given it by men of such moral stature as Roosevelt and Churchill, who understand perfectly that they are guardians not only of their own countries but also of the entire world. We shall not easily forget this declaration heard from the ocean, the same ocean from which it was made."

"And it is generous, for these men begin by renouncing territorial expansion for their respective countries."

"The chief difficulty, as always happens, is its practical application. Broad programs are generally very attractive. The trouble begins when they start putting them into practice. Let us take a real case as an illustration. Take your own country, Poland. According to the rules just laid down, all territory dominated by the Nazis shall be freed. But what about that occupied by the Russians: does the same thing apply there?"

"I should think so, for they said they don't want any territorial changes, except those freely agreed to by the interested countries. And that territory was occupied by force."

"That is true, but what countries does it mean? The interested countries, or the countries whose transfer is being sought? Suppose that Russia refuses to give back the occupied Polish territory and it is impossible to reach an agreement between the Polish and Russian governments: don't you think that the will of the people living under a government or State which is not their own, or which they do not like, is the thing that should be respected and consulted? Take another case. In very difficult circumstances for Czechoslovakia, after she had been invaded and taken over by Hitler, you Poles invaded a portion of this country on the pretext that the inhabitants were Poles. It was not exactly an appropriate time for such an action, even though you may have been right and the people were of Polish origin. Don't you think it would have been more suitable to wait and let the people most concerned in the transfer express their own desires? In cases like these, the practical regulation of the desires of the people is a very delicate matter, and a set of rules must be laid down which will open a channel through which the will of the people can flow. This would be an aid to liberty and to necessary national or spiritual homogeneity of a country, and thus would help to preserve peace. Of course, to carry all this out, there must be a powerful and respected international authority and machinery for forcing its decision on recalcitrants; but no one today doubts the necessity of such an authority. It is a human requirement."

"I agree with you, Dr. Alvarez," my Polish companion answered; "but I give even more weight (since you have led the discussion to more practical ground) to the most important problem of all, that of man and his individual liberty in relation to the form of government of his country. For if the right of a people to choose the form of government which suits it best, according to one of the eight points, is not limited by a moral statute which will preserve the rights of the individual, we can easily have a return of the tragedy we are witnessing today. In the new society after the war, would a country be free to choose a tyrannical form of government for itself, one which failed to recognize the most elementary rights of man? Would a regime like the Nazi one, or anything similar, be permitted? I believe what people are apt to forget in these times: that it is not States that need protection but individual men, persons of flesh and blood who live in these States. For what is the State useful if it does not serve the development of man and the natural societies which seek to perfect themselves beneath the protection of the State? For this reason it is hard for me to believe that they would forsake man by giving all-embracing liberty to the countries to choose, perhaps, antihuman governments. To come to that, it's hardly worth while to spend so much blood."

"I think I can see in the declaration which we have just heard a difference between the words 'form of government' and 'regime.' Perhaps they chose the former in order to define the faculty of each country to choose for itself the political form of government which it deems most suitable.

"That is to say that these words refer more to the external form of sovereignty, and to its free expression by a country, than to its internal constitution.

"On the other hand, you will have noticed in the sixth clause they speak of peace which will allow all countries to live securely within their borders, and which will give to all men of all countries of the world (observe the importance of these words) the faith that in the future they will be able to live free from fear and from want. You must understand that the promise of such a peace cannot be accomplished solely by the overthrow of the Nazis, as the signers of the Charter say, if anti-democratic regimes are to be allowed in other countries. The oppressed people of those countries would find themselves deceived not only because of the insincerity of the promises but because their enormous sacrifices would have been rendered useless. And that is why I believe that the concepts of the rights of nations have a Wilsonian meaning and refer intentionally to small oppressed countries. In this respect the Anglo-Saxon policy has been constant and practically unanimous."

"It seems strange to me that you who are an American should take such interest in European problems, especially those of small nations. For in general in America these problems don't exist, and even the concept of nationality has a different meaning," replied my companion.

"It is that very contrast which has always attracted me," I replied, dissembling yet again. "If the European and American concepts of these things are different, they are a reality which one ought not to forget, and which ought to be respected if one is not to act mistakenly. Europe is the cradle of many countries, each one of which is jealously guarding its own home. This fact produces much good and a deep-rooted love of country, but also great evils and defects. One of these is exclusiveness and the constant quarreling, like neighbors who live together constantly. In America the countries have been formed by mixed emigrations, and they have had to find formulas for living together which have had very interesting and advantageous practical results. Each person sacrificed his original nationality and changed it for a citizenship which as time went on acquired new characteristics so strong as to create a new concept of nationality. And in time they showed the same abilities and made the same mistakes as Europe for they are all men, and Nature's laws are the same for all. But, generally speaking, in America there is a broader vision, and that is why they look with such wonder at Europe's rankling problems. Both concepts have their advantages and their disadvantages. There is, however, an agreement on principles among men of good will in both latitudes. The concept of man and his liberty, a country's right to freedom, condemnation of force, disapproval of all kinds of imperialism, the necessity of international order based on freedom—these are all common principles felt as strongly in one hemisphere as in the other, and producing conferences and agreements as important as that which Roosevelt and Churchill have just signed. Today's agreement will have an enthusiastic reception throughout the world because it is an answer to universal human needs and worries, and because there will be hope for a universal application of its principles."

6

We had been at sea just twenty-four days when we caught our first glimpse of the Brazilian shores. We were looking at America. We had reached the promised land.

As an "American," my importance grew, the closer we got to Rio. All my companions began asking for my help. The Polish couple had American visas which expired the 30th of August, and the boat would not dock until the 27th. How could they reach the United States in three days? To that, they had to add a Brazilian visa to disembark. If they could not get it, their situation was grave, for they had a return visa for Sweden and would be forced to make the trip back again in the same boat. Those people were truly to be pitied.

"Help us, Dr. Alvarez, help us," the wife begged me, "for if they won't let us disembark in Rio I will throw myself into the sea before returning to Sweden. I would rather die than be put in a concentration camp."

"Calm yourself, madam. I am sure everything will turn out all right here," I answered like an amiable protector.

I had to laugh at myself in the role of protector, thinking that I might well end up in prison myself if the police should become aware of my true identity and decide to put an end to the joke of Dr. Alvarez. How surprised my protégés would be!

On the morning of the 27th of August we reached the marvelous Brazilian capital. My traveling companions were very nervous. I had to pretend not to be, for here was another frontier and another customs to be passed. I could leave the vessel, but not so my poor traveling companions. Some relatives who had come out to meet them in a small boat announced that they had been unable to get the Brazilian visas. There was no way for them to reach America except by plane, and all the seats were taken. Moreover without the Brazilian visa they could not leave the ship. They were so discouraged they cried. I begged the police to let them leave so that they could try and make some arrangements. They consented to it. The Polish couple took the plane that night for New York. How? I don't know.

When we first set foot on South American soil I felt like bending down and kissing it. Here was a free land, something I had not seen for a long time.

7

The irregularity of my position made it advisable for me to leave Brazil as soon as possible. My arrival was known to my friends in New York and Buenos Aires, but they kept it a closely guarded secret. Any indiscretion might do me a great deal of harm as it would be a case of falsification of documents. I had to go on keeping my true identity a secret.

They had some very good news for me. Mr. Stevenson, the former British Consul in Bilbao, to whom I had written when he was in Moscow, was now Consul General in Rio. When I went to see him he recognized me at once in spite of my mustache and greeted me with great feeling. Through him I got into contact with the American

Embassy as it seemed to me necessary, and the polite thing, to explain my real situation. As I had no documents to prove that I was really Aguirre, Stevenson supplied proof. I was received with great cordiality. They promised to call me from the Embassy as soon as they received instructions from Washington.

Meanwhile my wife's Venezuelan passport had lapsed. She needed it to leave Brazil, where we were still using our fictitious names.

We made a trip to the Venezuelan Consulate. When the Consul saw that Madame the widow of Guerra was from Mérida, he said:

"I come from Mérida too, but it is strange that I don't recognize these names. What was your father's name?"

"José," answered my wife, while the Consul looked at us perplexedly.

Then followed a series of questions which my wife answered calmly enough. Apparently all the personnel of all the Venezuelan consulates were from Mérida. Bad luck for my wife. The Chancellor in Berlin was also from Mérida. The Consul was completely mystified by this countrywoman of his who had left Venezuela at the age of three and never returned and knew no one in Mérida. He said:

"Well, since this passport was issued in Antwerp I will consult the Ambassador tomorrow to find out whether a confirmation from Caracas is necessary to renew it."

Fortunately the matter was soon cleared up, thanks to the intervention of the Dominican Minister. I had paid him a visit in order to greet him in Dr. Despradel's name. I told him our story and our difficulties. We shall never be able to forget what the Dominican Ministers have done for us.

Several days passed. I received a telephone call from New York. There was wonderful news for me. I had been appointed visiting professor to Columbia University. The news filled me with emotion. I couldn't go on talking. Something had risen from my heart to my throat. How much I had to thank America for! Cast out of my own country, harried and pursued across half of Europe, in America they not only gave shelter but welcomed me with respect and appreciation. But the honor was not done for me as an individual. It couldn't be. It was for the Basque people, for their secular history of liberty, for their clear conception of democracy, and for the blood bravely spilled in defense of it.

A little later they called me from the American Embassy. Few times have I felt such satisfaction as in that first conversation with the Ambassador, Mr. Caffery. A Catholic and a democrat, like myself, he was a representative of the most powerful democracy on earth, while I was a poor fugitive, a man who had been defeated, but who nevertheless was proud of being the honorable representative of one of the oldest democracies on earth.

"I am glad to be able to tell you," he said, "that I have just received instructions to grant both you and your family permanent residence in the United States. And congratulations on your appointment to Columbia University."

"Mr. Ambassador," I replied, "I should like to express my gratitude both for myself and for my country, for the significant honor which you have done me, and I wish you would send my thanks to the President. Because I know that this honor is not for me but for my country."

Twice I had the pleasure of talking with Ambassador Caffery. With our similar ideologies it was very easy for us to reach an almost identical point of view. It seemed to me that the world had spun around.

I decided to visit Montevideo and Buenos Aires. All my friends and compatriots sent me a perfect stream of enthusiastic invitations from the various political groups of those countries who wanted to show me their esteem and friendship. Both Caffery and Stevenson thought it would be wise to go to another country to resume my own name. Uruguay offered me every kind of facility. There Dr. Alvarez would be sacrificed.

When we reached Rio Grande do Sul, we found the Uruguayan National Congressman, Iturbide, the Uruguayan Consul in Rio Grande and Mr. Uriarte, representing the Basques in Montevideo, waiting for us.

On the 9th of October the little train which joins Rio Grande do Sul with the Uruguayan frontier carried us across the rest of Brazilian territory.

In the last Brazilian station I noticed a young priest wandering around on the platform as though he were looking for someone. I saw he had a little Basque flag pinned to his chest, so I called to him in Basque. He got on the train and embraced me with great feeling. He had not recognized me because of my mustache. He was an exiled member of a Basque religious order, Father Irizar, who lived with other members of his order in a near-by town in Uruguay. All the fathers wanted to go to the frontier to meet me when they read in the papers of my arrival; but as they hadn't enough money they drew lots, and Father Irizar had the luck to represent all the others.

When we reached the frontier they took me by the arm and escorted me across, without formalities of any kind. It was a frontier coup d'état. It was a scene of great emotion. My wife saw her father, and he saw his grandchildren again after a long and tragic separation. There I embraced my colleague in the government, Aldasoro, whom I had not seen since our hours of struggle.

The Uruguayan authorities showered me with attentions.

In the hotel of that frontier town, on the 9th of October, 1941, Dr. Alvarez ceased to exist. But with scissors and razor in my hand, before beginning to cut off my mustache, I said to the reflection I saw in the mirror: "Goodbye, Dr. Alvarez! Thank you, a thousand times—thank you!"

IV

GERNIKA'S MESSAGE

TO AMERICA

CHAPTER IX

["These Are the Times That Try Men's Souls"]

In one sense my book might have ended here.* The "agur" (goodbye) with which I bade farewell to my intimate friend and comrade Dr. Alvarez could have been the closing word. But I should have remained unsatisfied; for I should still have held, bottled up inside me, a small store of ideas and lessons learned which it would have been selfish to keep to myself. What we have learned may hold a very useful lesson for others, and it seems to me a duty to share it with them. We owe it to our respective countries and above all to humanity. Our patriotism must be universal in spirit, for if we allow it to become egotistical and petty it will only serve once again as a pretext for strife among nations.[1]

*[Editor's note: The remainder of the book is devoted to an explication of José Antonio de Aguirre's political and moral philosophy, what he modestly refers to here as "a small store of ideas and lessons learned." Actually, he has shared some of these ideas with us already, as he has used the extended conversations in earlier parts of the book to articulate a number of important themes.

In this first section of part IV, to page 318 (below), Aguirre's principal themes include the following: nationalism (Aguirre's preferred word is "patriotism") is a perfectly valid precept by which to live (a Basque nationalist could not believe otherwise); but nationalism must be "universal in spirit," not "egotistical and petty." How we are to overcome the tension inherent in a contradictory term such as "universal nationalism" remains, unfortunately, elusive even to the end of Aguirre's book. World War II, he goes on, is a great ideological war between two diametrically opposed conceptions of life. Thus, it is more correctly understood not as an international war but as a universal civil war. These two great ideological forces are mutually exclusive; they do not admit of compromise. One is either for liberty or against it, for rationality or for irrationality. Unfortunately, he has discovered much confusion, both in Europe and America, about the true ideological nature of the war. The Spanish civil war is a prime example of this confusion. For example, the threat of communism was used as a scare tactic to persuade Americans to support Franco. Franco's reason for rising was demonstrably not to defeat communism since the coup plotters had begun to plan their uprising as early as 1931, before communism became a threat in Spain. Another scare tactic was the portrayal of Franco as the defender of the Catholic faith, or of Christianity in general, against the forces of atheism. The reality was that the devoutly Catholic Basques were fighting to defend their culture, which obviously included Christian faith. Finally, in a long passage that was added to the English version, Aguirre addresses the nature of Soviet communism under Stalin. Here Aguirre argues, somewhat naively, that because Stalin had signed the Atlantic Charter the Soviet Union was committed to liberalization, a belief that seriously underestimated what another decade of Stalinist rule would produce.]

When I set foot on South American soil I breathed for the first time in many long months the invigorating air of freedom and felt the strength and universality with which liberty endows even the smallest of men. Liberty gave depth and meaning to the tributes which I received. In spite of my own personal insignificance, the men of South America saw in me a symbol of persecuted liberty, and to that they rendered homage. For them, my story represented the epic of a tiny nation with a great soul which had freely shed its blood in defense of liberty.

Having lived for so long in a world of fear and flight and entreaty, everything which I have felt and lived since coming to America seems like a dream, that wonderful dream one has in the lands of oppression. There has been sincere friendliness in the pressure of the hands that have shaken mine, and a smile of understanding and solidarity on the faces of all those with whom I have spoken. To a son of the old world this is quite a novelty, for in Europe there is often more of courtesy than of friendliness, and smiles are studiously measured to correspond with the ideas of the person greeted. The word *simpatía* (friendliness, "niceness"), which is difficult to translate into English, seems to me to symbolize American character. It is more striking to me than the Statue of Liberty or Manhattan's towers of Babel. And united to this quality, there is generosity, a spirit of independence, simplicity, frankness, in a word, youthful exuberance. These qualities are common to all Americans, and I have found them equally among the passengers on the subway and among the highest magistrates of the land. But there also exists here in America the same phenomenon which we have seen in Europe. The war of propagandas has produced some of the same confusion here as there.[2]

The reason for this may be found in ignorance and sometimes in a blameworthy lack of interest, but above all there seems to be confusion over the principles for which this war is being fought.

It seems to be difficult for many people to realize that this war is an ideological struggle, a fight to the death between two diametrically opposed conceptions of life in which the spiritual destiny of all humanity will be determined. This is no mere struggle for the conquest of territory but one for the conquest of souls. For this reason the war we are living through today is more than just another international war. It is a universal civil war whose fronts are so constantly shifting that they not only pit nations against each other but divide the peoples internally as well.[3]

This is the most profound and terrible ideological struggle that humanity has ever witnessed. Today there is only one choice: to be with liberty or against it. On one side are those who believe that the world is peopled by rational beings, who have the right to govern themselves by standards based on respect for liberty and the dignity of the individual and on collaboration and friendly understanding between nations; on the other side are those who, in their pessimistic conception of life, can conceive of no other doctrine than that of force. For some, man is a creation of God whose defects can be cured in time if he is allowed a healthy liberty; for others, man is no more than a degenerate and mischievous being, a creation of the powers of evil, who can be domesticated only by whiplash or gunshot. For the former, tolerance and law are the only standards of government; for the latter, coercion, abuse, and brute force are the only rules of conduct.[4]

["By the Sword Ye Shall Perish"]

A typical example of the ideological confusion existing today is furnished by the attitude of certain people toward the Spanish case, which was and still is one of the chief causes of that confusion.

I happened to be present at the annual dinner of the History Department of Columbia University in New York. Among others seated at my table there was one woman teacher. We were talking of the war, as I suppose the other tables were also; even professors can descend to the world of reality at times. I was very interested in the opinions expressed by my colleagues, but what struck me most was the rabid anti-Hitlerism of the lady professor.

"Anything is permissible which will serve to defeat Hitler," she said, "—alliance with Stalin, or with the devil himself if it were necessary. But he must be smashed."

Everyone applauded the energy displayed by our colleague of the weaker sex.

Then someone began asking me about my adventures in my trip through Germany. I started to tell them a few of the incidents which I had lived through. At about that time the lady began to realize who I was. Though we had been introduced, as so often happens neither one had understood the name of the other. Suddenly she interrupted me.

"Then you must have been fighting against Franco?"

"Yes, madame," I replied, rather startled by the question.

"Ah, then you were very much mistaken."

This left me very much disconcerted, but I replied rapidly with a smile which I hoped had a softening effect on my words.

"Like yourself, madame, like yourself."

"How like me?" she burst out, amazed.

"Of course, since you have just finished saying that you are body and soul against Hitler."

The professor looked at me a moment, and then, as one who begins to see dimly, she answered:

"Oh! Now—I think I begin to understand."

For this rabid anti-Hitlerite, Franco still represented order, and we, his adversaries, were the representatives of disorder, communism, and atheism. Can it be possible that there are still people capable of asking whether the heroes of Elgueta, of Artxanda and of the Nabarra are not vicious criminals instead of valiant patriots who were defending the liberty of their country against unjust aggression? Why, then, sing the praises of the Czechs and Norwegians for their resistance? Only because they were attacked by Hitler? In that case, would an aggression not perpetrated by Hitler cease to be an aggression?

Dear reader, if such an outstanding case of obvious ideological confusion can occur in the History Department of the famous Columbia University of New York, what greater confusion must there not be among other folk who have no time for such learned studies?

The protagonist of the story I am going to tell next happens to be a wealthy American businessman, as young in spirit as in body. One fine day, at the beginning of our war against Franco, he called a meeting of a group of New York bankers and announced his plan of going to Bilbao, where he had many friends, to redeem certain securities which the Americans owned, deposited in the Basque banks. The bankers were horrified at his plan. "You must be crazy," they told him, "for not only are those securities lost for good but the Reds will surely murder you."

But in spite of these dire predictions the agreeable Mr. Minnings turned up one morning in my Presidential office in Bilbao.

"Mr. President," he said, "I know very well what kind of people the Basques are, but I want my friends in New York to know too. Will you grant me one request?"

"Certainly," I replied. "I would like very much to be able to demonstrate the regard we feel here both for yourself and for the United States."

"Well, my request is this: that you hand over to me the American securities deposited in the Basque banks."

"Nothing more than this, Mr. Minnings?"

"Nothing less, Mr. President."

I spoke by telephone with our Minister of Finance, Eliodoro de la Torre, and in a short time Mr. Minnings was in possession of the securities. And if my memory does not serve me ill, they amounted to something like two million pesetas.

A few days later when Mr. Minnings came to bid me goodbye, he was beaming with satisfaction as he said: "At last I have a really good argument to convince the bankers of Wall Street of the heroic struggle which this country is putting up for its liberty. For, believe me, if I arrived and began telling them of your ancient race and original language, and that you are one of the oldest existing democracies, or any other such details, they would pay no attention at all, probably fall asleep. But if the first thing I do is to produce these securities and fling them on the table, then they will listen with respect—especially when I tell them that you handed them over to me at a time when you had not even money to buy arms or feed your blockaded people. This you did because you are neither *Communists* nor *thieves*, as has been said of you, and because you love the United States, a land of liberty. I feel sure that more than one of those bankers will ask me just where this Basque country is situated, so that they can invest their money there after the Civil War."

The tragic death of Mr. Minnings in an automobile accident, shortly after his return to the United States, not only deprived us of a true friend of the Basques, but left us without means of knowing the reaction of the Wall Street bankers on receiving their securities. But I am sure that they would think twice before investing their money in the Basque banks, precisely because of the triumph of Franco, whom they admired and whom they may even have supported with their money because they believed him the "defender of order."

This story serves very well to illustrate the effect produced on certain well-off or moneyed groups by propaganda which makes use of the Communist scarecrow. All this talk serves as an efficient smoke screen to keep people from realizing the true extent of the disaster which has occurred in those countries employing such propaganda. "Fear Communism, which will bring ruin to the country," they cry in horrified tones, when it is they themselves who have brought down ruin, hunger, and desperation on their own people.

When General Franco revolted, the world was inundated with a propaganda of horror and frightfulness. They justified their military rebellion by saying that Spaniards could "no longer live in Spain," that the Republic was "under orders from Moscow," that the *Red hordes* were burning, pillaging, and murdering.

The truth is that both the "Red hordes" and the "White hordes" were guilty of burning, pillaging, and murder. But when all the truth is known the world will be even more horrified by the bloody accomplishments of the "White hordes" than it was over the tales of "Red atrocities." I can state categorically that the victims executed by

Franco's regime are far more numerous than the victims made to suffer at the hands of certain hangers-on of the Republic. This statement may cause disbelief now; but when the time comes, and all the truth is known, reality will confirm me.

As a burnt offering to what principles was this disaster brought about? In the name of order? of anti-Communism? I can say definitely no, for I was a witness and in a certain sense an actor in events which reveal just the opposite.

The following took place in the summer of 1931, the Republic having been proclaimed on April 14 of that year. At that time the Basque country was carrying on a vigorous campaign for the recovery of its lost liberties. It was demanding that the Republic, based on democratic ideals, should recognize its autonomy which had been unanimously voted in assembly of all the Basque municipalities. But Basque aspirations were rudely denied. Influenced by an outmoded anticlericalism, the men of the Republic went so far as to call us the Vatican Gibraltar, stupidly confusing the real Christian ardor of the Basque people with the religious utilitarianism of certain Spanish Rightists.

In the meantime, the Monarchical elements were laying their own plans. Unable to realize their schemes through the suffrage, they decided to resort to the old Spanish custom of the *pronunciamiento* which had been used so often and so successfully in the past century. And to help them carry out their plan they thought of the Basques.

I was in the little town of Deba, where a great meeting of Basque young people had just taken place, when I received a note through a friend of mine from General Orgaz (the present commander in chief of Spanish Morocco) stating that he wished to see me. I granted his request, and we met in the house of a friend. I repeat, all this took place in August, 1931, and not in 1936. The General told me frankly that they were preparing an insurrection, and he wanted help from the Basques.

"If you will give me," he said, "those five thousand young men I saw marching yesterday in Deba, I will be master of Spain tomorrow."

For more than three hours I listened to the General outlining plans and arguments, based always on the use of force to implant a political regime according to his likings and ambition. He also listened to my replies, which were based entirely on respect for the will of the people.

Naturally, the General was full of promises for Basque autonomy, promises so generous and far-reaching that they aroused more suspicion than gratitude. In times such as these, promises are handed out freely and later conveniently forgotten. This was not the first time that we had received promises like this. And what had happened to us had happened to many others also.

Some days later, I had another interview of still greater importance. King Alfonso XIII, then in exile at Fontainebleau, had sent his private secretary, Marquis de las Torres, and one of the chiefs of his escort to negotiate with the Basques. Their object was the same as General Orgaz's: to gain the support of the Basque patriots for an insurrection which was being prepared. Well I remember the words of the royal messengers: "King Alfonso is anxious to make amends for past injustices inflicted on the Basques. You people know how to cling to your ideals even in times when the whole world deserted you." This was a slap at the Spanish Monarchists who were ready to abandon King Alfonso. "And for that reason you deserve different treatment. We have already begun to study the best method for restoring your *fueros*."

Now the *fueros* were the sovereign Basque laws and constitution—that is to say, the basic foundation of the national liberty—which had been stolen from us by the ancestors of Alfonso XIII. Thus it was no small thing which they were promising us.

In exchange for this they asked for our complicity in an insurrection for a cause directly contrary to popular sentiment. My reply that the Basques would fight only for their own liberty or in case of unjust attack displeased them greatly. Neither the Monarchists nor the militarists will ever forgive this refusal to fall in with their plans.

The Spanish conspirators continued scheming without us. General Orgaz founded a society known as the U.M.E. (Unión Militar Española) which was a semisecret organization composed of all those officers and military men who later were responsible for so much bloodshed in the Peninsula in their military revolt.

General Sanjurjo—the Franco of that time—revolted in Seville on August 10, 1932. His insurrection was put down in short order, and he was condemned to death by a tribunal and later pardoned by the President of the Republic, Alcalá Zamora. This generosity on the part of the Republic was completely misunderstood by the militarists and served only to increase their contempt.

Also I should not neglect to mention the trip which Señor Goicoechea, the Monarchist leader, and others of his persuasion, made to Rome in 1935. At that time they obtained from Mussolini promises of important economic and military aid for their proposed insurrection.

The sympathy of this dissatisfied group for Italy was well known. And when Hitler came to power in 1933, he was roundly applauded by the same elements who favored the use of force to impose *order* in their own country as well. But the type of order which they envisioned was incompatible with human dignity.

The Spanish military leaders had not been able to keep their fingers out of the Spanish pie for over a century, though naturally when they staged a revolt it was always on the pretext of "saving Spain." What occurred in 1936 is no more than a repetition, in a bloodier and much more horrible form, of the evil we have just pointed out, which had already caused over a hundred pronunciamientos and outbursts, as well as three major civil wars, in the preceding century.

They are twisting the truth when they say they rose up in arms in 1936 to save civilization from Communism. There was not the least talk of Communism in 1931 in the Peninsula, and in spite of this they were already planning and asking our help for a revolt as early as that year.

Here was no defense of civilization nor struggle against Communism. This was purely and simply an outburst of hate, resentment, and impotence on the part of those who, seeing themselves and their doctrines repudiated by the people, determined to impose them by force, from whatever source they could obtain it, and even though it meant the profanation of their country's soil by foreign armies.

The so-called Spanish Crusade has been and still is the focal point of confusion.

"What we cannot deny," an American priest once said to me, repeating what has been said so many times, "is that General Franco fought for Christian civilization; and even the Pope himself recognized this in a public note."

"There was such a note," I answered, "and I admit the intention of General Franco may have been as you say. But we must remember that this note was issued by the Vatican rather than by the Holy See of St. Peter, and it could not have been otherwise. It takes note of the intentions, but it does not say, for example, that the insurrection was legitimate, nor that this revolt against the established power was an act permitted a Christian. And there lies the crux of the whole matter. For the Spanish prelates themselves, in their declarations of 1931 and 1933, specifically forbade Spanish Catholics any resort to armed insurrection against the established power even though that power be persecuting the Church. And this doctrine was still in force on July 18, 1936."

"Well, that may be so, but we Catholics must respect the Papal note."

"Agreed, but you also should respect the fact that the Basques also were fighting and continue to fight for Christian civilization—in the first place because we feel it deeply, and in the second because in repelling unjust aggression we were acting in accord with a doctrine of natural right which is also Christian. It is exactly what you are doing now."

"Then how do you explain this extraordinary contradiction?"

"There really is no contradiction, but misinformation, when one discovers, as you are discovering now, this strange struggle between Christian civilizations. When I reached Paris after my departure from Santander, I was bombarded by twenty or more reporters. One of the naïve questions asked me was, 'But you who are a Catholic, haven't you been excommunicated by the Pope? Didn't you at least receive an admonition?'

"'Neither excommunication nor admonition,' I replied, for that was the truth.

"The reporters seemed very much surprised, for they also were living in that world of confusion produced by an excited propaganda. They did not know, for I did not tell them, that two years previous, at the beginning of the Spanish war, the Vatican had assured us through a reply by the then Subsecretary of State, Cardinal Pizzardo, to a request for an opinion made by the Basque Canon, Dr. Onaindia, that we had nothing to reproach ourselves for from a moral point of view. So that any Basque Catholic need have no further moral scruples in continuing the struggle against Franco, no matter how ardent his claims of leadership in a new Crusade.

"History will have an important role in future enlightenment on this question. For it is not a matter of dogma but of conduct. Surely there has never existed such a tangle of confused ideas and feelings as those springing from the Spanish Civil War. What a quantity of false information was served out to the world, especially the Catholic world! It was not for nothing that Cardinal Verdier said to me in Paris, 'The Church of Spain has jeopardized the Universal Church,' since it was not only Franco who so contributed to the spiritual upheaval in the Catholic world, but also the position adopted by the Spanish Hierarchy in siding with the military insurrection. The Spanish Church was truly a martyr in those early days when the wrath of the people overflowed all bounds. Of this there can be absolutely no doubt. If only the Church had continued in that role! What authority would it not possess today, if in the midst of its martyrdom it had preached peace and forgiveness instead of extending its blessing to those who had provoked the horrible conflict and called in the aid of the Nazis and Fascists. The outrages against it would have ceased on the spot, for the people are not such wild beasts as propaganda would have us believe. But instead it chose to ally itself publicly with the enemies of democracy, on the side of those who employed brute force to impose their doctrines on the rest of the country, and the people who understood this as an attack on themselves fought against it as an enemy power.

"Franco was supported and helped by every antidemocratic power in the world. And many Catholics appeared on the side of antiliberty, misled by the widespread confusion and lack of knowledge of the truth. I am sure that the Church of Spain, if it could go back today, would have chosen a different path. For confirmation of this you have only to read the words of tardy and implicit rectification which are issuing from their pens today. What they seem to say is, 'This is not what we had hoped for.'"

"Something similar is occurring to many today," the priest answered.

"Do you want to know the historic reason for the Church's action?" I responded. "They believed that the insurrection would triumph in fifteen days and never imagined that it would result in such a terrible and bloody war. The Basque Bishop Mujica confessed as much to me and confided that that had also been the opinion of the Primate of the Spanish Church."

"I have to admit," replied the American priest, "that there has never existed such a burning problem for Christian consciences, nor one which has caused such disorientation among American Catholics. Perhaps you Basques should have spoken sooner."

"We did speak, but no one believed us; instead, we were insulted and lied about."[5]

So great were the calumnies circulated about us that one day an American Catholic newspaperman said to me, "It is difficult to understand how you people could have opposed Franco, who was fighting for Christian civilization."

"What it is difficult for me to understand today," I answered him, "is how an American citizen can make such a deplorable mistake as to confuse Christian civilization with concentration camps, exile, and executions. If you really believe that this kind of 'Christian civilization' is that best suited for the United States, then I can understand your enthusiasm for our enemies; but I warn you that in this case you have made a mistake in the battle fronts, and your place is not exactly here."

We Christians have contributed greatly to what some have called the crisis of Christianity. But the fact that Christianity is passing through difficult moments does not mean that it has failed. Because men fall sick is no reason for denying the blessings of health; and the same we may say of Christianity. If we Christians have lost our prestige, it is only because we have departed from true Christianity. It is we who have failed, and not the doctrines of Christ. These are living today; they have never been excelled, and anguished humanity is again turning toward them after searching in vain through the paths of philosophic romanticism for some doctrine which could replace them. For though the mistaken actions of some poor Christians bring about misunderstanding of Christianity, they can never really change the eternal truth and excellence of its doctrines. Everything else may change and die, but Christianity will go on living.

[The Russian Sphinx]

[The Basques have been accused of Communism because we fought side by side with the Spanish Republic, which in turn was criticized for accepting the help of Russia. Well I remember the scandal among certain circles of Paris society caused by the reply of the intelligent Chinese Catholic Bishop, Mgr. Yupin, to the question, "How can the Chinese possibly accept aid from the Communists?"

"In the first place," reasoned the Bishop, "do you admit that the cause of the Chinese people is just?"

"Ah, yes, of course," they answered.

"Very well, since the most remote times, in the doctrines of our ancient sages, in that of Confucius, and in that of Christ who perfected Confucianism, we have always understood that a just cause should be defended and supported. Do you think that the U.S.S.R.—or Communism, if you prefer—is acting wrongly in supporting our cause? Does it not seem to you that the other countries should follow its example and lend us their help in fighting the unjust aggression of Japan?"

In spite of the clarity of this reasoning, many Parisians insisted on misunderstanding, for they were already prejudiced by violent and one-sided propaganda. For the Chinese prelate was speaking an eternal language which many are still incapable of understanding.

Later on in America I had a very interesting conversation on the subject of relations with the U.S.S.R.

"There is no doubt," one of those present told me, "that the entrance of Russia into the war on the side of the democracies has rather changed the outlines of this struggle for liberty. To make a strong alliance in time of war may in fact lead to compromising the future peace. For who can believe that the Soviet Union is fighting for liberty? In order to believe that, there would have to be liberty on Russian soil as well. The Soviet Union is a totalitarian system just as much as those others we are fighting against. A dictatorship of the people is none the less a dictatorship, and we cannot call it democracy. Neither Soviet propaganda which calls on democracy and speaks of itself as democracy's defender, nor the heroic struggle of the Russian people in their fight against Nazism, is enough to make us believe in the good faith of the Soviets. Their former pact with Hitler deprives them of all authority. The reasons of strategy, and the sense of realism of the present Soviet leaders, put forward to explain the pact, not only fail to convince us but on the contrary increase our anxiety. For who can be sure that in similar circumstances, if they were ever to occur again, this same realism would not play just such another trick on us? What is your opinion of this grave problem?" he asked me. "And how would you solve this contradiction which carries so much confusion to so many souls?"

"The problem of an alliance with the Soviet Union," I said, "should be met courageously, penetrating deeply into the reasons and causes for it and above all judging doctrines and actions from an ethical point of view."

"It is exactly from this point of view that I posed the question," interrupted the man who had spoken first.

"There are many people," I replied, "especially those who give no importance to the spiritual values of life, for whom the problem of an alliance with Russia poses no special difficulty. It is merely a matter of convenience or added power. All those who are with us in the fight are welcome, they say. The important thing is to defeat Hitler. And in their way they are right, for Hitler must be defeated. But this is not enough. For that reason, when you ask them if liberty is not going to suffer through this alliance, or what the future organization of humanity will be like, usually they shrug their shoulders, as much as to say that for the time being they cannot be bothered with such questions. They live only in the present. These are the so-called practical people who have caused so much harm to humanity with their self-centered egotism."

"That is all very well, but it still leaves us with the difficulty of defining the place of the democratic idea in the present struggle."

"That is why we must go even deeper in our analysis. Now the Soviet system, which is not all-out Communism, is a totalitarian regime. It is ruled by one party and forbids the organization of other parties with different opinions. Dictatorship as a permanent system is their mode of government. This is a truth stronger than any good wishes or interested silence, and it places the U.S.S.R. in the ideological camp of the dictatorships. Even though there has been internal evolution, and even though, personally, I am certain that the U.S.S.R. will some day exercise positive and beneficial influence on the future of humanity, we must recognize that today the U.S.S.R. is politically a totalitarian state. This must be clearly understood and frankly stated so that we may not walk blindfolded into the future.

"When Hitler attacked the U.S.S.R. he chose his own adversaries: on the one hand, the democracies; on the other, Soviet Russia. Thus grew up the natural alliance between those who had been attacked, for we ought not forget that Russia also was the victim of unjust aggression. Later Russian adherence to the Pact of the twenty-six nations and her acceptance of the Atlantic Charter marked important advances toward her acceptance of the principles of liberty."

"But many of us are extremely doubtful of the sincerity of these acts," this gentleman interrupted again.

"I know that, but your doubts cannot detract from the significance of the acts. So far it has been democratic thinking which has won the day. The Atlantic Charter and the Pact of the twenty-six nations contain a doctrine of liberty completely opposed to totalitarianism. And these documents have been signed by representatives of the U.S.S.R. We certainly have cause to congratulate ourselves, for so far it is the democratic countries who have laid down the rules and the U.S.S.R. which has corrected, after a fashion, its former doctrinal position. Does the Russian signature mean nothing? Is it a manifestation of *realism*? I do not know, but at least there exists today a program for liberty to which all the democratic world adheres, and

Russia is included in this adherence. And it is this program for freedom, and not one derived from more or less Communist or totalitarian principles, which is serving as the guide for the present and the future. I pray God that there is no change in an opposite direction in the future leadership of the world! For this reason the entrance of Russia into the war by the side of the democracies has not meant a weakening of democratic principles; but, on the contrary, it has extended their sphere of influence, since the Russian signature, that of a nondemocratic country, has been added to those of the democracies in proclaiming these principles. Will it carry out in its own land the principles of liberty which it has endorsed? That is another problem, but the mere possibility of such an occurrence is in itself an advance in the right direction."

"I think you have the right answer," put in one of the others present. "Moreover, we must not forget that the U.S.S.R. is fighting a just war, and that it was also the victim of violent aggression by Hitler. And if this were not enough there is the fact that it is fighting by the side of the democratic countries and therefore by the side of liberty also."

"That is true in spite of the fact that this line of reasoning is merely amusing to practical realists. For these are the very reasons able to unite and move the peoples of the world."

"I agree with you completely," said another in the group. "Fear and passion are capable of twisting everything. The case of Russia is absolutely clear to me in its present position. I think both countries, the U.S.S.R. and the U.S.A., should help each other, loyally and fully. I am not afraid of the ghosts of Communism which some people invoke to scare us out of cordial relations. I am very much more afraid of our own inconsistency and of our spiritual cowardice."

"There lies the greatest problem of all," I answered. "Will the universal ideas defended today be used for universal good? That is to say, will they be applied to all men and all nations equally, or will they be belittled and reserved for the chosen few? Will the democratic leadership of the war remain firm in its resolves? Or will it waver and cease to serve as a landmark for the hopes of the world, forgetting its friends and compromising with the enemy and its accomplices? If this should happen, then it would mean not disillusion but complete and final despair."]

The Meaning of This War*

*[*Editor's note:* For the next 16 pages or so, Aguirre takes the reader through an analysis of the three principal problems whose solution, he asserts, depends on the outcome of the war. In his discussion of these three problems, Aguirre places himself squarely in the tradition of contemporary European Christian democracy, a movement he was so active in leading after the war. The first problem, the so-called democratic problem, leads Aguirre to defend the idea of democracy even though individual democratic leaders may not have fulfilled their obligation to carry out its precepts. Democracy has not failed, he asserts; men have failed to live up to its ideals, especially the principle that democracy depends on individual moral rectitude. But democracy, he says, depends on "disciplined liberty." Too often, democratic institutions have been undermined by their enemies who hid behind, or took advantage of, the protections offered by political freedom. Thus, Aguirre confronts the question that democratic theorists have wrestled with since the time of Plato; namely, how can a system based on freedom protect itself against those who do not obey its rules? "Those who would make use of liberty in order to strangle it," he writes, "have no right to organize themselves nor enjoy its benefits." It would appear, then, that in Aguirre's ideal democratic state, anti-democratic groups such as Fascists and Communists would be denied the right to organize and enter into the contest for power.

Aguirre's second problem involves what he calls "the social question." (Interestingly, in the Spanish version this discussion is headed "The Social Question and Communism," a title that much more clearly shows how Aguirre linked the two.) In this section, Aguirre describes what he sees as a "social revolution compatible with liberty," a movement to assure every person at least a minimum of security and economic well-being. This movement is to be applauded, first because it will keep the youth of the world from pursuing fascism or commu-

nism, second because the doctrine of Christ does not permit the exploitation of one man by another. Aguirre concludes this section with
some predictions of the future of communism and of the Soviet state.
His views of a softening, liberalizing Soviet system seem significant in
the context of the *glasnost* era of the 1990s; but in the context of Sta-
linism, he was surely naive.

The third great problem to be resolved by World War II would be
"the problem of nationalities," a question that obviously had great rele-
vance for the Basques. Aguirre here makes the point that "nations are
formed by God." Individual and social liberty is not enough if the national soul is not respected. Ironically, while the war did help resolve
the problem of nationalities to some degree by hastening the disin-
tegration of European colonialism and thereby leading to the creation
of many new nation-states in Africa and Asia, in Europe the war did
practically nothing to change the fortunes of ethnic nations in France,
Britain, or Spain. In fact, by leading to Soviet domination of Eastern Europe, the war also prevented the timely resolution of the festering nationality problems in Yugoslavia, Czechoslovakia, and indeed in the
Soviet Union itself. And as far as the Basques were concerned, some
improvement in their status in Spain would not be achieved until thirty
more years had passed and Franco had died.]

There are three main problems of the future which will be decided by this war: the democratic problem, the social problem, and
the problem of liberty for the nations great and small who desire it,
and their coordination in some workable organization.

We have often heard it said that democracy has failed. But this is
not true. Those who have failed are the men who were incapable of
understanding that democratic institutions are based primarily on
ideals of moral rectitude. Man is, more often than not, a creature
of his environment chiefly because he lacks the inner strength to
rise above the misery which surrounds him. For this reason, when
men weaken and fail, especially in the political field, it is the ideals
which they have embraced, and not the men themselves, which are
blamed. Since man is essentially a spiritual being, it is difficult for us
to mark out a line of separation between him and the universal ideas

which he accepts, but which belong to all humanity. For example, a Daladier or a Reynaud can fail, and with him the interpretation which he has given the democratic idea. But the failure of these men does not mean that the universal conception of democracy has failed also. Although all the democrats in the world might fail, democracy itself would remain a grand human ideal serving notice to the world that that which has failed is not democracy but the men who abused or falsified the ideal. Doctrine is one thing and sacrilege another, in spite of the fact that without the one the other could not exist. It would be absurd to lay aside truth merely because millions of men tell lies daily. A king may embody the monarchical institution, but it is not the king who creates the monarchy but the latter which makes kings of men. In the same way it is democracy which makes democrats of men, but not always successful democrats. If they misuse democracy it is they and not democracy who have failed.

Another mistake which happens frequently is that of confusing democracy with its mockery, such as certain institutions—chiefly the parliamentary system—which, because they have injured democracy, need basic reforms. A democracy can perfectly well exist without a parliamentary system of the type we know today; it cannot exist without some means of representation which will answer to the free and legitimate will of the people. That is, it cannot exist without liberty.

Totalitarians based their propaganda attack on democracy on the disorders occurring through the abuse of unlimited liberty, and on the state of unrest in certain countries produced by parliamentary institutions which mistook the tyranny of the majority for democracy. They were right in many cases, but they were completely mistaken when they denied that democracy and liberty are so intimately connected as to form a united whole. A society can constitute itself in whatever form it considers best, but it cannot do so without liberty. And by liberty I mean a disciplined liberty, which consists in each man being free to seek God after his own fashion, to guard over the manner in which his country is being run, and to choose freely, as a reasonable being, the men whom he wants to exercise the public functions of government.

The pessimistic conception of man, personified by all totalitarian ideas, is in reality a selfish doctrine put forward to cover the limitless personal ambitions of certain people. The totalitarian leaders use this concept of man as a degenerate and dangerous being to achieve their own dominant position. Many ingenious people have fallen into the trap of believing that a totalitarian regime is the best means to achieve and maintain order. But what order! Could there be greater disorder than that brought about by Nazism and its imitations? Jails and concentration camps are full to overflowing with unhappy people who are often no more than suspects. The citizen who lives in his house or walks through the streets—a kind of slave on a holiday—is constantly shadowed by fear and suspicion, for the carefully organized system of espionage is no respecter of homes and teaches the children that it is their patriotic duty to denounce their fathers for the good of the State. No, this is not order; this is terror, the absolute negation of order.

That is why those of us who have lived through tragic experiences in the totalitarian countries know that this is a disease which can only be cured by liberty. And because they believe in their future liberation there is still hope in the subjugated countries of Europe, and this includes half of Germany also. This confidence in the future coming of liberty is the only thing which upholds them, and because of it there are still smiles in the midst of so much sorrow.

In the humblest homes, in those which know privation, and which today have dropped everything to take up their rifles, I have found a conception for the future: "We want democracy to triumph because it means liberty; but future society must guard it with the following precept: *Liberty is a universal patrimony. But those who would make use of liberty in order to strangle it have no right to organize themselves nor enjoy its benefits.*"

I think we are all willing to admit this principle. But what future guarantees will men have that their liberty will be respected? Are we to continue thinking that human dignity is a private concern of each nation, leaving to each the power of deciding whether men shall be free or no?

I have a very intelligent friend who used to say to me that no future peace will be perfect unless the treaty which crowns the triumph of liberty begins with these words:

ARTICLE I. Man is a rational being born to be free. By virtue of this, in no part of the world and by no authority or State, can the following rights be denied him. [Here he enumerates a long list of rights.] The International Society will assure the universal application of this article.

My friend is a stanch defender of man and goes very far in the rights which he would assign him. But I still think he is right, for he often says that man is worth far more than the territorial boundaries of the States.

It will be truly disheartening if, after the sacrifice which humanity is making, we still fail to recognize the existence of man. For individual man is rather like a tree in the forest—he becomes lost in the group. And it would be no less disheartening if, once victory was won, man should still not enjoy the benefits of the four freedoms envisaged with great human understanding by President Roosevelt. This would be as true in China as in Russia and India, in Europe as in America, in the huge British Empire as in tiny Euzkadi. For a man is no less a man, be his country large or small. The future peace of the world must not be jeopardized by opportunism or so-called "realism" nor for reasons of an economic nature. For surely liberty for all men is a more worth-while and, in the long run, a more profitable aim than increased production in cotton or petroleum.[6]

The Social Question

A phenomenon has been taking place in the last few years which is both curious and noteworthy: the ebbing of Marxism, and on the other hand the growth of a sense of social responsibility. As the influence of Marxist philosophy decreases we note a growing conviction among men of the need for profound social reform.

But the mass of working people and the youth who are fighting today feel no attraction toward the materialistic interpretation of history nor a dictatorship of the proletariat, philosophic-political conceptions at odds with the doctrine of liberty. What they want is a social revolution that would be compatible with liberty. That is to say, they are seeking security.

In this respect we can observe a change of feeling which would not have been understood nor even possible twenty years ago. It took but a few years, one might almost say a few months, after the close of the last great war for a deep and terrible disillusionment to engulf the young generation of that time. All their heroic sacrifice in the trenches had gone for nothing. The doors of life were slammed in their faces. And the struggle for their daily bread became even harsher and more difficult than before the war. Of what use then had been their great sacrifice?

With the failure of the peace and the triumph of egoism, whole generations of young people, unable to find work and with an empty future staring them in the face, took refuge in the doctrine of force. Communism, Nazism, and Fascism were quick to take advantage of their despair and won over the young people by the thousands. Their desire to live was the supreme argument, and left them no time for philosophizing. The leaders of the democracies were busy discussing boundaries and plebiscites, too busy to remember that the most urgent need was for real peace among nations and an opportunity for every man to gain a living decently and honestly.

Today people are turning once again to liberty, which has been trampled on by the dictatorships, and toward new confidence in the leaders of this fight for liberty. This faith and confidence must be justified and upheld if the social revolution which is inevitable is to be kept within reasonable bounds. For this reason the confidence which the masses feel in their present democratic leaders is of fundamental importance. We are moving in the direction of new social forms. It is impossible to ignore this or shut our eyes to reality. What we must do is accept the fact and, if possible, give ourselves up to the work of building these new forms, for they are based on human need and on justice. We must not let it happen again that the new generations which are giving up so much to fight for liberty return from the battlefield to find the doors of opportunity closed against them. We must not let disillusionment and despair settle on the souls of those who believed they were opening up a new future at the points of their bayonets, a future which would assure every honorable and hard-working man at least a minimum of well-being, and where opportunity is left open to any man of merit and intelligence to rise as high as he can.[7]

Can it be true that the systems of liberty have exhausted all possibilities for solution of these problems? I deny it absolutely. One of the main jobs of the free world after victory is won is to prove that it is capable of finding a satisfactory solution to this or any problem.[8]

I like to recall the simple regime in some of the tiny villages of my country where, after all the necessary public works have been done and debts paid up, they divide up the total expenses of the village among the neighbors according to their means. It seems to me that the simple wisdom of these men who live so close to the soil and to reality might find some application in the running of bigger societies.

Many are the discussions I have had on these practical questions. Especially do I remember the conversations with certain financiers in my own country who were attempting to prove by studies and other data that the social reforms introduced into my own family's business enterprise—today in the hands of General Franco—were dangerous and anti-economical. I never believed them, and reality proved me right. We tried many social innovations: among others, the family salary—a 10 per cent increase on marriage and the birth of each child; worker's participation in the profits (the worker's salary was counted as capital, and he received the same dividend as the stockholder); free medicines and medical attention, etc. And there was no perceptible injury to the business. When we were studying ways of putting into effect a plan whereby after twenty years each worker would own his own house, and another reform concerning old-age pensions, the war interrupted us, and workers and employers united in a common struggle in defense of their country's liberty.[9]

On another occasion, the Basque delegates presented a bill to the Madrid Parliament in 1935. In this bill we asked the legal establishment of the family salary and the worker's participation in social benefits, after 5 per cent interest had been assured to capital. They did not even permit a discussion of the bill in Parliament, even though the Basque deputy who presented it cited the social doctrines of Popes Leo XIII and Pius XI in defense of it, an argument which should have carried some weight with the Rightist leader, Gil Robles, at that time in the government. In fact one of the Rightist deputies who later joined Franco's rebellion even exclaimed, "If you continue to invoke papal doctrines as an argument to rob us of our own, we shall be forced to turn schismatic."

There are many Christians in the world, both in Europe and in America, who would rather turn schismatic than accept even such simple social reforms. They are unable and do not wish to understand the reality of the social problem. That is why so many of them turned to violence and embraced the Nazi, Fascist, and Falangist doctrines, thinking that these regimes were going to save them from "Communism and its accomplices." They considered us its accomplices, those of us who believed that the doctrines of Christ do not admit of hypocrisy nor the exploitation of man by man. These social classes who believed in Hitler and Mussolini and glorified Franco have found out to their dismay that the dictators also have a social program. And they have carried out many aspects of it, and no one is granted the right to protest or turn schismatic, as the deputy expressed it. For this reason so many people who originally sympathized with totalitarianism out of fear of Communism now find themselves disillusioned once more.

Fear of Communism. I like to ask those who say they fear it just what they have done to avoid it. For a negative position against anything is incapable of solving problems.

The case of the U.S.S.R. deserves careful study. The mere fact that it has survived in a hostile world for twenty-five years should provide food for serious thought. Many have been surprised by the heroism and discipline of the Soviet peoples in their fight against the forces of Hitler. They forget that twenty-five years of doctrinal education with all frontiers closed to external influence have completely formed the thought and feeling of a whole generation. All those under forty have known no other regime, or can remember but dimly the previous one. Moreover they know—and in this they are right—that this regime has meant social liberation for their parents. And they believe, for so they have been told, that this can only happen in the U.S.S.R.

I have never been able to understand the viewpoint of those who would get around a problem by pretending that it does not exist. The Soviet experiment is truly a reality, and one which has triumphed. If it were merely a social experiment—that is to say, an experiment in more or less advanced social reforms—I am sure the world would look on it with greater tranquillity and satisfaction. But it is a whole conception of life in which liberty is left out of account. Certainly there has been a great deal of evolution and day-to-day advance. It is also true that the Soviet regime and the purely Communist doctrine have been growing father apart as the former grows and evolves. When liberty—at least those fundamental liberties proclaimed today—finally penetrates into the Soviet conception of life and is accepted and applied to its own people (and the people will impose this some day) I am sure that it will be hailed as one of the greatest contributions to human society and certainly the most interesting social experiment yet tried. Day by day the Soviet regime is becoming more peculiarly Russian and losing that "international" trend with which its Communist origin once endowed it. The constant impact with reality and, above all, with living men has had the effect of softening the clear-cut outline of the early bigoted Soviet conception.

Man himself is the greatest enemy of oppression, whether it be political or social. His deepest instincts cry out for liberty. His intelligence demands an outlet for his initiative. That is why those of us—for I count myself one—who are following the course of Soviet evolution from an interested and dispassionate point of view are gratified to note that here, also, man is beginning to triumph. The Stalin Constitution of 1936 is already a noteworthy advance. The steps which the reality of the war are forcing the U.S.S.R. to take are another advance in the right direction. The recognition of private property and inheritance rights, the progress toward freedom of religion, and even "stakanovism" are all triumphs of man over the materialistic conception of life which is an integral part of true Marxism.

The rising spirit of liberty in the U.S.S.R. is one of the most important and significant happenings occurring in the world today. The weight of centuries of evolution toward liberty and man himself are all pushing in this direction. And I am sure that in the end man will triumph.

Communism in the rest of the world is going to suffer a rude shock after the war. The Communist groups in the other countries of the world have taken their cue from Moscow, not only as regards doctrine but also in regard to political action and orientation. It was difficult to understand in 1939 how the Communists of the world could follow the Russian line even against the interests of their own countries. Overnight the slogan "Nazi-Fascist beast" took on a different meaning, and the war which the attacked democracies were fighting became an "imperialistic struggle." The cause of liberty suffered greatly from this ideological about-face. But today the early slogan is again in use, and this time the cause is just.

Whether it was justified or not, the Soviet State was acting exclusively in its own interest; but those who changed their attitudes and action with each shift of Soviet policy were certainly lacking in loyalty to their own countries. For this reason, it seems to me, the Communist movement outside Russia is going to find itself in a difficult situation in the future.

It is very possible that many of the reforms and social experiments of the totalitarian countries may be found feasible for incorporation into the future social fabric of the world. They also spring from the deepest needs of man. For in all countries, whether democratic or totalitarian, there is the same anxiety and the same aspiration for security, well-being, and work for all.

Many people dream of the great synthesis which will bring us to the solution of the future. I dream of a return to the principles of the Sermon on the Mount and early Christianity, which has no connection at all with the type of "Christianity" which we see, for example, in dictatorial regimes with its opportunist egotisms. It seems to me that the hour of true Christianity must be very near. So many people with an awakened sense of the spiritual world and of liberty are turning toward it, and others who believe in the doctrines but have not practiced them feel the need of bringing their lives into harmony with the eternal precepts of Christ.[10]

The Problem of Nationalities

During the past centuries man has been carrying on a struggle for his political liberty. He demanded a guarantee of respect for his human rights, and from this demand arose first the granted charters and later the constitutions which were signed and sworn to by the monarchs. But once these had been granted man began to understand that his liberty would never be complete if he did not also achieve social and economic emancipation. Until this was achieved his situation would remain precarious. He needed equality before the law and a guarantee of at least that minimum of economic well-being so necessary if man is to be truly a man and not a slave to economic circumstances. This struggle is still being carried on today, and it is one of fundamental importance for the future peace.

But this rising curve in man's fight for liberty does not stop here. There is yet another problem which cries out urgently for a just solution. Europe, the cradle and seat of the different countries and civilizations, today is witnessing a new resurgence of nationalities. Individual and social liberty is still not enough if the national soul of each country is not respected. A people that feels itself to be a nation cannot endure oppression by another nation, nor can it stand by patiently and allow itself to be deprived arbitrarily of its national heritage. Nature itself rises up to oppose this form of abuse and oppression.

In discussing this question it is well to keep in mind one fact which is often forgotten: State and nation are not one and the same thing. Poland, for example, was a nation both before and after her independence—that is to say, her emergence as a State. The same is true of many other nationalities, whether they are States or not. And one of the most important problems which the future peace must solve is this problem of the nations. For nations are formed by God, and States are political creations—sometimes just, sometimes unjust, like all the works of man.[11]

The great absolutist empires believed they had stifled the longings of the peoples under their rule and attempted by brutal assimilation to wipe out the different nationalities which they included. Persecution of the native culture and the forceful imposition of a foreign culture, exile or execution for the patriots of these subjugated nationalities—these and other methods were employed by all the great powers. But in spite of everything the will of the nations to live kept on growing and triumphing. In the nineteenth century the Balkan peoples began to gain their independence. In the twentieth century the central European peoples and the Irish gained theirs. But there are other peoples who are still awaiting their hour of liberation. And the Basque nation is one of these.

"How confused the whole problem appears!" an American writer, interested in this subject, recently said to me. "For Hitler, also, wishes to appear as the redeemer of oppressed nationalities. What effrontery!"

"The evil is not so much that he wishes to appear as a liberator but in the fact that he wants to liberate those peoples oppressed by his adversary while he himself crushes out all peoples who oppose his schemes," I answered.

"But what good is it," argued the writer, "for him to recognize a Slovakian state, more or less under his control, or the precarious sovereignty of Croatia, or similar claims to independence, if at the same time he makes slaves of the Poles, the Czechs, the Norwegians, and so many other peoples who were once free nations?"

"All this is true, but it is not as confusing as you think. In the first place it is pretty well accepted by all that a nation has a right to exist and govern itself freely. This right has been established in the Atlantic Charter and in the five points of Pope Pius XII, and even Hitler admits it. But on the other hand, and in spite of the acceptance in principle of this right, many of the great powers of the world have not thought it necessary to apply it within their own territories, though they may preach it to others. So, for example, at the end of the last war we all witnessed Ireland's struggle for freedom. Why should Poland have been granted its independence, and not Ireland?

"Such contradictions, or other injustices, lead only to desperation on the part of the oppressed peoples. And this is exactly what Hitler is doing today when he grants liberty to the Slovaks with one hand and oppresses the Czechs with the other. Up to now the great powers have been apt to grant or withhold this right according to the degree of friendship felt for the weaker peoples. The Basques are well acquainted with this phenomenon. How many Spanish newspapers of Nazi tendencies have not attacked Russia and England on the question of oppression of the Poles and the Irish—singularly enough they don't mention Germany—while they applaud the imprisonment of Basque patriots for demanding liberty for their country, a liberty which the Basque country enjoyed long before even the birth of Poland or Ireland."

"Here in America," I was told, "we feel tremendous sympathy for all the causes of freedom. Any country which is fighting bravely for its liberty receives our help and moral backing. This time, I hope that the principles of liberty will be applied universally, for every country which is truly a nation has a right to freedom as every man has a right to demand respect for his dignity and personality."

This conversation left me thinking about America's role in helping to solve the three great problems of the world: the restoration of liberty to the nations; the restoration of democracy within nations, and the social-economic problem. My mind flew back again to those who are still struggling to free their country from domination. Just a few days before, I had received word of the death of a Basque sailor in a torpedoing in the Caribbean Sea. He was one of those who had fought so valiantly on the Basque fishing boat Bizkaya beside the glorious Nabarra. "He died while accomplishing his duty," wrote my informant. "He might have died in Basque waters, but he died in the Caribbean. In both places he was serving the cause of liberty."

In contrast with this episode I am going to quote from a conversation with a very cultivated European gentleman. He was a defeatist, and his pessimism went much deeper than anything an American can imagine.

"Rest assured," he said, with that self-confidence typical of the scion of an old country, "that this is the hour of the great nations. Sovereignty will only be granted to those capable of defending it. All the little nationalities and their demands for freedom are nothing but a bother to the big nations in times like these."

"And just what do you mean by little nations?" put in an American professor.

"Those who need outside help to maintain their security," replied the European.

"Then we are all little nations with the possible exception of one," answered the American. "Do you consider France, for example, a little nation? It was unable to defend itself. And what do you think would have happened to England if the Nazi aggression had continued and America had refrained from sending aid? Would you classify it also as a little nation? And what would have happened to Russia without our help? In the face of reality your definition becomes meaningless, for we are all in need, to greater or lesser extent, of outside help. When peace and decency are at last restored to the world, then great and little nations can live in security. We cannot deny the right to existence to any nation, for this right does not depend on the size of its territory but on its national soul and will to live. How does this strike you other Europeans? Do you agree with me, or with this gentleman?"

"I must confess that this time it is the American who has best expressed my own convictions, and the European who has left me untouched," answered a philosopher from Central Europe, expelled from his university for preferring Plato to Hitler. "I cannot accept a pessimistic concept of life. I have always believed that a nation has a right to live not so much because of its size as because of the very fact of its being a nation and, as such, a powerful contributor to the cultural inheritance of mankind. Any other point of view would simply mean agreement with the barbaric Nazi philosophy that neither the weak nor the imperfect have the right to participate in the creation of life. But isn't that exactly the reason why we are fighting this terrible war—to wipe out forever the brutal doctrine that might makes right? And consider, my friend, how many noble souls and geniuses have sprung from the little countries of the world."[12]

Later he added, smiling, "A nation, like a woman, must never be judged by its size."

"It is only through some such point of view as yours," I said, addressing myself to the first European, "that one can understand the complacency of certain writers—fortunately they are few—in accepting as natural the sacrifice of certain small nations. Today they are discussing the case of Poland and the Baltic countries; and, without in the least being aware that they are sabotaging the whole doctrine of liberty for which the peoples of the world are fighting, they bow to so-called *realism* and argue in favor of ceding these countries to Russia if she so desires."

"America will never accept such a solution unless it is based on the expressed will and desire of the interested peoples," the American stated emphatically.

"Well, you people have almost convinced me," said the pessimist. "Certainly that kind of realism doesn't exist in small countries. On the contrary, they are the first to suffer by it. And if it is really going to be accepted as the natural form of procedure it is better to know it in time, so that we may lock ourselves within our houses."[13]

How many countries and how many millions of men have already been brutally crushed by the totalitarian countries! For the most part, they are small countries who only wished to live their own lives—respected throughout centuries—unmolested and at peace with the rest of the world. These are countries which, in spite of their tiny size, have contributed generously to the cultural wealth of the world. Most people viewed with sympathy the heroic gesture of these little countries who dared to stand up and fight against the colossal might of the totalitarian steam-roller. But their forces were small, they received little material aid, and in some cases were completely abandoned to their fate. At times, it was geography which was to blame; at others, lack of foresight or understanding.

The totalitarians kept repeating to each of these countries in turn: "Your fight is useless, for no one will come to help you. They will laud you in the columns of their newspapers, but they will not help you. It is better to give up the fight in time; otherwise we will level your cities and you will have to flee through the world while your so-called friends remain peacefully behind their ramparts, for they really don't care what happens to you."[14]

We must never forget that the victory of the big powers will have been achieved at the cost of the heroic sacrifice of the small nations. Before the destruction of Coventry, Gernika was destroyed; before Paris fell, Warsaw perished; and long before Manila was taken, Athens was lying beneath the heel of the oppressor. The way for the treacherous attack on Norway, Denmark, Belgium, Holland, and later Greece and Yugoslavia had long since been paved by the indifference of the world to the unjust attacks on Ethiopia, China, Albania, and the Spanish Republic, including the autonomous peoples of Euzkadi and Catalonia.

London and Washington were not the first to be attacked, but that constellation of smaller States which formed a defensive ring around them. No one should be surprised, therefore, if from this group of little nations arises a cry for justice and generosity of action.

If after victory the world is to be run by the standards of a business undertaking, it would be such a blow to human aspirations that no one would be able to avoid the certain catastrophe of still another war in the near future. Not all the force and vigilance of the victors could prevent it. Nothing but justice, applied in time, would be able to stop it.

However, to those who still think that calculation and self-interest can rule the world, after so much blood and suffering and ruin, it is well to repeat the words of a certain Uruguayan diplomat:

"Those who regard the world as an immense business opportunity for the exclusive benefit of either America or the British Empire or Russia or anybody, are terribly mistaken. For it is the concern of all men and all nations, and therein lies the grandeur of the Ideal. If it were not so, millions upon millions of human beings, feeling themselves cheated and deceived, would rise up and unite behind the first man on horseback who presented himself, welded by hate and fear and disillusionment into an offensive might more terrible than any known before."

This present conflict is more than just a war: it is a revolution. And let us be thankful that it is, for the revolutionary wars are always those which bring about the triumph of principles over interest. There is no need to be frightened at the mere mention of the word "revolution." But we must accept the reality without haggling over it, and face inevitable change with courage and hope.

The Latin Versus the Anglo-Saxon World*

*[Editor's note: For the next 6 pages or so, Aguirre discusses what he calls (in the words of the Spanish-version title of this section) "the third enemy front: the Latin Union." The central theme of this section is that the Latin axis of Rome–Vichy (France)–Madrid–Lisbon–Buenos Aires was at war against democracy even if most of the Latin countries formally maintained their neutrality in the war. Aguirre's thesis is that the Latin Union would try to bring together the countries already united by common culture, religion, language, and history, and to form them into a powerful bloc motivated by their common desire to defeat international communism. In advancing the cause of anti-communism, these countries would also attempt to promote their brand of authoritarian regime, complete with state religion, state unions, and the suppression of individual liberties.

A bit more of a historical perspective would have helped Aguirre understand better the economic and social dynamic of the countries linked to the Latin Union. For the most part, these are countries that political scientist A. F. K. Organski labeled "syncratic states" in his book The Stages of Political Development (New York: Knopf, 1965). These countries, such as Italy under Mussolini or Spain under Franco, are all societies in which industrial development became arrested and stunted before the emergence of a strong and influential industrial bourgeoisie. The course of modernization is controlled, therefore, by an unnatural coalition (hence the term "syncratic," for rule by coalition) of forces both in favor of, and opposed to, industrialization. The consequence of this is authoritarianism, usually of the corporatist variety. The advantage of this kind of perspective is that it shows that Latin fascism (in contrast to the German variety) is a problem that will be solved by a successful industrialization effort, and that, in turn, takes time, perhaps several generations. Indeed, the recent history of not only Italy, Greece, Spain, and Portugal, but also of Argentina and Brazil, supports this kind of interpretation, which perhaps explains why the Latin Union never really presented much of a threat to anyone, except to the people of the Latin countries themselves.]

In speaking of the war, we usually think of two battle fronts, the Atlantic and the Pacific, and two chief adversaries, Hitler in Europe and Japan in Asia. The third enemy and the third front is generally forgotten or at best given only slight importance. I am referring, of course, to the Latin Front—or, more concretely, the Rome-Vichy-Madrid-Lisbon Axis and its attempted tie-up with Buenos Aires. It is also known as the Latin Union. Its material organization has not been perfected as yet, but the spirit and meaning of this movement is unmistakable. The danger of this third front lies in the very fact that it tends to be ignored or glossed over or so well disguised that it is not even recognized for what it is: a hidden enemy.[15]

A few years ago when Mussolini was classed as a comic opera star who had not yet precipitated his people into a tragic war, Rome was the recognized head of this movement. In France, also, there were many, in the antidemocratic and so-called nationalist sectors, who sympathized strongly with its ideals. In Spain, the incipient Falangist movement proclaimed Rome as the Latin capital. Some of the pseudophilosophers and directors of the Falange went so far as to state that, as in early Christian times Catholicism owed its existence to Paul of Tarsus, so today its chief defender was Benito Mussolini. Thus the confusion began with a show of homage and waving of incense. Pity the Catholic Church if it can count on no better protector than the Duce!

In Europe, the same in Italy as in France, Spain, and Portugal and I think we may say Belgium also, a pro-Latin campaign is being carried on today by all those elements who are either outspokenly or surreptitiously opposed to democracy and liberty. This campaign, so innocent-seeming from the outside—based as it is on the sisterhood of the Latin peoples, affinity of culture, order, etc.—has in reality far other and more sinister designs.

The Latin Union is attempting to tie those countries whose civilization and physiognomy have been more or less influenced by Catholicism into a comprehensive organization with the following characteristics: (a) it hopes to create a powerful Latin block of future influence which will be able to counteract the Germanism which it expects or hopes to see triumph; (b) it uses the anti-Communist slogan more or less to suit its convenience; (c) it is essentially anti-democratic; (d) it stands for the radical suppression of all individual liberties; (e) it would introduce the corporative state and obligatory syndicates in the social realm, and is autocratic in the economic realm; (f) it is trying to make use of the Catholic religion as an integrating element in its civilization, and (g) it is attempting to use the influence of the Latin-European Axis to win over Latin America.

The endeavor to create a block of sister nations with a similar civilization is easily understandable. We could even accept their anti-Communist doctrines, in spite of the fact that we have little faith in the efficacy of negative programs. But what really gives this movement away completely is its organized fight against liberty.

Two important consequences can be noted immediately: one, the connection with the Axis, in whose ideological orbit and sphere of influence the movement lies; the other, the imitation of totalitarian procedures, such as exile, concentration camps, prison, seizure of the property of political opponents, shootings, and executions.

The influence of the Portuguese dictator, Oliveira Salazar, who has the advantage of greater moderation in his procedure, and whose prestige is recognized even by his adversaries for his success in administration of the State, is strongly felt by the other members of this antiliberty block. The Portuguese ruler is trying to organize the Latin world and hopes sincerely to extricate it from the spiritual influence both of the Anglo-Saxon world and of the German. He hates democracy, but he fears a German triumph. Latin America plays a big part in his plans, and in her he puts his hope for the future.

I spoke with one of the Portuguese Premier's close collaborators, in the boat which brought me from Buenos Aires to the United States. I rather suspect that his propaganda trip through South America, with the object of winning over these peoples to the idea of a Latin Union, had not been too fruitful, especially in Brazil. We talked about the Latin world and its organization. I argued with him, saying that a problem of this nature could only be solved on a basis of liberty because countries organized into regimes of violence would be incapable of creating any real and constructive relationship. He, however, did not believe in liberty, nor that anyone would fight for it.

"Do you really believe that England is fighting for liberty? No, she is fighting exclusively for her own interests," he told me.

"For both things," I replied. "It is extraordinary that you who have a Treaty of Alliance with England can doubt it," I added with an irony which made him smile.

I continued to question him. "Your position is becoming more difficult," I told him. "The Hitler menace detracts from the strength of your ideas. For this is a question of ideas and positions—especially if America enters the war, as seems inevitable. What, in your judgment, will be the position of Spain and Portugal, now that Vichy France is a conquered country?"

"Spain won't be able to avoid war, sooner or later, and we will do all we can to remain neutral. Everything depends on Hitler," he answered.

My ideas seemed to be confirmed. If these countries of the Latin Union are unable to make their own decisions over whether or not they are to be involved in the struggle, and if they do not wish to organize themselves to oppose Hitler's aggressions, then what purpose can this union with its antidemocratic ideology have, other than that of serving totalitarianism and weakening the spirit of certain masses of popular opinion in order to keep it from joining the struggle for liberty? The Rome-Vichy-Madrid-Lisbon Axis, whose tentacles are reaching out already toward Buenos Aires, represents itself as an association of so-called Christian nations, supposedly organized on Christian principles, whose aim is to safeguard Christian civilization. This kind of talk, which like a mirage is capable of misleading countless souls, is the chief basis of all its propaganda. I will not deny that there are many honest and sincere men among its advocates. What I must assert is that, because of the means employed and the antidemocratic ideology, the chief result so far is the setting up of a third front against liberty which is as dangerous as either of the others. On this front no shots have yet been fired; but from it spring confusion and discord, discouragement and demoralization, and the fighters for liberty find themselves defeated from the rear. That is why we must count it as an enemy and combat it with all the means in our power.

It does not require any stretch of the imagination to understand what I am saying. A study of the propaganda used by those countries who, though calling themselves Christian, are more apt to use the methods of Judas, would be sufficient. I am referring especially to those countries who have kept their neutrality even though it is neutrality in name only.

In my opinion, a thorough knowledge of the ideology and propaganda of those countries which, like Franco Spain, lie within the orbit of totalitarianism is at least as important as the discovery of a cache of arms by any Nazi-type center or organization anywhere in the Americas. Without the ideological danger there would be no need to fear such an organization.

I can state as a positive fact known to me, although I cannot at present be more explicit, that all the official instructions given by totalitarian Spain to those organizations or undertakings working abroad were those of a totalitarian nation preparing for war. There is not one which could mean the slightest adherence to the cause of liberty. There is no real desire to enter the war; to say that would be a misstatement of fact. But ideology is a powerful force, and the fear of a victory for freedom is stronger than any desire for peace. When the democracies have triumphed, they will not have to undertake the job of overthrowing one by one the shameful totalitarian regimes that exist in Europe. The people in each country will see to that. But the democracies may have to take a hand in seeing that the aroused peoples—whose injuries have been almost unbearable—do not convert justice into injustice when the day of liberation finally comes. They know as well in Vichy as Madrid, and they suspect in Lisbon, that the downfall of Hitler and Mussolini would bring about the overthrow of their friends and all those who owed their existence to totalitarianism.

That is why every defeat for the Allies is looked upon by these governments as a victory for themselves; *for, although their belligerency against the Allies is not declared, they are at open war against democracy.* This position might not have been so anomalous when democracy was accepted as one thing and liberty another; but today the difference exists no longer, for where democracy is swept away liberty perishes with it.

From this position of the Latin Union arises the indirect aid furnished to the totalitarian powers—more direct aid is given individually. This aid is mainly spiritual and consists of clouding the atmosphere in the democratic circles, aiming chiefly at those timid democrats who are more worried by the dangers of democracy than impressed by its benefits.

The Italian leanings of the so-called "national" elements in France, before Italy was a belligerent in the war, caused untold damage to the morale of the country, weakening it appreciably. When this current of sympathy toward Italy on the part of the antidemocratic elements finally blossomed out in the "revolution" represented by Vichy, its effect was felt as far as Canada. If in place of the defeatism which led to the compromise of Montoire, the spirit of resistance of the true French patriots had triumphed, the reaction in French Canada would have been totally different.

I was told by an eminent French philosopher, after one of his visits to Canada, that there are still many who maintain publicly that this is exclusively an imperialist war, and so great is their confusion that they state that the only reasonable and dignified position is that of Vichy and it is the British Empire which is mistaken. From this position to that of desiring a victory for the totalitarians is but a step.

Some time ago I was introduced to a French diplomat in the service of the government of Marshal Pétain. He was criticizing American democracy with what seemed like rather childish resentment, as we stood watching a military parade, one of those organized in New York before the entrance of the United States into the war.

"You see what these democracies are like," he said, among other sneers at the organization of the parade—which, to tell the truth, was anything but perfect. "There go the Negroes separated from the whites. With such distinctions still being made, it is difficult to believe that the war is being fought for democracy."

His argument with its scrupulous respect for orthodox democracy was really very amusing.

"In spite of the defects which you are pointing out," I answered pointedly, "these colored soldiers are a thousand times freer than the citizens enslaved by Hitler's regime and by the other dictators who imitate him. That is why they are willing here to fight for freedom even though the practical application of democracy may not be perfect. If we did not accept this, we would have to side with Hitler, don't you agree?"

"No. With Hitler, no!" he exclaimed spontaneously, thus revealing the true French spirit he carried within. "But doesn't it seem to you that what they are really fighting for is their own interests exclusively and their imperialist designs?"

"Well, let us suppose so," I answered. "Then which side would you choose?"

Timidly, like one who has received an order which he dislikes or of which he is unconvinced, he replied with lowered voice, "An organized Latin world might be a solution—"

"Based on dictators?" I answered rather brusquely. "Based on constant criticism of those countries which are fighting for liberty? And with the aid of concentration camps?"

Our conversation was interrupted at that point by the wife of the diplomat, who, on seeing the mathematical precision of the West Point cadets marching by, exclaimed sardonically: "I must telegraph *le Maréchal* that the Americans have at last learned to march."

I should have been happy to answer that lady by saying that these well-trained and disciplined boys from West Point not only knew how to march well but also believed in the ideals symbolized by their flag, a quality which had been lacking in many of the heads of the French army and which caused the demoralization and downfall of a magnificent people. And I might have added that it was ideas like those of her husband which, filtering into and poisoning the mind of a people, will end in armies marching soulless toward defeat. But I chose instead to change the conversation, and we ended up speaking of such subjects as oriental art.

The Christian Dictatorships*

*[*Editor's note:* This entire section, which in the English version runs nearly 10 pages, appears to have two aims, both of which are actually continuations from the preceding section on the Latin Union. The first objective is to clarify the numerous misunderstandings that had arisen among American Catholics and church leaders concerning the true nature of the Franco dictatorship and the underlying causes of the Spanish civil war. Aguirre's longer-term purpose was apparently to convince church leaders in the U.S. to withdraw their support from the Franco regime and to give assistance, moral and otherwise, to the Basque government-in-exile. The second purpose of this section is to deal with the apparent anomaly of Catholic leaders espousing dictatorship. This issue caused European Christian democrats a good deal of trouble in the 1930s and 1940s; but in the aftermath of the war, at least in Europe, dictatorships were so discredited that the church's position was unambiguously pro-democracy.]

The use to which the Latin Union has put the tremendous Christian potentiality, principally of Catholicism, has wrought untold damage in the minds and consciences of people all over the Americas.

It is my contention that many Americans, and principally the Catholics, as much in North America as in South America, have been the victims—and still are, to a considerable degree—of the deceitful guile of the *Christian dictatorships*. The Latin Union exerts a tremendous power of attraction over many religious minds since it is composed of nations whose thought and orientation are mainly Christian. For that reason those who believe that the truth and profundity of religious ideas are in direct proportion to the public power of their protectors, have put all their hopes for the future in this union.

The cause for which the members of the Latin Union and Nazi totalitarianism are struggling is one and the same. I cannot conceive today of any possibility of separating the two. The Latin Union is Nazism's most powerful ally, and its most useful, since it spreads jealousy and confusion in the minds of neutral and Allied peoples. Loyalty and enthusiasm for the Christian dictatorships have placed thousands in a most difficult position today. How can an American Catholic applaud Franco and at the same time oppose Hitler? Franco is confident of Hitler victory; he has cast his lot with him now and has even promised to send a million men to "fight Bolshevism." This is the great pretext. But the system is the same: dictatorship, antiliberty. Adherence to those regimes which have compromised Christian doctrine through the use of force, both to gain the control of the nation and to keep it, acts like strong poison: (a) it arouses instinctive sympathy for any strong dictatorial regime which acts as a "barrier against Bolshevism"; (b) it creates a strong antidemocratic atmosphere; (c) it leads imperceptibly toward strong sympathy with the Axis, which is backing the Christian dictatorships not because they are Christian but because they are dictatorships; (d) and as the reverse of the medal it also leads to an attack on the democracies, the "allies of Bolshevism," for to those people the U.S.S.R. means only Bolshevism.

Those who extol the regimes of Franco and Pétain necessarily lose some of their own fervor for liberty, for it can never be forgotten that these regimes have installed dictatorships as a permanent system. A dictatorship of the moment may have some slight justification; but as a permanent system, never. Even democracies have made provisions in their laws for the granting of extraordinary powers under certain specified circumstances.

But such is not the case with the Christian dictatorships. Sympathy for these regimes springs from a mistaken idea of them and a twisted conception of religious spirit. It is only possible to comprehend this attitude if we admit that the sympathizers are probably mistaken in their understanding of the situation. What American, and more particularly Catholic, could want for his own country a regime like the Spanish, where political opponents are "eliminated" merely because they are opponents, thrown into prison, herded into concentration camps, or at best relieved of all their worldly goods? We should have to go back in history many centuries to find anything similar. Only the ambition of certain oligarchies made use of this type of regime for their own convenience and aggrandizement.

It is neither honorable nor just to drag the magnificent ideal of religious faith through the mud by linking it with these miserable caricatures of dictators. The Catholic of America cannot side with the forces of antiliberty, and much less can he compromise his faith by confusing it with the antidemocratic interests of the Latin Union. When this mask of solicitude for Christian civilization is torn away and the air is cleared of myths, what is left? Nothing is left but an inhuman regime against which one must act with firmness and vigor, proclaiming that Christianity, a doctrine of liberation, must not be confused with dictatorships and divorcing Christians from all sympathy for totalitarianism. Then, in the noble fight for human dignity and the liberty of the peoples of the earth, it could never happen again that a believer could desire for others a regime which he himself would find intolerable. How would he feel if tomorrow a Protestant dictatorship should sweep by force from American soil all external signs of Catholicism, or if a Catholic dictatorship should do the same with all the other American denominations?

And, to give an example in civil affairs, how would he like it if a single political party should humiliate the American people by obliging them to join its ranks or enter a concentration camp? Only through ignorance can I conceive of an American pledging his support to the Christian dictatorships. And how greatly has democratic faith already been weakened by this harmful sympathy! For too often we are apt to forget that this is not a purely theoretical debate in a literary society but a merciless war on whose outcome our whole future and even more our children's future depend.

Give to the Christian world that support which it so urgently needs today! And this can only be accomplished by a sincere Catholicism and Christianity which fights for liberty with banners unfurled, aware that liberty itself, without need of further protection, can help it carry out its lofty mission towards all humanity. It was in this sense that Pius XII spoke. His Five Points for a lasting peace have nothing whatsoever in common with the doctrines of totalitarian regimes nor with those of the Christian dictatorships. Thus in London they were accepted as the basis for the common declaration made by the heads of other Christian faiths as well as the Jewish faith.

What is truly deplorable is the crisis in charity which is occurring in the Christianism of those countries adhering to the Latin Union. Why is it that the leaders of the dictatorships seem to lack all sense of humanity when they achieve power?

In Belgium I had a chance to talk to the Basque Bishop, Dr. Mujica, exiled by Franco, about just this subject. Dr. Mujica was in his see, Vitoria, when the military rebellion broke out. The Basques of that region, like those of Navarre, were taken completely by surprise and were totally defenseless, and so fell the first day into the power of the rebels. Then began the bloodiest persecution of those defenseless Basques, and the Spanish rebels could not even pardon priests and members of religious orders, in their anti-Basque fury.

Dr. Mujica told me that the number of murders committed by these "crusaders" reached such proportions, and so horrible was the passion and fury displayed, that the alarmed Cardinal Primate of Spain, Dr. Goma, called a meeting in the house of Dr. Mujica in Vitoria to which he also invited the Basque Bishop of Pamplona. They were horror-stricken at the number of assassinations that had taken place in Alava and Navarre alone. Dr. Mujica asked them: "Can it be possible that the number of assassinations has risen to seven thousand, as I have been assured, in these two regions where no fighting at all has taken place? If this is so, then it is nothing but cold-blooded murder which cannot be tolerated."

The Prelates decided to take energetic measures. While they were still holding their meeting, a captain in Franco's army was ushered in. He was a sincere and responsible person who, owing to his position, had very exact information of the happenings. He was extremely indignant also over the extent of the crimes. Cardinal Goma asked him, "Is it possible that in Alava and Navarre seven thousand persons have been murdered?"

"Many more than that, Señor Cardinal, many more," replied the Franco captain, who was unwilling to reveal the exact number, for the very memory of it shamed him.[16]

It is unjust to lay the blame for all the excesses committed in the war at the door of the Republicans, as has been done in the Spanish case. The crimes committed deserve condemnation, whoever the perpetrators. Those which occurred on the side of the Republic compromised the good name and prestige of its leaders, who were insulted and slandered because of them. But those which occurred on the other side compromised Christ himself. And from this fact arises the protest of Christians all over the world who, with complete knowledge of the occurrences, have dared to break the guilty silence surrounding them and in all good faith proclaim that no one is justified in compromising Christ.

Only by recognizing that this crisis in charity occurring in the Catholicism of dictatorial Spain has spread to that of other countries as well can one explain the enthusiasm shown for those men who, with the help of Moors, Germans, and Italians, took up arms for the purpose of "saving Christian civilization." Not once has any of these men, either in speeches or in official notes and declarations, expressed the slightest pity or concern for those victims of unjust aggression, many of them executed or simply murdered in defiance of all standards of human justice and decency. I once asked Cardinal Goma why the execution of the fifteen Basque priests and the exile, persecution, and imprisonment suffered by hundreds of others was so shrouded in silence. In his reply he attributed the execution of some and persecution of others to culpable political activities on their part. If this were true, what possible argument remained for the Spanish Hierarchy in their protest against the execution of so many priests at the hands of the Republican extremists, whose excuse was that the Spanish priests were actively aiding a revolt against the legitimate regime?

But the silence has persisted. Calumny and slander of their adversaries has continued even when it is well known that in many cases there is not a bit of truth in the accusation.

Those who believe in the rule of brute force and are completely lacking in any sense of humanity may well applaud and extol a regime which wreaked such moral and material havoc on its road to power and, when once victorious, continued shooting and hanging systematically all those whom it considered dangerous to itself, and established concentration camps for any who dared to dissent from the line of thought which it decided to impose on all. But how can anyone calling himself Christian dare approve of such procedures? For, though we have the gift of prophecy and understand all mysteries, and though we have all faith so that we could remove mountains—how long ago was this said to Christians!—and have not charity, we are as nothing.

It must be frankly confessed that we Christians lack the courage and decision to attack these evils, because we are lacking in faith—faith in the power of the spirit which needs no machine guns to spread over the earth the blessings of Christianity, faith in our own doctrines which are being jeopardized by the very inconsistency of our conduct.

I have come from the battlefields, from the lands of sorrow and sacrifice, where sincere confessions are heard, and where men who have been despoiled of all earthly goods lift up their eyes to the Highest with hearts and thoughts purified by what they have lived through. I have spoken with people of every conceivable ideology who have suffered as I have, and I have been able to approach them free from all suspicion and fear. From these contacts, forged by suffering into a fraternal bond, I have received my greatest consolation as a Christian, for out of these contacts I have become convinced that men are seeking a return to moral standards and eternal principles which no human inventions envisaging only material welfare can possibly give them. And I have seen men turn to Christ who had long since forgotten Him and at times had denied Him. What a far-reaching and lofty reaction of the human spirit today! If only we Christians can be worthy of this hour when Christendom is coming into its own! For this we need deep faith, a profound sense of social responsibility, a firm line of conduct, because we are in the front line of the battle for liberty. We must unite in brotherhood with all the other Christian groups, and with all men who believe in human dignity, helping to persuade those who are still unconvinced, never jeopardizing the cause of liberty by vacillating action or confused thought. Above all, we must never allow ourselves the delusion of thinking that cannons were invented to impose a doctrine—still less a doctrine of love, peace, and charity. If we make use of cannons now, we have been forced to do so, in defense of our civilization endangered by those who have set up dictatorships—be they called pagan or Christian—and who believe in violence as the only means of preventing human wickedness, which according to them consists mainly in not thinking as they do.

In the last few paragraphs I have been addressing myself mainly to those who respect Christianity, with special thought for my Catholic coreligionists. Through plain speaking I have hoped to expose for them the hoax of the so-called Christian dictatorships and help them understand clearly that the time has come to call a halt to the confusions and malicious results arising out of mistaken sympathy for these movements, a confusion which has perhaps caused more spiritual damage in the Americas than anywhere else. Many will be able to understand at last that the Basques, in taking up arms to defend their country against aggression, did so not because they were confused or deceived, but because they saw their duty clearly and were willing to take the consequences. They—the Basques—well understood that in defending their own liberty they were also fighting for Christian decency, which is the patrimony not only of the Basques but of all the world. Through their sacrifice they have made a notable contribution to world comprehension of the fact that Christianity and Catholicism must never be confused with dictatorship. If we have succeeded in casting a single ray of light on so much darkness we will count ourselves well repaid for all our sacrifice and suffering.

The emphasis on *order* in the totalitarian countries has been apt to mislead that timid element among the bourgeois who are fearful of

Communism. The propaganda carried out in the name of a "crusade" has exerted a strong attraction over Catholic and Christian elements. There is also a third group who have been influenced more or less by the "wait and see" attitude.[17]

Some time ago in Washington I was talking with an agreeable diplomat from the State Department. He seemed very much amused by my manner of looking at things.

"You certainly are definite in your ideas, aren't you? Apparently you would have us break off relations with any country which did not please us—"

"No, I am not as positive as you think. What I do say is that to wait too long and gloss over and forgive too much the actions of those who deserve nothing from you may finish by alienating those who believe and trust in you. It may be advisable to maintain relations with those opposed to you, but it would be extremely imprudent not to be able to recognize your friends."

"But to return to the subject," the diplomat continued, "don't you believe that those countries which you term the Latin Union are not so much within the orbit of the Axis as moved by fear of it, and that one day they also may join the ranks of the United Nations?"

"If you are referring to the people and not to the governments of those countries I should say that they are already with the United Nations; but if you are referring to the governments and not the people I should say, categorically, no. They may preserve a false appearance of neutrality, if you like, or keep quiet in case of an attack by Hitler—but join the ranks of the democracies? Never! Can you imagine Laval passing over to the democratic side, or Franco fighting for liberty? What I cannot conceive, and surely you cannot either, is that the Free French would ever support Laval, or that the exiled Spaniards and the Basques would proclaim Franco as their leader—for reasons of decency among many others."

The diplomat laughed quite frankly and took up the argument thus: "Don't you think that the course of the war may take a hand in changing the mistaken orientation of these regimes?"

"You have only to look at the propaganda they are using," I answered. "*It is either this* (they are referring to their own regimes) *or*

Communism. With this dangerous simplification they state their position. We, who know them well and have fought against them, know that they will never change. For their position is not based on calculation—even though calculation does enter their schemes at the moment—but on a conception of government which considers itself responsible to History alone. You can see what that means. For although their ideological friends may annoy them at times—even the Axis does not always please them—they are agreed in their violent concept of government for the peoples, and they know that they will triumph or fall together."

"But don't you think it likely that these regimes may become more humane as time passes and thus make it possible to draw closer to the democracies as I have suggested?"

"Naturally, it can happen. But in that case the dictatorial regimes of the Latin countries would cease to be what they are now. If this should come to pass, it would be accomplished by other men chosen by the people; but by no means would it be the work of those men who have launched their peoples on a course so contrary to the popular will, so dangerous and so filled with terrible memories."

"You are absolutely right," the diplomat answered. "I agree with you completely, but there are still some who think the opposite. I am afraid that only a disagreeable reality can open the eyes of these stragglers."

"I am very glad to hear you say that," I replied, "for if my talk has amused you I, at least, am happy to have heard an American diplomat express himself in these terms."

Hispano-Americanism Versus Pan-Americanism

The problem of South America is more than anything else a spiritual one. It ought to be solved through conviction and not through fear. And I am not using the word "conviction" in any metaphysical sense. Even a trade agreement can result from it. Everything depends on the spirit in which it is carried out. For there is certainly a tremendous difference between a pact among equals and collaboration among friends and a measure carried out in imposition of the will of the strongest.

The sense of their own dignity is very strong among South American republics, even among those who have not shown themselves as yet very gifted in the field of government and pacification of their own peoples. They seem to have conserved a great deal of that quixotic spirit which will tolerate no slight to their dignity or honor, even though, like Don Quixote, they interpret it after their own fashion. No one who has listened to the South Americans can doubt the reality of this statement. It should never be forgotten that the souls of these countries have been formed almost exclusively by occidental Latin culture. From it springs the enormous influence wielded over the Latin American countries by their motherlands. Everything occurring in their ancestral homes finds its echo in the young republics.

You have only to glance through the pages of history to become aware that the South American continent is a natural link with the Latin Axis of Rome-Vichy-Madrid-Lisbon. Common cultural bonds which are rooted in the spirit of these nations are more powerful than geography or any material commercial interests. Pan-Latinism existed long before Pan-Americanism, and in this lies the danger.

"The Spanish War," one of the most distinguished political personalities of these republics once told me, "has made a deeper impression here than any other universal happening in the last few years. For this reason, whatever can be done to drive out confusion and clear up the atmosphere would be of inestimable benefit to the whole continent."

And he was right. I have already drawn attention to the natural bewilderment which a cleverly exploited propaganda has succeeded in spreading through the United States. But among South American countries, owing to their closer ties with Latin European countries, this confusion has been aggravated by passionate sympathy with one side or the other. Among large sections of the people the peninsular cause was and still is *their cause*. And because of the universal repercussions of the struggle—due mainly to the opposing principles which are being fought over—sympathy for Franco's side or for the Republican side has been a strong determining factor in the present position of the South American peoples, whether they will lean toward totalitarianism or liberty. I will not say that there are no exceptions, nor that there have been no changes of heart and notable rectifications, but I must affirm that the fifth column which is active in South America today in one way or another, whether through organized action or individual sympathy, and which is mainly responsible for that weakening of the love of liberty in those countries, had its beginning in Franco's school during the Spanish Civil War.

A great deal has been written about the Nazi penetration of South America and about the contacts and connections it maintains with all kinds of totalitarian organizations both in Europe and in America. This penetration is a reflection of, and was made possible by the spiritual environment created by, a clever propaganda. Totalitarian propaganda carried on during the Spanish war, with its talk of *established order* (ignoring, naturally enough, its victims), the necessity for a strong government, which leads sooner or later to dictatorship, its emphasis on the Communist danger, which it saw in any liberty-loving person or organization, exerted the greatest attraction over those timorous and conservative elements of society, and inflamed the hopes and ambitions of that little group of oligarchs who dreamt of permanent power in South America.[18]

This turbid atmosphere can only be lifted by a constant effort at enlightenment of those sectors which have been influenced by adverse propaganda. The mysticism of totalitarianism must be combated by the mysticism of liberty. This doctrine of liberty can count on a great deal more support than is commonly supposed, since it can rely not only on those elements commonly called democratic but also on large spiritual groups which are influenced by Christianity. This doctrine of liberty, in proclaiming human dignity and decency in the international field as the end and aim of the war, will unite in its ranks all men of conviction, who will in turn aid in winning over the weaker and less decided members of society.

The Atlantic Charter loses all significance if it is not applied equally to all lands bordering on this ocean. South America is one of the basic pillars in the future reconstruction of the world. It is one of the arms which reach out toward Europe from the south, just as, from the north, a current of Anglo-Saxon liberty is flowing toward and around that vast Atlantic rampart of occidental civilization. If either of these two currents of influence—that which flows toward the United States, bringing with it the civilizing spirit of the Scandinavian countries, the Anglo-Saxon, or the German, or that which flows from the Latin countries to the coasts of the American Republics, through the channels of a common culture—if either of these two currents, I repeat, should be based on anything but liberty, proclaimed and applied in all the respective territories, then the immediate result would be a dangerous loss of equilibrium. The Atlantic Charter without South America would be reduced to an Anglo-Saxon charter. It would lack that universality so important for the welfare of all in the present struggle, and it would be no guarantee of peace.

The struggle between Pan-Americanism and Hispano-Americanism—which through a dangerous derivation is today called *Hispanidad*—has a very important bearing on the present conflict. Only liberty, firmly established in all the territories bathed by the waters of the Atlantic, can counteract the effect of this war, whose significance is too often ill understood and hazy in people's minds.

The aims of Pan-Americanism are liberty for all the countries of the American continents, and solidarity based on mutual respect, answering to geographical, economic, and spiritual needs, for the benefit of all. Hence its underlying principle is liberty. Hispano-Americanism proclaims the solidarity of the Spanish-speaking American countries with the mother country, Spain, for the greater development of those bonds which history and culture have forged between them. It would really be better to call it Latin-Americanism since it includes the influence exerted on South America by all the Latin countries, chiefly Spain and Portugal but also Italy and France. However, the word *Hispanidad* seems to be in vogue today, and it is a word which provokes suspicion among many people in both North and South America.

No one should be surprised by this warning, for to understand the nature of the Hispano-American doctrine which Hispanidad is attempting to spread through South America you have only to look at the ruling spirit in Spain today. Actually Pan-Americanism and Hispanidad are the antitheses of each other. The first represents the concept of liberty; the second, through cultural and other links, spreads an atmosphere of violence and dictatorship. The first unites all America in liberty and mutual respect; the second divides America, pitting the republics of the South against those of the North. This division is not brought about in the name of culture, for culture cannot divide where liberty exists, but is produced by a violent conception of life which tends to disorganize and separate the peoples of the hemisphere. We can see this same phenomenon occurring in the religious field where the Catholicism of the South is set against the Protestantism of the North, in spite of the fact that tolerance and mutual respect are perfectly capable of resolving these conflicts, as they have done in the United States. In the political field Hispanidad stands for *authoritarianism* and *order* as opposed to *discredited democracy*, the ally of Bolshevism.

The danger, then, of Hispano-Americanism lies in its origin, in the source from which its doctrines spring. If there were no Fascism in Italy or Falangism in Spain, would there be any justification for our extreme concern over Nazi maneuvers in South America or over those Hispano-American doctrines which are more or less allied to totalitarianism? Surely not. If there were no Latin bridge over which Nazi propaganda flows so easily, that propaganda would be rendered harmless. No South American could swallow Nazism raw; but when it is cooked up with Latin ingredients, he finds it palatable enough. The Germans are well aware of this, and with characteristic audacity lose no time in taking advantage of it. They well know that the dictatorships of the Latin Union serve as their most powerful ally and means of ideological penetration, undermining the rearguard of the democracies, and they exploit them to the full with an astuteness which is one of their major characteristics.

At a dinner which was given for me by some of the intellectuals of Montevideo, I referred to this subject in the following words:

"I don't know whether my appreciation of events is correct or not—on this I would like your opinions—but I believe that if, in place of a regime of violence and oppression like the present one in Spain today, completely given over to the whims of totalitarianism, there existed a regime of freedom, where individual men were free and the different peoples of the Peninsula were allowed to develop their national spirit in liberty, then there would be no danger for you, in those ties of solidarity which might spring up between the peoples of the Peninsula and the countries of America. For the liberty existing among those peoples and the peoples of South America would be a bond of security and not one of fear, a reason for affection and not suspicion . . ."

I remember that they did not let me finish the paragraph; it was interrupted by deafening applause, applause which expressed their complete approval of my words. Later in commenting on these ideas they told me: "It is true that the Peninsula peoples are linked to those of South America by a common culture; but culture is permeated by spirit, and the spirit of those who control the Peninsula today constitutes a grave danger for our countries. Oh, if only there existed that spirit of liberty such as you have described! What a different situation for all!"

Others at the dinner added: "Neither Spain nor any other of the Peninsula peoples holds a meaning for us without liberty. Franco's system and America's are incompatible. Only liberty is capable of uniting peoples, and only through liberty can there be established a bridge of mutual esteem and understanding which will link us to Europe."

Yes, the bridge of the North and the bridge of the South, the two arms which will seal the Atlantic Charter in the Occident, but only if all the countries are organized in a system of liberty. Without this there will never be peace and security.

Up to now it has been the European continent which cast its influence, sometimes for good, other times for evil, over the American continent. In the last century, while the reactionary Holy Alliance was crushing all semblance of liberty in Europe, its victims were taking refuge in America. Today that story is repeating itself but with greatly heightened drama and violence.

Once more liberty is finding a refuge in America, and the arms of the Atlantic have folded in upon this continent from the north and from the south. It is part of the American tradition that liberty should find asylum on these shores; but no other doctrine, attempting to insinuate itself in the name of a common civilization, language, or history, can find a place in that tradition. The mission of America is to prevent these deceptive relationships from serving as a vehicle for systems of oppression and cruelty which are incompatible with the dignity of man and of the American peoples. For that reason it drew up its bridges, and the Atlantic became more and more difficult to cross. But that mission will remain incomplete if, instead of merely isolating itself from the perilous doctrines of Europe, America does not let down the bridges once again to go to the aid of those desperate peoples awaiting liberation in Europe.

Here I am going to pause for a moment to bring to the reader's attention the fact that what he has read so far and what follows hereafter was all written and completed before May, 1942, when the cause of democracy was still hanging in the balance. It was the time when a victorious Hitler was planning his advance on Stalingrad and the Caucasus, when Rommel's troops were still in a position to cut the Suez Canal, when Allied arms and diplomacy were still wavering on the defensive and the Axis dominated all Europe, spreading confusion with its propaganda among all the countries of America.[19]

It was at this time, also, that Franco was assuring Hitler that the victory was already won, promising him a million men for the Eastern Front to end the Bolshevik menace, denouncing the Jewish-democratic peril, lauding Mussolini, and aiding totalitarian propaganda in South America. It was the time when many in the democratic countries were wondering whether it would not be better to give in, for they had not the courage to face totalitarian insolence and apparent invincibility. Two years have passed since that time, and the balance has swung decisively in favor of the cause of liberty. But none of the events which have occurred has in the least modified our appreciation of the situation made in 1942; in fact they stand confirmed.

Hitler reached Stalingrad but was stopped at its very doors by the legendary heroism of the Soviet troops. The invincible power of German might was broken and buried in Stalingrad, and the whole picture of the Eastern Front was changed. From that moment humanity received assurance of its future victory. And what of the internal evolution which has been going on in the U.S.S.R. since that time? Everything seems to confirm the ideas already outlined here. The U.S.S.R. is becoming both more Russian and more occidental as a result of its close daily contact with the democracies. The human factor is becoming stronger and making itself felt more and more in this evolution. The dissolution of the Comintern, the reconciliation with the Orthodox Church, the degree of religious liberty now allowed, the greater autonomy given the Soviet republics, and finally the abandonment of the "Internationale" and the substitution of a real Russian anthem—all these are clear and gratifying symptoms. Even if all this were merely "tactical," the concessions are so significant that, sooner or later, we can expect the triumph of man over dictatorial bureaucracy; it is the triumph of human liberty. The Teheran meeting is a further step in this evolutionary process toward liberty, and the Soviet signature represents acceptance of the future organization of the world on democratic lines. As the occidental ideals of liberty of the democracies grow clearer and firmer, the U.S.S.R. continues to give its assent to these ideals. And although we are still far from perfection—because many would like to see the word made flesh—a great advance has certainly been made along that road. This is a process which all democrats should encourage, making certain that the future also is guided by high moral law. For it might well happen that, as the early primitive communism of the Soviets diminishes, so the heat of victory may bring with it a resurgence of the old imperialism of the time of Peter the Great and Catherine.

Perhaps the remedy lies in the occidental nations, who by abandoning their old policies of suspicion and neglect, and showing a new appreciation of and gratitude toward the peoples of the U.S.S.R. for their heroism and magnificent accomplishment, could open a new era of successful collaboration. And this they must do without wavering in their principles, standing firm in their application of the moral law—based on universal justice, the opposite of calculated egoism or utilitarianism, and applied equally to all whether great or small. They must deny "realism" when it departs from the moral law. There is a type of realist—self-satisfied and smug—that you can never find among the people who have suffered or among the soldiers in the trenches. You can find him in the salons and in the rearguard, in places where the truth about the war is generally ignored and where unconsciously the seeds of a third war are being planted.

To prevent such disaster and to enforce the moral law, the armies of the United States and Great Britain have liberated not only North Africa but half of Italy as well and are well on the way to Rome and other suffering parts of Europe. Allied diplomacy has graduated from the waiting stage to launch a full offensive in step with its victorious armies, and the Anglo-Saxon world is assuming more and more definitely its role of a universal redeeming force. At the first push one of the greatest of totalitarian fictions, Mussolini, fell, dragging with him the Fascist regime of Italy. The Latin Axis is also badly damaged with the fall of what was considered its leading spirit, but its influence continues to be felt as far as Buenos Aires. It does not detract from the original good intentions of the Argentinian leaders to say that totalitarianism, especially of the "Christian" variety, is continuing its intrigues, seeking a possible future refuge for the hour when democracy shall triumph throughout the world.

The situation of the Spanish dictator is gloomier yet, the more so as his cloak of grandeur has completely slipped off. What a comedown for the chivalrous and quixotic spirit of Spanish genius, which they loved so to proclaim, their present ungraceful scrambling about must be!

Feverishly searching for a hypocritical and tardy way out, bungling about, and abasing himself in all the chancelleries and diplomatic salons of the democratic countries (despised but yesterday), the Spanish Caudillo and his followers have demonstrated only too clearly that their heroic mien and much-vaunted gallantry were only put on to combat their defenseless compatriots. To brag that

Spain owes them the precarious peace she now enjoys, after having climbed to power over the piled corpses of a million brother Spaniards, is not only monstrous; it is cowardly. Their fall will be even more contemptible than Mussolini's, for at least he sought refuge in the end with his friend in evil, Hitler. But Franco is not even capable of that loyalty in misfortune. Let his country be witness. Sweden and Switzerland, for example, were able to maintain their neutrality without insulting democracy, remaining democratic themselves. But the Spain of General Franco, antidemocratic in its essence, boastful and insulting when Hitler's armies had the upper hand, is today frantically seeking some means of escape from the ruin which threatens it, trying to take advantage of the necessities of Allied strategy, and caring little that it has reduced the country to a state of absolute insignificance in the international realm by its undignified scurryings to and fro.

But Franco's new-found tact and accomplishments will gain him nothing in the end. He formed the Iberian pact when things just began to go badly for the totalitarian group. Today, London's agreement with Portugal and the subsequent occupation of the Azores have put an end to this pact, to all intents and purposes. Tomorrow, the process of decomposition of Franco's state will reach its height, for the people themselves will take over. In spite of the original purpose for which it was formed, that of escaping from the war and maintaining dictatorships within the Peninsular territory, the Iberian pact was nevertheless an interesting experiment which may find application in the future. But any future union among the Peninsular nations must be based on systems of democracy and liberty. On the following pages of the original text, which we now resume, the reader will find this idea worked out in greater detail, under the heading of "The Iberian Problem."

The Iberian Problem*

*[Editor's note: This section, "The Iberian Problem," is the most faithfully translated portion of the entire book. It appears to have been trans-

lated from the Spanish version practically verbatim. In the section, Aguirre deals with the assimilationist history of the Spanish state, as well as the religious, social, and nationalities policies of the Second Republic. He foresees as a solution a confederation of Iberian peoples, but does not go beyond this vision to propose—as have many other Basque nationalists—a "Europe of the Peoples," a confederation of ethnic nations stretching from the Atlantic to the Urals. In fact, in the years since Aguirre wrote, the solution actually attempted to resolve Spain's ethnic nationalities "problem"—the autonomous community system contained in the 1978 Spanish constitution—does not remotely approach his vision of a confederated Iberia, much less the total sovereignty demanded by many Basques.]

There is one problem of perennial interest whose importance, it seems to me, is not sufficiently recognized here in America. I am referring to the problem of the Iberian Peninsula, and by that I do not mean Spain alone.

The Iberian Peninsula is not composed of a homogeneous people, as so many believe, but is made up of a group of several peoples. Besides the Spanish there are the Portuguese, the Galicians, the Catalans, and the Basques. With the exception of the Basques they are all Latin peoples.

The Iberian Peninsula, situated between the Pyrenees and the Strait of Gibraltar, its coasts bathed by the waters of both the Atlantic and the Mediterranean, forms a natural bridge between Europe and Latin America and is also an important artery of communication between Europe and Africa. Besides its privileged geographical position we must take into account the tremendous influence over South America of Peninsular thought, thanks to the powerful vehicles of the Spanish and Portuguese languages.

The importance of the Peninsula in its relations with South America is so great that we can say that without the Iberian Peninsula, the Latin Union—the Rome-Vichy-Madrid-Lisbon Axis—would be impotent and meaningless; and its very presence in the Union is enough to insure the realization of its designs for America. What I mean to say is that the Latin Union in its proposals for American domination must act through the Iberian Peninsula, since Italian and French influence make themselves felt only through the medium of Peninsular culture. Hence it is easy to understand the deep influence which the political constitution of the Peninsula and its way of thinking have over Latin America—an influence which merits special attention particularly today.

It is my firm belief that perhaps the most powerful reason which prevented the various leaders of Argentine opinion from breaking off relations with the Axis at the same time as the other American republics was the ideological position of Spain and Portugal.

I used to ask South Americans the question, "Do you think that Argentina would have objected to breaking relations with the Axis if the Iberian Peninsula had had a free government and declared itself on the side of the Allies?"

"No objection whatsoever," they would reply, "for, more than any fear of attack from such distant countries as Germany, or Japan, the position of Argentina has been influenced by spiritual reasons born of a desire to show her own independence of initiative and personality and also reluctance to having some day to break off relations with Spain."

That is why there has been such a careful fostering of the bridge between Madrid, Lisbon, and Buenos Aires, which would be all very well if liberty prevailed at both ends of the bridge.

The present political structure of the Peninsula constitutes a danger for America because of the pernicious example and influence it exerts over the republics of oligarchical tendencies. The Atlantic Charter, whose principles are the foundation for a world organization based on liberty, will be unable to achieve its purpose unless the peoples of the Iberian Peninsula are organized as free peoples in regimes of liberty. For this is the natural complement of the South American problem. With the cooperation of the Peninsula, success would be assured to the Atlantic Charter, and that important part of the world would serve as cement in building the world of the future.

The type of danger just outlined does not exist in the North of Europe, where the countries from Scandinavia through Belgium (Germany excepted) have preserved their democratic spirit. There remains France, whose misfortune and present regime we can consider as transitory evils, because she still possesses a wealth of spiritual reserve in spite of the catastrophe. For she who was once the mother of liberties will not allow her sons to remain long in slavery.

For every kind of reason, doctrinal, political, economic, and social, the entire humanity is now entering into a constituent period whose depth and extension it is difficult to foresee. In all likelihood the programs existing today will appear worn-out and antiquated in the times which are ahead. And like all the other peoples of the world, those of the Iberian Peninsula will have to enter a new stage in their existence. I consider it useful to devote a few words to this topic.

Since Spain determined on becoming a nation, mistaking its geographical boundaries with those of the Iberian Peninsula, it entered into a period of decadence which has not yet ended. Spain could not understand that its universal role was leadership and coordination rather than assimilation of the Iberian and South American nations. That is why the Spanish Crown lost its colonial empire. It could not or did not wish to comprehend that a transition from the absolutist to the liberal era of the nineteenth century could not be made without a complete fulfillment of those liberal principles which it proclaimed. Thus, in attempting to assimilate the different peoples of the Peninsula, it deprived them of all liberties. It had no wish to follow the road pointed out by the times, that of transforming the confederation of peoples united by the crown, which was the political structure then existing, into a community of free nations united in a common civilizing purpose. Instead, influenced by a false Jacobinism, it preferred a policy of violent and senseless assimilation, completely opposed to its own interests and to history itself, which resulted in a century and a half of disturbances and civil strife. The Spanish State which was formed in the nineteenth century was unable to establish itself on lasting foundations, and for this reason it has failed. On one side the ideological struggle between so-called liberalism and reactionary ideas, on the other side the frustrated attempts at assimilation of other peoples who are distinct nations in their own right, and finally the cult of force which has been born of impatience—all these have led the Spanish State to a situation differing very little from that of the Austro-Hungarian Empire at the end of the First World War.

It was unable to follow in the path of the British Empire. An English diplomat said to me a few years ago: "We learned a great deal when the United States declared their independence. Since that time London has decided that it was much juster and more expedient to be a leader of nations. And thus grew up the British Commonwealth, which, with all its defects, is still a constructive human achievement, capable of being perfected still more."

The Spanish Crown of the nineteenth century, imbued with a kind of provincial liberalism, which it neither felt nor assimilated, suppressed by violence, among other things, Basque sovereignty in the year 1839. Thus, at one stroke it swept away one of the solidest and most ancient monuments to liberty, organized in constructive democratic forms.

Moreover, it carried out these oppressive measures while still enthusiastically proclaiming liberal ideas—apparently without realizing the inherent contradictions of its words and policies—and lost its colonial empire through lack of foresight and inability to provide for the free growth of the latter. Spain has never seriously believed (and this fault has been widespread throughout the world) that liberty is a coordinating force, and that oppression makes for discord and lack of harmony. And this was so even when its most eloquent speakers proclaimed the opposite.

Centralist Jacobinism and reactionary imperialistic oppression ruled the Spanish State by turns during a century and a half. More than a hundred uprisings and three civil wars make up the unhappy balance of recent and contemporary history of the Spanish State, resulting in the word "pronunciamiento" becoming so common that it has been introduced into the dictionaries of all countries.

And this wild succession of upheavals and revolts, unparalleled throughout the world, has dragged in its train a people like the Basques who, because of their secular democratic education, have been unable to stomach this verbal Jacobinism or tolerate unitarian oppression. The centralist regime, imposed by one or another of the leaders of the State since the time when the Spanish Crown lost sight of its true role as coordinator of nations and instead attempted either to assimilate or to exterminate them in an effort to create a false national unity, is responsible for Spanish decadence and for the fear and suspicion of the Peninsular peoples. In its blindness, it undertook a policy of pettiness which, lacking all breadth of vision or nobility, not only paralyzed action but provoked disaffection as well.

It fell to the Republic, born in 1931, to attempt to set right the historic injustices. It should have done this in straightforward fashion without sidestepping or vacillation. The achievements of the Republic were notable in many respects; but in too many cases it showed a sad lack of decision. It gave the people a real sense of partnership in the public welfare; it carried out a work of real value in the cultural field, and gave the public an honest administration. But in a democratic sense it failed to implant a real tolerance and respect which should permeate the life of a State, and without which the most perfect institutions are as nothing. The early preoccupation of certain Republican leaders with ancient quarrels and the desire to stamp out *clericalism* grew to the proportions of a real obsession. Feelings were inflamed to such a pitch that the religious problem became practically insoluble; and they even went so far as to make provisions in the Constitution (Article 26) for the dissolution of the Order of the Jesuits. This was a compromise measure taken to prevent the constitutional expulsion of all the other religious orders.

As a deputy in the Constitutional Cortes I had the opportunity of observing the number of hours and speeches and sessions of Congress devoted solely to this one subject, and the extremes to which the timidity of these Republicans led them. They were completely unable to use their prestige and authority in imposing commonsense standards of tolerance and prudence or in introducing a more intelligent and farsighted policy for the guidance of a people momentarily led astray by the impassioned propaganda of an outmoded anticlericalism. They could not foresee the reaction to their policy, which was naturally immediate and violent.

Admittedly there were abuses which needed correction; but they would have done much better to authorize the executive power to take the necessary steps, and by establishing a policy of tolerance for all they would have disarmed their opponents before things got out of hand. Later, it was too late.

I myself have first-hand knowledge of some of these abuses, as I was a witness to the tremendous difficulties encountered, in 1931, by the Papal Nuncio, Mgr. Tedeschini, and the Catalan Cardinal, Vidal y Barraquer, in their efforts to get the Spanish Rightists to accept certain principles and solutions which would have made possible a reconciliation with the newborn Republic. But this is just what the Spanish Rightists did not want. The excessive measures of the Republicans served them as marvelous propaganda.

By the year 1935 any solution at all was impossible. In that year the Pope named Mgr. Tedeschini (then serving as Papal Nuncio in Spain) a Cardinal, and had granted the power of crowning him with the Cardinal's hat to the President of the Republic, Señor Alcalá Zamora. The ceremony was celebrated with great solemnity in the Presidential Palace. Only two of the 474 members of the Cortes—myself and the other Basque representative—were present at that ceremony. The Rightists refused to go because they resented Mgr. Tedeschini's well-meant attempts at bringing about their collaboration with the Republic. The Leftists refused to attend for fear that their presence might be interpreted as showing clerical leanings. What in other parts of the world would have been considered a solemn state occasion was here no more than a new pretext for intolerance.

The fact was that the democracy written into the laws and institutions had not yet reached the man in the street. Without mutual respect and tolerance the most carefully planned institutions will fail. Although it seems like a paradox, the Republicans were too timid to impose respect.

In other countries, those problems are solved through tolerance and mutual understanding. In Spain the religious problem is so out of focus as to be almost a clinical case. It can be solved only by men of high vision who refuse to be influenced by either Jacobin anti-clericalism or the inquisitorial fervor of the overly pious. A Leftist who is tolerant enough to attend the crowning of a Cardinal, or a Rightist who proclaims that the Church should never take sides in an armed revolt against the constituted government—either of these two would be capable of solving the question.

In April, 1933, on a trip through Andalusia, my train happened to stop at the little town of Marmolejo. I was struck by the immense stretches of beautiful irrigated land in which only grass was growing. Mystified, I asked a porter to whom these lands belonged, and why they were not being cultivated. The man replied rather timidly:

"They are the lands of the Duque del Infantado, and they are not being cultivated because the Duque is very angry over this business of the agrarian reform."

"But many families must have worked in these fields. Isn't it so?"

"Many, señor," he replied, "and they are all without work today."

"But hasn't the village sent any protest to the authorities?" I questioned.

"No, I don't think so—as it concerns the Duque . . ."

Two years after the proclamation of the Republic we still found cases like the one described, due to fear of the Duke or fear of someone else. The Spanish Republic was altogether too timid in its application of social principles. While intolerable strikes abounded, many of them actually harmful to the public welfare, certain privileged positions were still tolerated, which would be inconceivable in any other country with normal development. This was as true in the industrial field as in the agrarian. They did not have a well-defined, consistent social program.

It must be added in behalf of the Republicans that they were confronted with the most violent opposition on the part of the conservative classes which made up the Rightist groups in the Cortes.

Their conception of social responsibility was so backward and so egotistical that, had the Republicans passed fiscal decrees similar to any of those existing in England, United States, or France before the war, for example, they would have been classed as absurd measures of expropriation, inspired by Moscow.

The moment the Radical-Right coalition came into power in 1933, "starvation salaries" once more made their appearance in

Andalusia, which in their turn helped precipitate the Popular Front triumph in 1936. For some time now, those conservative and Rightist elements who supported General Franco's revolt have been criticizing the attempted social regime of the Falange. This organization, whose ranks have been swelled by former syndicalists and Communists, had long been urging a social transformation following the example of the Italian and German regimes.

This problem can only be solved—within the limits of human possibility—by those who face it squarely and courageously, who recognize that it is a demand of the times and a matter of pure justice, and who are able to make it clearly understood by all that an unauthorized political strike causing undeserving hardship to many is as criminal as wealth amassed at the cost of the misery of others.

The Spanish Republic was equally timid in its approach to the fundamental problem of the different Peninsular peoples, who were demanding a historic rectification of past wrongs, and with it their liberty. Spanish centralists rose up en masse to protest. They could not tolerate the idea of granting even partial liberties to these peoples.

Neither Basque nor Catalan Home Rule was granted in time, and even these modest Statutes did not come up to the basic and commonly accepted standards for the solution of the national problems. There was tremendous opposition and constant haggling over them among the authorities. The proposals for political autonomy of these peoples were shoved around from commission to commission, from the Parliament to the country, from the country back to the Parliament. The Catalan minority in the Constitutional Cortes twice left the Parliament in protest against the obstinate lack of comprehension of the Spanish deputies. This happened a full year after a Catalan plebiscite had triumphantly voted for Home Rule. At the same time the Basques were being called the Gibraltar of the Vatican by those very members who later were to find us fighting at their side against the totalitarian coalition.

This attitude gave rise to a provision in the Basque autonomous constitution whereby if the Spanish Republic should break off relations with the Vatican the Basques could still maintain them, since the great majority were Catholics; and the provision did not carry with it the forfeit of any of the individual liberties guaranteed by the Republican Constitution. This measure, which seemed perfectly reasonable to all the cultivated persons whom we have consulted, was greeted with a storm of protest in the Parliament of Madrid and in the pages of the sensational press. In such an atmosphere of inflamed excitement the most delicate problems were debated. But, at least, in the Republican era they were debated. In the previous period they were not even recognized, much less discussed.

It cannot be denied that the most serious-minded of the Republican leaders were anxious to effect acceptable, human solutions of problems which, like the religious or the social problems, had such a profound influence over Spanish society. They had the best of intentions concerning the problems of nationality, but their proposals were frustrated by men of lesser caliber and understanding and by intransigent organizations. But I repeat, their intentions were honest as their lives were honest. One may criticize the Republic for its many mistakes and errors, but it ought to be loudly proclaimed that the Republican period was one of the most honest if not *the* most honest in all the history of Spanish politics. And my assertion can be taken at its face value because I myself suffered deeply and bitterly for the cause of my Basque fatherland during all the Republican period.

But all that belongs to the past and now we are facing the future. The Iberian Peninsular problem is no longer one of personalities, nor political parties, nor parliamentary debates; it is a problem of peoples.

The Peninsular peoples, like all the other peoples of the world, stand today on the brink of a future immanent with change. The march of events is swift, and woe to him who attempts to stop it in its course. That is why I feel that reality has grown beyond the problem usually spoken of as the "Spanish question," and that now it is a problem of the Iberian Peninsula, that is to say of Spain, Portugal, Euzkadi, Catalonia, and Galicia and their coordination and organization. They must look to the future world for the form which this organization will take, leaving the past behind and breaking down ancient molds. In accord with present-day trends of thought, the future is pushing them toward a confederation of Iberian peoples.

This problem will be meaningless if it is not given a more universal focus, looking toward America on the one side, and on the other toward a closer understanding with Europe. Through uniting in freedom, these needs of the future could be met, for American suspicion would melt away when it was understood that the bridge between the continent and the Peninsula serves only to unite the two in systems of liberty. And on the other hand a well-balanced Peninsular structure could keep in step with Europe. Later it could be incorporated into that organization hoped for by all of the old continent, an organization of common aims and purposes, more or less federal in form, which will unite the big and little nations in universal undertakings.

Many people, especially Spaniards and Portuguese, are made very apprehensive by the mere mention of a Peninsular problem. Others, Europeans and Americans, appear very much surprised at the existence of such a problem. They were brought up to accept certain opinions as eternal truths, and any change in the established order of things is viewed with alarm. It is my belief that more can be accomplished through clear thinking and plain speaking, approaching each problem in a spirit of harmony and generosity, than from a fearful shrinking from the changes which the future will inevitably bring. For the Iberian problem is not one of mere whims but one which nature itself has implanted. Many people seem to forget that only through liberty and mutual respect, and not through oppression, can anything of a permanent nature be constructed.

In discussing the future of Europe, how can one conceive of any process of coordination of the continent, whether through federations or any other system, without including the Iberian peoples? How can one discuss plans for coordinating the Scandinavian countries, or the Central European, or the Balkans without relating them to still more extensive projects? Could the nations of the Iberian Peninsula remain outside a European organization?

Here is the problem of the future which it would be stupid to deny or neglect. It is my belief that a coordination and organization of the

Iberian Peninsula, based on the national liberty of each of its peoples, which would accord perfectly with the principles which are being evolved for the future, is probably the last chance we shall have to correct those historic mistakes, for which we are all more or less responsible. Such a solution would be in accord with the will of the peoples and would make possible the necessary prospective collaboration between them. Moreover, an adequate solution of this problem would have an immediate and beneficial influence over the future spiritual orientation of Latin America.

If the intolerance and complacence of these more or less dictatorial regimes, so at odds with the principles of liberty for which the rest of the world is fighting, continues to deny or ignore the legitimate demands of the Peninsular peoples, then a new era of violence will result. If a peaceful and orderly method of solving the problem is denied them, then the peoples will rise up determined to seek by other means the liberty for which they thirst.

For liberty is the last prerogative which a people will give up. Especially when so much blood has already been shed in its defense.

The Mission of America*

*[Editor's note: This concluding section of the English version is a composite of two separate discussions from the Spanish version. In the Spanish version, the section entitled "Misión de América" appears much earlier (pages 381 to 387 in that version), between the discussions on the nationalities problem and the Latin Union. In the English version, this material begins on page 000 with the quote from Franklin Roosevelt and ends at the bottom of page 000. The Spanish version concludes with a section entitled "Message from the Basques Who Sing and Suffer" ("Mensaje de los Vascos que Cantan y Sufren"). This material is interrupted by the "Misión de América" passages from pages 373–376, and then resumes with the two concluding paragraphs of the book. The most striking aspect of this conclusion is the almost total, sublime faith Aguirre places in America to come to the relief of Europe, and to rescue it from the grip of tyranny. Of course, he is

really talking here to all Americans, both north and south; but clearly his hopes were that the United States would defeat fascism and go on to restore democracy to the other countries where it had been suppressed—most importantly, of course, Spain. Unquestionably, the recent history of the Basque people would have been decidedly different if the United States had risen to this challenge.]

On April 5th of the year 1526 our ancestors held a meeting, or *Batzarra* (Congress), beneath the Tree of Gernika, for the purpose of reforming the *Fuero,* or Constitution. They delegated the task of studying and drawing up the reform to a committee, or what we call today a parliamentary commission. This commission presented its work "having made a careful study of the old Fuero, omitting laws which had become superfluous and adding those which had become useful through custom or whatever seemed wise to them in the sight of God and their own consciences." They added later that they were meeting "in conformity with the power granted them by the General Council to draw up the reform of the old Fuero . . . that they had discussed each article and law of the new Fuero and were agreed that it conformed to the privileges and liberties, the customs and usages of Biscay."

Thus simply the Constitutional Junta, meeting in Gernika in 1526, concluded the legislative reform of their constitution. Among other provisions, it forbade the use of torture, and even of detention for misdemeanor, unless the person were called beneath the Tree of Gernika. It prohibited the giving of titles of nobility and declared all Basques to be equally noble, and equal before the law without exception, and proclaimed that any decree, whether by the King or by any other authority, should be disregarded if it ran contrary to liberty.

In this atmosphere of liberty the Basque people lived and had their being. Their standards did not derive from the will of any single man, call him King or Señor, but from the legislative organs representing the people, who in all their history had known no other way of life.

In 1839, this liberty and this way of life were forcibly taken from them by the Spanish Monarchy in the first of a series of attempts at assimilation of the peoples under its rule.

After a century of struggle the Basque people finally achieved autonomy, and in 1936 I had the honor of taking the oath of office beneath the Tree of Gernika, thus renewing the tradition of our forefathers and commencing again our history of liberty.

But this did not last long. Both the government and the Basque people were scattered to the four corners of the earth like ashes blown by the winds. The bombers of Hitler and Mussolini, at that time serving Franco, destroyed Gernika; but they could not destroy the spirit of the Basque people.

The same Basque government which I appointed under the Tree of Gernika in 1936, and the same government which opposed with all the force in its power the unjust totalitarian aggression and invasion of our soil, that government is now living in exile. There are only two missing. One, who was treacherously handed over to Franco by a disloyal aviator, was shot. The other died of fatigue and exposure in his flight from the Germans at the time France fell.

There are Basques living under all the skies of the world, wanderers in many lands. But though they live in exile they do not despair, for they have faith that the future will restore liberty to their beloved country. Scattered though they may be, they are united in spirit behind their government in the continuing battle for freedom. They fight and they wait, as their ancestors had to do so many times, for the storms of history to pass and leave them free once more.

Hope rises from their hearts to their lips like a song from heaven. That is why the Basques are always singing. Basque songs, as old as those which the wind sings to the oaks of Aralar, have been heard even in the concentration camps of the Sahara. For the ungrateful Vichy, forgetting that the Basques had worked and fought for the true France and remembering only that they were enemies of Hitler and Franco, imprisoned many there. But even the prison guards were touched by these songs, and they let many escape and sail for America.

Many others are still suffering in Franco's jails, but they are let out occasionally to sing in near-by churches.

One day in the Cathedral of Palencia during the celebration of a High Mass an unknown choral group was heard. Those present in the church were so impressed by the beauty of the singing that they began to ask where the chorus came from. "From Dueñas prison," was the reply. "These are Basque priests condemned to prison . . ." And when Mass was finished these holy men returned to the prison where they had been condemned for the sole misdeed of loving their country.

Basques continue to sing even when they are marching to their death. A young man who had succeeded in escaping from Franco Spain into France told me the following story: One morning in an old house near the cemetery where he had taken refuge, he was awakened by a magnificent chorus of young voices singing the Basque Hymn of the Gudaris. Convinced that this was a hymn of victory, he rushed out of his hiding place to greet the singers. He was hastily pulled back by his protector, who told him that it was a wagonload of Basque prisoners going to their execution. "We often hear that song at daybreak," he said. They listened to the stirring chorus as it died away in the distance. Then came the sound of shots, and the singing and the singers were stilled forever.

There is no suffering or sacrifice great enough to crush the soul of a people who know they are fighting for justice and liberty. Our battle was even harder and more thankless than most, for we were completely alone, and instead of aid and understanding we received only contempt from those who ignored us. There are many today who suffer as we suffered, but at least they are not alone and do not have to bear the insults and misunderstanding which made our struggle bitter indeed. But the same sorrow and the same faith unites us to those people, and the same firm resolve to fight through to victory.

And here in America the same spirit is felt. The American people, born to peace and carried against their will into war, are finding new spiritual reserves of courage and fortitude as the task which faces them becomes more difficult and more bloody. Keeping time with their factories and shipyards, the American conscience is producing a spirit of sacrifice and a will to victory.

And I thank God that this is so. Because—

Listen well, American reader. Others may hide it from you, but I must tell it to you in all frankness. This war, the most terrible and cruel in all history, will weigh more heavily on your shoulders than on any others. In dollars, war material, tears, and blood your country is going to have to spend more than any other country to win this war. And if you ask me why, I will tell you: "Just as once you astonished the world with your skyscrapers and your ingenious inventions, so today you have been given the greatest and most noble role in all history—that of saving mankind, through saving liberty."

"This generation of Americans," said President Roosevelt in 1936, "has an appointment with destiny." These words were never truer than today when America is charged with the performance of one of the loftiest missions. Freedom itself sought refuge on these shores, and America opened its arms and welcomed it. From that moment its responsibility became greater than that of any other country in the world. Its mission is to preserve this great spiritual refuge to which suffering humanity has entrusted all its faith and hope for future liberation.

This is no time for egoism nor for casting the blame on others. America is facing now one of those magnificent tasks which history from time to time assigns to countries which are capable and worthy of fulfilling them.

"The attitude of Americans toward themselves and toward all other human beings," says Dorothy Thompson, "the fact that we are a race of races, and a nation of nations, the fact of our outlook upon two oceans—and the miracle of the creation of this country out of stock that for such a large part represents the frustration of European dreams and the rejection of human material—all these combine to make us a messianic people, with a feeling of mission not only for ourselves but for the world."[20]

On the crowded roads of Europe I have seen human beings fall fainting with these words of hope on their lips: "America and England will save us." Those mothers with their children in their arms, those old people who were not even allowed to finish out their years in peace, those broken families and improvised hearths beneath the stars have one supreme hope: "America and England will be our salvation, or if not ours at least that of our children." And they are right to speak thus, for their countries have served as a first line of defense and England and America have promised to set them free.

There are millions of people throughout the world who have suffered for liberty, and who are only sustained in their captivity by this same hope. From the ruins of Gernika and the bombed English cities, through the bloody roads of Europe, to the concentration camps and ghettos of Poland and the burnt-out fields of Russia there arises one cry of hope from those who only accept such suffering because they believe that liberty will be restored to all humanity.

Just as today the airplane has decreased the size of the world, so also has the radio. Ideas and their impacts travel around the world in a few hours, leaving no part of humanity untouched. Whoever remains unaware of this modern solidarity is preparing the way for his own ruin.

The interest of America is at one with the interest of the whole world, or it is meaningless. And this is the heart of the problem which is troubling the greater part of humanity, in whose wounded spirit faith still burns with the hope of liberation and triumph.

In Belgium, in Sweden, and even in Germany itself, countries which I have traveled through since the war, they look to America, because they believe in her. And this faith which the countries feel for America takes living form in the figure of President Roosevelt. It would be hard to find in the pages of history a leader of greater universal prestige or moral authority. There have been many famous leaders, both military and political, in various epochs. But the peoples living in their times feared them even though they admired them. Providence has assigned a role of such universality to President Roosevelt, not because the peoples fear him but because they have placed all their hopes on him, especially those who are writhing beneath oppression. Never has a ruling figure received so many expressions of loyalty and allegiance as the American President. In Germany, in Italy, in the Iberian Peninsula, in the Central European countries, in France, in Scandinavia, the figure of President Roosevelt has acquired such moral stature that only those of us who have actually been in these oppressed lands can bear full witness to it.

When I was in Buenos Aires and Montevideo I heard constant expressions of loyalty and faith in the American President. When a

Uruguayan diplomat, at a meeting of the most outstanding intellectual leaders of his country, proclaimed amid thundering applause
the need for union among all lovers of liberty "under our leader,
Roosevelt"—these were his exact words—I understood that this
phrase held a much deeper significance than mere flattery or adula-
tion. It put into words a universal feeling of faith in this man and
what he stood for and, because of him, faith in his country also. In
Buenos Aires I heard similar expressions of confidence from people
of all social classes and the most mixed political beliefs. Never before
in history was one man granted such universal confidence and,
because of it, such tremendous responsibility toward the world.[21]

By far the greater part of the human race has already pledged its
allegiance to the spirit of the Atlantic Charter. The putting into
effect of the principles contained in the Charter will mean the end of
totalitarian tyranny. The men who worked out this Charter have
obtained for it the adherence of every nation now fighting for
liberty. This banner of hope and liberty must continue to float on
high until the final day of victory. There must be no vacillation but
only an iron will to fight on, brushing aside those weak and timorous
souls who are unable to comprehend that by their suicidal actions
they are courting the very evils they fear most.

A spirit of frank and burning optimism should guide humanity in
these difficult times. We should strive to emulate the iron temper of
the British Prime Minister, who alone sustained the spirits of his
people in those dark days of Dunkirk when the Allied troops were
scattered and fleeing before the advancing might of the Nazis. The
confidence and optimism which is expressed and felt in every speech
and note and action of the American President should become a
beacon for all humanity, spreading its light across all the dark corners of the world. For this war, more than anything else, is a struggle
of wills.

Our principles are clearly set forth, our purposes are high, we
have the will to win, and we will win. And when the hour of victory
arrives, it must be crowned by a just application of those high
principles for which the world is fighting, without discrimination or
mean bargaining. And herein lies the greatest of the responsibilities
falling to the leaders of the fight for liberty. And America's re-

sponsibility is the greatest of all. I am sure that, if a contrary spirit should today gain control of the destinies of the world, a deathlike silence would reign over all the concentration camps and oppressed countries of Europe and spread over the rest of the world like a mantle of despair. The silent people would watch with indifference the uncurbed gallop of the totalitarian horsemen who would soon sweep away all before them like riders of death.

The generations who have known such sorrow, and those who have yet to live through it, are determined once and for all to seek the establishment of a moral law for humanity—a moral law which would prevent the breaking of promises among nations as well as among men and restore decency in human relations of every kind, reminding us once more that we are rational beings capable of rectification.

And this is the mission of America: to bring about decency in the world, to make sure that the principles proclaimed to the world are applied to the full in practice, and to prove that honor and integrity are living forces and gangsterism is dead.

The present generation of Americans must have thought many times of those magnificent words of President Lincoln in his Gettysburg address: "that we here highly resolve that these dead shall not have died in vain, that this nation, under God, shall have a new birth of freedom, and that government of the people, by the people, for the people, shall not perish from the earth."

And because we believe firmly that America will carry out the high mission that has been entrusted to her, we ask God to bless her, to shed His light upon her and guide her.

Everything depends on you, American, more than on any one else. Because you are a new man, a symbolic fusion of all the races of the earth, all those who have fallen for the cause, all those who suffer and hope rely on you to carry to fulfillment their dreams of liberty.

And you will not fail them, for in your new heart the blood of all these peoples still beats strongly. And on the day when your mission is accomplished, the Tree of Gernika—universal symbol—will once more cast its shadow over a free land.

Notes

CHAPTER I

1. The material in chapters I and II appears in the Spanish version on pp. 85–119, after the historical material on Basque origins and nationalism.

2. The preceding paragraph contains considerable graphic detail concerning the bombing that does not appear in the Spanish version.

3. In the Spanish version, the preceding discussion is followed by a paragraph in which Aguirre tells an anecdote about several Jews who, "following the commercial instincts of their race," were selling cigarettes at twice their market price to others caught in this makeshift concentration camp. This anecdote, as well as others at a later point in the book, were deleted from the English version, perhaps out of a concern that they could be interpreted as antisemitic. At a more appropriate point below, I shall discuss why this was an unwarranted concern, but one brought on by the understandable pressures and tensions of the war and its accompanying horrors.

CHAPTER II

1. The following anecdote appears in the Spanish version, but with much less detail and without the quoted material. The translators appear to have taken some poetic license with the original.

2. The date cited in the Spanish version is May 22, 1940.

3. In the Spanish version, this story about the traitorous French Basque, Ibarnegaray, is developed in much greater detail that goes on, in fact, for some 3 pages. The French minister is referred to as "*un mal vasco*" ("a bad Basque"), and his efforts to punish the Spanish Basques to ingratiate himself with General Franco are described at length. For a Basque nationalist such as Aguirre, of course, there was no greater sin than to betray one's own countrymen; but the English translators apparently felt this episode deserved less space in the English version.

4. The following several sentences appear here in much greater detail, complete with quotations, than in the Spanish version, where the encounter is passed by in only the most general terms. It is as if the English translators were trying to provide more dramatic detail for the American reader.

CHAPTER III

1. In the Spanish version, the historical background developed here in chapter III actually begins the book and occupies the first 80 or so pages. The American translators apparently felt this material would detract from the drama of Aguirre's narrative, so it was moved in the English version. As one might expect with a book of this sort, some liberties were taken with historical fact. In the Carlist wars, for example, many Basques from the larger coastal cities such as Bilbao and San Sebastián sided with the liberal forces that favored centralization and unification of the Spanish state. No doubt they did so for reasons having to do with the economic interests of the growing Basque middle class. Whatever the reason, it is not accurate to depict the Carlist wars as a battle between Basques and Spaniards.

The first several pages of this chapter contain material not in the Spanish version, apparently to help the American reader identify with the subject better. The long quote from John Adams, for example, is not in the Spanish version. On the other hand, there are substantial passages deleted from the Spanish version. An example would be the paragraphs about the ancient Basque language, Euskera, that appear on pp. 13–14 of the Spanish version, but which have been deleted from the English version.

It is also noteworthy that in the English version the Basques are referred to as a race or in racial terms a number of times. In the Spanish version, Aguirre (at least in this segment) did not use the word "race" at all to describe the Basques. He much preferred to refer to them as a "people" or a "nation."

2. *Portugal and Galicia with a Review of the Social and Political State of the Basque Provinces* . . . (London: John Murray, 1836). [Author's note.]

3. John Adams, *A Defense of the Constitution of Government of the United States of America* (London, 1794), v. I, pp. 18–19. [Author's note.]

4. At this point in the Spanish version, there are 4/5 pages that do not appear in the English version at all. Some of this material deals with events surrounding the launching of the Basque Government in October 1936; but the bulk of the narrative—some 4 pages—discusses the arrival of a sizable quantity of weapons, small arms, and rifles, as well as artillery, from two unlikely sources: Nazi Germany (sold through the black market) and Soviet Russia. Apparently the American translators thought it better not to reveal this kind of detail to their American readers.

5. *The Tree of Gernika* (London, 1938), pp. 12, 395. [Author's note.]

6. At this point in the Spanish version, Aguirre devotes two full pages to a discussion of the parallels between the bombing of Guernica and the attack on Pearl Harbor. One wonders why the American translators chose to delete these passages when they would have bolstered strongly their effort to make the book a significant and meaningful message to an American

audience largely ignorant of the simple facts of the Basque struggle, much less of its larger significance in the unfolding war in Europe. The following excerpt from the Spanish version will give the flavor of what was deleted: "If Pearl Harbor was a terrible blow for the Americans, the reader can understand what the destruction of Guernica, the living symbol of all that was most beloved by us, meant for the Basques. . . . Between Pearl Harbor—a purely military objective—and Guernica—a purely civilian objective— there is an intimate relationship that becomes more real after having lived through the five years that separate them; both are painful landmarks of a new savage, cowardly war tactic, since if Guernica was the first trial run of totalitarian destruction, Pearl Harbor has been the last, the beginning and the end of a tragic chain of collective slaughters, perpetrated by those who hid behind the cowardice and pride of the powerful nations, to attack first the weak, and then finally the strong." And so on.

7. The battle of Elgueta occupies pp. 41–47 in the Spanish version; in the English version, it is reviewed in one brief paragraph.

8. Reprinted by permission of C. D. Lewis. [Author's note.]

9. The material enclosed here in quotes is presented in the Spanish version not in quotes, but rather as if they were the thoughts of Aguirre himself.

10. The following material on pp. ooo–ooo is set aside and given much expanded treatment in a section (part III) of the Spanish version titled "In the France that Went to the War with the Soul Divided." In this section of the Spanish version, which covers pp. 73–86, Aguirre describes in great detail how the French people were confused about the true purpose of the war and therefore were unable to support their government in its resistance against Nazi Germany. In both his own words and in conversations he reports with others, Aguirre emphasized that the French people did not understand the Basque struggle as being a battle between freedom and dictatorship. They (the French) were so obsessed with the threat of communism that they were unable to muster the internal strength necessary to resist Hitler and his confederates in the French Fascist parties. This internal division of France is noted briefly in the English edition, but downplayed considerably compared with Aguirre's Spanish version.

CHAPTER IV

1. At this point in the Spanish version, Aguirre describes a conversation with the rector of the Jesuit college, which is deleted from the English version, probably because of the rector's pro-German and anti-British sentiments. The rector proclaimed his belief that the war on the continent was already over, that the French would soon give up, and that Britain would

soon be invaded. The rector was also of the opinion that, unlike the situation in World War I, the German soldiers were behaving themselves this time with admirable discipline. Aguirre, needless to say, was incredulous in the face of such naïveté. This is one of several such conversations he describes in the Spanish version to drive home one of the central themes of the book: namely, that many people in Europe did not understand the true nature of the Hitler menace until it was too late.

CHAPTER V

1. At this point in the Spanish version (pp. 155–156), Aguirre devotes a paragraph to the three-person intelligence network that connected him to Basque political leaders and provided him with precious information. According to Aguirre, this network had even reached inside the Spanish embassy in Brussels. For some reason, the book's American translators saw fit to delete this paragraph. The network appears in action in the next several pages of the English text (pp. 136–138).

2. The preceding paragraphs are only a brief and superficial summary of Aguirre's account in the Spanish version (pp. 165–168) of the discussion with the Flemish nationalist. Not only did the Flemish activist believe that the struggling ethnic peoples of Europe would find more support for their cause among Nazi Germans than among the Western democracies; he was also scathingly critical of the pre-war government of Belgium, a regime he accused of corruption and cowardice. He also warned Aguirre and his companions against believing any promises made by the British, who would offer anything to any ethnic group to secure their support in the war, but who would betray these promises as soon as the war was over. Germany, on the other hand, despite its treatment of countries like Norway or Czechoslovakia, could be counted on to provide adequate autonomy and representation to ethnic nations such as the Flemish. By the end of the discussion, however, Aguirre had managed to put the Flemish representative on the defensive by recalling Germany's pact with Stalinist Russia and the resultant sacrifice of numerous small countries. Very little of this conversation was kept in the English version, perhaps because of the criticism of Britain and Belgium, two American allies.

CHAPTER VII

1. For the next 40 to 50 pages, the translator has provided a fairly faithful rendition of the Spanish text into English. A few significant changes and

deletions are noted where they occur, but in general there is little that needs annotation for the next 50 pages or so. This change suggests that a different translator worked on this portion of the book.

2. The reader has, in the preceding paragraph, a short and succinct statement of the ideology of Christian democracy that Aguirre and others attempted to defend in European politics after World War II. Central here is the idea that human beings do not exist solely in the material sense or realm, but achieve their humanity by extending their existence into the realm of the spirit as well. Thus, material reforms, while important, are not enough. Freedom of people to pursue the spiritual values of their choice is essential if they are to be truly free. While Christian democracy regained considerable influence in certain parts of Western Europe (such as West Germany) after the war, on the whole Christian democratic parties are not a major force across Europe today, forty-five years after the end of the war. In post-Franco Spain, efforts to create a Christian democratic centrist party failed; and only Aguirre's party, the Basque Nationalist party, retains some elements of Christian democracy in its ideological tenets. Even the Basque Nationalists, however, have cast off a considerable portion of their pre-war ideological principles, perhaps sensing that battles between the church and lay society, so important in Spain before 1975, are of relatively little significance in a largely secularized society like that of Spain in the 1980s and 1990s.

3. For reasons that will be obvious, the translator has deleted several lengthy passages in which Aguirre comments on the refusal of the American diplomat to assist him in his efforts to escape the clutches of the Nazis. I quote some of the deleted passages to give the reader some idea of Aguirre's sense of outrage at this treatment of his case:

"'I cannot get it into my head that an American Minister can act in this way. Do you understand the horrible situation of men like me? In some cases, we are beaten individuals who must be shoved aside because we are undesirable and useless guests; but in other cases ... we rise to the category of a delicate problem whose resolution requires instructions from superiors. This is a sad concept that we have of a man in danger. In the face of bureaucratic instructions, it's not worth anything, absolutely nothing. These are problems of the heart, and not of bureaucratic regulations. ...

"'I believe in America, and I believe that you will save the freedom of the world; but if a contrary spirit were to infiltrate these countries, all their moral recourse would emerge broken ... This is what has happened in Europe. The insolidarity of the peoples is a consequence of the insolidarity of individuals ... How many peoples of Europe, especially the small ones, revolve today in the orbit of the Axis because their rights were undervalued. You do not want to understand that in those small peoples is where freedom has its most fervent admirers, because they are alive thanks to it [freedom]. And instead of taking advantage of all these forces jointly, which is considerable, they are abandoned and in many cases disillusioned.'

"Throughout the day I have not been able to get out of my mind the answer of the United States Embassy in Moscow, their denial to deliver to my friend Stevenson a letter that represents life and death to me. . . . And I can only recall those words of Walt Whitman . . . in the preface to *Leaves of Grass:* 'The largeness of Nature and of this Nation were *monstrous* without a corresponding largeness and generosity of the spirit of the citizen.' Yes, all the natural greatness of the American nation would be monstrous if there were no greatness in the spirit of its citizens." (In the Spanish version, this sentence from Walt Whitman appears in English, with emphasis supplied by Aguirre himself.)

4. These comments of Aguirre about the Spanish king Alfonso XIII are accompanied in the Spanish version by a reference to the king's "extraordinary obesity." The ending sentence of the paragraph, about the aspirations of the monarchists for a restoration of the monarchy, is followed by this sentence: "But the will of the people is lacking, which is no little matter." These remarks are deleted from the English version.

5. This comment about the Hitler-Stalin pact is accompanied in the Spanish version by several paragraphs in which Aguirre sharply criticizes Stalin for what Aguirre describes as "cold calculations" and "machiavellianisms." He continues: "If the rest [of the world's leaders] are thinking of following this road, better that they be discovered in time, to avoid the shedding of innocent blood." These paragraphs are deleted from the English version.

6. In the Spanish version, we learn that the film Aguirre went to see concerned the Irish rebellion against England. "It is the first time," observes Aguirre, "that I have heard applause in a movie theater in Germany. A people who will not applaud for Hitler or for their soldiers on parade will applaud for the Irish struggle for their freedom. It made me think. While they enslave Czechs, Poles, and Norwegians, and they destroy Guernica, attacking the Basques like many other peaceful and innocent peoples, here they applaud because Ireland wants to be free. It runs against common sense." These remarks are deleted from the English version.

7. At this point, and for at least the next 50 pages, the translator exercised considerable literary license in creating the English version. For example, the preceding sentence reads more accurately as follows: "When my friends leave, I feel more alone." Not as dramatic, perhaps, as the American translation, but more faithful to Aguirre's true state of mind, at least when he wrote the Spanish version.

8. In the Spanish version, this comment about the need to invade the

European Continent is followed by this sentence, deleted from the English version: "But there is no doubt that air power can destroy the morale of this people who have believed everything their leaders have told them."

9. The *txapela*, or beret, is a national Basque headgear which distinguished the Carlists in the last two civil wars. Franco adopted it as part of the Falangist uniform when the Carlist forces joined him. [Author's note.]

10. These sentences, which do not appear in the Spanish version, are another example of the translator's literary interpretation of Aguirre's state of mind while in Germany. Nothing in the Spanish version suggests he felt himself "at the breaking point."

11. Again the translator has taken extraordinary liberty with Aguirre's prose. The Spanish version reads, simply: "Today I have had a very great satisfaction." The net effect of many of these interpretative decisions by the translator is to distort the highs and lows of Aguirre's mental state during his time in Germany. No doubt he was distressed; who in his position would not be? But the Spanish version is probably a more accurate picture of an intelligent and resourceful man working hard to extricate himself from a serious predicament.

12. In the Spanish version, Aguirre ends this passage with a different supplication: "My God, my God, why have you forsaken me?" It is not clear why the translator thought it necessary to change Aguirre's words here.

13. At this point, the Spanish version describes a fairly lengthy conversation between Aguirre and the Panamanian consul to Berlin, which is deleted from the American version. In the conversation, the consul complains of the way he and other Latin American diplomatic representatives are mistreated by the German government. Despite their neutral status, the Latin Americans are tightly restricted in their travel as well as in their use of telephone and mail services. Aguirre has little sympathy for the complaining Panamanian. He tells the consul that if all the Latin American representatives would band together in a joint protest, Berlin would be forced to remove or relax these unwarranted restrictions. The Panamanian agrees, but laments that the Latin American diplomats are too divided among themselves, and too self-conscious about their small size and their weakness; they would never agree to participate in such a move. Aguirre seizes the opportunity to draw the reader's attention once again to the failure of the European democracies to stop Hitler through a united effort.

14. The English version deletes the entire diary entry for April 24. In the Spanish version, the entry relates a conversation Aguirre had with several Latin American diplomats concerning the low level of public morality he found in Germany and in Nazi-occupied Europe in general. The conversation was deleted probably because Aguirre cited as evidence for his statement the case of a prominent Latin American who was making a fortune in

Belgium in the black market. Upon being discovered by the German authorities, he was released with little more than a mild reprimand.

15. The following paragraph provides yet another example of literary license. The Spanish version ends the sentence with the observation that the Spanish government could not get away with its lies about a leader—in this case, the Catalan, Companys—who had been freely elected by his people, and execute him for crimes that he had not committed. There is no reference in the Spanish version to the "kettle of water" that will "boil over eventually to scald them for their treachery."

16. The English version deletes the diary entry for May 7, in which Aguirre relates a conversation with a Chilean diplomat living in Germany. The thrust of the conversation is that the Nazi dictatorship was having a stultifying effect on artistic expression and on free thought in general, a mistake that cost the Germans dearly in the long run. It is not clear why the passage was deleted from the American version.

17. The reference here is to German manufacture of 3,000 *airplanes* per month. In the Spanish version, the word for airplane is "aparato," which has been clumsily rendered here as "machine."

18. More literary license. In the Spanish version, the first two sentences of this diary entry—about Aguirre's not being able to sleep, etc.—do not appear. The entry begins much more matter of factly, with the telephone call from the Venezuelan minister.

19. Psalm 106 in the Douay Version. [Author's note.]

20. The English version omits at this point a diary entry by Aguirre in which he relates a conversation with several Latin Americans about the flight to England of German leader Rudolph Hess. There is speculation that Hess fled to England to try to arrange a separate peace with the British, since the Germans had apparently decided to open a second front with the Soviet Union. The consensus of the group is that the opening of the Russian front will mean the downfall of the Germans.

21. In the Spanish version, Aguirre does not end this chapter here, but continues on for three more pages with a lengthy description of his impressions of Nazi Germany. Now on Swedish soil, he cannot resist some parting shots at the famed—and, for him, mythological—German efficiency and invulnerability. He begins this section by apologizing to the reader if his account of his travels through Nazi Germany has seemed too dull and routine. The fact is, he says, the Gestapo is just like any other bureaucratic organization, full of inefficiencies and surprisingly easy to fool. Germany, he claims, is one of the easiest countries in the world in which to practice espionage because its leaders have too much blind faith in the efficiency of its police and its counterintelligence service. With these comments, Aguirre continues one of the central themes of the book; namely, that Germans are

not supermen, and they can be defeated through an opposition that is united and determined. Aguirre admits that outwardly Germany appears to be calm and normal; but this apparent tranquility masks a terrible system of "blood and oppression," as well as the forced flight from their homeland of millions of human beings. Aguirre ends this section by observing that "the struggle consists of conquering and smashing the totalitarian adversary and all his friends *without exception*" (obviously meaning Franco). Force, he says, is the only language they understand. "Poor Europe," he writes, "now waits for the just force that will finally conquer the brute force." It is not clear why these passages were deleted from the English version.

CHAPTER VIII

1. The preceding paragraph contains a very brief summary of some of Aguirre's anti-German comments which, in the Spanish version, occupy some 3 pages and come at the end of the preceding section.

2. This account of the dialogue between Aguirre and Petterson has been changed substantially from the Spanish version. For example, there is no mention in the Spanish version of the bombing of Guernica or of Petterson's deep concern over the fate of the Basques. On the other hand, the Spanish version does contain about a page of dialogue between the two men that in the English version is summed up in a sentence.

3. This passage in the English version is quite a bit shorter than in the Spanish version, and it omits an additional criticism voiced by Swedish workers of the Soviet system; that is, as Aguirre puts it, "above all, what sickened them the most was the lack of freedom [in the Soviet Union]." Given the desire then strong in the United States to depict our Soviet allies in a positive light, it is not surprising that passages like this were toned down or deleted entirely.

4. For the next 5 pages, Aguirre reports on a lengthy conversation with a Protestant minister in which the relative threats of the Nazis and the Soviets are assessed. As the reader will see, the minister believes nazism to be by far the greater threat to Western civilization. Again, the flaws (from the point of view of liberal democracy) in Stalinist Russia are played down in keeping with the prevailing mass opinion of the time. The reader will notice that these long conversations are appearing with greater frequency as Aguirre nears the end of his journey and of his book. For the most part, the translations of these conversations are, like this one, faithful to the Spanish original. I have no doubt that most of these conversations took place more or less as Aguirre records them; on the other hand, it strains our credulity to believe that a man in his circumstances (fleeing the oppression of a police

state, with a wife and two small children, headed toward an uncertain future) would have the time, presence of mind, or energy to record in such great detail the contents of conversations that were casual and unplanned. One must conclude, then, that much of what we are reading in the words of others are in fact some of the most important ideas of President Aguirre, at least as of the early to mid-1940s.

5. At this point, the English version omits a fairly lengthy conversation between Aguirre and Petterson about the will and the ability of Sweden to resist German pressure once war began between Germany and the Soviet Union. Petterson feels that his country can resist for a short time, but that eventually it will be overwhelmed by the much stronger Germany. Aguirre takes advantage of this conversation to return to one of his favorite themes: if the small democracies had only stood up to Hitler earlier, the war could have been avoided.

6. Once again the English version omits an exchange between Aguirre and Petterson about the ability of Sweden to maintain neutrality in the face of German pressure. It is clear that Aguirre, so close to escape and yet still in such a vulnerable position, has become nearly obsessed with the fateful decisions to be taken by Sweden. Once again he expresses his view that the three Scandinavian countries would have stood a better chance against Hitler if they had remained united. It is not clear why the translators chose to delete this passage, or the one preceding, that incorporated such an important message.

7. At this point in the narrative, Aguirre introduces what was becoming the central issue in his life: overcoming the intense competition from thousands of other refugees who were struggling to escape to America, to free themselves from the threat of Nazi Germany. Like Aguirre and his family, if they failed in this struggle they faced the certainty of the concentration camp and the high probability of death. Also like Aguirre, they were ready to use any means at their disposal to secure one of the extremely rare passages aboard one of the few passenger ships that dared the Atlantic crossing. A short paragraph appeared in the Spanish edition in which Aguirre simply describes the problem: too many desperate people trying to crowd into a very few cabins. For some of these refugees, like Aguirre, political influence was their trump card; for others, including many hundreds of Jews, their great wealth was their chief resource. Under these circumstances, it is entirely understandable that Aguirre's frustration and desperation might lead to some unkind remarks about Jews. These comments have all been deleted from the English version.

8. At this point the following passage appears in the Spanish version: "They were trying to throw us out to give our tickets to more influential persons. Principally Jewish elements and Central European politicians,

certainly unfortunate and in danger, but especially fearsome because of the resources that they could mobilize among their well-situated friends."

9. The Spanish version included the following sentence at this point: "We simply cannot leave him (Alvarez) alone if we want to beat the Jews in this fight."

10. In the Spanish version, arrival in America was described as "the strong desire of so many people in Europe who are persecuted because they think in a different way from those who run things, or because they have a nose with these features or the others." [This latter remark might be interpreted as referring to Basques, since it is often said that one of the Basques' most prominent facial features is the nose. However, in the current context, it is more likely that Aguirre is referring to a physical stereotype of the Jews. Apparently the translators thought so as well, since they deleted this sentence from the English version.]

One can only speculate about the reasons behind the systematic deletion of the remarks referred to in notes 7, 8, 9, and 10. If one of the purposes of producing an English-language edition was to secure the support of influential persons in the United States and Britain, then it certainly would have been risky to retain such comments. No matter how understandable they might have been in the circumstances of the moment, they could easily be misconstrued as indicating that Aguirre was antisemitic. It is also of interest that one of the chief translators of the book, Nea Colton, was described by one of the leading historians of the Basque diaspora as "the Jewish writer." Perhaps she was simply exercising her literary license to expunge passages that she sensed would lead to misunderstandings among American or British Jews. (See Koldo San Sebastián, *El Exilio Vasco en América, 1936–1946* [San Sebastián: Txertoa, 1988], p. 67.)

CHAPTER IX

1. The English version omits here a paragraph in which Aguirre expresses his appreciation to the "American Continent," especially Uruguay and Argentina, for not only saving his life, but honoring him and the nation he represents, thereby overcoming much of the terribly negative propaganda that had been spread throughout America about the Basques and their cause.

2. The English version here omits two paragraphs in which Aguirre asks, more or less rhetorically, why the United States waited so long to enter the war. "How is it," he asks, "that this nation, that feels in its soul the injustices and beatings committed against others, was not able to foresee that the violence unleashed in far-off countries would one day reach its coasts? But

this is not an evil exclusive to America . . . In every country I have visited I have seen the same phenomenon. It is not an evil of one nation or another, but a poison that attacks the very roots of twentieth-century civilization, without distinction of race or religion."

3. At this point, there are several long paragraphs in the Spanish version in which Aguirre observes that the war is as much an internal struggle of opposed ideas as it is an international war. This internal struggle explains why the opposition rearguard in any country takes on so much importance. "Many here in America are closer to the adversary than they are to the principles that inform the public institutions of their country. . . . For them it is nothing more than a war of imperialisms, for which the principal responsible parties are Great Britain and the United States."

4. The Spanish version contains a paragraph here deleted in which Aguirre expresses his concern over the continued confusion about the purposes of the Second World War. He wants to mark off the ideological boundaries of the rearguard just as the trenches define the enemies at the front. There is too much at stake for people to continue to be guided by "murky definitions and indecisive stances." This observation leads, then, to the discussion that follows about the ideological confusion surrounding the Spanish civil war.

5. The English version omits here several long paragraphs in which Aguirre complains of the numerous lies and misrepresentations about the Basques that have been spread throughout America. One of the most pointed examples involves the Vatican's criticism of the Basque government for sending a number of Basque children to refugee camps in the Soviet Union. Aguirre's heated response deserves to be cited at length: ". . . of the 30,000 Basque children who went into exile, only 1,000 went to Russia, responding to the generous invitation of charitable Soviet organizations, and after the documented signature of their parents who gave their consent. Why didn't the Catholic media that attacked us . . . imitate the attitude of the French and Belgian Catholics . . . who took in thousands of our abandoned children? Why didn't you American Catholics open your arms to our poor children, who after all were Catholics, and who could not be blamed for the errors of their parents, if indeed there were any?" The American priest to whom these questions are directed can only respond "I assure you this is the first time I have learned of these things." To which Aguirre responds "I'm not surprised."

6. At the end of this section, the English version omits two paragraphs in which Aguirre compares the advocates of democracy today with the situation faced by Jesus' disciples, who sought the "Kingdom of God" and created thereby a civilization of freedom and justice.

7. At this point, Aguirre delivers a strong sermon to the Western industrial democracies about their obligation to help people find work that will

assure them a minimum level of well-being. At this point, the English version omits his observation that "we are marching toward new social forms" that must absorb into the work force the hundreds of thousands of young men who fought to defend their country, and who will soon be returning to continue their lives.

8. The English version here omits this comment by Aguirre: "I have always thought that the material goods that were more than humanity needs—what constitutes the surplus—are much more than what is necessary to eliminate poverty. It is not economically impossible, but rather a question of organization and of social reform."

9. Here the Spanish version contains these sentences, deleted from the English version: "From the factory to the trenches, from the trenches to exile, my convictions have always been the same. Democracy failed to find solutions to the social question because it did not want to find them, or because pride took over completely the political leadership and prevented it." These remarks taken together suggest a fairly strong commitment by Aguirre to social and economic justice, a stance that in the 1940s could have equated with socialism. I would guess that that had something to do with the decision to delete these comments from the English version.

10. The Spanish version includes here a paragraph deleted from the English version in which Aguirre points out that "the time has passed for comfortable situations and vacillations." Either we bring about the needed social reforms he has described "or we will have to give way to other men and to other concepts that will know how to convince others with greater conviction than we, because they never stopped working for their goal."

11. Aguirre here comments that the national question is different in Europe from what it is in the Americas because of the "perfectly differentiated" nature of nations or peoples in Europe. In the Americas, in contrast, there were no ethnic peoples with a heritage of differentiation among one another (or even, one might have added, awareness of one another for the most part). On top of this native population was imposed another culture, that of the European explorers and colonizers. As a result, national differences were not as sharply drawn in the New World as they were in Europe; and consequently the national question will prove much more difficult to resolve in Europe than it was in the Americas. These comments were deleted from the English version.

12. In the Spanish version, Aguirre quotes the speaker as adding a number of significant figures in history who were either Basque by birth or by ancestry, including St. Ignatius of Loyola, the founder of the Jesuit order; Simon Bolivar; and Juan Sebastián Elcano, the navigator who assumed command of Magellan's fleet after Magellan was killed in the Philippines, and so became the first person to circumnavigate the world.

13. At this point in the Spanish version, Aguirre relates a lengthy conver-

sation in which the alliance between the United States and the Soviet Union is debated. While several of the participants doubted the sincerity of the Soviets and their willingness to undertake the steps toward liberalizing their regime which Stalin had pledged, Aguirre, as we have already seen, was strong in his defense of the alliance. Far from being a sheer necessity in the struggle against Hitler, the alliance between the U.S. and the USSR could prove to have lasting positive consequences for the world. The second portion of this deleted section (the entire deletion covers some 7 pages in the Spanish version) contains some thoughts from Aguirre regarding the tension between national interests and the achieving of some lasting structure of world government. This part was deleted probably because it includes a conversation with an American who avows to be interested in his country, and his country only; and with a British diplomat who fails to show the proper respect for the higher values at stake and the interests of those small countries that often are called upon to defend these higher values.

14. The English version deletes at this point a long passage of more than 2 pages in which Aguirre takes Britain and the United States to task for having failed to block Hitler's aggression earlier, when they could have done so with far less loss of life. Aguirre's writing at this point becomes intensely personal: "I have seen on the roads of Europe dying human beings fall while their lips pronounced these words of hope: 'America and England will save us'. Those mothers dragging their children along, those elderly persons who had seen the peace of their final years shattered, those broken families, those homes improvised under the stars, they still had a supreme hope: 'America and England will be our salvation, or in any case of our children'." Aguirre's message in this passage is clear: "Either America's interest becomes that of the entire world, or it makes no sense whatever." It is not surprising that the American translators decided to delete this and similar passages at this point, and to introduce them below (p. ooo of the English version) in a much more pro-American context.

15. This section begins in the Spanish version with two paragraphs in which Aguirre tells the reader why he is addressing this topic. "We must know well where to find the enemies of freedom, those that appear defined, and even more those that hide their designs with studied deception; these are the most dangerous." Of course, it is the Latin Axis countries to which he is referring.

16. Aguirre devotes several paragraphs at this point in the Spanish version to the issue of prisoner exchanges in the civil war. When the war broke out on July 18, 1936, it caught many people by surprise. Consequently, several supporters of both sides were caught on the "wrong side" of the battle lines. Many of these people were imprisoned and treated extremely harshly—sometimes even executed without trial—simply for their beliefs.

Aguirre made a major effort to exchange all the prisoners then held in Basque jails for these supporters of the republic then held by Franco's forces. These efforts were largely unsuccessful, as Aguirre here relates. It is not clear why this material was deleted from the English version.

17. The Spanish version devotes about 1 page at this point to the failure of the diplomacy of the Western democracies to resist the expansion of the Axis, a theme amply developed below. In the deleted paragraphs, Aguirre criticizes Western diplomats for not countering the aggressive foreign policy of Nazi Germany.

18. The English version here omits several paragraphs in which Aguirre sharply rebukes leaders of the Catholic church in Latin America for their support of the Franco dictatorship, and for the Christian dictatorships in general.

19. In the Spanish version, the preceding note to the reader was printed in italics to highlight the fact that it represents events and ideas that post-date Aguirre's completion of the main text in May 1942. The section runs up to the subhead entitled "The Iberian Problem."

20. *The Pocket Book of America,* ed. Philip Van Doren Stern, p. 144. Reprinted by permission of Dorothy Thompson. [Author's note.]

21. At this point in the Spanish version, Aguirre criticizes those Americans who want nothing to do with the war, or with politics in general. In the course of these several paragraphs, he relates a conversation with an American banker who is quoted as saying ". . . for us there is only one enemy, the greatest of all, and that is Roosevelt." These passages were deleted from the English version.